MONSOON

ROBERT D. KAPLAN

MONSOON

THE INDIAN OCEAN
AND THE FUTURE
OF AMERICAN POWER

RANDOM HOUSE

NEW YORK

Published in the United States by Random House, an imprint of The Random House Publishing
Group, a division of Random House, Inc., New York.

RANDOM HOUSE and colophon are registered trademarks of Random House, Inc.

Library of Congress Cataloging-in-Publication Data
Kaplan, Robert D.
Monsoon : the Indian Ocean and the future of American power / Robert D. Kaplan.
p.   cm.
ISBN 978-1-4000-6746-6
eBook ISBN 978-0-679-60405-1
1. United States—Foreign relations—Indian Ocean Region.
2. Indian Ocean Region—Foreign relations—United States.
3. Indian Ocean Region—Strategic aspects.   4. National security—United States.
5. National security—Indian Ocean Region.   I. Title.
DS341.3.U6K374 2010
327.730182'4—dc22   2009049752

Printed in the United States of America

www.atrandom.com

2 4 6 8 9 7 5 3 1

First Edition

To
Grenville Byford

Gradual, inexorable, and fundamental changes . . . are . . . occurring in
the balances of power among civilizations, and the power of the
West relative to that of other civilizations will continue to decline.

—SAMUEL P. HUNTINGTON
The Clash of Civilizations and the Remaking
of World Order (1996)

PREFACE

THE RIMLAND OF EURASIA

The map of Europe defined the twentieth century: from Flanders Fields to Omaha Beach to the Berlin Wall to the burned villages of Kosovo; from the Long European War, lasting from 1914 to 1989, to its bloody aftershocks, Europe was the center of world history. Momentous trends and events happened elsewhere, to be sure. But great power politics, from the collapse of Old World empires to the bipolar struggle between the United States and the Soviet Union, had more to do with Europe than anywhere else.

It is my contention that the Greater Indian Ocean, stretching eastward from the Horn of Africa past the Arabian Peninsula, the Iranian plateau, and the Indian Subcontinent, all the way to the Indonesian archipelago and beyond, may comprise a map as iconic to the new century as Europe was to the last one. Hopefully, the twenty-first century will not be as violent as the twentieth, but, to a similar degree, it could have a recognizable geography. In this rimland of Eurasia—the maritime oikoumene of the medieval Muslim world that was never far from China's gaze—we can locate the tense dialogue between Western and Islamic civilizations, the ganglia of global energy routes, and the quiet, seemingly inexorable rise of India and China over land and sea. For the sum-total effect of U.S. preoccupation with Iraq and Afghanistan has been to fast-forward the arrival of the Asian Century, not only in the economic terms that we all know about, but in military terms as well.

Recently, messy land wars have obscured for us the importance of seas and coastlines, across which most trade is conducted and along which most of humanity lives, and where, consequently, future military and economic activity is likely to take place as in the past. It is in the littorals where global issues such as population growth, climate change, sea level rises, shortages of fresh water, and extremist politics—the last of which is affected by all the other factors—acquire a vivid geographical face. What the late British historian C. R. Boxer called Monsoon Asia, at the crossroads of the Indian Ocean and the western Pacific, will demographically and strategically be a hub of the twenty-first-century world.[1]

Half a millennium ago, Vasco da Gama braved storm and scurvy to round Africa and cross the Indian Ocean to the Subcontinent. Writes the sixteenth-century Portuguese poet Luiz Vaz de Camões about that signal moment:

> This is the land you have been seeking,
> This is India rising before you. . . .[2]

Da Gama's arrival in India initiated the rise of the West in Asia. Portuguese seaborne dominance eventually gave way to that of other Western powers—Holland, France, Great Britain, and the United States, in their turn. Now, as China and India compete for ports and access routes along the southern Eurasian rimland, and with the future strength of the U.S. Navy uncertain, because of America's own economic travails and the diversionary cost of its land wars, it is possible that the five-hundred-year chapter of Western preponderance is slowly beginning to close.

This gradual power shift could not come at a more turbulent time for the lands bordering the Indian Ocean's two halves, the Arabian Sea and the Bay of Bengal: at the top of the Arabian Sea is Pakistan; at the top of the Bay of Bengal is Burma, both highly volatile and populous pivot states. Analysts normally don't put those two countries in the same category, but they should. Then, of course, there is the whole political future of the Islamic world from Somalia to Indonesia to consider. Besides their proximity to the Indian Ocean, so many of these places are characterized by weak institutions, tottering infrastructures, and young and restive populations tempted by extremism. Yet they are the future, much more than the graying populations of the West.

As the late Belgian scholar Charles Verlinden once noted, the Indian Ocean "is surrounded by not less than thirty-seven countries representing a third of the world's population," and extends for more than 80 degrees in latitude and more than 100 degrees in longitude.[3] I can only visit a few points along the Indian Ocean's seaboard and see what is currently going on—so as to further illuminate a wider canvas, and to show what a world without a superpower looks like on the ground.

The Indian Ocean region is more than just a stimulating geography. It is an *idea* because it provides an insightful visual impression of Islam, and combines the centrality of Islam with global energy politics and the importance of world navies, in order to show us a multi-layered, multi-polar world above and beyond the headlines in Iraq and Afghanistan; it is also an idea because it allows us to see the world whole, within a very new and yet very old framework, complete with its own traditions and characteristics, without having to drift into bland nostrums about global-ization.

The book begins with a broad strategic overview of the region. Then I move on to individual locations along this great seaboard. Oman is my principal reference point, where I consider the ocean's medieval history, as well as the legacy of the first Western power, the Portuguese; there, too, I ponder the perennial relationship between the sea and the desert, and how each leads to different political paths. Then I focus on massive Chinese harbor projects smack in the heart of zones of regional sepa-ratism in the case of Pakistan, and of ethnic rivalry in the case of Sri Lanka. In Bangladesh, I write about the interrelationship of climate change, extreme poverty, and Islamic radicalism. In India, I focus on Hindu extremism, which is being overcome by economic and social dy-namism. In Burma, I report on the collision between India and China over a devastated and resource-rich landscape, and the challenges it pre-sents for Western powers like the United States. In Indonesia, I explore the relationship between democracy and a vibrant, syncretic Islam, so different from that in Pakistan and Bangladesh: for Islam, as I learned in many of these places, is more intelligently considered against the back-drop of a specific landscape and history. Finally, I consider Chinese naval expansion originating in the eastern end of the Greater Indian Ocean, and at the western end take a peek at African renewal through the prism of Zanzibar. Everywhere I attempt to describe the ceaseless currents of his-torical change as they shape the contours of the new century. It is the in-termingling of challenges in each place—religious, economic, political, environmental—rather than each challenge in isolation, that creates such drama.

The "monsoon" of which I speak is more than just a storm system (which it sometimes comes across as in the English-language lexicon); it is, too, a life-affirming and beneficial climatic phenomenon, so necessary over the centuries for trade, globalization, unity, and progress. The monsoon is nature writ large, a spectacle of turbulence that suggests the effect of the environment on humankind living in increasingly crowded and fragile conditions in places like Bangladesh and Indonesia. In a densely interconnected world, America's ability to grasp what, in a larger sense, the monsoon represents and to recognize its manifold implications will help determine America's own destiny and that of the West as a whole. Thus, the Indian Ocean may be the essential place to contemplate the future of U.S. power.

CONTENTS

PART III

PART I

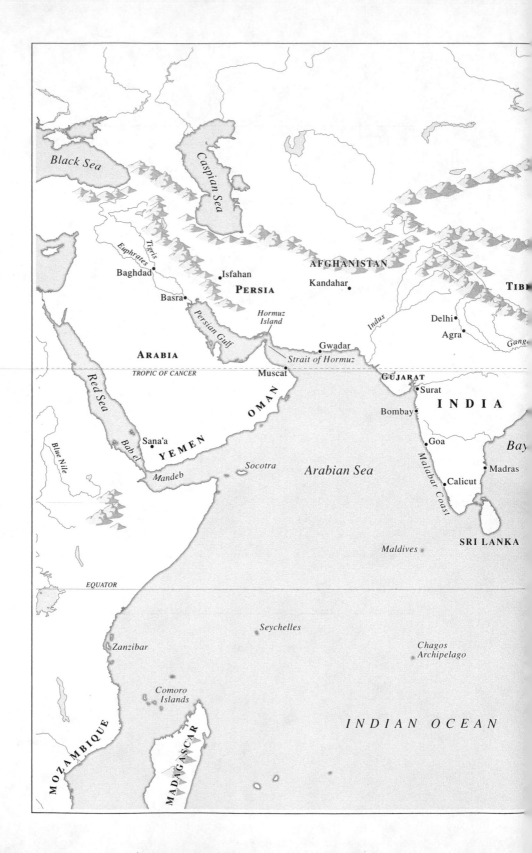

Black Sea

Caspian Sea

Euphrates

Tigris

Baghdad

Isfahan

AFGHANISTAN

Kandahar

TIB

PERSIA

Basra

Persian Gulf

Hormuz
Island

Indus

Delhi

Agra

Gang

Gwadar

ARABIA

Strait of Hormuz

TROPIC OF CANCER

Muscat

GUJARAT

Red Sea

O M A N

Surat

INDIA

Bombay

Sana'a

Bab el

YEMEN

Goa

Blue Nile

Malabar Coast

Bay

Socotra

Arabian Sea

Madras

Mandeb

Calicut

SRI LANKA

Maldives

EQUATOR

Seychelles

Chagos
Archipelago

Zanzibar

Comoro
Islands

INDIAN OCEAN

MOZAMBIQUE

MADAGASCAR

Beijing

Huang He (Yellow R.)

C H I N A

KOREA

J A P A N

Chang Jiang (Yangtze River)

Okinawa

TROPIC OF CANCER

ENGAL

Mandalay

BURMA

lkata
alcutta)

Hong Kong

TAIWAN
(Formosa)

PACIFIC

OCEAN

Rangoon
(Yangon)

THAILAND
(SIAM)

CAMBODIA

*South China
Sea*

Luzon

PHILIPPINES

Manila

ngal

daman
slands

Nicobar
Islands

Strait of
Malacca

Aceh

Mindanao

Palau

Malacca
Singapore

Sumatra

Borneo

Sulawesi

EQUATOR

I N D O N E S I A

Krakatoa

Batavia
Java

Timor

Scale at Equator

0   400 miles

0   400 km

NEW HOLLAND
(AUSTRALIA)

CHAPTER ONE

CHINA EXPANDS VERTICALLY, INDIA HORIZONTALLY

l Bahr al Hindi is what the Arabs called the ocean in their old navigational treatises. The Indian Ocean and its tributary waters bear the imprint of that great, proselytizing wave of Islam that spread from its Red Sea base across the longitudes to India and as far as Indonesia and Malaysia, so a map of these seas is central to a historical understanding of the faith. This is a geography that encompasses, going from west to east, the Red Sea, Arabian Sea, Bay of Bengal, and Java and South China seas. Here, in our day, are located the violence- and famine-plagued nations of the Horn of Africa, the geopolitical challenges of Iraq and Iran, the fissuring fundamentalist cauldron of Pakistan, economically rising India and its teetering neighbors Sri Lanka and Bangladesh, despotic Burma (over which a contest looms between China and India), and Thailand, through which the Chinese and Japanese, too, may help finance a canal sometime in this century that will affect the Asian balance of power in their favor. Indeed, the canal is just one of several projects on the drawing board, including land bridges and pipelines, that aim to unite the Indian Ocean with the western Pacific.

On the Indian Ocean's western shores, we have the emerging and volatile democracies of East Africa, as well as anarchic Somalia; almost four thousand miles away on its eastern shores the evolving, post-fundamentalist face of Indonesia, the most populous Muslim country in the world. No image epitomizes the spirit of our borderless world, with its civilizational competition on one hand and intense, inarticulate yearning for unity on the other, as much as an Indian Ocean map.

Water, unlike land, bears no trace of history, no message really, but the very act of crossing and recrossing it makes this ocean, in the words of Harvard professor of history Sugata Bose, a "symbol of universal humanity."[1] There are Indian and Chinese, Arab and Persian trading arrangements creating a grand network of cross-oceanic communal ties, brought even closer over the centuries by the monsoon winds and, in the case of the Arabs, Persians, and other Muslims, by the haj pilgrimage.[2] This is truly a global ocean, its shores home to an agglomeration of peoples of the fast-developing former "third world," but not to any superpower: unlike the Atlantic and Pacific.[3] Here is the most useful quarter of the earth to contemplate, pace Fareed Zakaria, a "post-American" world in the wake of the Cold War and the conflicts in Afghanistan and Iraq.[4] Rudyard Kipling's turn of phrase "east of Suez"—from the 1890 poem "Mandalay," which begins in Moulmein in Burma, on the Bay of Bengal—applies more than ever, though few may realize it.

Cold War military maps highlighted the Arctic, owing to the geography of the Soviet Union and its principal ports. Former president George W. Bush's so-called war on terrorism underscored the Greater Middle East. But the geopolitical map of the world keeps evolving. The arc of crisis is everywhere: a warming Arctic could even become a zone of contention. Because the entire globe is simply too general an instrument to focus on, thus it helps to have a specific cartographic image in mind that includes the majority of world trouble spots, while at the same time focusing on the nexus of terrorism, energy flows, and environmental emergencies such as the 2004 tsunami. Just as phrases matter for good or for bad—"the Cold War," "the clash of civilizations"—so do maps. The right map provides a spatial view of world politics that can deduce future trends. Although developments in finance and technology encourage global thinking, we are still at the mercy of geography, as the artificiality of Iraq and Pakistan attest.

Americans, in particular, are barely aware of the Indian Ocean, concentrated as they are, because of their own geography, on the Atlantic and the Pacific. World War II and the Cold War confirmed this bias, with Nazi Germany, Imperial Japan, the Soviet Union, Korea, and Communist China all with Atlantic or Pacific orientations. This bias is embedded in mapping conventions: Mercator projections tend to place the Western Hemisphere in the middle, so the Indian Ocean is often split up at the far edges of the map. Yet, it is this ocean to which Marco Polo devoted almost an entire book of his travels near the end of the thirteenth century, from Java and Sumatra to Aden and Dhofar. Herein lies the entire arc of Islam, from the eastern fringe of the Sahara Desert to the Indonesian archipelago; thus it follows that the struggle against terrorism and anarchy (which includes piracy) focuses broadly on these tropical waters, between the Suez Canal and Southeast Asia. The Indian Ocean littoral, which takes in Somalia, Yemen, Saudi Arabia, Iraq, Iran, and Pakistan, constitutes a veritable networking map of al-Qaeda, as well as one of disparate groups smuggling hashish and other contraband. Indeed, Iran has supplied Hamas by a sea route from the Persian Gulf to Sudan, and then overland through Egypt.

Here, too, are the principal oil shipping lanes, as well as the main navigational choke points of world commerce—the Straits of Bab el Mandeb, Hormuz, and Malacca. Forty percent of seaborne crude oil passes through the Strait of Hormuz at one end of the ocean, and 50 percent of the world's merchant fleet capacity is hosted at the Strait of Malacca, at the other end, making the Indian Ocean the globe's busiest and most important interstate.

Throughout history, sea routes have been more important than land ones, writes Tufts University scholar Felipe Fernandez-Armesto, because they carry more goods more economically.[5] The sea silk route from Venice to Japan across the Indian Ocean in the medieval and early modern centuries was as important as the silk route proper across Central Asia. "Whoever is lord of Malacca has his hands on the throat of Venice," went the saying.[6] Another proverb had it that if the world were an egg, Hormuz was its yoke.[7]

Today, despite the jet and information age, 90 percent of global commerce and two thirds of all petroleum supplies travel by sea. Globalization relies ultimately on shipping containers, and the Indian Ocean accounts for one half of all the world's container traffic. Moreover, the Indian Ocean rimland from the Middle East to the Pacific accounts for 70 percent of the traffic of petroleum products for the entire world.[8] Indian Ocean tanker routes between the Persian Gulf and South and East Asia are becoming clogged, as hundreds of millions of Indians and Chinese join the global middle class, necessitating vast consumption of oil. The world's energy needs will rise by 50 percent by 2030, and almost half of that consumption will come from India and China.[9] India—soon to become the world's fourth largest energy consumer after the United States,

China, and Japan—is dependent on oil for more than 90 percent of its energy needs, and 90 percent of that oil will soon come from the Persian Gulf by way of the Arabian Sea.* Indeed, before 2025, India will overtake Japan as the world's third largest net importer of oil after the United States and China.[10] And as India must satisfy a population that will be the most populous in the world before the middle of this century, its coal imports from Mozambique, in the southwestern Indian Ocean, are set to increase dramatically, adding to the coal that India already imports from Indian Ocean countries such as South Africa, Indonesia, and Australia. In the future, India-bound ships will also be carrying enormous quantities of liquefied natural gas across the western half of the Indian Ocean from southern Africa, even as it continues to import gas from Qatar, Malaysia, and Indonesia. This is how African poverty may be partially assuaged: less by Western foreign aid than by robust trade with the richer areas of the former third world.

Then there is China, whose demand for crude oil doubled between 1995 and 2005, and will double again in the coming decade or two, as it imports 7.3 million barrels of crude daily by 2020—half of Saudi Arabia's planned output.† More than 85 percent of that China-bound oil will pass across the span of the Indian Ocean through the Strait of Malacca: the reason China is desperate for alternative energy routes to the Pacific, as well as overland ones into China from Central Asia, Pakistan, and Burma.[11] The combined appetites of China, Japan, and South Korea for Persian Gulf oil already make the Strait of Malacca home to half of world oil flows and close to a quarter of global trade.[12]

"No ocean is in need of strategic stability more than the Indian Ocean, which is arguably the most nuclearized of the seven seas," notes the defense analyst Thomas P.M. Barnett. "Among the nuclear powers whose navies ply this ocean are the United States, the United Kingdom, France, Russia, China, India, Pakistan, and Israel."[13]

---

* The Persian Gulf is responsible for 57 percent of the world's crude oil reserves.

† In January 2004 the China Petrochemical Corporation signed a contract with Saudi Arabia for the exploration and production of natural gas in a nearly 15,000-square-mile area of the Empty Quarter, in the south. As air pollution becomes an increasingly serious problem in China because of the burning of dirty fossil fuels, China will turn to cleaner natural gas. Geoffrey Kemp, "The East Moves West," *National Interest,* Summer 2006. In any case, China's oil consumption is growing seven times faster than that of the U.S. Mohan Malik, "Energy Flows and Maritime Rivalries in the Indian Ocean Region" (Honolulu: Asia-Pacific Center for Security Studies, 2008).

The Indian Ocean is where the rivalry between the United States and China in the Pacific interlocks with the regional rivalry between China and India, and also with America's fight against Islamic terrorism in the Middle East, which includes America's attempt to contain Iran. Whenever U.S. Navy warships have bombed Iraq or Afghanistan, they have often done so from the Indian Ocean. The U.S. Air Force guards Iraq and Afghanistan from bases in the Persian Gulf, and from the island of Diego Garcia, smack in the center of the Indian Ocean. Any American strike against Iran—and its aftershocks, regarding the flow of oil—will have an Indian Ocean address. The same with responses to any upheaval in Saudi Arabia; or in the teeming, water-starved tinderbox of Yemen, home to twenty-two million people and eighty million firearms.

The U.S. Navy's new maritime strategy, unveiled in October 2007 at the Naval War College in Newport, Rhode Island, both states and implies that the navy will henceforth seek a sustained, forward presence in the Indian Ocean and adjacent western Pacific, but less so in the Atlantic. The U.S. Marine Corps "Vision and Strategy" statement, unveiled in June 2008, covering the years to 2025, also concludes in so many words that the Indian Ocean and its adjacent waters will be a central theater of conflict and competition. Along with its continued dominance in the Pacific, the U.S. clearly seeks to be the preeminent South Asian power. This signals a momentous historical shift away from the North Atlantic and Europe. The United States may not control events inside the "big sandbox" of the Middle East, but, as the military analyst Ralph Peters suggests, it will compensate by trying to dominate the doors in and out of the sandbox—the Straits of Hormuz and Bab el Mandeb: choke points where the naval presence of India and China will be expanding alongside America's own.

India's and China's aspirations for great-power status, as well as their quest for energy security, have compelled them "to redirect their gazes from land to the seas," write James R. Holmes and Toshi Yoshihara, associate professors at the U.S. Naval War College. Meanwhile, as Holmes and Yoshihara also note, there are "lingering questions over the sustainability of American primacy on the high seas," something that has guaranteed commercial maritime stability for decades, and has, therefore, been taken for granted, even as globalization itself has depended upon it.[14] If we are entering a phase of history in which several nations will share dominance of the high seas, rather than one as in the recent past, then the Indian Ocean will play center stage to this more dynamic and unstable configuration.

While China seeks to expand its influence vertically, that is, reaching southward down to the warm waters of the Indian Ocean, India seeks to expand its influence horizontally, reaching eastward and westward to the borders of Victorian age British India, parallel to the Indian Ocean. Chinese president Hu Jintao, according to one report, has bemoaned China's sea-lane vulnerability, referring to it as his country's "Malacca dilemma," a dependence on the narrow and vulnerable Strait of Malacca for oil imports from which China must somehow escape.[15] It is an old fear, for Ming China's world was disrupted in 1511 when the Portuguese conquered Malacca. In the twenty-first century an escape from the Malacca dilemma means, among other things, eventually using Indian Ocean ports to transport oil and other energy products via roads and pipelines northward into the heart of China, so that tankers do not all have to sail through the Strait of Malacca to reach their destination. This is just one reason why China wants desperately to integrate Taiwan into its dominion, so that it can redirect its naval energies to the Indian Ocean.[16]

The Chinese military's so-called string-of-pearls strategy for the Indian Ocean features the construction of a large port and listening post at the Pakistani port of Gwadar on the Arabian Sea, where the Chinese could monitor ship traffic through the Strait of Hormuz. There could be another Chinese-utilized port in Pakistan, at Pasni, seventy-five miles east of Gwadar and joined to it by a new highway. At Hambantota, on the southern coast of Sri Lanka, the Chinese seem to be building the oil-age equivalent of a coaling station for their ships. At the Bangladeshi port of Chittagong on the Bay of Bengal, Chinese companies have been active in developing the container port facility, where China might also be seeking naval access. In Burma, where the Chinese have given billions of dollars in military assistance to the ruling junta, Beijing is building and upgrading commercial and naval bases; constructing road, waterway, and pipeline links from the Bay of Bengal to China's Yunnan Province; and operating surveillance facilities on the Coco Islands deep in the Bay of Bengal.[17] A number of these ports are closer to cities in central and western China than those cities are to Beijing and Shanghai. Such Indian Ocean ports, with north-south road and rail links, would help economically liberate landlocked inner China. China is reaching southward and westward, evinced by a seemingly improbable railway it hopes to construct linking its westernmost provinces—across some of the highest terrain in the world—to a copper-producing region of Afghanistan south of Kabul.

Of course, one must be extremely careful in judging China's actions in this region. What the Chinese actually plan for the Indian Ocean is still far from clear and open to debate. Some in Washington are skeptical of the whole notion of a string-of-pearls strategy. Overt bases do not conform with China's nonhegemonic, benign view of itself. The Chinese are rarely seeking outright control, standing by, as in the case of Gwadar, as the Port of Singapore Authority prepares to run the facility for decades to come. (Though, as one Singaporean official told me, his country is tiny and thus no threat to China at Gwadar.) Many pipeline routes originating in these ports go through what are presently politically unstable areas, so China is in no rush to go forward with some of these plans. Indeed, partly out of security concerns, the Chinese have shelved a multibillion-dollar coastal oil refinery at Gwadar. Nevertheless, given the dictates of geography and China's historical ties to the Indian Ocean region, about which I will elaborate, something is clearly going on. It isn't the port projects per se that are critical, because all of them are motivated by local development realities and only secondarily concerned with China. Rather, what is interesting and bears watching is China's desire for access to modern deepwater ports in friendly countries along the southern Eurasian rimland, where it has invested considerably in economic aid and diplomatic outreach, thus giving Beijing a greater presence along Indian Ocean sea lines of communication. Guarding these lines makes for a major bureaucratic sales argument in Chinese power circles for a blue-water oceanic force.[18] The real lesson here is the subtlety of the world we are entering, of which the Indian Ocean provides a salient demonstration. Instead of the hardened military bases of the Cold War and earlier epochs, there will be dual-use civilian-military facilities where basing arrangements will be implicit rather than explicit, and completely dependent on the health of the bilateral relationship in question.

China's long-term quest for a presence in the Indian Ocean in order to project power and protect its merchant and energy fleets is evinced by its well-heeled, very public commemoration of the historical figure of Zheng He, the fifteenth-century Ming dynasty explorer and admiral who plied the seas between China and the East Indies, Ceylon, the Persian Gulf, and the Horn of Africa. A Muslim eunuch of Mongolian origin who was captured and castrated as a little boy for service in the Forbidden City and rose up through the ranks, Zheng He took his treasure fleet of hundreds of ships with as many as thirty thousand men—including doctors, interpreters, and astrologers—to Middle Eastern shores to trade, exact tribute, and show the flag.[19] China's much renewed emphasis on this Indian Ocean explorer and his life story says, in effect, that these seas have always been part of its zone of influence.

At the same time that China is asserting itself, India is looking to increase its regional influence from the Middle East to Southeast Asia. The first foreign visit of Admiral Sureesh Mehta, formerly chief of the Indian naval staff, was to the Gulf countries to the west, where trade with India is burgeoning. And as India booms, so also will its trade with Iran and a recovering Iraq. Take India and Iran, two littoral states, one dominating South Asia and the other the Middle East. Americans are not accustomed to seeing them in the same category but on a crucial level they are. Iran, like Afghanistan, has become a strategic rear base for India against Pakistan, as well as a future energy partner. In 2005, India and Iran signed a multibillion-dollar deal under which Iran will supply India with 7.5 million tons of liquefied natural gas annually for twenty-five years.[20] Though never fully ratified, the deal has been pending, and it likely will move forward at some foreseeable time. Likewise, there has been talk of an energy pipeline from Iran through Pakistan to India, a project that would go a long way toward stabilizing Indian-Pakistani relations, as well as joining the Middle East and South Asia at the hip. India has also been helping Iran develop the Chah Bahar port on the Arabian Sea. This is one more reason the U.S. attempt to isolate Iran is untenable. In the past, American power depended on divisions within Eurasia, so many a country needed to go through Washington to get its interests served. But the long-term trend here is of greater integration, thus freezing out the United States to some extent.

It is often forgotten that for hundreds of years, India has enjoyed close economic and cultural ties with both Persian and Arabian shores of the Gulf. Approximately 3.5 million Indians work in Gulf Cooperation Council countries and send home $4 billion annually in remittances. A major impetus for India's current maritime buildup in the Indian Ocean was the humiliating inability of its navy to evacuate its citizens from Iraq and Kuwait during the 1990–91 Gulf crisis.[21]

Concomitantly, India is expanding its military and economic ties with

Burma to the east. Democratic India does not have the luxury of spurning authoritarian Burma, because its neighbor is rich in natural resources and threatens to be completely taken over by China if India stands aloof and does nothing. In fact, India hopes a nexus of east-west roads and energy pipelines will ultimately give it soft power dominance over the former territorial India of the Raj, which encompassed Pakistan, Bangladesh, and Burma.

Yet competition between India and China, caused by their spreading and overlapping layers of commercial and political influence, will play out less on land than in a naval realm. Zhao Nanqi, when he was the director of the general staff logistics department in the Chinese navy, proclaimed: "We can no longer accept the Indian Ocean as an ocean only of the Indians."[22] This attitude applies particularly to the Bay of Bengal, where both nations will have considerable maritime presences, owing to the closeness of Burma as well as the Andaman and Nicobar islands, possessed by India near the entrance of the Strait of Malacca. Conversely, India's and China's mutual dependence on the same sea lanes could also lead to an alliance between them that, in some circumstances, might be implicitly hostile to the United States. In other words, the Indian Ocean will be where global power dynamics will be revealed. Together with the contiguous Near East and Central Asia, it constitutes the new Great Game in geopolitics.

The Cold War forced an artificial dichotomy on area studies in which the Middle East, the Indian Subcontinent, and the Pacific Rim were separate entities. But as India and China become more integrally connected with both Southeast Asia and the Middle East through trade, energy, and security agreements, the map of Asia is reemerging as a single organic unit, just as it was during earlier epochs in history—manifested now by an Indian Ocean map.

Such a map, in which artificial regions dissolve, includes even landlocked Central Asia. While the Chinese develop a deepwater port at Gwadar in Pakistani Baluchistan, only a hundred miles farther to the west, inside the Gulf of Oman, the Indians, as I mentioned, along with the Russians and Iranians, are developing the port of Chah Bahar in Iranian Baluchistan, which is already a forward base for the Iranian navy. (The Indians have also encouraged a new road from Chah Bahar to the southwestern Afghan province of Nimruz.) Both Gwadar and Chah Bahar, which lie on major maritime shipping routes close to the Gulf—and might be expected to be in fierce competition with each other—may one day be linked by feeder roads and pipelines to oil- and natural gas–rich Azerbaijan, Turkmenistan, and other former Soviet republics in the heart of the Eurasian landmass. And by helping to build a highway connecting Afghanistan's main ring road with Iranian ports, India has potentially ended Afghanistan's reliance on Pakistan for its outlet to the sea. It is access to the Indian Ocean that will help define future Central Asian politics, according to S. Frederick Starr, a Central Asian area expert at the Johns Hopkins School of Advanced International Studies in Washington, D.C. To be sure, part of Iran's appeal to India is as a viable transit state for Central Asian gas. Moreover, Indian and Pakistani ports have been touted as "evacuation points" for Caspian Sea oil.[23] In this way, the destinies of countries as far away from the Indian Ocean as Kazakhstan and Georgia (which either have hydrocarbons or are transit routes for them) are connected with it.

A particularly critical country in this regard is Afghanistan, through which natural gas from the Dauletabad field in Turkmenistan may one day flow en route to Pakistani and Indian cities and ports. This is in addition to other energy pipeline routes between Central Asia and the Subcontinent of which Afghanistan is right in the middle. Therefore, stabilizing Afghanistan is about much more than just the anti-terrorist war against al-Qaeda and the Taliban; it is about securing the future prosperity of the whole of southern Eurasia; as well as easing India and Pakistan toward peaceful coexistence through the sharing of energy routes.

The point is, as not only Asian but African populations, too, continue to increase and become more prosperous through the enlargement of middle classes, trade and energy routes will burgeon in all directions, both on land and at sea, leading to a multiplicity of organizations and alliances. That is why in the twenty-first century the Indian Ocean constitutes a vastly different map than the one of Europe and the North Atlantic in the twentieth. The earlier map illustrated both a singular threat and a concept: the Soviet Union. The aim was simple: defend Western Europe against the Red Army and keep the Soviet navy bottled up near the polar ice cap. Because the threat was straightforward, and the United States the paramount power, the U.S.-led North Atlantic Treaty Organization (NATO) became arguably history's most successful alliance. Of course, one might envision a NATO of the seas for the Indian Ocean, comprising South Africa, Oman, India, Pakistan, Singapore, and Australia, with Pakistan and India bickering inside the alliance much as Greece and Turkey do inside NATO. But such an idea represents an old model that does not quite capture the meaning of what the cartographic image represented by the Indian Ocean is all about.

While it may form a historical and cultural unit, in strategic terms, the Indian Ocean, like the larger world we are inheriting, does not have a single focal point; it has many. The Horn of Africa, the Persian Gulf, the Bay of Bengal, and so on are all burdened by particular threats with different players in each arena. Then, too, there are the transnational threats of terrorism, natural disasters, nuclear proliferation, and anarchy. Any future Indian Ocean alliance will be like the present NATO alliance, looser and less singularly focused than during the Cold War years. But given the size of this ocean—stretching across seven time zones and almost half the world's latitudes—and the comparative slowness at which ships move, it may be very hard for a multinational navy to even get to a crisis zone in adequate time. It is easily forgotten that the principal reason the United States played such a leading role in the tsunami relief effort off the coast of Indonesia in the Bay of Bengal in 2004–2005 was that it happened to have an aircraft carrier strike group in the vicinity. Had that carrier strike group, the *Abraham Lincoln,* been in the Korean Peninsula, where it was headed, America's response to the tsunami would have been less adequate. This is why a single alliance system is a backward way of looking at the world.

It is more productive, instead, to think of a multiplicity of regional and ideological alliances in different parts of the ocean and its littoral states. There is already evidence of it. The navies of Thailand, Singapore, and Indonesia, with the help of the U.S. Navy, have banded together to deter piracy in the Strait of Malacca. The navies of India, Japan, Australia, Singapore, and the United States—democracies all—have exercised together off India's southwestern Malabar coast, in an implicit rebuke to China's design on the ocean, even as the armies of India and China have conducted exercises together near the southern Chinese city of Kunming. A combined naval task force, comprised of the Americans, Canadians, French, Dutch, British, Pakistanis, and Australians, patrols permanently off the Horn of Africa in an effort to deter piracy.

The Indian Ocean strategic system has been described by Vice Admiral John Morgan, former deputy chief of naval operations, as like the New York City taxicab system, where there is no central dispatcher—no United Nations or NATO—and maritime security is driven by market forces; coalitions will appear where shipping lanes need to be protected, just as more taxis show up in the theater district before and after performances.

No one nation dominates, even as the U.S. Navy is still quietly the reigning hegemon of the seas. As one Australian commodore told me: imagine a world of decentralized, network-centric sea basing, supplied by the United States, with different alliances for different scenarios; whereby frigates and destroyers of various nations can "plug and play" into these sea bases that often resemble oil rigs, spread out from the Horn of Africa to the Indonesian archipelago.

The U.S. military, with its sheer size and ability to deploy rapidly, will still be indispensable, even as the United States itself plays a more modest political role, and other, once-poor nations rise up and leverage one another. After all, this is a world where raw materials from Indonesia are manufactured into component parts in Vietnam and supplied with software from Singapore, financed by the United Arab Emirates: a process dependent on safe sea-lanes that are defended by the U.S. and various naval coalitions. The Indian Ocean may not have a unitary focus, like the Soviet threat to the Atlantic, or the challenge of a rising China in the Pacific, but it certainly does constitute a scale model of a global system.

And yet within this microcosm of a radically interconnected global system, ironically nationalism will still flourish. "No one in Asia wants to pool sovereignty," writes Greg Sheridan, foreign editor of *The Australian*. "Asia's politicians have come up through hard schools and amid hard neighbors. They appreciate hard power; the U.S. position is much stronger in Asia than anywhere else in the world."[24]

In other words, do not confuse this world with the one of the United Nations, which in any case is partly an old construct with France having a seat on the Security Council but not India. India, Japan, the United States, and Australia sent ships steaming to tsunami-afflicted zones in Indonesia and Sri Lanka in December 2004 without initial reference to the U.N.[25] Overlapping configurations of pipelines and land and sea routes will lead more to Metternichean balance-of-power politics than to Kantian post-nationalism. A non-Western world of astonishing interdependence and yet ferociously guarded sovereignty, with militaries growing alongside economies, is being tensely woven in the Greater Indian Ocean. Writes Martin Walker, senior director of A. T. Kearney's Global Business Policy Council:

> The combination of Middle Eastern energy and finance with African raw materials and untapped food potential and Indian and Chinese goods, services, investments and markets looks to be more than just a mutually rewarding triple partnership. Wealth follows trade, and with wealth comes the means to purchase influence and power. Just as the great powers of Europe emerged first around the Mediterranean Sea until the greater trade across the Atlantic and then across the Pacific produced new and richer and more powerful states, so the prospects are strong that the Indian Ocean powers will develop influence and ambition in their turn.[26]

And so this ocean is once again at the heart of the world, just as it was in antique and medieval times. To consider that history, and to explore the ocean part by part, let us begin with Oman.

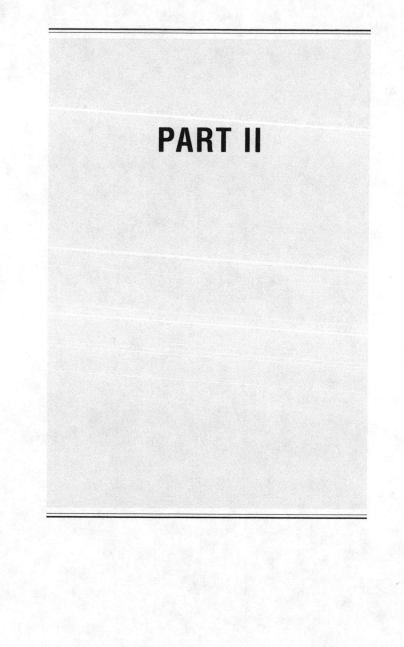

PART II

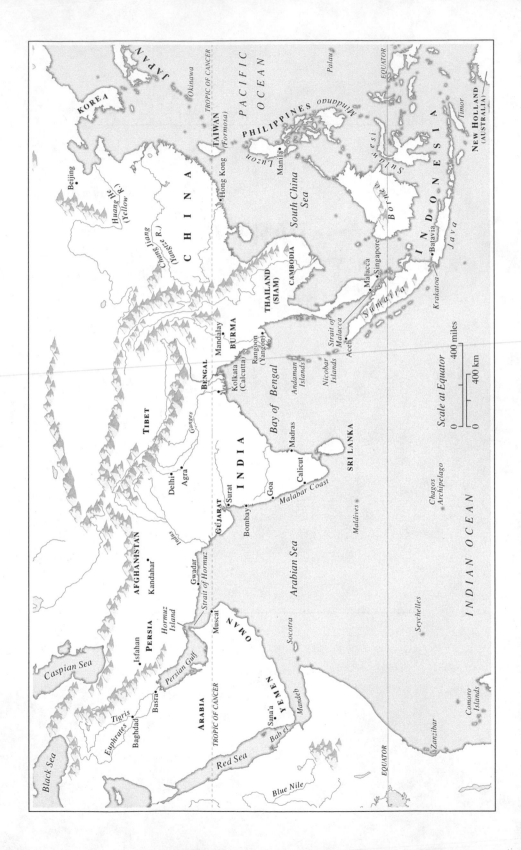

CHAPTER TWO

OMAN IS EVERYWHERE

The southern shore of the Arabian Peninsula is a near wasteland of igneous colors, with humbling plains and soaring, knife-edged formations of dolomite, limestone, and shale. Broad, empty beaches go on in all their undefiled grandeur for hundreds of miles. The hand of man seems truly absent. The sea, though mesmerizing, has no features to stimulate historical memory, so the vivid turquoise water suggests little beyond a tropical latitude. But the winds tell a story. The monsoon winds throughout the Indian Ocean generally north of the equator are as predictable as clockwork, blowing northeast to southwest and north to south, then reversing themselves at regular six-month intervals in April and October, making it possible since antiquity for sailing ships to cover great distances relatively quickly, with the certainty, perhaps after a long sojourn, of returning home almost as fast.*

Of course, it was not always that simple. Whereas the northeast monsoon, in the words of the Australian master mariner and unwearying Indian Ocean traveler Alan Villiers, "is as gracious, as clear, and as balmy as a permanent trade . . . the southwest is a season of much bad weather." So it was occasionally necessary in parts of the ocean for sailing ships to use the northeast monsoon for their passage in *both* directions. But the

* So dependable has been the monsoonal system that its inability to arrive has constituted a historical event. To wit, in 1630 the failure of the rains in certain parts of India—Gujarat, the Deccan, and the Coromandel coast—led to a million deaths from drought. John Keay, *The Honourable Company: A History of the English East India Company* (London: Harper-Collins, 1991), pp. 115–16.

Arab, Persian, and Indian dhows* could well manage this, with their huge lateen rigs lying as close as 55 to 60 degrees in the direction of the soft northeast headwind—sailing right into it, in other words.† This is almost as good as a modern yacht and a considerable technical achievement. The importance of it was that India's southwestern Malabar coast could be reached from southern Arabia by sailing a straight-line course, even if it did involve the discomfort of what seamen call "sailing to weather."

Despite the occasional ferocity of the southwest wind, the discovery of the monsoonal system, which so easily favored trip planning, nevertheless liberated navigators from sailing too often against the elements.[1] So the Indian Ocean did not—at least to the same degree as other large bodies of water—have to wait until the age of steam to unite it. From a sailor's point of view the wholesale shift in wind direction twice a year over such a large area is fairly unique. Elsewhere, the winds shift in strength and somewhat in direction with the seasons, but not to the degree of the Indian Ocean monsoons. The other major ocean breezes, the northeast and southeast trades in the tropics and the westerlies in the middle latitudes, remain throughout the year, as do the doldrums around the equator.

Thus, it may have been here off the coast of southern Arabia, with its clear starlit nights, plentiful stores of fish, and virtual absence of rivers, where the art of open-water sailing developed.[2] Both East Africa and India were remarkably close in terms of sailing time. Indeed, the winds have allowed the Indian Ocean from the Horn of Africa four thousand miles across to the Indonesian archipelago—and all the barren stretches of desert and seaboard in between—to be for much of history a small, intimate community.

And that means, it was early on a world of trade.

I was in the region of Oman known as Dhofar, near the Yemeni border, almost in the middle of the southern shore of Arabia. It is an abstract can-

---

* The smaller dhow, used for fishing, is called a *mashua*, a name from India; the larger kind, used for cargo and passengers is a *jahazi*, from a Persian word.
† Alan Villiers, *Monsoon Seas: The Story of the Indian Ocean* (New York: McGraw-Hill, 1952), pp. 3, 6, 56–57. The wind situation was even more complex in the Bay of Bengal, whose eastern coast was partially closed by the northeast monsoon. See Sinnappah Arasaratnam, *Maritime India in the Seventeenth Century* (New Delhi: Oxford University Press, 1994), p. 4.

vas of ocean and rock, an utter desert in the dry winter months save for the hardy frankincense tree erupting in solitude out of the ground. I cut into the bark of one, picked off the resin, and inhaled the interior of the Eastern Orthodox Church. But long before the emergence of Christianity, burning frankincense (*lubban* in Arabic) was used to freshen family clothes, bless people, keep insects at bay, and treat many ills. Lumps of the resin were added to drinking water to invigorate the body, especially the kidneys; it was thought to kill disease by activating the immune system and warding off evil spirits. Frankincense sweetened every funeral pyre in the ancient world and was used to embalm pharaohs. This resin was found inside the tomb of Tutankhamen in Luxor, and we know it was stored in special rooms under priestly guard in the Hebrew temple at Jerusalem.

Intrinsic to the Roman, Egyptian, Persian, and Syrian lifestyles, frankincense was to antiquity what oil is to the modern age: the basis for economic existence, and for shipping routes. Dhofar and nearby Yemen exported three thousand tons of the resin annually to the Roman Empire in the Mediterranean.[3] Sailing ship after ship laden with frankincense, aided by the sure and steady monsoon winds, traveled southwestward toward the entrance to the Red Sea, en route to Egypt and Rome, and eastward to Persia and India. Months later, when the winds shifted, the ships returned to Dhofari and Yemeni ports, loaded now with ivory and ostrich feathers from Africa, and diamonds, sapphires, lapis lazuli, and pepper from India. Tribal maritime kingdoms in southern and southwestern Arabia—Sabaean, Hadhramauti, Himyarite—grew rich from their individual strips of this incense highway. Until about 100 B.C. the fulcrum of trade between East and West was here, in this seeming wasteland in southern Arabia. Arabs, Greeks, Persians, Africans, and others mingled to do business amid this halfway house of transshipment in the days before direct sailings between Egypt and India.[4]

The summer monsoon from the south, known locally as the *khareef,* brings rain that will turn these now desolate hillsides of western Oman where I stood a miraculous jungly green. But an even wetter climate in antiquity allowed for more fresh water and thus an urban civilization, culturally sophisticated because of the oceanic traffic. Driving along the shore, I found a stone hut where an Arab in a flowing *dishdasha* and embroidered cap brewed me tea in Indian masala style, with milk, spices, and a heavy dose of sugar. Earlier, in a small restaurant, I had coconut mixed with curry powder and the local soup flavored with chili peppers and soy sauce—again the mundane influences of India and China here in Arabia, for I was closer by sail to the mouth of the Indus than to the mouth of the Euphrates.

I visited the crumbly ruins of Sumhuram, a wealthy Dhofari port at the heart of the frankincense trail, one of the wealthiest ports in the world between the fourth century B.C. and the fourth century A.D. Inscriptions at the temple of Queen Hapshetsut in Luxor mention the Al Hojari variety of white frankincense from here, considered the best in the world, and mentioned by Marco Polo in his *Travels*.[5] This frankincense was famous as far as China.

At one point the Chinese city of Quanzhou imported almost four hundred pounds of frankincense per year from Al-Baleed, another Dhofari seaside settlement near Sumhuram, whose city wall encloses the remains of more than fifty mosques from the medieval age. The ruins at Al-Baleed are more extensive than those at Sumhuram, allowing me to mentally reconstruct the great city that it was. A major settlement from as far back as 2000 B.C., Al-Baleed was visited by Marco Polo in 1285 and twice by the Moroccan traveler Ibn Battuta, in 1329 and 1349, both of whom arrived and departed by sea. The Chinese admiral Zheng He sailed his "treasure ships" across the Indian Ocean to Al-Baleed in 1421 and again in 1431, where he was received with open arms.* Writing much earlier, in the late tenth century, the Jerusalem-born Arab geographer Al-Muqaddasi calls ports in Oman and Yemen the "vestibule" of China, even as the Red Sea was known as the Sea of China.[6] Going in the other direction, Omanis from Dhofar and other regions of southern Arabia had been arriving in China since the middle of the eighth century A.D. In later centuries, a population of Arabs from the Arabian Peninsula would make the northwestern Sumatran port of Aceh, at the other end of the Indian Ocean in the distant East Indies, the "Gateway to Mecca."[7]

It was, indeed, a small ocean.

"Oman is everywhere, in China, India, Singapore, Zanzibar," Abdulrahman Al-Salimi, an Omani government official, told me over a welcoming ceremony in the capital of Muscat, featuring rose water, dates, sticky glutinous *halwa,* and bitter cardamom-scented coffee served out of a

---

* Treasure ships were warships carrying small-caliber guns, bombs, and rockets.

brass pot. He wore a white turban and *dishdasha*. The minister of religious endowments, whom I also met, wore a bejeweled dagger (*khanjar*) at the middle of his waist. This is a land of consciously reinforced tradition that is not insular; rather the reverse, such customs are linked to a seaborne national identity, forged over the millennia, of interacting with—not withdrawing from—the outside world. Oman is an example of how globalization at its best is built on vigorous localisms that can survive the onslaught of destructive commercial forces. What may appear medieval to the awestruck, first-time traveler actually fits well with the modern world.

The northeastward journey from Dhofar to Muscat takes twelve hours over an unceasingly flat, gravel- and lava-strewn desert bordering the Empty Quarter of Saudi Arabia, parallel to the sea.* Throughout most of the past, such a journey would have been accomplished under sail. As seafarers, Omanis are in many ways the ultimate Arabs. So influential have they been throughout history that the Arabian Sea—the northwestern quarter of the Indian Ocean—was formerly known as the Sea of Oman. The legendary Sindbad the Sailor might have been an Omani from Sohar, though he was based out of Basra, in Iraq. Sindbad's Homeric voyages of the eighth through the tenth century are another testament to the smallness of this great ocean, owing to the winds and the sailing skills of the medieval Arabs and Persians. The Kingdom of Mihraj in Sindbad's first voyage has been likened to Borneo in the South China Sea; the monstrous bird of his second voyage has been compared to birds near Madagascar; the Island of Apes in the third voyage was considered by the twelfth-century Arab geographer Idrisi to be Socotra, between Yemen and Somalia; and the cannibal land of the fourth voyage has been thought to be the Andaman Islands in the Bay of Bengal, if not even farther-afield Sumatra.

Another great Omani seafarer, Ahmad ibn Majid, might have navigated Vasco da Gama's ship from Kenya to India in 1498 (more of him later).† The Omanis dominated the slave trade, and ran an empire along the Swahili coast in East Africa through the early nineteenth century.

---

* The very waterless barrenness of the Empty Quarter was another reason that drove the Omanis to the sea.

† Though many scholars confirm this, there is still some confusion as to the identity of da Gama's pilot; one expert identifies him as a Gujarati. Satish Chandra, *The Indian Ocean: Explorations in History, Commerce and Politics* (New Delhi: Sage, 1987), p. 18.

They held the port of Gwadar on the Arabian Sea in Baluchistan (south-western Pakistan) until 1958. Indonesia has Omani communities, the forebears of which helped spread Islam into the Far East.

Likewise, you can find traces of all these places in Oman. The souks of Muscat are filled with a nineteenth-century Hindu community from Rajasthan and Hyderabad. The styles of women's dresses and the embroidered caps of the men bear influences from Zanzibar and Baluchistan. Music and dance are Zanzibari in character. Chinese porcelain is ubiquitous. The bakers are Yemeni and Iranian. Many of the businessmen are Gujaratis from northwestern India. The shields and coats of armor of Omani soldiers of old demonstrate the influence of India and of the Zulus from South Africa. Loan words from all these places influence Omani Arabic, and many Omanis speak Arabic with a Swahili accent. Globalization happened in Oman and the rest of the Indian Ocean in antiquity and in the early medieval era long before it did in other places, leading to an extraordinary level of sophistication.

The Arabs are known in the West as a desert people, susceptible to the extremities of thought to which deserts give rise. But they have also been a great seafaring race, as the frankincense trade and the historical experience of Oman demonstrate, the very harbingers of cosmopolitanism, who have been sailing these waters for thousands of years before Vasco da Gama. When looking at the entire period of Islamic expansion, "one fact stands out," writes the Dutch-American scholar André Wink in his encyclopedical series, *Al-Hind: The Making of the Indo-Islamic World,* "the growth and development of a world economy in and around the Indian Ocean—with India at its centre and the Middle East and China as its two dynamic poles—was effected by continued economic, social and cultural integration into ever . . . more complex patterns under the aegis of Islam."[8]

The "Saracens," as the British geographer Sir Halford Mackinder referred to the Arabs a century ago, "created a great empire by availing themselves of the two mobilities permitted by their land—that of the horse and camel on the one hand, and that of the ship on the other. At different times their fleets controlled both the Mediterranean as far as Spain, and the Indian Ocean to the Malay Islands."[9] The trapezoidal geography of the Arabian peninsula favored this development. Long coastlines bound Arabia on three sides: from the Gulf of Suez all the way down the

Red Sea to the Strait of Bab el Mandeb ("The Gate of Tears"), then north-eastward for 1250 miles to the Gulf of Oman, along what was in earlier eras the most fertile, populous parts of the peninsula (Yemen, the Hadhramaut, and Dhofar); and finally back north up the Persian Gulf to the Shatt el Arab in Iraq. The Shatt el Arab led to the Tigris, and hence to Baghdad, so during the Abbasid Caliphate, from the eighth to the thir-teenth century, until the Mongol devastation, Baghdad was connected via the Indian Ocean to China, since for much of history communications were often more easily accomplished by sea than across inhospitable deserts.

Moreover, commerce in Arabia was encouraged by the nearby shores of Africa to the west and the Iranian plateau to the east, for in the enclosed, protected waters of the Red Sea and Persian Gulf, constant seafaring brought the Arabs into intimate contact with two antique urban civilizations—those of Egypt and Persia. The Persians, in partic-ular, originally dominated the long-distance sailing trade with the East. In the sixth century B.C., Darius I "ordered a reconnaissance of the seas from Suez to the Indus," for there was much sea traffic between the Achaemenid dynasty in Persia and the equally thriving Mauryan dynasty in India.[10] Later, during the Sassanid dynasty in Persia, just prior to the coming of Islam, it is likely that Persian ships were in Chinese ports. In fact, the Persians, who under the Sassanids were a major Indian Ocean power, appear in Chinese documents throughout the late seventh and eighth centuries as owners of ships at Canton.[11] By this time, under the Arab-Persian cultural unity effected by the eclectic medieval Abbasid Caliphate in Baghdad, Arab and Persian sailings across the Indian Ocean from Africa to the Far East became nearly indistinguishable, falling under the general rubric of Muslim trade and exploration.

The aptly named Persian Gulf was the oldest open-water route of hu-mankind, from where it was possible to sail along the coast of Sindh (southeastern Pakistan) and Hind (India) without losing sight of land—that is, if one chose not to use the open ocean route from Oman to India, aided by the monsoon during half the year. For it was southern India that served as the "hinge" uniting the two great basins of the Indian Ocean—the Arabian Sea and the Bay of Bengal.[12] From South India or Ceylon it was a straight shot with the monsoon winds all the way to the Far East, close-hauled on a port tack. From the Persian Gulf to Sumatra in the In-donesian archipelago it was a relatively quick seventy-day journey—

twice the speed of sail travel in the Mediterranean, owing again to the monsoon.[13] And in another direction, from Yemen and Oman it was a comparatively short and easy sea journey southwestward to East Africa. Indeed, East Africa's Swahili coast was drawn intimately into the Islamic maritime sphere after A.D. 1200, and by the end of the fifteenth century at least thirty African coastal towns had been established by Muslim immigrants from southern Arabia.[14] It was as if every group was present everywhere around this ocean.

As noted, in classical times the towns of southern Arabia, to quote the late scholar George F. Hourani, were "the *entrepots* of all intercourse" among Africa, Egypt, and India. The ambassadors whom Ptolemy II of Egypt exchanged with the Mauryan emperors Chandragupta and Asoka of India, and "the Indian women, oxen, and marbles which he displayed in his triumphal procession" in 271 or 270 B.C., were likely transshipped at Sabaean, that is, at Yemeni ports.[15] According to the *Periplus of the Erythraean Sea* (Greek for "Sailing Around the Red Sea"), a document of the mid-first century A.D. compiled by the equivalent of a master mariner, Arab merchants were reportedly active in antiquity in Somaliland, East Africa, and near the mouth of the Indus River valley (today's Pakistan). Seemingly desolate and remote Arabia was at the heart of civilizational contact, and it was all on account of sailing.

The coming of Islam in the seventh century encouraged this seafaring trade. Islam is an ethical faith that provides an entire framework for social and economic interaction. What's more, as the scholar Patricia Risso explains, Islam is "portable." It is "not identified with a certain locale where animistic spirits dwell, or with temples belonging to particular deities," as has been the case with Hinduism. Thus, Islam was particularly "well suited to merchants who needed to conduct complex transactions and to travel." It encouraged networking because it is a unifying culture that centers around elements such as the Koran, communal prayer, regulations on family life, and dietary restrictions against pork and alcohol. Such elements brought the faithful together in social groups. Indeed, in the early Islamic centuries the haj pilgrimage functioned in part as a trade fair, as Muslim merchants came together in Mecca to make deals. Islam's "intermingling and coexistence" with Hinduism and Buddhism, writes the scholar Janet L. Abu-Lughod, lent a "coherence" to the Indian Ocean world that at times even the much smaller Mediterranean—divided rather than united by the winds—lacked.[16] This mercantile community, which adapted particularly well to new norms and traditions, impelled Islam eastward through the Southern Seas, giving it hegemony over much of the Afro-Eurasian land mass.[17]

Muslims dealt in slaves and ivory in East Africa, in pearls and gold in the Persian Gulf, in rice and cotton in India, and in silk, tea, and porcelain in China.[18] Islam not only sustained far-flung Muslim merchant communities throughout the Indian Ocean, but also attracted converts in the process. This had a pragmatic side, since by converting to Islam an African or Asian merchant could raise his credit value among the Arabs. In Burma, whose western coastline the Arabs would penetrate eventually, the ethnic Arakanese of the region often would take an Arab name in the interests of commerce. Arab merchants converted Indians, too, and together, through their own peripatetic movements about the ocean, established Islamic communities from Mogadishu to Malacca—that is, from Somalia to Malaysia. (This was all in stark contrast to Christian missionary communities who would not have much to do with trade, and whose interests were at times inimical to those of European trading companies.)[19]

Helping the expansion of Arab trade in the Indian Ocean was not just the rise of Islam, but of China, too. The Mohammedan state at Medina was established in 622; that of the Tang dynasty in China in 618. The Tang regime reinvigorated the bureaucracy, brought strong central government to China, and aggressively sought to develop maritime trading links to the south in the Indian Ocean. The situation was analogous to the moment in antiquity when the Roman Empire ruled in the west of the Indian Ocean and the Han dynasty in the east. Until the influx of Islam, Chinese merchants were comfortable dealing with Hindu and Buddhist Indians, but afterwards, under Tang tutelage, they came to be more comfortable with Muslim Indians, Arabs, and Persians.[20] Thus began a pattern of strong commercial relations between the various medieval Muslim dynasties (the Damascus-based Omayyads and especially the Baghdad-based Abbasids) in the west, and the Tang and succeeding dynasties of the Song and Yuan in the east, a pattern lasting for hundreds of years. Only later, in the fifteenth century, when China turned inward and trading opportunities were fewer there, did Muslim merchant power begin to wane. But with the large empires at either end of the Indian Ocean commercially interdependent, peace reigned generally, along with free trade.

Besides the desire for the ubiquitous frankincense, the search for luxury items like metals and medicinal herbs spurred trade between distant parts of Asia. In addition, India sold rice and cotton to China, and China sold tea in return. When da Gama arrived in Calicut, in India, he was dazzled by the maritime traffic that arrived from "China to the Nile."[21] The Muslim trading system was central to this medieval process of globalization, just as American-style capitalism has been to the post-modern form.

The Muslims were truly everywhere. Within a few years of the advent of Islam in the seventh century, the explorer Sa'ad ibn Abi Waqqas, sailing from Ethiopia, built a mosque in the Chinese city of Quanzhou. In the early fifteenth century an Indian Muslim piloted Admiral Zheng He's treasure fleet from India to Dhofar and on to Yemen, from where the admiral, a Muslim, too, became the first high Chinese official to make the pilgrimage north to Mecca.[22]

However, though the Muslims—Arab, Persian, and Indian—dominated, the Indian Ocean was not only theirs. Traders from all countries and religions took advantage of the ocean's unique environment. Even before the coming of Islam, Malays from the eastern seas, in present-day Malaysia and Indonesia, sailed as far west as Madagascar and East Africa at the opposite end of the Indian Ocean, bringing cinnamon and other spices.* Known as Waqwaqs because of the type of outrigger canoes they used, these heathens covered the distance of thirty-five hundred miles in about a month because of the winds.[23] Hindus, too, were also spreading their rituals, icons, and language around these littorals. A thriving trade brought Indian traders, mainly Hindu, all over the South Seas, creating a "Sanskrit cosmopolis" in the early Middle Ages throughout South and Southeast Asia.[24] Indeed, throughout medieval and early modern history, India's southeastern Coromandel coast was in close contact with Burma and the Indonesian archipelago, as well as Persia in the opposite direction.

The ocean constituted a web of trade routes. It vaguely resembled what our world of today increasingly looks like with its commercial and cultural interlinkages. Because the Indian Ocean is the sum of its parts,

---

* Excavations in Kenya have uncovered Iranian pottery from the Sassanid era of late antiquity, as well as Chinese Yueh pottery, attesting further to the great sailing distances covered. Charles Verlinden, "The Indian Ocean: The Ancient Period and the Middle Ages," in Satish Chandra *The Indian Ocean: Explorations in History, Commerce and Politics* (New Delhi: Sage, 1987), p. 50.

broken up as it is into subunits—the Arabian Sea, the Bay of Bengal, and so forth—the "natural condition" was for "several locally hegemonic powers to coexist," writes Abu-Lughod.[25] The ocean was neutral, in other words. No one state power dominated, certainly not any kingdom in Europe.

In the medieval centuries, Western hegemony still lay in the future; just as today, American naval hegemony, to the degree that it exists—the last phase of the rule of the West across these seas—may, as the years and decades advance, lie increasingly in the past.

CHAPTER THREE

CURZON'S FRONTIERS

I n 1907, soon after his return to England from India as viceroy, Lord George Nathaniel Curzon delivered the annual Romanes Lecture at Oxford. The subject he chose was "Frontiers," of which he had a lifetime of experience, first as a younger man traveling along the boundaries of the British Empire in Asia, and later as a diplomat involved in determining the empire's borders in Turkestan.[1] Curzon spoke about every kind of natural frontier: seas, deserts, mountains, rivers, and forests; and every kind of man-made one: walls and ramparts, straight astronomical lines on a map, marchlands, buffer states, protectorates, hinterlands, and spheres of influence. He named seas and secondly deserts as the most "uncompromising" and "effective" of frontiers, noting that England lost America, Spain lost Cuba and the Philippines, Napoleon lost Egypt, and the Dutch and Portuguese lost their coastal empires in Asia all, ultimately, because of the "interposition" of seas. As for deserts, he pointed out that the Gobi Desert protected China to its northwest, Bukhara and Samarkand were "shielded by the sandhills of the Kara Kum," the Middle East was for long periods relatively cut off from India by the "broad wastes" of Persia and Turkestan, and black Africa cut off from the rest of civilization by the Sahara to its north.[2]

Of course, seas could be navigated and deserts spanned by railroad and camel caravans, and Curzon listed numerous examples of this. Indeed, the ways in which seas separate humanity are obvious. It is the ways in which they connect civilizations that are crucially revealing, particularly when assessing such a strategic and crowded arena as the Indian Ocean. The same holds true for deserts, which are much more than just impassable frontiers, even without railways, Curzon's reasoning to the contrary. The effect of deserts on the destiny of nations is more subtle than that of oceans; after all, it was not only the existence of a desert to the east of Mesopotamia that formed a barrier between the Middle East and the Indian Subcontinent, it was also a matter of different cultures and languages or dialects, which arose because of numerous factors, not all of them geographical. Moreover, we should not exaggerate this kind of barrier, for history is full of Arab and Persian migrations across deserts. The desert stretching from Syria south into peninsular Arabia may have proved to be even less of a divider of peoples, as Arabic is spoken throughout. This north-south Arabian desert has been traversed by tribes and roving bands that intimately have affected the destinies of all the areas through which they have passed.

Hence, we have the story of Oman, a microcosm of the world of the western Indian Ocean, because, like other places on and near the Arabian Sea—Somalia, the Gulf sheikhdoms, the provinces of Baluchistan and Sindh in Pakistan, and the northwestern Indian province of Gujarat—Oman constitutes a vibrant albeit thin band of humanity existing between sea and desert, subject to the immense influences of both.

Oman is sort of an island; albeit not literally. Reversing in this case Curzon's neat order of interposition, the desert has been even more of a frontier in Oman's history than the sea. Because of the predictability of the winds, thousands of miles of open ocean not only did not separate Oman from the pathways of humankind, but indeed brought it closer to its neighbors, even as more than a thousand miles of open desert to the north kept it isolated by land. From the sea has come cosmopolitanism; from the desert isolation and tribal conflict. Because seafaring communities have existed for more than two thousand years here, Oman, in the manner of Yemen, Egypt, and Mesopotamia, constitutes an age-old cluster of civilization. Oman is not a relatively recent creation of history like the Gulf sheikhdoms, which came about mainly because they lay along the Indian Ocean trade and communications route of Great Britain, the nineteenth century's greatest maritime power: "Petty Arab chiefships" is what Curzon called the Gulf states, "established in order to prevent slave-raiding on the adjoining seas."[3] Nor is Oman the product of a family in the twentieth century like Saudi Arabia. Oman's ruling dynasty, the Al Bu Sa'ids, have been in power longer than the United States has been a country. Yet, despite its longevity, the animosity of the tribes in the desert have kept the Omani state weak or nonexistent for long periods, often resulting in domination by the most proximate great power, Iran. The sea, its winds, and good harbors have provided the foundation for a venerable state, whereas the desert has often come close to destroying it.

Oman, it is said, is the land of five hundred forts. In fact, I traveled from one Arab *qasr* (fort) to another in the desert that lurks just behind the deepwater harbors, a landscape kneaded over the eons by the wind and seismic disruptions into excruciating and beautiful forms. Each fort boasts a clean, mathematical singularity, towering over twisted hilltops and naked precipices. But it is the repetition that is instructive. As appealing as the museum restorers try to make them—decorating the rooms with carpets, porcelain, native jewelry, old pictures, and lovely latticework—the very number of these stone and mud edifices demonstrates the lawlessness of this wasteland over the centuries. Each fort signified a separate, self-contained society, where everyone from the governor on down to the children lived: with boiling date syrup, sticky and scalding, literally at the ready to be poured down through the narrow slits onto invaders. Thus, the desert was not simply an empty, impenetrable terrain that could be conquered only by a railroad, as Curzon suggests. Rather, it was sparsely but critically populated by nomadic tribes. Yet, lacking an urban focal point where a settled civilization could take root and thus provide political stability, it was also a landscape of anarchy.

The liberalizing influence of the ocean never truly penetrated into such a chaotic hinterland. Indeed, the deeper and broader the desert, potentially the more unstable and violent the state. The states of the African Sahel have been the starkest examples of this worldwide, and for long periods this was the story of Oman.*

* Nevertheless, we must be careful, since this interrelationship between geography and politics is never that cut-and-dried, and is full of contradictions. Actually, it can be a very fluid dynamic, particularly when great cataclysms occur. Just as conditions at sea occasionally can affect the desert interior, the reverse has been true. For example, in the thirteenth century, a sea route linked Canton in China with Basra in Iraq, from where goods were transshipped to Baghdad, and from there portered overland westward to the Mediterranean. Indeed, Basra functioned as Baghdad's port, giving the great medieval city of the Abbasid caliphs access to the Persian Gulf and Indian Ocean, and hence to the entire East. But in 1258 the Mongols, coming out of the desert, sacked Abbasid Baghdad and security broke down throughout Iraq. The result was that the sea route up the Persian Gulf became unfavorable, and Indian Ocean trade routes shifted from the Persian Gulf by Oman to the Red Sea by Yemen. Engseng Ho, Harvard University professor of anthropology, presentation for a conference on "Port City States of the Indian Ocean," Harvard University and the Dubai Initiative, Feb. 9–10, 2008.

So what has allowed Oman to emerge from decades and centuries of instability—the wages of its violent, desert hinterland—to become a stable and durable pro-Western state with its own highly trained navy deployed astride the all-important Gulf of Hormuz? And what can we learn from this that is applicable to the entire Indian Ocean region?

A number of factors feed into Oman's present cohesion as a state. It has a population of less than three million. That, combined with significant oil and natural gas reserves, has enabled the building of roads and other infrastructure enhancing the role of central government. This is in stark contrast to neighboring Yemen, which has a population of twenty-two million in a similar amount of territory, and is far more riven by mountains. Yemen is a much weaker polity, its central government has difficulty accessing vast reaches of the country, and must keep peace through a fragile balance of tribal relations, since no one tribe or sect has been able to establish an identity for the Yemeni state. The unsettling aspect of Yemen is the diffusion of power rather than the concentration of it. Since antiquity, the Wadi Hadhramaut, a hundred-mile-long oasis in southeastern Yemen surrounded by great tracts of desert and stony plateau, has maintained, through caravan routes and Arabian Sea ports, closer relations with India and Indonesia than with other parts of Yemen.* Unlike Oman, Yemen has remained a vast, unruly assemblage of tribal kingdoms.

Moreover, Oman's happy situation owes less to Western precepts of technology and democracy than to the reinvigoration of certain feudal practices and, relatedly, the unusual personal qualities of its absolute ruler, Sultan Qabus bin Sa'id. In and of itself, Sultan Qabus's Oman constitutes a rebuke to Washington notions of how the Middle East and the world should evolve. Oman shows how the path to progress in the non-Western world is indeed varied and at odds with some of the ideals of the liberal West and of the Enlightenment. It demonstrates, too, how individuals, as I learned throughout my travels about the Indian Ocean, determine history to the same degree as do seas and deserts: for good and for

---

* The Nizam of Hyderabad, in south-central India, recruited his bodyguards exclusively from among Hadhrami tribesmen. I have written extensively about Yemen elsewhere—see Robert D. Kaplan, *Imperial Grunts: The American Military on the Ground* (New York: Random House, 2005), ch. 1, and Robert D. Kaplan, "A Tale of Two Colonies," *The Atlantic*, April 2003.

bad. Sultan Qabus's singular achievement has been to unite Oman's two worlds: its Indian Ocean world and its Arabian desert one. Some historical background is in order.

Oman was unstable for long periods because although its official borders extend only around two hundred miles inland, such borders have been largely meaningless. In fact, its desert hinterland has extended much deeper, stretching into today's Saudi Arabia and beyond. After the population of present-day Saudi Arabia itself, Oman was likely the first region in the Arab world whose people converted to Islam. But because Oman was located on the fringes of the Arabian desert, by the Indian Ocean, it became a refuge for dissidents, notably the Ibadis, the followers of Abd Allah bin Ibad, a seventh-century Kharijite teacher from Basra.

The Kharijites (from an Arab word meaning "to go out") repudiated the religiously impure nature of the Islamic world's first dynasty, that of the Damascus-based Omayyad caliphs, who relied on conquered non-Muslims for their administration. The Kharijites, who championed jihad against their enemies—Muslim and non-Muslim alike—represented the "most extreme form of tribal independence," writes the scholar Bernard Lewis: "they refused to accept any authority not deriving from their own freely given and always revocable consent."[4] The Kharijite Ibadis of Oman rejected the hereditary Omayyad caliphs in favor of democratically elected imams. And yet these Ibadis were less fanatical than other Kharijites: they forbade the killing of other Muslims and were tolerant of non-Ibadis.[5] Oman became a breeding ground for Ibadi missionaries, particularly after the collapse of the Omayyad caliphate in A.D. 750. However, the problem was that although Ibadi Islam united the interior of Oman by giving it a sectarian identity, it divided it in another sense; the democratic nature of the Ibadi imamate led to many bloody disputes. Rent by genealogy and political-religious factions, Oman's two hundred–odd tribes fought continually among themselves in the desert, even as the coast prospered from Indian Ocean trade.

Thus, while goods piled up at the harbors, the tribes in the interior suffered incursions from the desert farther to the north.[6] Iran, the great power across the Gulf, took advantage of this weakness and instability, intervening to arrange truces between the tribes.* In 1749, Ahmad bin

---

* In fact, Persian influence in Oman goes back to antiquity. The *falaj* irrigation system—a system of tunnels, small dams, and storage tanks—was brought to Oman by Persian settlers in the seventh century B.C., as part of the expansion of the Achaemenid Empire.

Sa'id Al Bu Sa'id, the progenitor of the present Omani dynasty, united the warring factions and was hence able to expel the Persians. But thereafter Oman went into a decline. In 1829, Sultan Sa'id bin Sultan left Muscat itself for his empire to the south across the Indian Ocean in Zanzibar, off the coast of East Africa, which the Omanis had gradually established over the years owing to the swiftness and reliability of the monsoon winds. Subsequent British domination of Omani affairs played on the feebleness of Oman's coastal rulers who, while able to govern Zanzibar two thousand miles away—as well as plant their flag at the East African ports of Lamu and Mombasa, and at points deep in the African interior—were unable to withstand tribal attacks from their own close-by desert.

And there were other problems for Oman. The British Royal Navy enforced the abolition of the slave trade, the profitable East African part of which had been controlled by Oman.* The age of steam would make Omani sailing vessels, collectively known to Europeans as dhows, partially obsolete.† And the opening of the Suez Canal shortened the distance from Europe to India, undermining the importance of Muscat and other Omani harbors as Indian Ocean transshipment points.

Then, in 1913, the clerics and tribal leaders of the interior launched an uprising against Muscat, determined to restore an Ibadi imamate that would better represent the Islamic values of the desert. With British help, the coastal sultanate in 1915 beat back an assault by the three thousand desert tribesmen. Negotiations dragged on, with fighting on and off. There was an economic blockage of the interior. Ultimately, in 1920 the two sides signed a treaty whereby the sultan and the imam agreed not to interfere in each other's affairs, in effect rendering Muscat and Oman— the coast and the interior—two separate countries. Peace reigned for thirty-five years, until the lure of oil deposits in the interior led to new battles between the forces of the sultan and the imam, in which Saudi Arabia backed the tribes in the desert and Great Britain the sultan on the

---

* It should be said that on the whole, the Omani slavers were not nearly as cruel as their European counterparts. Rather than enforce a living death upon the poor Africans they captured, they often integrated them into their families, clothed them, and provided them with wives, according to the laws of Islam.

† This was particularly galling, given that around the turn of the nineteenth century, Oman was a sea power second only to Great Britain in the northern Arabian Sea. Richard Hall, *Empires of the Monsoon: A History of the Indian Ocean and Its Invaders* (London: HarperCollins, 1996), p. 355.

coast.[7] Though the British-backed Sultan Sa'id bin Taymur eventually prevailed, it turned out to be a Pyrrhic victory. A separatist rebellion broke out in Dhofar in the 1960s, and was hijacked by Marxist radicals. This occurred just as the sultan withdrew from politics, keeping the country isolated from the outside world and shunning development. The old divides between coast and interior, sultanate and imamate, thus persisted. In effect, into the latter half of the twentieth century, Oman was less a state than a geographical expression.

The road to true statehood began only in July 1970 when, with the assistance of the British, the reactionary Sultan Sa'id was overthrown by his son Qabus in a nearly bloodless coup: there was a brief gun battle and the old sultan was wounded in the foot before being dispatched to exile in London. The twenty-nine-year-old Qabus offered a general amnesty to the Dhofari tribesmen. He built wells, roads, and bridges in their desert region. Tribal guerrillas who surrendered were retrained by the British and turned into an irregular unit of the country's armed forces.[8] The new sultan also began an intensive campaign of meetings to win over both his extended family and his tribe, in addition to the Dhofaris, to his rule. It was a classic, counterinsurgency strategy-of-sorts, and over time it worked. By 1975, the insurgency in the desert was over and Oman was poised for development as a modern state.

Indeed, quelling anarchy means starting with clans and tribes, and building upward from those granular elements, just as Qabus did. In the desert particularly, it is all about the tribes. Historically, both Marxist and liberal intellectuals, in their efforts to remake societies after Soviet and Western models, have tragically underestimated these traditional loyal ties existing below the level of the state. A realist like Saint Augustine, in his *City of God,* understood that tribes, based on the narrow bonds of kinship and ethnicity rather than on any universalist longing, may not constitute the highest good; but by contributing to social cohesion, tribes nevertheless constitute a good in and of themselves. Qabus intuited this, and cobbled together a nation out of disparate tribal elements—plagued by the division between sea and desert—through the inspirational power of medieval tradition.

Sultan Qabus fashioned a neo-medieval system that comprised elements of democracy, built as it was on regular consultation with tribal elders, so even as he maintained absolute power, few decisions were arbitrary. This approach restored the link between the former imamate of the interior and the sultanate of the coast that had been rent for so much of history. Qabus was also sly. In the 1970s the *dishdasha,* the long traditional white shirtdress worn by men throughout the country, was going out of style in favor of Western polyester dress, when he more or less made the *dishdasha* mandatory. This step, together with the celebration of traditional architecture, honored rudiments of cultural unity throughout the coast and desert that assisted nation building.

There really is no ruler in the Middle East quite like Sultan Qabus. Today he is a slim septuagenarian who is unmarried and lives alone, almost as a recluse. There is a studied remoteness about him. He plays the lute and the organ and loves Western classical music, which he also composes. (He has started the Middle East's only classical symphony orchestra made up of indigenous musicians.) He has institutionalized his rule through the building of well-functioning ministries, advanced the status of women, built schools throughout the interior, worked to protect the environment, and outlawed hunting. One Western expert of the Arab world said that in private audiences, the sultan, a Sandhurst graduate, is the "best-informed, most thoughtful, most well read and articulate leader—in both Arabic and English—in the Middle East; he is the only one in the region you can truly call a Renaissance man," the personification of the cosmopolitanism that has accompanied Indian Ocean societies.

One former high-ranking American official observed that there is a breadth of strategic thinking to Sultan Qabus that is comparable to Singapore's Lee Kuan Yew. Indeed, the world has been fortunate over the decades to have two such enlightened and capable rulers governing at the two most critical choke points of the Indian Ocean, by the Strait of Hormuz in the west and the Strait of Malacca in the east. It is almost as if, like Lee's Singapore, Sultan Qabus's Oman is too small a country for the talents of such a leader. Sultan Qabus, it is said, can discuss the Israeli-Palestinian conflict in detail from both points of view, has worked hard to cultivate a good working relationship with the Iranians even as he has provided the United States with a military access agreement that helped rid Afghanistan of the Soviets and Kuwait of the Iraqi army, and later allowed for as many as twenty thousand American troops to temporarily stage in Oman prior to the invasions of Afghanistan and Iraq. In 1979 his was the only Arab state to recognize Anwar al-Sadat's peace agreement with Israel. Given that the deep-draft parts of the Strait of Hormuz that are essential for oil tankers are entirely in Omani territory—making Oman's own strategic interests identical to those of the outside world—Sultan Qabus would seem to be, with all his talents, the perfect go-between for the Americans and Iranians, and, for that matter, between the Americans and the Arabs in the case of the Israeli-Palestinian conflict. Yet the sultan, in keeping with his quasi-reclusive style, has shunned the role, retreating to his books and music like an elderly Victorian gentle-man, for whom courting publicity would be a sign of weak character.

He grants few interviews. His public appearances are modest in number. He is not in the newspapers cutting ribbons every day like other dictators, nor are photos of him present to an obscene degree as has been the case with dictators such as Saddam Hussein in Iraq or even Hosni Mubarak in Egypt. There is no cult of personality per se surrounding Sultan Qabus. Instead, there is an unreal, Stepford-like quality to contemporary Oman. There is very little military or other force to be seen in the country, in contrast to the security guards and concrete Jersey and Texas barriers that guard entrances to hotels and other buildings in Saudi Arabia. Almost every adult here is in native dress, smiles, and talks altogether positively of the ruler, though only when asked; and when asked about democracy or freedom, says, as an Omani friend told me, "What is this freedom that you talk about that we don't have?" And given the demonstration that the United States has provided in Iraq, with all its attendant violence, you cannot blame the Omanis their incredulousness at the question.*

Indeed, Americans have had a tendency to interpret democracy too legalistically, strictly in terms of laws and elections. They put perhaps too much stress in the act of voting itself, an interpretation of democracy which can inhibit American power rather than project it. In some societies, particularly in the Middle East, democracy is a matter of informal consultation between ruler and ruled, rather than an official process. Where would America's position in the Middle East be without the likes

---

* In general, it seems that Oman lacks political freedom but largely respects human rights. The U.S. State Department's 2008 *Human Rights Report* on Oman notes that while the government is centralized in the sultan's authority, "In October 2007 approximately 245,000 registered voters participated in generally free and fair elections" for the Majlis as-Shura. Similarly, rights of press, speech, assembly, and religion are restricted. However, basic human rights are largely respected. There were no reports of arbitrary or unlawful killings by the government, no reports of politically motivated disappearances, and the government "generally observes" prohibitions on arbitrary arrests and detentions.

of the monarchs of Oman, Jordan, and Morocco, not to mention other nondemocratic rulers who nonetheless fight anti-Western extremists? The future of American power necessitates an understanding of other people's historical experiences, not just its own. Americans believe, because of their own generally happy history, in a "unity of goodness," that all good things flow from the same source, such as democracy, economic development, or social reform.[9] But Oman shows that something Americans believe is a bad thing—absolute monarchy—can produce good results.

Oman demonstrates that whereas in the West democracy is an end in itself, in the Middle East the goal is justice through religious and tribal authority, which comes together in the person of the sultan. There is also the realization that, thank God we're not Saudi Arabia, with its unappealing and repressive monarchical style; thank God we're not Yemen, with its Wild West, partially democratic tribal anarchy; and thank God we're still a real place, unlike Dubai.

Oman's serenity is curiously aided by its Ibadi form of Islam, which is neither Sunni nor Shiite (and is also practiced in pockets of North and East Africa). Although the Ibadis, because of their democratic-cum-anarchic tendencies, fell into discord in previous eras, Ibadism, like a many-sided jewel, can also stress conciliation, the avoidance of conflict, and the importance of saving face. There is a calming, Buddhist aspect to Ibadism. It represents the opposite of jihadism. Here the few dissidents have been co-opted and work for the government. Ibadism is another factor, like the *dishdashas,* the distinctive turbans, bejeweled daggers, and architecture that help construct national unity.

Moderate amounts of oil and new discoveries of natural gas have also helped provide for Oman's political and social tranquillity. The sultan has leveraged this by conservative fiscal planning, whereby budgets are calculated according to oil prices much lower than the world rate, providing for extreme surpluses. He himself lives in a style below that of many an American CEO. There is a small-scale elegance to his palaces, and no fleets of limousines and jetliners accompany top Omani officials. The excesses of other oil-rich Gulf states are absent here.

The sultan's very tact, evinced by the modest style of his rule, and his shyness in cutting a larger figure on the international stage—almost in the minimalist manner of Scandinavian prime ministers, and in direct contrast to bombastic rulers like Iran's Mahmoud Ahmadinejad and

Venezuela's Hugo Chávez—may attest to the vulnerability he feels. Oman's eerie perfection may work precisely because it does not attract attention within the region.

Yet the sultan now faces a vaguer threat to his regime: acceleration of change that threatens to end Oman's relative isolation. Half the population is under twenty-one, and increasingly more young people are dressing in Western clothes and wearing baseball caps. Because of higher insurance rates for shipping inside the Persian Gulf, and the threat to oil supplies in the narrow Strait of Hormuz, more transport links are being developed between Dubai and Omani ports beyond the strait, so the brash Dubai model of development is spreading more quickly in Oman. And while the Dubai model is often criticized within the region for going too far in the direction of westernization, it is also, like globalization itself, insidiously appealing. Partly to create jobs for all these young people and partly to diversify the economy, the sultanate is now being forced to move in the direction of mass tourism, filling up the unspoiled coast with holiday villages for Europeans that will, in turn, affect Oman's carefully preserved traditional culture.

This wrenching change will transpire as the sultan, rumored to have diabetes, enters his seventies with no heirs to the throne. The hope is that the family and wider tribal elite, through a series of *shura* (councils), can agree on a qualified candidate. No one in Oman is suggesting a national election, even as the process by which a new sultan is chosen will be inherently consultative and therefore democratic. Oman does not fit easily within the strictures of Washington, D.C., policy debates, whose backdrop is the power of individuals in mass democracies. Yet democracy cannot be dismissed out of hand. The extreme centralization of authority that characterizes Oman works well only in the hands of a vigorous and enlightened leader. But what happens if—or when—power shifts to a less vigorous or enlightened one? Then such extreme centralization can signal disaster. Nondemocratic countries like Oman often evince efficiency when things are going well, but when problems arise in such systems the population, especially if it is young, can become quite restive. While I stayed here as a guest of the government and, like all the Middle East specialists I knew, was impressed with the achievements of this relatively little known, benign ruler, I nevertheless worried about Oman. It was a bit too perfect. I was attentive to the stirrings of democracy in Iran and Burma, and the return of it in Bangladesh, and despite the Arab world's dismal record in this regard, I felt that continued economic progress would ultimately initiate freer societies everywhere. Information technology and an emerging global culture demanded it. How would Oman react to the pressure in the years to come? The next few decades here might be less serene than the present.

Though from the government's point of view, as explained to me by the minister of religious endowments, Abdullah bin Mohammed al Salmi, the fundamental question is the relationship between tribal and state authority. Thus, by melding the Ibadi imamate of the desert to the coastal sultanate, his country is conducting a great, democratic experiment.

Nothing symbolizes that marriage between local tradition and Indian Ocean worldliness so much as the Sultan Qabus Grand Mosque in Muscat, completed in 2001. In other countries with absolute rulers, such a project could easily have degenerated into a monument not to culture and religion, but to the oppressive power of the dictator, exuding not eclecticism but giganticism.

I am thinking of the mosque of Saddam Hussein in the Mansour district of Baghdad and Romanian dictator Nicolae Ceauşescu's House of the Republic in Bucharest, both half completed at the time each ruler was toppled; architectural monstrosities both, that, in their inhuman dimensions, seemed to crush everything around them, and were, therefore, essentially fascist. The Qabus Mosque is different. Though it is truly large—the site covers 3281 feet by 2789 feet, with a main minaret almost 328 feet high—from every angle it is of manageable, intimate proportions, while at the same time exuding an elegant monumentality. To walk through the courtyards, along the arcades, and under the pointed sandstone archways so graceful that they have the lightness of swift pencil lines drawn on paper, is to take an aesthetic dream-journey from one end of the Islamic world to the other, from North Africa to the Indian Subcontinent, with a slight detour to Central Asia and with a heavy accent on the Iranian plateau. There are the sharp, soaring archways reminiscent of Iraq, the tiered and balconied minarets reminiscent of old Cairo, the dazzlingly intricate latticework and painted windows evocative of Iberia and the Maghreb, the carved wooden ceilings of Syria, ceramic tiles that recall mosques in both Uzbekistan and the Hejaz of western Saudi Arabia, the alternating white and dark gray stone arcades of Mamluk Egypt, the beige sandstone walls of India (from where the stones come), and, of course, the handwoven carpets and mosaic floral designs of Iran. Images of Greek Byzantium, Safavid Iran, and Mughal India flow together here, anchored by a dome with gold embossed fretwork that evokes the daring abstract modernism of the twenty-first-century Gulf itself. This is less a celebration of Oman than of Oman's place in a cultural and artistic continuum stretching thousands of miles in either direction. Beauty and proportionality are the principal intents, rather than the legitimation of the ruler-builder, whose picture is rarely to be seen in the complex. Though it is a mosque and religious complex, the tone is clearly one of inclusion. The world is welcomed. It is the spirit of the ocean more than of the desert.

Yet this benign spirit, a product of the trade and other civilizational contacts of the medieval Islamic centuries—strangely reaching fruition in the twenty-first century in the person of Sultan Qabus himself—does not, of course, prevent the ocean from becoming a zone of conflict and competition among great powers, for whom the importance of Oman must only grow.

Although Oman's influence declined with the age of steam, it is now recovering with newly enlarged container ports. From the blank desert of Dhofar a mass of gargantuan gantry cranes are visible from miles away, at the port of Salalah. Salalah, whose downtown, with its large outdoor markets and eateries exudes the sweaty African-like intimacy of nearby Yemeni towns across the border, is becoming a major global transshipment center for A. P. Moller-Maersk, one of the largest container terminal firms in the world.* A similar expansion has occurred at Sohar, at the other end of Oman, Sohar was home to Sindbad the Sailor and Ahmad ibn Majid; now Sohar constitutes one of the world's largest port development projects, as well as maritime and industrial hubs, with investments of more than $12 billion. Sohar is able to handle containerships with fifty-nine-foot drafts, and boasts petrochemical, metals, and logistics complexes.

A look at the map shows why all this is happening. The oil hub of the world, the Persian Gulf, is increasingly crowded and dangerous. Not only a possible war between the United States and Iran threatens it, but also a

* It is more commonly known as Maersk Sealand, a Danish firm.

plethora of terrorist scenarios that could involve one or a number of containerships or oil tankers. Moreover, with the rise of India and China, the Gulf is not just a lifeline to the West, but to the East as well. If the Gulf were ever closed to shipping, the ports close by, connected to it by railways and oil pipelines, would therefore become ever more vital—ports like Oman's Sohar, which sits just outside the Strait of Hormuz. Oman, a beacon of stability, is being configured as the Gulf countries' alternative link to the outer world. Though twenty-first-century Dubai may be the true successor to nineteenth-century Aden—the great coaling station of the British Empire in the Indian Ocean—Dubai, inside the Gulf, is geographically vulnerable. And because going to Dubai involves a detour for transoceanic container shipping, it is more of an air transshipment hub than a sea one.[10] Meanwhile, Salalah in Dhofar has the added advantage of being near the midpoint of the southern end of the Arabian Peninsula, almost equidistant between the Indian Subcontinent and the Red Sea: the perfect transshipment point both in antiquity and in the twenty-first century. Unlike Dubai, no geographical detour is involved for shipping routes, and consequently Salalah—with its repair, bunkering, warehousing, and freight station facilities—services more than fifteen hundred vessels per year, with consistent double-digit growth for port revenues over the past decade. Railways and pipelines culminating at massive port complexes have finally conquered the anarchy of the desert, leaving the sea—itself conquered from time immemorial by the monsoon winds—as the final victor.

CHAPTER FOUR

"LANDS OF INDIA"

Muscat, Oman's capital, is a series of whispering, fairy-tale bays. Jetties elbow their way out into the water that turns a hypnotic silver-blue at dusk. The white harborscapes composed of Mughal and Persian architecture, with green and gold domes, huddle against steep, jagged mountains the introspective color of gray. There are no modern buildings with ugly signage to destroy the spectacle. India feels very close, but nearby Dubai with its Disney-style globalization feels half a world away.

In the main bay out of which Muscat has grown, crawling up two rocky outcrops like the horned backs of reptiles, are the blotched walls of two Portuguese forts, Jalali and Mirani, constructed in 1587 and 1588, respectively, to strengthen the Portuguese hold on the Gulf against the Ottoman Turks. Together they flank Sultan Qabus's Al Alam Palace. Dominating the harbor with their humbling symmetry, these two forts appear charged with meaning. They recall the bulwarks and "cyclopean" dimensions of Portuguese forts in Hormuz, Malacca, Macao, Mozambique, and particularly Diu, off northwestern India's Kathiawar Peninsula in Gujarat.[1] With their three-foot-thick outer walls, curved battlements, circular towers and spiral stairways, cavernous rooms and mazes, they are pieces of superb architectural engineering that conjure up the whole fantastic story of the Portuguese. It is not only Oman whose shores are graced by Portuguese remains, but much of the entire Indian Ocean littoral.

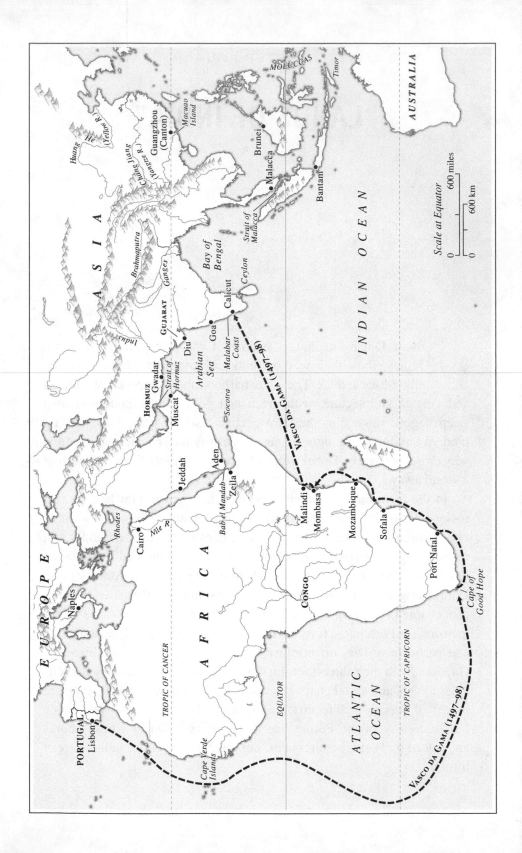

The Indian Ocean began its modern history as a Portuguese imperial lake. Within two decades of Vasco da Gama's voyage in 1498, the Portuguese came to dominate the most important sea routes and trading networks between East Africa and modern-day Indonesia.[2] This is not to say that the Portuguese were the first distant power to have a presence in the Indian Ocean—very far from it—only that they were the first to do something comprehensive with it.

In fact, Europe's involvement with the Indian Ocean has a deep basis in antiquity. The ancient Greeks sailed as far south as Rhapta, located somewhere on the East African coast near Zanzibar. The Greeks were also familiar with Ceylon, of which Claudius Ptolemy gives a description in his *Geographia,* and they sailed up the Bay of Bengal into the mouth of the Ganges not far from present-day Kolkata (Calcutta).[3] In the first century B.C. the Greek navigator Hippalus plotted a direct route from the Red Sea to India by observing the workings of the monsoon winds, the knowledge of which he passed on to the Romans.*

Every year, "about the time of the summer solstice," writes Edward Gibbon, a Roman commercial fleet, aided by the monsoon, sailed from Egypt to India's southwestern Malabar coast by way of Arabia, returning in winter, after the winds reversed, with a cargo rich in silks, precious stones, wood, ivory, exotic animals, and aromatics like frankincense.[4] Christianity may have been introduced to the Malabar coast (which Ptolemy describes) in late Roman times.[5] And along the farther-removed Coromandel coast in southeastern India, archeologists have found Roman amphora containers and coins.[6]

Fifteen hundred years later, the Ottoman Turks had a presence on the Red Sea in Yemen and on the Persian Gulf at Basra in Iraq. By seizing Yemen they were able to close the Red Sea to the rival Portuguese. The Turks launched raids against the Portuguese as far afield as East Africa. Yet their attempts to solidify a strong presence in Arabia in and around the Persian Gulf and to establish one in India ultimately came to naught,

---

* Hippalus may have been an Egyptian-Greek, though there is some confusion over whether he existed. The exact date of his discovery is uncertain. The workings of the monsoon may have been known about since Nearchus, an officer in Alexander's Macedonian army, sailed back from India in 326 B.C. Hourani, *Arab Seafaring,* p. 25; Donald B. Freeman, *The Straits of Malacca: Gateway or Gauntlet?* (Montreal: McGill-Queen's University Press, 2003), p. 12; Charles Verlinden, "The Indian Ocean: The Ancient Period and the Middle Ages," in Satish Chandra, *The Indian Ocean: Explorations in History, Commerce and Politics* (New Delhi: Sage, 1987), p. 32.

even as they controlled northern Arabian Sea shipping routes for significant periods in the sixteenth century. It was the Portuguese who can claim credit for ultimately thwarting Muslim Turkish ambitions.[7] But though the Ottomans clearly recognized the importance of the Indian Ocean—indeed, they were obsessed with competing globally with the Portuguese—they were too much of a land-based empire to sustain operations in its tropical waters. Battling the Venetians in the Mediterranean and the Austrian Hapsburgs in central Europe, with their resources in Constantinople, so far from the Indian Ocean, they were limited. The Indian Ocean became in due course a sideshow for them.[8]

Contrast all these efforts with those of the Portuguese, whose soldiers and mariners occupied Goa on the western coast of India in 1510, Malacca in the Malay Strait in 1511, Hormuz (near Muscat) on the Persian Gulf in 1515, and Colombo in Ceylon in 1518. Only twenty-three years after rounding the Cape of Good Hope, the Portuguese reached Java. The European fort design in Asia was of Portuguese origin. By 1571 there were some forty Portuguese forts and outposts like Jalali and Mirani in the Greater Indian Ocean, challenging and in some cases controlling the trade routes to the Levant, the Persian Gulf, the Arabian Sea, the Bay of Bengal, and East Asia.[9] Portuguese carracks and galleons might have been clumsy by the standards of ships that would appear in the seventeenth century in the Mediterranean, but by combining lateen sails and square rigging, and by putting artillery aboard ships, they were vastly superior to the Turkish, Egyptian, and Malayan corsairs in oared galleys and single-masted foists—as well as to the Chinese "junks" and Arab dhows—that they met in the Indian Ocean in the sixteenth century.*

This seaborne world empire was the bounty of obsessed adventurers: men ruthless for wealth, heroic to the point of fanaticism, freighted with the cruel mental baggage of the Middle Ages, and intoxicated with a poignant love for the Virgin Mary. Faith and greed went together. The Portuguese stole, but only from those whom they saw as the corrupt of God. Such an iron faith brought them through many an ocean storm, as well as through months upon months in battering seas; their troops deep in the hull, beset with malaria and scurvy, packed together in the hundreds. Between 1629 and 1634, of 5228 soldiers who left Lisbon, only 2495 reached India alive, most dying of sickness, exposure, or ship-

---

* "Junk" is the anglicized form of the Southeast Asian term *jong,* a range of advanced Chinese vessels that were developed by the Song dynasty in the tenth century.

wreck.* The story of Portuguese travel to and from India is biblical in its record of suffering.

The Indian scholar and statesman K. M. Panikkar describes Portuguese maritime expansion in the Persian Gulf and South Asia as an attempt to "get around the overwhelming land power of Islam in the Middle East," and thus to break out of the " 'prison of the Mediterranean.' "[10] Along with this dry strategic logic came a hot-blooded Catholic religious fervor. Panikkar reminds us that the spirit of the Crusades lingered much longer in Iberia than it did in Europe proper. In Iberia, Islam was not a mere "distant menace" but a close threat, owing to the existence of Muslim kingdoms that still flourished on Portugal's doorstep. "Islam was the enemy and had to be fought everywhere."[11] This fact, more than any other, explains both the cruelty and ferocity of so much Portuguese behavior in the Greater Indian Ocean. Indeed, as one Portuguese historian of the era, João de Barros, writes, justifying the awful deaths meted out to local populations:

> The Moors . . . are outside the law of Jesus Christ, which is the true law which everyone has to keep under pain of damnation to eternal fire. If then the soul be so condemned, what right has the body to the privileges of our laws?[12]

Arguably, Portugal's efforts in the Indian Ocean constituted nothing less than an Eighth Crusade. While the previous seven had focused on the Levant (the Muslim lands abutting the eastern Mediterranean), this one sought conquests much farther east, where of the four great empires in the region—Ottoman Turkey, Safavid Iran, Mughal India, and Ming China—three were Muslim.[13]

These factors came together in the myth of *Infante Henrique,* or Prince Henry the Navigator, who "imbibed early in his life," writes Panikkar, a spirit of "militant Christian mysticism" combined with a "bitter hatred" of Islam. As a young man in 1415, Prince Henry organized a successful expedition against Ceuta in Morocco—the first ever Portuguese attack on Islam's African base. This carried deep significance since Ceuta was the place from where Islam had entered Iberia in 711.

---

* The voyage from Lisbon to Goa in India usually took six to eight months nonstop. A.J.R. Russell-Wood, *The Portuguese Empire, 1415–1808: A World on the Move* (Baltimore: Johns Hopkins University Press, 1992), pp. 37, 58, 59, 73, 119, 219.

From then on, at least according to the myth, Henry lost interest in limited military actions and began to plan a grand strategy to outflank the Islamic world from bases in the Indian Ocean. This strategy carried the added benefit of undermining the middleman role played by the Arabs in the Eastern spice trade. Thus, Prince Henry, this myth continues, developed an obsession with India, which led, in turn, to an interest in sailing and navigation. To his castle and fortified camp on the Cape of Sagres—jutting out on three sides into the windswept Atlantic, on Portugal's and Europe's southwestern tip—Henry was said to have invited "mathematicians, cartographers, astronomers, and Moorish prisoners with knowledge of distant islands."[14] Amid the wild tableau of one ocean, plans were laid to conquer another.

In fact, as Oxford scholar Peter Russell writes in *Prince Henry "the Navigator": A Life,* contradicting Panikkar and others, much of this simply was not true. Henry conceived of India as only what is today the Horn of Africa, and no farther. Though much the crusader, Henry probably did not have a developed concept for outflanking the Muslim world, and he did not retire to Sagres to study cartography and navigation.[15] But the myth of Henry that grew after his death is true in the way that myths often are: they reveal the authentic motives and desires of a people, in this case of the Portuguese.

In addition to searching for grains, gold, and spices, the Portuguese truly did have a desire to outflank Islam, made more intense by the Muslim Turkish conquest of Greek Christian Constantinople in 1453.* So it is ironic that Prince Henry comes down to us through history not as a character in the story of the Crusades—which he actually was—but as a benevolent figure in the age of discovery, whose school of navigation (which might have never existed) laid the groundwork for the pathbreaking global journeys of Portuguese mariners.

Prince Henry died in 1460. Building on Henry's store of knowledge in organizing expeditions down the Moroccan and Mauritanian coasts, in 1483, Diego Cão was able to sail from Portugal as far south as the Congo River in Africa. Finally, five years later, it was a hitherto obscure mariner, Bartolomeu Dias, who rounded the African continent and brought Portu-

---

* But as Fernand Braudel points out, the Turkish occupation of Egypt and Syria did not occur until after Vasco da Gama's voyage, and thus outflanking the Turks was only a part of Portugal's crusading spirit against the world of Islam. Braudel, *The Mediterranean and the Mediterranean World in the Age of Philip II,* vol. 2, pp. 667–68.

gal into the Indian Ocean for the first time. According to one story, it was Dias who named the Cape of Good Hope, for he hoped to return there and reach India on a succeeding voyage. But Dias died on another voyage when his ship broke apart in the South Atlantic. It would be Vasco da Gama in 1497 who passed the cape with four square-rigged ships and sailed up the East African coast to Malindi, in present-day Kenya.

In Malindi, hundreds of years of Arab knowledge of the Indian Ocean—its winds and currents and haunts—were gathered into the head of one man: an Omani-born navigator, Ahmad ibn Majid, who agreed to help da Gama. Majid had sailed the Indian Ocean for half a century, and was a veritable Arab cultural repository of the seas.* He knew the best entry points to the mouths of the Tigris and the Indus, the way to negotiate the shoals off Mozambique, and the best landfalls in India and on both sides of the Red Sea.[16] Because the Arab world was so loose and diversified, in East Africa, so far from Iberia and the Middle East, the Portuguese could collaborate with an Arab like Majid, even as they planned to outflank the Arabs elsewhere on the map.

Whether it was Majid himself or another pilot perhaps recommended by him, an Arab pilot helped da Gama cross the Indian Ocean from Kenya to Calicut on India's Malabar coast in just twenty-three days in the spring of 1498, a spectacularly quick journey made possible by the winds of the southwest monsoon.† (Compare this to the late sixteenth century, when it took two months just to cross a stretch of the Mediterranean from Venice to the Holy Land.) Rather than "find" India, which the Greeks, Romans, and Arabs had done long before, the Portuguese put Europe back into intimate contact with it, for it was not so much Asia that da Gama had rediscovered for Europe as the wind system that brought him there.

There could not be a clearer case than this "discovery" of one civilization building upon the knowledge and skills of another. After all, it was not only the specific help provided by Majid from which the Portuguese benefited. In a more general sense, it was the Arabs and Jews

---

* Not just the Arabs, but the Indians, too, had long before explored the Greater Indian Ocean from East Africa to Borneo, beyond the Strait of Malacca.

† They arrived on May 20. The voyage back took four months because the winds were in the wrong direction. Almost half the crew was lost and the survivors were crippled with scurvy. Felipe Fernández-Armesto, *Pathfinders: A Global History of Exploration* (New York: Norton, 2006), p. 180.

who had bequeathed maps and astrolabes (precursors to sextants) to the Portuguese, so medieval mapmaking reached its zenith with these Iberian mariners.*

By opening the sea route from Europe to the East, Portuguese mariners went a significant way toward ending the isolation of the different branches of humankind. Of course, this process was helped along by the Silk Road and other land routes across Asia. But with the general collapse of Mongol power in the fourteenth century, which preceded the more specific decline of the Timurid Empire—not to mention the rise of Safavid Persia at the turn of the sixteenth-century that caused tensions with the Ottoman Empire—these trans-Asian land routes became less secure, and their further weakening was foretold by the ability of the Portuguese to reach the East more easily by sea.[17] With the establishment of this maritime route the East was pulled into European rivalries to a degree heretofore unseen. For the first time there was a truly vibrant world history, rather than strictly a European, or Indian, or Chinese one.[18] One region could no longer be written about without reference to another.

The more specific effect of da Gama's rounding the Cape of Good Hope was that it diminished the importance of the Mediterranean in favor of the much vaster Indian Ocean, with its even richer civilizational links.[19] As great as da Gama's accomplishment was, however, it was strictly one of application and endurance: obviously, a level of endurance that is almost inconceivable in our age, when the idea of months and years at a time in the scurvy-ridden hold of a ship is something that belongs to the level of the phantasmagoric. Truly, it was an achievement of character, though the Portuguese empire in the Indian Ocean emerged not as a direct consequence of da Gama's voyage at all, but as a result of the vision, that is, of the intellect—and of the endurance—of another mariner: Afonso d'Albuquerque.

D'Albuquerque had made the voyage around Africa to India shortly after da Gama, where he made the strategic decision to prop up friendly rulers on the Malabar coast. He saw immediately that an area as vast as the Indian Ocean could not be controlled permanently by a small and distant country like Portugal, unless Portugal established not only bases but

---

* The astrolabe was a thick bronze plate with an arm that moved on an axis, used for measuring the elevation of known stars in order to calculate the latitude and time of day. It appeared in the second half of the eighth century in Baghdad, built by Muhammad ibn Ibrahim al-Fazari, and was used by Ahmad ibn Majid.

also an overseas civilization there. It was not enough for Portugal to control the principal egress points: the Cape of Good Hope and the Straits of Bab el Mandeb, Hormuz, and Malacca. It needed a capital city of its own in India, which D'Albuquerque established at Goa, south of present-day Mumbai (formerly Bombay) on India's western Konkan coast, which would grow into a great outpost of cathedrals and fortresses. In order to hold and develop Goa, cemented by his implacable hatred of the Muslims, he formed a strategic alliance with the Hindu empire of Vijayanagar. D'Albuquerque put every Moor in Goa to the sword; though he was a man of great accomplishments, he should not be romanticized.

This viceregal "Caesar of the East" took Hormuz and captured Malacca, from where he sent out expeditions to scout and control the East Indies, to the extent possible. He built a fortress on the island of Socotra to partially block the Strait of Bab el Mandeb and deny Arab traders the capacity to reach India via the Red Sea.[20] His desire to deny Muslims use of the entire ocean ended up straining Portuguese resources to their utmost. Operating thousands of miles from any home base, he never had control of more than four thousand sailors and a small fleet of ships, and he did all this while a relatively old man in his fifties and beyond.[21] D'Albuquerque wrested a tenuous empire out of the horrid expanse of the seas. It is something that, in strategic terms, a global maritime system, loosely led by the Americans, with help from the Indians, and hopefully the Chinese, now has no choice than to try to achieve.

Yet, despite D'Albuquerque's accomplishments, much remained as it was. Change around the Indian Ocean seaboard even in the heyday of Portuguese imperialism was gradual. "Indigenous empires and trading states remained dominant and largely unaffected by Europeans scurrying . . . at their edges," writes the scholar Felipe Fernández-Armesto.[22] There were a few Portuguese forts on the coast of Oman, but none in the desert interior. At the same time, though, the Portuguese were able to block the Red Sea to Muslim shipping, in keeping with their strategy to outflank the forces of Islam. And they defeated the Mamluk (Egyptian) fleet in the Arabian Sea.[23] But while the high seas might have been Christian, much of the coastlines and all of the interior were not.

As the first of the modern empires, Portugal's was not only the weakest, but also the most medieval. Its navigators pried open the doors to the wider world, but at a savage cost. The Portuguese did not so much discover the East as launch a "piratical onslaught" upon it, breaking up, however slowly, the web of mutually profitable and peaceful maritime commerce that for centuries had bound the Arab and Persian worlds with the distant Orient. Indeed, the process that led China and Japan into hostile isolation was born of their bitter experience with the Portuguese. Yet, it wasn't really the modern West that the peoples of the East came to know through the Portuguese, but Europe of the late Middle Ages.

Portuguese sensibilities were further brutalized by nearly a century of ferocious fighting for control of Morocco, which had turned their soldiery into a veritable frontier society.[24] With the Portuguese, modern-style mission planning went lock and key with a worldview that at times represented the worst of the Inquisition. In the minds of these sailors, because the Orientals were heathens, they felt no shame in recounting their stories of pillage. Writes the late British scholar J. H. Plumb:

> They butchered crews of captured Moslem dhows, slinging some from the yardarms for target practice, cutting off the hands and feet of others and sending a boatload of bits to the local ruler, telling him to use them for curry. They spared neither women nor children. In the early days they stole almost as often as they traded. . . . the children of Christ followed the trade of blood, setting up their churches, missions and seminaries, for, after all, the rapine was a crusade: no matter how great the reward of Da Gama . . . and the rest might be in this world, the next would see them in greater glory.[25]

Da Gama sought "Christians and spices." Thus, he filled his ship with pepper for the voyage home, while sinking a merchant ship off the Indian coast filled with seven hundred Muslim pilgrims from Mecca.[26] Muscat was sacked and burned by D'Albuquerque in 1507. Portuguese freebooters occupied parts of Ceylon and Burma, and sold tens of thousands of the inhabitants into slavery. Such deeds, coupled with conquest on the scale that the Portuguese managed to achieve, required a narrow certainty of belief. If "doubt," as T. E. Lawrence writes in *Seven Pillars of Wisdom,* is "our modern crown of thorns," then the Portuguese were just short of being modern.[27] C. R. Boxer, the late British scholar, notes that despite their momentary misgivings, "The certainty that God was on their side, and that He would and did intervene directly on their behalf" was a pivotal factor not only, as he writes, in the capture of Ceuta in Morocco in

1415, but also throughout the course of the fifteenth and sixteenth centuries, as the Portuguese groped their way down the western coast of Africa and beyond.*

Believing themselves a chosen people destined to be the sword of the faith, the Portuguese show us a religious nationalism as doughty and often extreme as any in history.[28] Portugal's spectacular and sweeping conquest of the Indian Ocean littoral falls into a category similar to that of the Arab conquest of North Africa nine centuries earlier. In the post-national West, we would do well to remember that morale is still the key to military victory: in particular, a morale fortified by a narrow, unshakable conviction, which often has been the product of religion and nationalism. What the medieval Arabs and the late-medieval Portuguese once embodied challenges us to this day. To a significant extent, American power will depend on how it confronts fanatical enemies who believe more firmly than it does.

Portugal's was both a slaving empire and a military one. Unlike the Spanish in the New World who, following the conquest of Mexico and Peru, ran their holdings through civilian administrators (at least in the beginning), the great majority of male Portuguese who sailed from Lisbon to India's western coast went out as soldiers. "This is a frontier land of conquest," wrote a Franciscan missionary friar from the vantage point of late-sixteenth-century Goa.[29]

That frontier—everything beyond the Cape of Good Hope, from the Swahili coast of East Africa to Timor in archipelagic Indonesia—was called India by the Portuguese, or the Estado da India (State of India). Indeed, the entire sprawling East was also referred to as the Indies or the lands of India for, as we have seen, Arab, Persian, Hindu, and other traders had turned it into a recognizable cultural system, unified and in a very palpable sense made smaller by the predictable monsoon winds.

To understand further how the Portuguese were able to establish themselves so quickly throughout this quarter of the earth, one needs to realize that while a climatic, cultural, and trading system did unite the shores

* Boxer's critical view of the Portuguese expressed in his masterwork, *The Portuguese Seaborne Empire,* has been challenged in some respects by the scholar Holden Furber, who saw close cooperation between Asians and Europeans during the age of sail. Ashin Das Gupta and M. N. Pearson, eds., *India and the Indian Ocean, 1500–1800* (Kolkata: Oxford University Press, 1987), p. 131.

of the Indian Ocean, in political terms this vast region was in a state of incoherence and semi-chaos even, with congeries of small and weak states, susceptible to conquest or influence by an enterprising outsider. As we have seen in the case of Oman, while the sea united, the hinterlands often brought chaos.

No map during any point in history could surpass that of the early-sixteenth-century Indian Ocean in its cultural and political variety. It was a map of controlled anarchy. Going from west to east, there were the Swahili city-states of the East African coast; most importantly Kilwa, Mombasa, Malindi, and Pate. Arabic was, so to speak, their cultural lingua franca, mixed with a veneer of Persian. Moving north up the coast and swerving along Arabia, the Portuguese encountered Oman and a number of other states and tribes, some independent, but most under the sway of the Mamluks (converted Muslim slaves who ruled in Egypt, Syria, and the Hejaz from the thirteenth through fifteenth century). Heading east over to the Persian Gulf, the new Shia Safavid dynasty in Iran was expanding inland, and on the verge of a collision with the Sunni Ottoman Turks that would soon exhaust both powers. India proper was on the eve of the Mughal conquest from Turkic Central Asia, and was thus still divided between Hindus and Muslims. In northern India, there were the Muslim principalities of Gujarat, Delhi, and Bengal. Other Muslim sultanates in the southern Deccan plateau region warred with one another and with the Hindu empire of Vijayanagar (with which D'Albuquerque formed his alliance for the establishment of Goa). Arab and Persian traders were spread throughout India's coastal regions and Ceylon, which, in turn, was divided between the Buddhist Sinhalese and Hindu Tamils.

As for the region corresponding to present-day Southeast Asia, it was, in Boxer's words, "occupied by a number of warring states whose kaleidoscopic shifts of fortune cannot be followed even in outline." Going down the Malay Peninsula in the direction of Indonesia were the kingdoms of Patani, Singora, and Ligor under Siamese (Thai) political influence, "but also affected by Chinese cultural and commercial contacts." Malacca was the peninsula's wealthiest sultanate, its rulers having converted to Islam in the fourteenth century, though Hindu traders were welcome in the port. The main islands of the Indonesian archipelago were themselves divided among warring, petty states. As for China, under pressure from Japanese pirates and Mongol nomads, it had effectively retreated from the Indian Ocean in which it once had a great presence, owing to the eunuch admiral Zheng He.[30]

If the reader is confused, that is the whole point. Just as the Islamic conquest had occurred against a vacuum of power in seventh-century Arabia and North Africa—back then a stretch of weak Byzantine and Berber holdings—the Portuguese onslaught throughout the Indian Ocean took place during a period of weak principalities and distracted empires such as Ming China, Safavid Persia, and Ottoman Turkey. Furthermore, during the age of sail, political hegemony over the Indian Ocean was rendered impractical because of the monsoon, which made one-way communications fast but round-trip ones exceedingly slow, as the winds did not shift for months at a time.[31] Ergo, the Portuguese did not so much conquer the East as fill a vast gap of authority within it, especially that of the retreating Chinese, thus moving the ocean into a new phase of history.

As bigoted and illiberal as they were in some important ways, the Portuguese could also be broad-minded, and it was this aspect of their collective personality that accounts for their most successful techniques of empire.* Eventually, diplomats, merchants, naturalists, and artisans joined the ranks of soldiers toing-and-froing between Lisbon, the Persian Gulf, and India. Many of the travelers were educated, inquisitive people who did not make the journey as a last resort. "The depth, breadth, and richness of intelligence-gathering by the Portuguese was a notable characteristic of their world," writes the Johns Hopkins University historian A.J.R. Russell-Wood. As the case with Majid shows, they relied on Arab pilots to cross the wider stretches of the Indian Ocean, and Arab, Gujarati, Javanese, and Malay pilots for voyages from India's Malabar coast eastward to Ceylon, Siam (Thailand), and the Southeast Asian archipelago. They employed indigenous troops, and gave great recognition to local skills and lore. They became connoisseurs of Indian objects, particularly furniture. "Seemingly there was no facet of the human experience which escaped the lynx eyes and keen ears of the Portuguese in their peregrinations," writes Russell-Wood.[32] And for as brutal as they could be, there were other times, particularly in Africa, when the Portuguese used force as a last resort, establishing their forts and trading stations

---

* Some scholars allege that the Portuguese were not much worse than the Dutch and the English in their behavior, and that Anglo-American arrogance is responsible for the negative image of Portuguese colonialism. Kenneth McPherson, *The Indian Ocean: A History of People and the Sea* (New Delhi: Oxford University Press, 1993), p. 267.

only after much negotiation.[33] Indeed, there is much the United States can learn from the positive sides of the Portuguese imperial character, which left a deep cultural imprint in Monsoon Asia, with many Catholic converts and the persistence of the Portuguese language in places like Sri Lanka and the Moluccas.

Intoxicated with their newfound wealth, the Portuguese let the gold slip through their fingers. The imperial booty was not directed toward modernization back home. Portugal remained an antiquated and crumbling little jewel, lacking a real bourgeoisie until the twentieth century. Think of the poverty of old age that may follow a youth of dissipated luxury and far-flung adventures. Think of Lisbon in "ragged majesty" in winter, in the words of its early-twentieth-century philosopher and poet Fernando Pessoa.[34] The Renaissance had only a brief flowering in Portugal, owing to the natural conservatism of the people, the Counter-Reformation in Europe, and the rise of the Jesuits and the Inquisition, all of which worked to snuff out the Enlightenment in this land far beyond the Pyrenees. In the Portuguese Indian Ocean empire, the only institutions of higher learning were the Society of Jesus and other religious orders, which were part of the Counter-Reformation. Meanwhile, the Muslims held on, secure in their far-flung diasporas that reached around the tropical seas from the Levant to the Far East. They simply outlasted the Portuguese, whose empire would later be "whittled away" by the Dutch and the English.[35] The Eighth Crusade ultimately failed: the result of an indigenous reality in Estado da India and the religious wars back in Europe, which divided Christendom against itself.

What the Greeks and Romans accomplished for the Mediterranean, the Portuguese did for the Indian Ocean: they gave it a literary and historical unity, at least in the mind of the West. Indeed, whereas Homer's *Odyssey* and Virgil's *Aeneid* constitute myths based on the memories of a vague long ago, *The Lusíads,* the epic poem of Portuguese naval conquest in the Indian Ocean by Luiz Vaz de Camões, relies on a specific historical event—Vasco da Gama's voyage to India—which occurred only a few decades before Camões wrote.

Camões's Vasco da Gama, unlike Odysseus or Aeneas, is more of a real man than a representational composite. Hence he is not romantic, or tragic, or even that interesting. As stated, da Gama's greatest trait is his sheer endurance: his ability to abide years of uncertainty, loneliness, and physical hardship—rotten food and "loathsome" scurvy on a churning ocean, cannonballs tearing at limbs in offshore battles—while his equals back in Lisbon enjoyed the convivial luxuries of home.[36] "Fearing all," as the poem says, "he was prepared for all."[37] In the midst of a storm, with the "seas gaping to hell," da Gama, "tormented by doubts and fears," has no one but God to turn to. He declares:

> Why, O God, do you now forsake us?
> Where is the offense? How are we to blame
> For this service undertaken in Thy name . . .
>
> As he uttered this prayer the winds howled,
> Butting like a herd of wild bulls,
> Lashing the storm to greater fury,
> And screaming through the shrouds;
> The fork-lightning never paused . . .[38]

They survive the storm to reach India. Because the adventures Camões relates are quite literally true, this story of the sons of Lusus (the mythical founder of Portugal) on the vast and uncharted oceanic wastes is in the final analysis more extraordinary than the "shore-hugging" epics of Greek and Roman antiquity.[39] As Camões himself asks in his poem, did Odysseus or Aeneas "dare to embark on Actual Oceans . . . did they see a fraction" of what da Gama saw?[40] It is hard to think of many other odysseys where the hardships seem to last as many months and years as was the case with the Portuguese in the Indian Ocean. Not until men journey to other planets are they likely to have such a painful, palpable sense of great and lonely distance over the revolving earth as did these Portuguese mariners.

In the poem, the giant ogre Adamastor, who stands watch over the Cape of Good Hope (the "Cape of Storms"), awakens in these sailors the fear and doubt over whether they have ventured too far. Yet they do not turn back. To be sure, The Lusíads encapsulates the essence of the Portuguese achievement of the late fifteenth and sixteenth centuries: to drag the West from a "limited Mediterranean outlook," in the words of the late Oxford scholar Maurice Bowra, "to a vision which embraced half the globe."[41]

Camões was the first great European artist to cross the equator and visit the tropics and the Orient. On "routes never charted" he was protected only by "frail timbers on treacherous seas."[42] His intense and intricate descriptions of the Indian Ocean and its fearful effects on men indicate just how well he knew it:

> Sudden, catastrophic thunderstorms,
> Bolts setting the atmosphere ablaze,
> Black squalls, nights of pitch darkness,
> Earth-splitting claps of thunder . . .[43]

There are, too, Camões's vivid descriptions of the East—that is, of the Indian Ocean littoral, or what he, too, simply calls the "lands of India." There are the sails made of palm leaves in Mozambique, and the bare chests and daggers of the inhabitants; the purple caftans of the people of Malinde and the golden collars and velvet sandals of their king. Then comes Dhofar, "source of the loveliest, most aromatic of all altar-incense." There is the Persian Gulf island of Bahrain, where "the ocean bed/Is bedecked with pearls, matching the dawn." There are the "spreading pavilions and pleasant groves" of the palace in India, the aromatic betel nut, the perfumes and peppercorns, the cardamoms and hot chilies and precious stones, and the "monstrous Hindu deities with their violent colors and many limbs." He describes the submarine plants of the Maldive Islands, the sandalwood trees of Timor, and the men of Burma who wear "tinkling bells" on their genitals.[44] Because the poet himself made the same voyage as da Gama, he crowds his epic with realism. Camões's description of feasting in the palace in Calicut evokes the fantastic descriptions of Aztec Mexico as seen by Bernal Díaz del Castillo, the chronicler of the Cortés expedition.

Camões was born in 1524 of Galician origin. He grew up in Coimbra in central Portugal and attended its great medieval university, where, because the classical spirit of the Renaissance had comprehensively penetrated, he was able to immerse himself in the literature of the Greeks and Romans. "The thoroughness of his teaching is apparent when we remember that he wrote his epic [replete with classical and other literary references] in the fortresses of Africa and Asia, far from books," notes the British scholar Edgar Prestage.[45]

On Good Friday 1544, in a Lisbon church, Camões fell in love at first sight with a thirteen-year-old girl, Caterina de Ataide, who ultimately rejected him. He then went through periods of depression, with thoughts of suicide. He might have fought a duel during this period. In any case, his indiscretions led to his banishment from court life. In 1547 he enlisted in the army and served for two years in Ceuta, where he lost his right eye in a skirmish with the native Moroccans. Back in Lisbon, where ladies mocked his disfigurement, he joined a gang of roughneck, bohemian youth, all the while hoping for a government appointment of some sort, but the palace turned him down. Then in a street fight he wounded a palace servant and was thrown in jail. In exchange for a pardon, he reenlisted for five years in the military and was dispatched to India. This was meant as a death sentence, given that his was the only one of four India-bound ships that arrived safely that year.

In 1553, six months after leaving Lisbon, his boat tied up in Goa, a Portuguese bastion of 100,000 founded by D'Albuquerque. From there, Camões went on combat missions along the coast to discipline petty Hindu and Muslim rulers. He took part in an armada that sailed back across the Arabian Sea and up the Red Sea and Persian Gulf, to rein in piracy, which throughout history had been a scourge in these waters. The next pirate hunt saw him in the Horn of Africa, the Gulf of Aden, and the East African port of Mombasa. Upon returning to India, he set sail again, this time eastward, to the Moluccas and Macao. His life reads like a chronicle of Portugal's policing efforts in its newfound Indian Ocean empire. All of these experiences he weaves into the final canto of *The Lusíads,* which manages to communicate both a spirit of exotic adventure and of a profound homesickness—that is, a unique sadness common to Portuguese mariners that they call *saudade.*

Camões had to rewrite much of his epic, which was lost in the mouth of the Mekong River in 1559 in modern-day Cambodia, after the boat he was traveling in as a prisoner from China back to India was wrecked. He had to swim ashore, clutching parts of his manuscript rather than his possessions.

Why he was imprisoned is unclear, most likely because of some intrigue or indiscretion in the violent, tumultuous frontier society he inhabited. By way of Malacca he was able to return to Goa. Finally released from jail there, he borrowed some money and made his way to Mozambique, where he was detained for two more years, unable to pay his debts. He had to beg his friends for food and clothes and for his passage home. The only wealth he had when he returned to Portugal in 1570, after an absence of seventeen years, was the finished manuscript of *The Lusíads*. Immediately upon disembarking in Lisbon, he visited his beloved Caterina's tomb. To the last he was a man obsessed.

Publication of the epic in 1572 won Camões a royal pension, but his troubles and heartbreak were not over. The poem calls for the rejuvenation of the imperial spirit just as King Sebastião's invasion of Morocco ended in disaster, with the destruction of the Portuguese army. A few years later, in 1580, Camões died of the plague in Lisbon, alone and unmarried, without even a sheet to cover him. He was buried in a borrowed shroud in a common grave. Three centuries later, what was believed to be some of his remains were transferred to the Portuguese national pantheon: the elaborate and spired Jerónimos Monastery in Belém, in western Lisbon. Here they lie in a sculptured stone tomb bathed in yellow light from the imposing stained-glass windows, right beside the tomb of Vasco da Gama, whom he had immortalized.

The stores of energy that drive *The Lusíads* are reminiscent of that other great Iberian epic, *Don Quixote,* published over three decades later, in 1605 and 1615. Both works were forged out of a crucible of extreme personal adventure and tragedy. In the way of Camões, Miguel de Cervantes enlisted in the army and fought in the naval battle of Lepanto in 1571 off the western coast of Greece, where his left arm was crippled by a wound. En route home to Spain four years later, he was captured by Barbary pirates and sold as a slave, eventually becoming the property of the viceroy of Algiers. After five years of captivity and several failed escape attempts, he was obliged to pay a ransom that financially ruined his family. Though the sensibilities of the two epics could not be more different—one a passionate salute to imperial conquest; the other a humorous parody of a knight-errant—both constitute a grand and audacious cinematic journey across the world map.

At the start of the poem, Camões makes the claim of how superior to the ancient Greeks and Romans are the Portuguese, to whom "both Mars and Neptune bowed."[46] Yet the poet pays tribute throughout his epic to the ancients by his very use of their classics. It is the ancient gods—full of beauty, enchantment, and brilliant contrasts—who help determine the voyage's outcome: Bacchus who seeks to thwart the Portuguese sailors; Venus and Mars who favor them. This deep involvement with Mediterranean mythology, according to the Oxford scholar Bowra, is what helps make Camões part of the secular Renaissance, even though his poem also can be read as an assertion of Christendom after a long period of Muslim ascendancy in the Mediterranean and the Levant.

Camões, like the Portuguese empire itself, is full of contradictions. He is the first of the moderns, and the last of the medievalists. He can be championed by Bowra as a humanist in his condemnation of the excesses of some of Portugal's own conquerors, although his portrayal of Muslims is often dark and unforgiving. He refers to "vile Mohammed."[47] To Camões, Islam is simply corrupt and barbarous, mixing "guile and falsehood."[48] The only virtuous Muslims are those who help the Portuguese, for the contest he depicts is nothing less than the struggle between light and darkness.[49] Camões attacks the Reformation for dividing Christians at a time when they should have been focused on the Islamic threat: instead of fighting the pope, he implies, they should have been fighting the Turks.

The poem celebrates Portuguese imperial conquest, but at the same time Camões can be ambivalent toward that very enterprise, for he rails against vanity and glory, and admits how the spreading of the Christian religion can lead to new horrors. As he writes:

> Delusions are possessing you,
> Already, ferocity and brute force
> Are labeled strength and valour . . .[50]

There was little pretty or romantic about the way Portugal yanked the Indian Ocean into contact with Europe and the West. It was a gruesome and grueling affair, full of pain and wonder and savagery. Camões's *Lusíads* illuminates it all. The poem is a reminder of how conquest almost always leads to heartbreak. The more they conquered, the less ground the Portuguese were able to hold. The Indian Ocean is small in a cultural sense, but too vast even in the jet age for one power to gain real sway over it. The Portuguese conquest, like the conquests of the Dutch and the British that followed, reflects both the dynamism and imprudence to which all empires are susceptible. It is a lesson the United States would do well to learn.

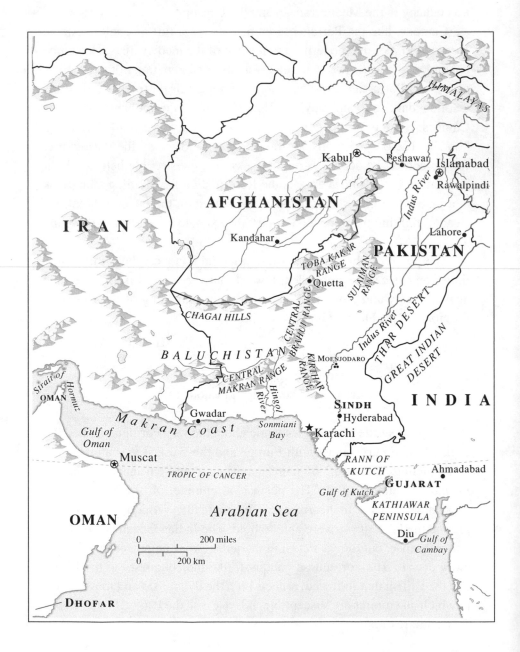

HIMALAYAS

Kabul ⊗   Peshawar
              Islamabad ⊗
              Rawalpindi

AFGHANISTAN

IRAN

Lahore

Kandahar

PAKISTAN

TOBA KAKAR
RANGE

SULAIMAN
RANGE

Quetta

CHAGAI HILLS

CENTRAL
BRAHUI RANGE

Indus River

THAR DESERT

BALUCHISTAN

MOENJODARO

GREAT INDIAN
DESERT

KIRTHAR
RANGE

CENTRAL
MAKRAN RANGE

INDIA

Strait of
Hormuz

OMAN

Hingol
River

SINDH

Gwadar

Sonmiani
Bay

Hyderabad

Makran Coast

Karachi

Gulf of
Oman

Muscat ⊗

RANN OF
KUTCH

Ahmadabad

TROPIC OF CANCER

GUJARAT

Gulf of Kutch

OMAN

Arabian Sea

KATHIAWAR
PENINSULA

0   200 miles

Diu   Gulf of
        Cambay

0   200 km

DHOFAR

CHAPTER FIVE

BALUCHISTAN AND SINDH

aps are inherently spellbinding, and one of the many delights of Camões is the way his poem draws you to them. Often when I have been in need of inspiration—or of an idea—I have consulted a map. Take the map of Pakistan's Makran coast, from the Iranian frontier eastward along the Arabian Sea to Karachi, near the border with India. The word "Pakistan" connotes the Indian Subcontinent, but geographically and culturally one may argue that the Subcontinent does not actually begin until the Hub River a few miles west of Karachi, near the Indus River delta. Thus, the four-hundred-mile Makran coast inside Pakistan constitutes a vast geographical and cultural transition zone, bearing a heavy imprint of the Middle East, particularly Arabia, for we are directly across the Gulf of Oman from Muscat. Makran was first invaded by Arabs in A.D. 644, only twenty-two years after the Hegira.[1] This transition zone, the frontier of al-Hind, which includes both the Makran coast and the adjacent interior, is together known as Baluchistan. It was through this wave-lashed alkaline wasteland that the 18,000-man army of Alexander the Great marched westward, from the Indus toward Persia, in the course of a disastrous retreat from India in 325 B.C.

Baluchistan, particularly the southern, coastal part, is a wild and woolly, Turko-Iranian, tribal stepchild of the Middle East that has chafed for decades under the domination of darker-skinned, urbanized, and, so it is alleged, sharper-in-the-ways-of-the-world Punjabis, who live close to the Indian border in Pakistan's crowded northeast, and who essentially run the Pakistani state. Yet, the teeming hills of humanity that mark the densely populated Indian Subcontinent feel far away here in *Arabian Pakistan*. To drive along the Makran coast is to experience the windy, liberating flatness of Yemen and Oman, with their towering, saw-tooth ramparts the color of sandpaper, rising sheer off a desert floor pockmarked with thornbushes. Here, along a coast so empty that you can almost hear the echo of the camel hooves of Alexander's army, you lose yourself in geology. An exploding sea bangs against a knife-carved apricot moonscape of high sand dunes, which, in turn, gives way to crumbly badlands of black slag heaps. This is a more baroque seaboard than Dhofar, and the record of the winds and seismic disruptions takes the form of tortuous folds and uplifts, as well as of deep gashes and conical incrustations.

For hours on end, the only sign of civilization is the odd teahouse, a partly charred stone hut with jute *charpoys* (beds) and musty, Iranian-packaged biscuits for sale along with strongly brewed tea. Historically, this is a wilder, less visited coastline than Oman, and thus less marked with the cosmopolitan influences of the rest of the Indian Ocean. Into these road stops, on old autos and motorcycles, screech Baluch tribesmen wearing Arab headscarves, speaking in harsh gutturals, and playing music that, with its rumbling rhythms, is much closer to the spirit of Arabia than to the introspective twanging ragas of the Subcontinent.

But be not deceived, Pakistan exists here. The highway from Karachi west to the Iranian border area is a modern one, with only a few broken patches left to be paved. Government checkpoints are frequent, and major air and sea bases are being developed, respectively, at Pasni and Ormara, from where Pakistan can counter India's projection of power into the Indian Ocean. Pakistan's government may not control the vast desert and mountain fastnesses of Baluchistan, with their rebellious and smuggling tribes and dacoits (bandits). But the government can be where it wants, when it wants: to extract minerals, to grab land, to build highways and bases.

Indeed, as the government builds roads and military installations, Baluch and minority Hindus are being displaced forcibly from the area, for both groups are suspected of harboring sympathy for India, which, truth be told, in Baluch and Hindu eyes, acts as a necessary counterweight to a Pakistani state that oppresses them.

Studying the map of "rugged and moldy" Baluchistan, as the first adventurers of the British East India Company called it, nothing stirred my imagination so much as Gwadar, a port town of seventy thousand close to the border with Iran at the far end of the Makran coast.[2] If there are great place-names of the past—Carthage, Thebes, Troy, Samarkand, Angkor Wat—and of the present—Dubai, Singapore, Teheran, Beijing, Washington—then Gwadar might qualify as a great place-name of the future.

Getting to Gwadar was not easy. A special permit, or "non-objection certificate," was required from the Pakistani Ministry of Interior. I waited nearly two weeks for one, and then was told I had been rejected. Thoroughly despondent, I was finally able to locate through an old friend a helpful bureaucrat who performed the seeming miracle of getting me the permit in two days. And so, because of the very difficulty in reaching the place, Gwadar was invested with great importance in my own mind before I even arrived.

Oman held Gwadar until 1958, when it ceded this western corner of the Makran coast to the new state of Pakistan. Gwadar immediately seized the imagination of Pakistani planners during the military rule of Ayub Khan in the 1960s. They saw Gwadar as an air and naval hub that would be an alternative to Karachi and that, when set alongside Pasni and Ormara, would constitute a string of Arabian Sea bases making Pakistan a great Indian Ocean power athwart both the Subcontinent and the whole Near East. Gwadar's ultra-strategic location would help liberate Pakistan from its own artificial geography, giving it in effect a new destiny. But the Pakistani state was young, poor, insecure, and with weak infrastructure and institutions. Thus, the development of Gwadar would have to wait.

The next people to dream of Gwadar, or at least of its coastal environs, were the Russians. The Makran coast was the ultimate prize denied them during their decade-long occupation of Afghanistan in the 1980s—the fabled warm water outlet to the sea that formed the strategic raison d'être for their Afghan adventure. From Gwadar the Soviet Union could have exported the hydrocarbon wealth of Central Asia, thus liberating the most landlocked portion of the Kremlin's empire. But Afghanistan proved to be the graveyard of Soviet imperial visions. Rather than expand the empire, it destroyed it. Gwadar, still just a point on the map—a huddle of stone fishermen's houses on a spit of sand—was like a poisoned chalice.

The story goes on. The 1990s in Pakistan were a time of successive democratic governments struggling to cope with the country's intensifying social and economic turmoil, aggravated by the spread of urban slum populations and the increasing scarcity of water. Violence was endemic to Karachi and other cities. But even as the Pakistani political elite turned inward, it remained obsessed with the related problems of Afghanistan and energy routes. The anarchy in Afghanistan in the wake of the Soviet troop withdrawal was preventing Pakistan from establishing roads and pipelines to the new oil states of Central Asia—routes that would help Islamabad consolidate a vast Muslim rear base for the containment of India. The final egress of this energy network would be Gwadar. So obsessed was Prime Minister Benazir Bhutto's government with containing Afghan chaos that her interior minister, the retired general Naseerullah Babar, conceived of the newly formed Taliban as a solution to Pakistan's problem. Bhutto's government provided the Taliban with money, weapons, vehicles, fuel, subsidized food, and volunteers from Pakistan's own Islamic madrassas, all of which eased the extremist movement's path to power in Kabul in 1996. The Taliban provided stability of a sort, but it was that of the grave, something that Unocal (Union Oil Company of California) and other firms, intrigued by building an energy pipeline from the Caspian Sea and Turkmenistan's Dauletabad natural gas field across Afghanistan to Pakistan's Indian Ocean ports like Gwadar, all found out to their dismay.

Then in October 1999, army general Pervez Musharraf took power in a bloodless coup precipitated by years of gross civilian misrule. In 2000 he asked the Chinese to consider funding the development of a deepwater port at Gwadar. A few weeks after 9/11, as it happened, the Chinese agreed. Thus, with little fanfare, Gwadar became an example of how the world began to change in the wake of the World Trade Center attacks in ways far different than Americans and the administration of George W. Bush ever imagined. The Chinese spent $200 million on the port project, completing the first phase on schedule in 2006. In 2007, PSA Singapore (the Port of Singapore Authority), was given a forty-year contract to run Gwadar port. It appeared that Gwadar was finally moving beyond the stage of dreams to become twenty-first-century reality.

So imagine now, a bustling deepwater port with refueling and docking facilities at the extreme southwestern tip of Pakistan, more a part of the Middle East than of the Indian Subcontinent, equipped with a highway and oil and natural gas pipelines that extend northeast all the way through Pakistan—cutting through some of the highest mountains in the world, the Karakorams—into China itself, from where more roads and pipelines connect the flow of consumer goods and hydrocarbons to

China's middle class fleshpots farther east.³ The pipelines would also be used to develop China's restive, Muslim far west; indeed, Gwadar looked poised to cement Pakistani and Chinese strategic interests.⁴ Meanwhile, another branch of this road and pipeline network would go from Gwadar north through a future stabilized Afghanistan, and on into Iran and Central Asia. In fact, Gwadar's pipelines would lead into a network extending from the Pacific Ocean westward to the Caspian Sea. In this way, Gwadar becomes the pulsing hub of a new silk route, both land and maritime: a mega-project and gateway to landlocked, hydrocarbon-rich Central Asia—an exotic twenty-first-century place-name.

But history is as much a series of accidents and ruined schemes as of great plans. And when I got to Gwadar, it was the pitfalls that impressed me as much as the dreams. What was so fantastic about Gwadar was less the futuristic vision mapped out for it than the present-day reality of the town itself. It was every bit the majestic frontier town that I had imagined, occupying a sweeping, bone-dry peninsula between long lines of soaring ashen cliffs and a sea the color of rusty tap water. The cliffs, with their buttes and mesas and steeple-like ridges were excruciating in their complexity. The town at their foot could have been mistaken for the sprawling, rectilinear remains of an ancient Near Eastern city: low, scabby white stone walls peeking up amidst the sand drifts and mounds of rubble. People sat here and there in broken-backed kitchen chairs, sipping tea under the shade of bamboo and burlap. Everyone was in traditional clothes; there were no Western polyesters. It evoked a nineteenth-century lithograph of Jaffa in Palestine or Tyre in Lebanon by David Roberts, with dhows emerging out of the white, watery miasma, laden with silvery fish thrown ashore by the fishermen, who were dressed in filthy turbans and *shalwar kameezes,* prayer beads dripping out of their pockets.*

Indeed, there truly was a dreamlike aura to Gwadar, owing to the haze that fused sea and sky into a unitary shroud. If Gwadar does develop as advertised, then the Western visitors who are trickling in now and then might be among the lucky ones, seeing it in its final days as a time-honored fishing town like Abu Dhabi, Dubai, and the other storied ports of the Persian Gulf as experienced by the British explorer Wilfred Thesiger in the 1940s and 1950s, just before Big Oil changed everything.

---

* Pajama-like trousers (*shalwar*) gathered at the waist and ankles, and worn underneath a long loose tunic (*kameez*).

"Here life moved in time with the past," Thesiger writes of Dubai, describing naked children romping in the shallows between the dhows alongside armed Bedouin, "Negro slaves," Kashgai tribesmen in their felt caps, and Somalis just off small boats from Aden. In Dubai, Thesiger felt ill at ease in his European clothes.[5] His description is a lesson in how rapidly things can change.

Meanwhile, the Chinese-built deepwater port with its neat angles, spanking new gantry cranes, and other cargo-handling equipment appeared charged with expectation, able to offer accommodations for the largest oil tankers, even as the complex stood silent and empty against the horizon, waiting for decisions to be made in the faraway Pakistani capital of Islamabad. I was shown a scale model of a vast housing project with tree-lined boulevards and a Marriott resort. "Come back in a decade or two and this place will look like Dubai. You won't recognize it," a businessman visiting from Karachi assured me. Yet Gwadar's airport was so tiny that it lacked even a conveyor belt for luggage.

Little seemed to be happening here, except at places like the fishermen's wharf. I watched as piles of salmon, trout, snappers, tiger prawns, perch, bass, sardines, and skate were dropped into straw baskets and put ashore through an ingenious pulley system. A big dead shark and a similarly large swordfish were being dragged by ropes into a vast, stinking market shed filled with fish, shiny and slippery, slapping on the bloody cement floor beside piles of manta rays. Donkeys, waiting patiently with their carts, stood at the ready to drag the mountains of fish away to smaller markets in town. Until the next building phase of the port and pipeline project began, traditional fishing was everything here. And the wharf was only part of the spectacle.

At a nearby beach I watched as dhows were built and repaired. Men used their fingers to smear the wooden seams of the hulls with epoxy while others, nestled next to scrawny dogs and cats, took long smokes in the shade. With all the talk of a geopolitical nerve center, here there were no generators, no electric drills, just craftsmen making holes with manual drills turned by bowlike devices, as though they were playing string instruments. A few men working for two months can build a forty-foot fishing boat that lasts about twenty years. The teak wood is imported from Burma and Indonesia. Cod liver oil is painted on the outside to make it waterproof. New boats are launched on the first and fifteenth days of the moon cycles to take advantage of the high tides. This was Arabia before the modern era.

As-Salem Musa, a turbaned Baluch graybeard, told me that his father and grandfather before him built boats. He fondly remembered the "freer" days of Omani control of Gwadar because "we were able to sail all around the Gulf without restrictions." He harbored both hope and fear of the future: change could mean even less freedom for the Baluch, as Punjabis and other urban Pakistanis swept down here to take over the city. "They don't have a chance," a Pakistani official in Islamabad told me, referring to the fishermen in Gwadar. "Modernity will wipe out their traditional life."

In the covered bazaar, amid the most derelict of tea, spice, and dry goods shops, with their dusty jars filled with old candy, I met more old men with beards and turbans who spoke with nostalgia about the sultan of Oman (Qabus's father, Sa'id bin Taymur), and how Gwadar had prospered under his rule, however backward it was in Oman. Many of these old men had dual Omani-Pakistani nationality. They led me through somnolent, burlap-covered streets and along crumbling mud-brick facades, past half-starved cows and goats hugging the shade of collapsed walls, to a small and round stuccoed former palace with its overhanging wooden balconies used by the sultan during his infrequent visits. It was like everything else in Gwadar, in some advanced stage of disintegration. The sea poked through at every turn, now a bottled chlorinated green color in the mid-afternoon.

At another beach there was the bizarre sight of donkeys—the smallest donkeys I have ever seen—romping out of the water and on to the sand, pulling creaky carts driven by little boys that were loaded down with fish just transferred from boats bobbing in the waves, which were flying a black, white, yellow, and green flag of Baluchistan. Miniature donkeys emerging from the sea! Gwadar was a place of wonders, slipping through an hourglass.

By contrast a few miles away, in vast tracts of desert just beyond town, a new industrial zone and other development sites had been fenced off, with migrant labor camps spread alongside, waiting for construction to begin. "Just wait for the new airport," another businessman from Karachi told me. "During the next building phase of the port complex you will see the

Dubai miracle taking shape." But everyone who spoke to me in terms of a business hub to rival Dubai neglected a key fact. The Gulf sheikhdoms, Dubai in particular, had wise, effective, and wholly legitimate governments that, because they had to rule only city-states without hinterlands, lacked all the weaknesses and disadvantages of Pakistan's various military and civilian regimes, which, in the course of the decades, not only had rarely proved effective, but were often perceived as illegitimate as well. Moreover, Pakistani regimes had to govern a sprawling territory of mountains and desert badlands, beset by constant wars and rebellions.

The Gulf states did not just happen; it was not destiny. It was the product of good government under ideal conditions, which Pakistan singularly lacked.

Whether Gwadar could become a new silk route nexus or not is tied to Pakistan's own struggle against becoming a failed state. Pakistan, with its "Islamic" bomb, its Taliban- and al-Qaeda-infested northwestern borderlands, its dysfunctional cities, and territorially based ethnic groups—Baluch, Sindhis, Punjabis, Pushtuns—for whom Islam could never provide the glue for a common identity, was commonly referred to as the most dangerous country in the world, a nuclearizing Yugoslavia in the making. So Gwadar was a litmus test for more than road and energy routes; it was an indication of the stability of the whole Arabian Sea region—that is, for half of the Indian Ocean. If Gwadar languished, remaining what for a Western visitor like myself was just a charming fishing port, it would indicate yet more disturbing trends about Pakistan that would affect neighboring countries.

As it turned out, no one ever did ask to see my non-objection certificate; I could have come here without one. But after a few days in Gwadar, I managed to attract the attention of the local police, who thereafter insisted on accompanying me everywhere with a truckload of black-clad commandos armed with AK-47s. Talking to people became nearly impossible, as my police escort immediately surrounded whomever I met. The police said that they were there for my own protection, but there was no terrorism in Gwadar, only poor Baluch fishermen and their families. While awkward to reach, Gwadar was nonetheless one of the safest places in Pakistan that I had been in nine long visits to the country.

The locals clearly did not like the police. "We Baluch only want to be free," I was told whenever out of earshot of my security detail. You might think that Gwadar's very promise of economic development would give the Baluch the freedom they craved. But more development, I was told, meant more Chinese, Singaporeans, Punjabis, and other outsiders who would turn the place into an authentic international port and transit center. Indeed, there was evidence that the Baluch would not only fail to benefit from rising real estate prices, but in many cases would be disenfranchised from their land altogether.

The respected Karachi-based investigative magazine *The Herald* had published a cover story, "The Great Land Robbery," which alleged that the Gwadar mega-project had "led to one of the biggest land scams in Pakistan's history."[6] The magazine detailed a system in which revenue clerks had been bribed by influential people from Karachi, Lahore, and other major cities to have land in Gwadar registered in their names at rock-bottom prices, and then resold to developers for residential and industrial schemes. In fact, hundreds of thousands of acres of land were said to be illegally allotted to civilian and military bureaucrats living elsewhere. In this way, the poor and uneducated Baluch population had been shut out of Gwadar's future prosperity. And so, Gwadar had become a lightning rod for Baluch hatred of Punjabi-ruled Pakistan. Gwadar's very promise as an Indian Ocean–slash–Central Asian mega-hub threatened to sunder the country further.

Pakistan's Arabian Sea coast has long been rife with separatist rebellion, with both Baluchistan and Sindh having rich, venerable histories as ethnic-geographical entities harboring fewer contradictions than the state that has existed here since 1947. For the Baluch and Sindhis, independence from Great Britain created a harsh irony: after resisting Punjabi overlordship for centuries they found themselves subject to Punjabi rule within the new state of Pakistan. Whereas the Punjabis venerated the historical memory of the Mughal kings of yore, the Baluch and the Sindhis looked back on the Mughals as symbols of oppression since, with the exception of the periods of rule by the Mughals, the medieval Arabs, and a brief interlude under Mahmud of Ghazna in the eleventh century, the Sindhis, for example, had been independent, ruled by their own local dynasties in the land they called Sindhu Desh.[7]

In fact, talk had revived of a future Baluch-Sindh confederation quietly supported by India. The two regions are complementary, with Baluchistan holding the natural resources and Sindh the industrial base. In recent decades the six million Baluch have mounted four insurgencies against the Pakistani military to protest economic and political discrimination. In the fiercest of these wars, from 1973 to 1977, some eighty thousand Pakistani troops and fifty-five thousand Baluch warriors were involved in the fighting. Baluch memories of the time are bitter. In 1974, writes the South Asia expert Selig S. Harrison, Pakistani forces, "frustrated by their inability to find Baluch guerrilla units hiding in the mountains, bombed, strafed, and burned the encampments of some 15,000 Baluch families . . . forcing the guerrillas to come out from their hideouts to defend their women and children."[8]

What Harrison calls a "slow-motion genocide" has continued in recent years, with thousands of Baluch in 2006 fleeing villages attacked by Pakistani F-16 fighter jets and Cobra helicopter gunships. This was followed by large-scale government-organized kidnappings and disappearances of Baluch youth. Recently, at least eighty-four thousand people have been displaced by the conflict.[9] Also in 2006 the Pakistani army killed the Baluch leader Nawab Akbar Khan Bugti. But as government tactics have grown more brutal, Baluch warriors have congealed into an authentic national movement, as a new and better-armed generation— emergent from a literate Baluch middle class in the capital of Quetta and elsewhere, and financed by Baluch compatriots in the Persian Gulf— have to a significant degree surmounted the age-old Baluch nemesis of feuding tribes, which outsiders like the Punjabis in the Pakistani military had been able to play against one another.

The insurgency now crossed regional, tribal, and class lines, the International Crisis Group reported.[10] According to the Pakistanis, the Indian intelligence services have been helping the Baluch, since the Indians clearly benefit from the Pakistani armed forces being tied down by separatist rebellions.[11] The Pakistani military has countered by pitting radical Islamic parties against the secular and nationalistic Baluch. In a region that has turned into a cauldron of fundamentalist rebellion, "Baluchistan is," in the words of one Baluch activist, "the only secular region between Afghanistan, Iran, and Pakistan and has no previous record of religious extremism."[12]

The Baluch number only 3.57 percent of Pakistan's 172 million people, but most of Pakistan's resources, including copper, uranium, potentially rich oil reserves, and natural gas, are in Baluchistan. Although more than a third of the country's natural gas is produced there, Baluchistan consumes only a fraction of it because of poverty, even as Pakistan's economy is one of the world's most dependent on natural gas.[13] More-over, as Selig Harrison explains, the central government has paid meager royalties to the province for the gas, and at the same time denied it development aid.

Thus, the real estate scandal in Gwadar and fears of a Punjabi takeover there come as culminations to a history of subjugation. To taste the emotions behind all of this, I met with Baluch nationalist leaders at the other end of the Makran coast, in Karachi.

The setting for the first meeting was a Kentucky Fried Chicken outlet in the Karachi neighborhood of Clifton, whose entrance was guarded by a private security guard with a shotgun and billy club. Such fast-food joints, with their overt American symbolism, have been sites of terrorist bombings. Inside were young people wearing both Western clothes and pressed white *shalwar kameezes,* with freshly shaven chins and long beards in Muslim religious fashion. Yet despite the clash of styles, they all had a slick suburban demeanor. Everyone had trays of chicken and Pepsi, and between bites were busy texting and talking on their cell-phones. Drum music blasted from loudspeakers: Indian-Pakistani Pun-jabi *bhangra.* In the midst of this upscale scene, five Baluch in soiled and wrinkled *shalwar kameezes,* wearing turbans and topis, stormed in with stacks of papers under their arms, including the copy of *The Herald* with the cover story on Gwadar.

Nisar Baluch, the general secretary of the Baluch Welfare Society, was the group's leader. He had unruly black hair and a thick mustache. His fingertips tapped on the table as he lectured me. "The Pakistani army is the biggest land grabber," he began. "It is giving away the coast of Baluchistan for peanuts to the Punjabis.

"The Punjabi army wears uniforms, but the soldiers are actually ter-rorists," he continued. "In Gwadar, the army is operating as a mafia, fal-sifying land records. They say we don't have papers to prove our ownership of the land, though we've been there for centuries." He told me that he was not against development and supported dialogue with the Pakistani authorities. "But when we talk about our rights, they accuse us of being Taliban.

"We're an oppressed nation," he went on, never raising his voice, even as his finger-tapping grew in intensity. "There is no other choice but to fight. The whole world is now talking about Gwadar. The entire polit-

ical establishment in this country is involved in the crime being perpetrated there."

Then came this warning: "No matter how hard they try to turn
Gwadar into Dubai, it won't work. There will be resistance. The future
pipelines going to China will not be safe. The pipelines will have to cross
through Baluch territory, and if our rights are violated, nothing will be secure."

This threat did not exist in isolation. Other nationalists had said that
somewhere down the road Baluch insurgents would ambush more Chinese workers and kill them, and that would be the end of Gwadar.[14]

Nisar Baluch was my warm-up to Nawab Khair Baksh Marri, the
chief of the Marri tribe of Baluch, who had been engaged in combat with
government forces on and off for sixty years, and whose son had recently
been killed by Pakistani troops.* Marri greeted me in his plush Karachi
villa, with massive exterior walls, giant plants, and ornate furniture,
where his servants and bodyguards rested on rugs in the garden. He was
old and wizened, with a cane, robes, and a beige-colored topi with wide
indentations that distinguished it from the kind worn by Sindhis. Before
us was a vast spread of local delicacies. Nawab Marri spoke a precise,
hesitant, whispering English that, when combined with his clothes and
the setting, gave him a certain charisma.

"If we keep fighting," he told me gently, "we will ignite an intifada
like the Palestinians. It is the cause of my optimism that the young generation of Baluch will sustain a guerrilla war. Pakistan is not eternal. It is
not likely to last. The British Empire, Pakistan, Burma, these have all
been temporary creations. After Bangladesh left Pakistan in 1971," he
continued, in his mild and lecturing voice, "the only dynamic left within
this country was the imperialist power of the Punjabi army. East Bengal
[Bangladesh] was the most important element in Pakistan. The Bengalis
were numerous enough to take on the Punjabis, but they seceded instead.
Now the only option left for the Baluch is to fight."

He liked and trusted no one in Pakistan who was not Baluch, he told
me. He thought little of the late Sindhi leader of the Pakistan People's
Party, Benazir Bhutto. After all, as he explained, it was under the government of her father, Zulfikar Ali Bhutto, in the 1970s, that "our people

---

* In November 2007, Pakistani security forces killed Nawabzada Balach Marri, the youngest
of Marri's six sons.

were thrown out of helicopters, killed in mass graves, burned, had their nails torn out, their bones broken . . . so I was not happy to greet her."

And what about Punjabi overtures to make amends with the Baluch? I asked. "We say to these Punjabis," he replied, still in his sweet regal voice, "leave us alone, get lost, we don't need your direction, your brotherliness. If Punjab continues to occupy us with the help of the American imperialists, then eventually our name will be nowhere in the soil."

He explained that Baluchistan overlapped three countries—Pakistan, Iran, and Afghanistan—and would eventually triumph as the central governments of all those lands weakened. In his view, Gwadar was just the latest Punjabi plot that would prove temporary. The Baluch would simply bomb the new roads and future pipelines leading out of there.

He was a man full of blunt insults, who abjured the give-and-take of politics, on which he seemed to have given up. As I was leaving his villa, it struck me that whether Gwadar developed or not depended signally on how the government in Islamabad behaved. If it did not make a grand bargain with the Baluch of the scope that would isolate embittered men like Marri and Nisar Baluch, then indeed the mega-project near the Iranian border would become another lost city in the sand, beset by local rebellion. Although, if it did make such a bargain, allowing Baluchistan to emerge as a region-state under the larger rubric of a democratic and decentralized Pakistan, then the traditional fishing village that I saw could well give way to a pulsing Rotterdam of the Arabian Sea, with tentacles reaching northward to Samarkand.

But nothing was destiny.

Whereas Baluchistan constitutes the easternmost limb of the Middle East, with its evocation of peninsular Arabia, Sindh and the snaking Indus River valley that territorially defines it mark the true beginning of the Indian Subcontinent, though, of course, history and geography are subtler still. Sindh, too, albeit to a somewhat lesser extent than Makran, is a transition zone with a long record of invasions. In particular, there were the Arab conquests in the eighth and ninth centuries, and consequent Arab commercial activity in the urban areas.[15] Perhaps the best way to think of the beginning of the Subcontinent is less of a hard border than a series of gradations.

Both the words "India" and "Hindu" derive from Sindhu, which in Persian became *Hind,* and, in Greek and Roman, *Ind.* The Indus (as it was called by these rulers of the Western classical world) and interior Sindh beckoned ever northward for hundreds of miles, from the sprawling urban city-state of Karachi on the Arabian Sea toward the fertile Punjab and the Karakorams—the dizzyingly steep "Black Gravel" range in Turkic, which adjoin the Himalayas.*

Karachi was a place of jarring aesthetics, unappealing at least to the Western eye. Whereas verticality is a sign of urban life in Europe—of venerable human settlement ascending upward in a confined and intimate space—Karachi was a horizontal city of the future, with many small neighborhood centers and comparatively little of a central core. From a rooftop barbecue restaurant, I gazed out at vast panels of sewage water egressing into the port, which was studded with dinosauric gantry cranes; and in the other direction I saw ranks of cruddy and cracked apartment blocks of undressed cement, festooned with drying clothes in an oily ash-smeared haze. Raggedy palms and mangrove swamps were bordered by heaps of cinder blocks. The city lacked any focal point or identifiable skyline. Mounds of garbage, rocks, dirt, tires, bricks, and withered tree stumps helped define the urban space. Private security guards were ever-present, along with liquor stores and radical Islamic madrassas that I had visited on previous trips here. Indeed, the city's very contradictions were one of its saving graces. Without the anchor of a substantive past, compared to other cities in the Subcontinent, Karachi has more possibilities to alter itself radically over the decades, taking advantage of global trends in urban living and architectural design. We all know about terrorist Karachi, which certainly is a reality, but a city of this size is many faceted. I was intrigued more than I was put off.

Karachi was a site of massive building projects financed by money from the Gulf, but no one project seemed to be architecturally coordinated with another. High marble fortress walls with buzzers and armed guards indicated how this was a city of hidden wealth. Glitzy stores and Western chain restaurants peeked out amidst sprawling slums that were, in turn, roamed over by armies of stray dogs and gray-breasted crows. Women in gold jewelry and fine gaudy silks shared sidewalks with hunchbacks and amputees. Because of the mishmash of poverty and wealth, neighborhoods were better and worse rather than good and bad.

---

* Punjab means "five rivers"—the Beas, Ravi, Jhelum, Sutlej, and Chenab—in the heavily Persian-influenced Urdu. They all have their origins in lakes in the Himalayas.

The better ones had hollow names like Clifton and Defense, evoking literally nothing.

With few vertical impediments, the Muslim prayer call swept like a tidal wave through the city's vast open spaces. Without a tradition like Lahore, and with significant inter-ethnic violence between Sindhis and *mohajirs* (Muslim immigrants from India), and between Pushtuns and Baluch, the future of this Arabian Sea port seemed open to two healing, dynamic forces: those of radical Islamic orthodoxy and of soulless materialism, the offerings, respectively, of Saudi Arabia and of Dubai. Truly, Karachi represented the other side of the moon from nearby Muscat, which, with its heavily zoned and blinding white, graceful Mughal-like ambience, bespoke—through a strong architectural tradition—a stalwart and enlightened state that protected its cities from the dark side of globalization, even as Karachi seemed to be devoured by it. The state, unlike in Oman, was little to be seen. In this sense, Karachi was the definitive Pakistani city. Unlike Lahore and the great Mughal metropolises of India, Karachi was an isolated seaboard settlement of 400,000 at the time of partition, and grew into a mega-city of 16 million without a prideful identity or past.

Half of Karachi's population lived in squatter settlements known as *katchiabaadis*. Barely 50 percent of the city's water needs were being met, and there were constant power outages, known locally by the quaint term "load-shedding."[16] And yet Karachi, I thought, might be saved by its very pluralism. It was a port after all, with a vibrant Hindu population and a community of Zoroastrians who exposed their dead to vultures on hills known as "towers of silence." No one sort of religious fundamentalism would go far here before being hedged in by other beliefs. The very fact of the sea, which brought to bear the various contradictory influences of the Indian Ocean, might ultimately protect Karachi from its worst aspects.

Despite the tradition of inter-ethnic violence, the city usually seemed peaceful. One day I drove out past the inland bays and salt ponds, past the derelict ancient storefronts with their scabby signage and cinder-block exteriors—the very essence of flatness and destitution—and found a throng of picnicking families on the beach at Manora headland, enjoying the pounding, sulfurous surf of the Arabian Sea in all its sudsy force, with no jetties to break up the wave formations. It was just after Friday prayers. The beach was clean, unlike most other places in Karachi, and children were taking rides up and down the shore on camels bedecked with colorfully embroidered saddles. Families were huddled in groups on the sand, smiling and taking photos of one another. Teenagers gathered at corroded drinks and fish stands. Some of the women were dressed in shapely, fashionable *shalwar kameezes* and wore makeup. Others were covered from head to toe in black.

The scene made me think of another one I had witnessed some years back at the Yemeni port of Mukalla, some 350 miles to the west of Dhofar. The beachfront in Mukalla was divided into two parts: one for men and teenage boys; another for women and their young children. The women were veiled and most of the men had beards. It was a serene communal space, with throngs of the proletarian faithful enjoying the first evening sea breezes.[17] The West, and the United States in particular, had no choice but to make its peace with such crowds. Here in its quiet understated way was global power, resting within a deep, anchoring belief.

Both beach scenes bespoke a simple intimacy, with this one here in Karachi somewhat more cosmopolitan. A Hindu temple—tawny, intricate, and dilapidated—stood sentinel in the background. Here was a vision of Karachi as a modest-sized, multi-confessional fishing community—a satellite of Mumbai and other cities on the western coast of India, something that before its architectural despoliation it was always meant to be. You could see that as soon as Karachi had been cut off from India proper because of the creation of Muslim Pakistan it had lost its organic connection to these other urban centers, and thus developed as an isolated Islamic city-state without the enriching advantage of a more variegated, partially Hindu soul. And so as vast as it had become, Karachi somehow lacked substance. Maybe globalization by way of Dubai and other Gulf cities was the answer after all. Karachi had lost India, but would gain the Gulf as its immediate neighbor.

Its young mayor, Syed Mustafa Kamal, talked of an information technology center that would make the city a transshipment point of ideas between the Gulf and Asia.[18] Yet, there were other visions of Karachi, not entirely contradictory with the young mayor's, but more in keeping with what the Baluch had in mind for their province. These visions, which saw Karachi as the capital of an independent or at least an autonomous Sindh, conceived of both Pakistan and India as not the last words in human political organization for the Subcontinent.

I was reminded that Sindh had been occupied for six thousand years, and by virtue of it being a racial mixture of Arabs, Persians, and other passing conquerors, it retained a strong cultural and historical identity. Sindh had been part of Bombay Presidency, a province of British India until 1936, when it became a province in its own right tied to New Delhi. Sindh joined Pakistan less because it was Muslim than because the new state promised Sindh autonomy, which it never got. "Instead, we became a colony of the Punjabis," was the refrain. For Sindhi nationalists, the Arabian Sea might yet return to its pre-Portuguese medieval past, as a place of regions and principalities, in which Kabul and Karachi were as united with Lahore and Delhi as Delhi was with Bangalore and the rest of south India. And in this firmament, aided by globalization, as they told me, the Sunnis and Shias of Sindh could deal, respectively, with Saudi Arabia and Iran without the intercession of Islamabad.

As unforgiving as some of these voices were, their anger had a reasonable focus, for it was directed against the extreme centralization of political life toward the populous Punjabi heartland that had robbed the state of Pakistan of vitality.

I met Ali Hassan Chandio, the vice-chairman of the Sindh Progressive Party, in an empty room with geckos on the walls. The monsoon wind blew through the open windows. We were located a few blocks from the site of a new mall and apartment complex to be built by a Dubai firm. Whatever was left of the past in Karachi was being wiped out. Chandio spoke to me of Mohammed Ali Jinnah, the founder of Pakistan, who had conceived of a state in which the various national peoples would be given their rights. But instead, Jinnah died soon after Pakistan's birth, and the military centralized power. "In India there have been no coups, while in Pakistan there has frequently been martial law. We want the Punjabi military to go back to the barracks. Sindhis should only be part of Pakistan if it is democratic like India. India," he emphasized, "despite all its wars and assassinations and other violence, is still the role model for South Asia." Like all the Baluch and Sindhi nationalists I met along Pakistan's Arabian Sea coast, he spoke openly in positive terms about India, which he and the others saw as their ally against the very state in which they felt themselves to be prisoners. Indeed, they all spoke to me about the need for an open border with the neighboring Indian state of Gujarat, India's most economically dynamic region, with a quarter of that country's investment. Gujarat's very proximity and strength made them aware of their own failure.

Bashir Khan Qureshi, the leader of the Sindhi Lives Progressive Front, met me in his home at Karachi's eastern edge. Plastic bags blew in the wind. Crows were ubiquitous. The ashtrays in the room overflowed. A fan blew loudly. A big and handsome man, he spoke easily above it.

"Pakistan is itself a breach of contract," he told me. He reiterated the whole history of the state from the minority Baluch and Sindhi point of view, paying particular attention to the secession of Bangladesh in 1971 and the inspiration the Bengalis there have given to the dreams of other minorities. One more coup in Pakistan, Qureshi said, and there would be civil war in Baluchistan and Sindh.

Maybe it was the bleak surroundings in this room, which seemed about to be submerged by the parched desert, but I distrusted his vision. It was too clear-cut. It worked only as long as you believed that Sindh was a cohesive and definable entity that could be neatly severed from Pakistan. But it couldn't, for Sindhis were a minority in Karachi itself. After partition, millions of Muslim Indians (*mohajirs*) had fled here and formed their own political groupings. Then there were the Pushtun, Punjabi, Hindu, and other minorities. As past violence showed, Sindhis might get their way here only through urban warfare. And that was to say nothing of the Sunni-Shia split within the Sindhi community itself, which had also periodically led to violence. Because of the vicissitudes of migration over recent decades, at least in Karachi Sindh had become something of an abstraction (as had the concept of Baluchistan in Quetta, because of the influx of Pushtuns). Like Gwadar, Karachi could emerge as an autonomous city-state of the future. And Sindh, as well as Baluchistan, could gain autonomy in a far more loosely controlled and democratic future Pakistan. But Pakistan as it currently existed, I felt, would not go so quietly into history. And the Mughal and medieval principalities of the past were only vague comparisons for what might come about, mainly because of the mixing of populations in the urban areas. Future decades would have to witness political structures of extreme subtlety.

Mohammed Ali Jinnah, the Quaid-i-Azam (father of the nation), the creator of the state that many have called the most dangerous and explosive in the world, is buried in the middle of a vast immaculately landscaped garden in central Karachi. So beautiful and perfect is the garden that once inside it you realize just how poor and chaotic much of the rest of the city is. The mausoleum itself is a bullet-shaped dome socketed into inward-sloping marble walls. The geometric design is so severe and cubistic it brings to mind all the too-neat abstractions of political ideology. Meanwhile, the flashy marble interior suggests a shopping mall, or the duty-free zone of one of the new airports in the Gulf. There is something both edgy and curiously vacant about the whole affair. Just as the tomb looked out of place amid Karachi's ratty mishmash, Jinnah's model-state has so far proved unsuited for the ground-level realities of a messy world.

In Pakistan, I detected three schools of thought about Jinnah. The first was the official one, which declared him a great twentieth-century hero of Muslim rights, in the vein of Turkey's Mustafa Kemal Ataturk. The second, shared by a few brave Pakistanis and more people in the West, was that Jinnah was a vain man and a failure who unwittingly gave birth to a monstrosity of a nation that was, in turn, linked to much of the violence in Afghanistan in recent decades. The third view, though, was the most interesting, and in its way the most subversive, as well as the most informed.

In this view, Jinnah was a complex man of India, a London-Bombay intellectual, the son of a merchant from Gujarat and a Parsee from Karachi. Like Ataturk, who had grown up amid the nourishing cosmopolitan influences of Salonika (rather than amid the narrower Islamic world of Anatolia which he came to rule), Jinnah was the product of a sophisticated cultural environment, that of Greater India, and thus was at heart a secularist. Yet he believed his Muslim state was needed to protect a minority from uncertain majority rule. As misguided and politically opportunistic as this might have been, it made room for a state that, though composed mostly of Muslims, might still maintain a secular spirit, much like Ataturk's Turkey. It would be informed by Muslim values without being necessarily ruled by Islamic law. Moreover, it might be a state with a high degree of provincial autonomy, in order to recognize the territorial-based nationalisms of the Pushtuns, Baluch, and Sindhis.

As I said, this view was the most subversive because it directly challenged what the ruling class in Islamabad—the generals and the politicians both—had turned the country into. Because Jinnah died in 1948, soon after Pakistan's birth, it is impossible to know what the country might have evolved into had he lived longer. But one can argue that key principles of the Quaid-i-Azam have been violated. Rather than a state with a moderate sensibility, Pakistan maintained a suffocating Islamic milieu in which extremism was rewarded with political concessions, while the military and political parties jockeyed for position with one another. Alcohol was banned and girls' schools in the rural areas were burned down. And as for autonomy, that was a myth that my meetings in Baluchistan and Sindh had made clear.

Jinnah's tomb was like a two-dimensional stage prop, just as Pakistan itself had all the artificial trappings of a state, with its Mughal-cum-Stalinist public buildings in Islamabad. But in the eyes of many of its ethnic peoples, it still lacked political legitimacy.

"The Indian Subcontinent has produced only one liberal, secular politician, Mohammed Ali Jinnah. [Mohandas] Gandhi was just a British agent from South Africa, a reactionary with a sweet tongue. Ever since Jinnah, though, we've been ruled by these gangsters who serve the Punjabis—the stooges of America. You know why the Indus is so low— because the Punjabis are stealing our water upstream. Sindh is the only ancient and legitimate state in Pakistan."

The speaker is Rasool Baksh Paleejo, a leftist Sindhi nationalist who had been imprisoned by both democratic and military governments in Pakistan. Before I met him in 2000, several people told me he was the most intelligent person in the city of Hyderabad (up the Indus, northeast of Karachi) with whom to discuss politics. In 2008, I returned to Hyderabad to see him again, to find out if his views had evolved or complexified. They hadn't. His house stood behind high walls at the end of a road near the desert; as with the first visit, I sensed an extreme isolation. He was still a man with a lean and sculpted face, and a thick mane of white hair. His house was a seedy, tumbledown affair with broken furniture and dirt all over the carpets. A corner of the sitting room was filled with pictures of Karl Marx, Friedrich Engels, Lenin, Ho Chi Minh, and Najibullah, the pro-Soviet leader of Afghanistan in the 1980s. When I had met Paleejo nearly a decade ago he told me of his voluminous readings of all the great works of Marxism. When I asked him this time what he had been reading recently, he mentioned Professors Stephen Walt and John Mearsheimer's book, *The Israel Lobby and U.S. Foreign Policy,* a controversial treatise published in 2007 claiming that excessive pro-Israeli influence has compromised American foreign policy.

He lectured me next about "criminal gangs," "Punjabi parasites," "imperialist pygmies," "Bush fascists," and "Jewish-capitalist-Taliban" who were all exploiting the Sindhi people. The *mohajirs,* Pushtuns, and Baluch were all "tools of America," he said. Then his voice calmed and he talked of a golden age of Mughal rule in the early modern era. "The Mughals were not bigots. They married Hindus. They had Hindu generals. They had no home, but were at heart Turkic nomads." He seemed to imply this was the era to which he wanted to return. If only Pakistan could disappear and dissolve into an even more pluralistic India, he rhapsodized.

Paleejo signified for me the end of the road of ethnic nationalism. He had reduced the whole world to an embittered, schematic conspiracy theory. He and the other Baluch and Sindhi nationalists I met were, ultimately, the products of a state under military rule for so long that it had allowed too little breathing space for the exchange of ideas, and thus for normal politics to take root. So instead of the give-and-take of normal politics came the hard divisions of ideology and us-versus-them irrationalities.

To be fair, military rule had not been accidental to Pakistan. Pakistan covers the desert frontier of the Subcontinent. British civilian administration extended only to Lahore, in the fertile Punjab, near Pakistan's eastern border with India. But the rest of Pakistan—the rugged border regions of Baluchistan and the North-West Frontier Province, the alkaline wastes of Sindh away from the Indus, and the Hindu Kush and Karakoram Mountains embracing Kashmir—has never really been subdued by the British or anyone else. Much of the area was grossly underdeveloped compared with the rest of British India, so when seven million Muslim refugees fled India to settle in this new frontier state, the role of the military, perforce, became paramount. Indeed, with tribal and ethnic identities so strong in these badlands, civilian politics when they were given a chance became a bureaucratic forum for revenge and unsavory trade-offs. Rather than barter water wells and tracts of desert as in the past, in the new state civilian politicians bartered flour mills, electricity grids, and transport systems. So the military was periodically obligated to clean house, which it pointedly failed to do, as it had emerged in its own right into a corrupt state-within-a-state, identified in the popular mind with one ethnic group, the Punjabis, thus fueling various fissiparous nationalisms.

But Pakistan had no choice now but to move beyond military rule, even if that meant, as it probably did, years and years of corrupt, ineffectual, and unstable civilian governments. For it was the very certainty of civilian rule, as unsatisfactory as it was, that had allowed for India's gradual emergence as a stabilizing, regional behemoth. Thus, it was Pakistan—unlike the Gulf states with their enlightened and efficient family dictatorships, and India with its venerable democracy—that had an especially arduous political future ahead of it. Consequently, like the troubled state of Burma at the top of the Bay of Bengal, Pakistan—in the middle of the littoral between the Persian Gulf and India—held the key to stability in the Arabian Sea region.

Yet, like the story of Oman, the coast did not exist in isolation. You had to travel inland to learn more. The map beckoned me northward, up the Indus into the heart of Sindh.

The Indus at Thatta, east of Karachi, is one of the last places to view the river before it breaks up into a vast delta along the Pakistan-India border. Here, it is said, Alexander's army might have rested before marching westward along the Makran coast. Just prior to the monsoon, I saw the Indus as a cracked and bleached landscape: a wide, putty-colored sea, swirling around sandbanks, deathly in color even by the standards of normal ash and cinder. It was a giver of life so joyless that heat was the only smell. Beyond Thatta, the Indus turns north for hundreds of miles, creating a densely populated river valley civilization comparable to those of the Nile and of the Tigris and Euphrates.

In Egypt, migration routes moved up and down the Nile, granting its political units stability and longevity. But the rivers of Mesopotamia, in the words of the early- and mid-twentieth-century British travel writer Freya Stark, rather than "parallel and peaceful to the routes of human traffic" like the Nile, were "obnoxious to the predestined paths of man"—that is to say, migration routes were at a right angle to the Tigris and Euphrates, making Mesopotamia susceptible to war and invasion.[19] So, too, with the Indus, which has seen many invasions. The Indus signals the western edge of the Subcontinent, from where its political unity was frequently breached by invaders coming out of the plateau and deserts of Afghanistan, Iran, and Baluchistan. It is thus a lesson in the feebleness of borders.

The Shah Jahan Mosque in Thatta bears witness to this. In 1586 the Mughal emperor Akbar the Great turned his attention to Sindh, overpowering local forces in a hard-fought battle on the Indus River. In 1593, after suffering further defeats, the Sindhi ruler of Thatta, Jani Bek, paid homage to Akbar at the emperor's court in Lahore. Indeed, it was the conquest of Sindh that strengthened Akbar's resolve to retake Kandahar in Afghanistan.[20] The eclectic nature of the Mughal Empire, which traversed modern borders from Iran to India, is deeply evoked by this mosque, built between 1644 and 1647 by Shah Jahan, Akbar's grandson, who also built the Taj Mahal in Agra. In the prayer halls you might imagine yourself in Isfahan or Shiraz, or even in Herat or Bukhara, so overt is the Persian and Turkic influence, with the vast variety of blue and turquoise faience and bright yellow arabesques. Then there is the austere and mathematical brick-and-mortar work, with its dazzling conches and quarter domes that are again reminiscent of the Near East and Central Asia. In this mosque you become aware of Sindh as a confection of all the desert and plateau lands to the west, from where came the invasions that had established Sindh's unique identity in the first place. Pakistan might have been created as a reaction to India, but as a frontier zone of the Subcontinent its material culture makes it a cauldron of the Greater Middle East.

A few minutes from the Shah Jahan Mosque is the necropolis on Makli Hill: tombs from the Samma, Arghun, Tarkhan, and Mughal periods, made of sandstone and glazed bricks. These, too, were dynasties with both Turkic and Mongol blood. And yet the tombs remind one of so many similar buildings in India, demonstrating that what we think of as Indian is itself a mélange of Near Eastern cultures.* Everywhere there are brick plinths, rectangular pillars, imposing ramparts, and cracked bulbous domes. The buckling, glazed brick is peeled away in layers, like old mascara, with faint touches of milky blue. These lonely monuments appear to soar into the clouds, each occupying its own little hill. Some, with their intricate fretwork, have an almost Byzantine stateliness. Others bear the proportions and complexity of the pharaonic buildings at Karnak. All stand in majestic separation from one another amid a destitute wasteland, with garbage everywhere, like at so many historical and cultural sites in Pakistan. It is as though in the last sixty years—unlike during the dynastic centuries recounted by these tombs—there has been no state here; nothing but marauders.

* Here took place another depredation of the Portuguese, who sailed up the Indus to Thatta and sacked the city, killing thousands, just because tribute was not paid.

The Indus turned north and I followed, through a pasty landscape smothered in dust that had been, in turn, created by the cracked mud, and which made everything appear to move in slow motion. Here was a truly antique riverine civilization: fields of wheat and rice, bananas and mango trees, and extensive date palm jungles, all sectioned by canals. There were the ubiquitous black and primordial water buffaloes, partly submerged in the mud; heartbreakingly frail donkeys pulling the most immense carts of wood, as nearby dromedaries hauled carts of bricks. Vast, seasonal encampments of Gypsies from Baluchistan and southern Punjab lined the road. They had come for the date palm harvest to make syrup and oils and other date by-products. Layered in mud, they looked no poorer than everyone else. The rice fields bore various translucent shades of lime and green, and women in garish and shimmering saris moved in statuesque formation along the embankments. Yet the scene as a whole was robbed of color because of the ashen skies that rarely culminated in rain.

The farther north I traveled away from the Arabian Sea, the hotter and more windless it became. The temperature hovered above 100 degrees Fahrenheit. The homes and rest houses I entered all had air conditioners that didn't work because of "load-shedding." Shops and cars were plastered with photographs of Benazir and Zulfikar Ali Bhutto. Sindh was the stronghold of the two slain former prime ministers: the daughter killed by an assassin's bomb and bullet in 2007; the father hung in 1979 by army dictator Zia ul-Haq. Yet these images did not necessarily denote loyalty: Many reportedly displayed the photographs and stickers out of fear that their property would be destroyed if they didn't. The photographs were insurance against rioters, I was told.

I reached Khairpur at night. There was nothing to the east of here except the Thar Desert that traverses the border with India. Before partition Khairpur had a large Hindu population. I discovered that the Muslims here had retained the Hindu custom of touching the foot of an elder upon greeting. It was a small gesture that added much to the sense of civilization in this crowded little city. I found the people at all levels warm and intimate, even though the heat was dense and heavy like water, and the hand of the state apparently absent except as an indifferent force of nature. There were tribal and clan feuds in the region, culminating in back-and-forth revenge killings in which the belligerents were armed with assault rifles, even as running water was a rarity. The reasons for these troubles were many, but the ultimate cause was the absence of development. I thought back to Gwadar, existing as a traditional culture in idyllic isolation from a rapacious state, living handily off the commerce of the ocean. While Gwadar felt itself threatened by modernity and the state's looming reach, by contrast interior Sindh constituted an entire civilization decaying because of overuse of resources, and so desperately required the hand of the state to help with its struggle with nature.

To the more practiced eye of William Dalrymple, a journalist, historian, and author specializing in the Subcontinent, who visited Sindh shortly after me, Sindh was actually "quieter and safer than it had been for some time."[21] Indeed, as he writes, the moderate Sufi culture of Sindh provides a mechanism for combating the religious extremism of other parts of Pakistan. The scholar André Wink concurs, noting that Sindh was historically a refuge for " 'dissidents' and 'freethinkers' " such as the Ismailis.[22] And as the Baluch and Sindhi separatist leaders never tired of telling me, theirs were essentially secular movements that owed nothing to Muslim orthodoxy.

All true, and yet my overall impression of Pakistan on this trip, taken near the end of George W. Bush's presidency in the United States, was one of neglect and threatening state failure. I had been here near the beginning of the Bush presidency, eight years earlier, and now could identify barely any progress in the intervening years. Because Pakistan and its stability had figured so prominently in Bush's foreign policy, the lack of improvement here constituted an indictment of his strategy, and an indictment of the diversion of resources to Iraq, a war I had supported early on. To be sure, I did not have to come to Pakistan to realize something so obvious. After all, I had been to both Iraq and Afghanistan periodically over the years, and reported on the chaos in both places. But to see such failure face-to-face, to see how vulnerable Pakistan was to upheaval after a hiatus of eight years, was to be faced with more unarguable facts.

To travel through Pakistan was to realize in a very palpable and visual sense how the United States could not possibly be in control of such broad historical processes as the future of an urbanized society of 172 million half a world away. Yet as the globe's preponderant power, America had the responsibility of at least trying to help wherever it could. In fact, America was heavily engaged in Afghanistan and Pakistan because of its own naked interests, following the attacks of September 11, 2001. But were the United States to sufficiently help stabilize Afghanistan in the years to come, that would only allow for the integration of the Indian Ocean–Central Asian region through energy pipelines, which would ultimately benefit China more than the U.S. In other words, the Gwadar port project may demonstrate more about the geopolitical world that awaits us than the hunt for Osama bin Laden.

The nearby ruins of the Bronze Age city of Moenjodaro ("The Mound in Front of" the Indus) stand as both a rebuke and a summation to everything around them. That Moenjodaro represented wealth and perfection in its age was a further reminder of the grim, poverty-stricken character of Indus valley civilization today—even as the ruins highlight the very agelessness of this valley and, therefore, its potential for regeneration. The square and oval shapes imprinted on bricks everywhere on the site declare a stunning geometrical flawlessness. Moenjodaro and Harappa farther upstream constituted the two major cities of Harappan civilization. Joseph A. Tainter, an American anthropologist and historian, describes Harappan culture as a "highly centralized society in which the state controlled many facets of daily living—milling grain, manufacturing bricks and mass producing pottery, obtaining firewood, and building residences."[23] In a slightly different interpretation, the historian of South Asia Burton Stein posits that Harappan cities like Moenjodaro were the core of "complex chieftaincies rather than unified states," and that each city was the "gateway" to an agrarian hinterland.[24] In any case, hard borders probably did not exist as they do now, even as a vast region from Baluchistan to Gujarat—that is, from southern Afghanistan to northwestern India—was united.

A series of excavations at Moenjodaro throughout the course of the twentieth century revealed about 120,000 square yards of an intricate dun and roseate maze-work of wafer-thin baked brick dating back nearly five thousand years, forming houses, streets, and canals. This represented only 10 percent of the ancient city near the banks of the Indus, possibly the largest city of its time in the world, twice the area of Roman London.[25] In the dark and humble museum, where I escaped momentarily from the heat, the faces of the figurines bear a distinct Sumerian look, with cropped beards and slitted eyes. A portion of the Sumer people had migrated here from Mesopotamia across the Iranian plateau and Baluchistan desert around 4500 B.C.[26]

I was drawn back to the site by a Buddhist stupa from the Kushan period of the second century A.D.—that is, sixteen centuries after Moenjo-daro's downfall. The stupa soars above the site as if it is the world's tallest building. Who needed the Empire State Building or the Burj Dubai when you had this inspiring stupa to gaze at? I thought. Though unconnected to Moenjodaro's Bronze Age civilization, the stupa fit in perfectly with the rest of the ruins, as though a Henry Moore sculpture, accentuating all the symmetry and neat angles of the site, yet electrifying in its stark and penetrating humanity. The stupa was the product of the Kushan dynasty, the easternmost of the Indo-European peoples, which ruled much of northern India, Pakistan, Afghanistan, and parts of Central Asia in the early centuries of the Christian era, and was notable as a force for toleration and syncretism, incorporating into its worldview the pantheons of the Greeks, Romans, Persians, and Hindus. It was an example of how cosmopolitanism, though identified with the Indian Ocean, need, of course, not be confined to it.

North of Moenjodaro lie Larkana and Garhi Khuda Baksh, the family mausoleum of the Bhuttos. This is one of the most harshly feudal parts of Pakistan, where, in the words of journalist Mary Anne Weaver, "families live in walled compounds, ringed by rifle sights; where landlords are often brutal and peasants are serfs; where women are in purdah, and men enjoy their whiskey and pheasant shoots."[27] The mausoleum's white domes make it visible from far away across the alternating desert and the farm fields with their persevering donkeys and water buffaloes. Upon closer inspection, the turquoise lines of the large white tomb were uneven, with white plaster and paint smeared a bit messily over the cracked blue faience. The walls were plastered over with shredded old posters of father and daughter, Zulfikar and Benazir. With the especially big posters of her, this Muslim holy place was replete with graven images. Indeed, there was a noteworthy Sufi-cum-Shiite air to the whole place—Zulfikar Ali Bhutto's tomb enclosed by pillars reminded me of the Ayatollah Khomeini's tomb in south Teheran, to which the faithful come to eat lunch and spend the entire day on the embroidered carpets. There was no landscaping here, no fine attention to detail. Rows of family coffins lay scattered on the floor. The prayer hall was humble, tribal. Benazir Bhutto had been educated at Harvard and Oxford, but there were no airs in this mausoleum. Here the common people ruled and were welcomed. Old men with beards sat around and threw rose petals on her coffin, draped in a carpet or two—a proper tomb would be built later on. Pendants and pictures of her were on sale, and newlyweds came to visit her tomb and pledge faithfulness.

Benazir Bhutto—a daughter of feudal Sindh despite her Western education—was a brilliant thinker and debater with no administrative ability to get anything done. Her two terms as prime minister of Pakistan in the late 1980s and 1990s were merely stations along the way to greater nationwide corruption and chaos that led eventually to the reinstitution of military rule. Yet, because of her rhetoric and promises, she was murdered by Islamists, who saw her as a dangerous symbol of democracy and moderation. But it would take more than symbols to rescue Pakistan, which desperately required the very governing ability that Bhutto lacked. In any case, should Pakistan have a bright future, it will be as a more decentralized state than it has ever been.

Civilizations are "fragile, impermanent things," writes the anthropologist Joseph Tainter.[28] In the Bronze Age, Moenjodaro survived as a highly centralized city-state within what was perhaps a loose and sprawling agricultural confederation. That could well be the future of what we call Pakistan, which will either live up to the deconcentrated cosmopolitan vision of its founder, Mohammed Ali Jinnah, or will decline further. That means, in one form or another, Baluchistan and Sindh must rise in significance, providing enriched local identities for the Arabian Sea ports along the Makran coast, whose own destinies will help determine those of cities far inland. The nineteenth-century traveler and linguist Richard Francis Burton, after a five-year sojourn in Sindh, wrote that the line of ports along the Makran coast, stretching to Iran, would make it possible to "easily collect the whole trade of Central Asia," with Bombay "as the point to which all these widely-diverging rays would tend."[29] Such a vision, though an imperial one at the time, could yet have a prospect in an age when current frontiers will become increasingly frail.

CHAPTER SIX

THE TROUBLED RISE
OF GUJARAT

If the spirit of modern India has a geographical heartland it is Gujarat, the state in the northwest bordering Sindh in Pakistan. Mohandas Karamchand Gandhi, the Mahatma (Sanskrit for "Great Soul") was a Gujarati, born in Porbandar on the Arabian Sea in 1869. The signal event of the Indian independence movement, which has attained the status of a foundation myth, was the Salt March that Gandhi, joined by thousands, led in March 1930 across Gujarat from the Sabarmati Ashram 241 miles south to Dandi on the Gulf of Cambay. Here, in defiance of British law, Gandhi picked up a handful of salt on the beach, challenging the prohibition against the collection or sale of salt except by the colonial authorities. "Next to air and water, salt is perhaps the greatest necessity of life. It is the only condiment of the poor," Gandhi wrote. So "I regard this tax to be the most iniquitous of all from the poor man's standpoint. As the independence movement is essentially for the poorest in the land, the beginning will be made with this evil."

Gandhi's identification with the poor was intrinsic to his universalist philosophy, which was best condensed into the following statement, perhaps the most politically revealing he ever made: "I do not believe in the doctrine of the greatest good of the greatest number. It means in its nakedness that in order to achieve the supposed good of 51 percent, the interest of 49 percent may be, or rather should be, sacrificed. It is a heartless doctrine and has done harm to humanity. The only real, dignified human doctrine is the greatest good of all."

So to protect the poor against the ravages of capitalism, which bene-

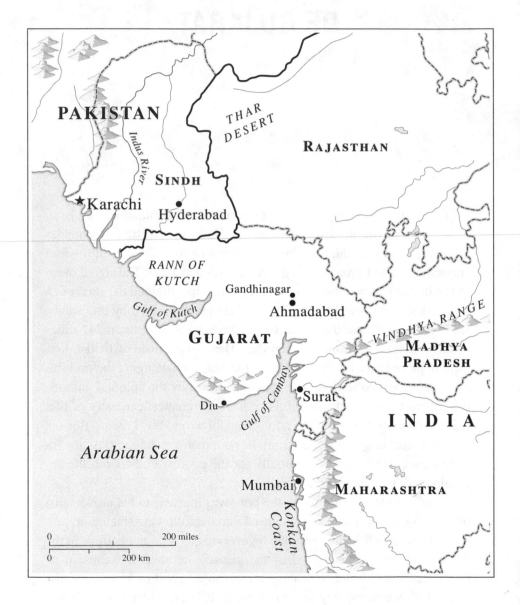

fits only the majority rather than everyone, India would adopt socialism after independence. More to the point, though the Hindus would dominate numerically, the rights of tens of millions of Muslims would not and must not be trampled on. Indeed, though India is swathed in an aura of religiosity and mysticism, the "greatest good" necessitated that the conscience of the new nation and the ruling Congress Party would be avowedly secular. Gandhi's rustic, semi-naked appearance notwithstanding, he is symbolic of the universalist spirit of the Indian Ocean, which he transferred in large measure to India's party of independence.

But the spirit of India has undergone an uneasy shift in this new era of rampant capitalism and ethnic and religious tensions, which arise partly as violent reactions against the very homogenization of societies that globalization engenders. Gujarat, among the handful of Indian states most identified with the long commercial history and traditions of the Indian Ocean, has found itself once again at the heart of what is roiling India, and this time what singularly menaces its rise to great global power status.

Let me be clear: I am very bullish on India, believing that its democracy has demonstrated sufficient elasticity to withstand future outbreaks of insurrection and localized anarchy to a degree that China's authoritarian system may not be able to match. India's democracy is ultimately a moderating force. Moreover, India is the birthplace of several religions: Hinduism, Buddhism, Jainism, and Sikhism. Jews, Zoroastrians, and Christians have lived in India for hundreds and thousands of years. The Tibetan Dalai Lama has resided here for decades. India has elected three Muslim presidents. It is nothing if not free and eclectic. Hence, consider the following as a long and cautionary tale, not a prediction of India's demise but, rather, an investigation into what might still go wrong with the country's otherwise extraordinarily hopeful story.

India is home to 154 million Muslims, the third largest Muslim population in the world after Indonesia and Pakistan. Tolerable inter-communal relations are the sine qua non of Indian stability and ascendancy, for throughout India and particularly in a mercantile state like Gujarat, Hindus and Muslims must interact in business transactions daily. India has more to lose from extremist Islam than arguably any other country in the world. Yet, in Gujarat—as well as in some other places in India—Hindus and Muslims have lately begun to segregate themselves. Children have left schools that lay on the wrong side of inter-communal lines, and are growing up for the first time without friends from the other religion. Muslims in significant numbers have turned their back on the rich Sub-continental tradition of religious syncretism and begun dressing in beards, skullcaps, and burkas. "The Hindu-Muslim divide here is worse than at any time since the partition," lamented historian Dwijendra Tripathi, who lives in Gujarat. Not coincidentally, this is occurring even as Gujarat booms economically, with brand-new malls, multiplexes, private ports, and highways, positioning itself as a pulsing region-state athwart Indian Ocean trade routes.

And yet Gujarat's religious tensions have a more specific source than merely the rigors of economic development. They stem from "2002," as everybody in Gujarat and the rest of India simply refers to it. That year in the local lexicon has attained a symbolism perhaps as resilient as the word "9/11" has to Americans. It connotes an atrocity that will not die, that has been etched deeply into the collective memory, becoming a myth in its own right that constitutes a hideous rebuke to Gandhi's Salt March. The notoriousness of these events is all the more shocking given that India regularly experiences spectacular violence among religious groups, castes, and tribes, yet these somehow all dissolve into the larger, messy stew that is this country's admired democracy.

What human rights groups here label the "pogrom" had its origin in the incineration of fifty-eight Hindu train passengers on February 27, 2002, in Godhra, a town with a large Muslim population that is a stop on the rail journey from Gujarat to Uttar Pradesh, in north-central India. The Muslims who started the fire were apparently the victims of taunts by other Hindus from Gujarat, who had previously passed through the station, en route to Ayodhya in Uttar Pradesh, to demonstrate for a Hindu temple to be built on the site of a demolished Mughal-era mosque. It was at this juncture that the recently installed chief minister of Gujarat, the Hindu nationalist Narendra Modi, immediately decreed February 28 a day of mourning, so that the funerals of the passengers could be held in the streets of Ahmedabad, Gujarat's largest city. "It was a clear invitation to violence," writes the *Financial Times* correspondent in India, Edward Luce, in his book, *In Spite of the Gods: The Strange Rise of Modern India*.[1] "The Muslim quarters of Ahmedabad and other cities in Gujarat subsequently turned into death traps as thousands of Hindu militants converged on them." In the midst of the riots, Chief Minister Modi quoted Newton's third law: "Every action has an equal and opposite reaction."

The statement removed all restraint from the killers. Mobs coalesced and raped Muslim women, before pouring kerosene down their throats and the throats of their children, who were then set on fire. The males were forced to watch the ritualistic killings before they, too, were put to death. The figures and some of the details of what happened are subject to great controversy. Some reports claim that as many as 400 women were raped, 2000 Muslims murdered, and 200,000 more made homeless throughout the state.

The killers—again, according to some reports—were dressed in saffron scarves and khaki shorts, the uniform of the RSS, the Rashtriya Swayamsevak Sangh (Organization of National Volunteers), the umbrella group of the Hindu nationalist movement, and came armed with swords and gas cylinders. The rioters were also equipped with electoral registers and computer printouts to identify Muslim homes. They even had the addresses of Muslim-owned businesses that had hidden behind Hindu business partners. Luce, the influential writer Pankaj Mishra, and many others have observed that the high degree of planning and efficiency to the murders indicated official culpability. "Surveys were done some weeks before indicating where Muslims lived," said Prasad Chacko, who runs a human rights nongovernmental organization (NGO), in Ahmedabad. "The police were complicit. There was the attitude of waiting for a pretext to let people vent their feelings. The quality of the killings, if not the numbers, indicate a state-sponsored genocide."

Indeed, the police stood by and observed the killings, and in some cases, according to Human Rights Watch, helped the rioters locate Muslim addresses. As for the 200,000 made homeless, the Gujarati state government provided little or nothing in the way of relief, or compensation for the loss of life and businesses. Many secular NGOs stayed on the sidelines, afraid to incur the wrath of the central authorities. Muslim charities—Jamaat-e-Islami, Tabliqe Jamaat, and Jamiat Ulema-e-Hind—provided for the shelters, and these organizations subsequently became a vehicle for the radicalization of young Muslims in the wake of the carnage. Modi, whom the riots had made a household word throughout India, later called the Muslim relief camps "baby-making factories."[2]

"The events of 2002 have reverberated years later because of the involvement of the Gujarati state authorities in the killings, and the fact that until this day there has been no public remorse," Sofia Khan, the head of a local Muslim NGO, told me. "There has been no moral reckoning," declared Ramesh Mehta, a retired judge. As one Hindu activist coldly rationalized to me, "If the train in Godhra had not been burnt, the riots would not have happened." His was an attitude I heard particularly from educated Hindus throughout Gujarat. While it is true that Indian political parties have for decades played the communal card—one could argue that the Congress Party stoked anti-Sikh violence after Indira Gandhi was assassinated by her Sikh bodyguards in 1984—there was a particular blatancy and transparency in the way that the Gujarati authorities helped orchestrate anti-Muslim violence. And afterwards, as Johanna Lokhande, an activist who helps victims of the massacre, told me, the local government was "averse to the whole idea of providing justice."

More tellingly, 2002 continues to echo precisely because of Chief Minister Modi's very success as a politician in the intervening years. He has never apologized, never demonstrated regret of any sort for 2002, and has thus become a hero to the Hindu nationalist movement, reelected several times as chief minister. Furthermore, his seeming incorruptibility, his machine-like efficiency, and his penchant for dynamic leadership of the government bureaucracy have lately made Gujarat a mecca for development, garnering more internal investment than any other state in India. To travel to Sindh and then to Gujarat is to comprehend at a very tangible level how Pakistan is a failed state and India a very successful one, with the ability to project economic and military power throughout the Indian Ocean region. And this impression, as imperfect as it may be, is to a significant extent due to the way Modi has governed.

Migrants, both Hindus and Muslims, from throughout India have been streaming into Gujarat in recent years to find work at its expanding factories. There is an element of Lee Kuan Yew's Singapore in Modi's Gujarat. What's more, his hypnotic oratory, helped by a background in the theater, has led some to compare him to Adolf Hitler. Modi is not only the most dangerously charismatic politician in India today, he may be the only charismatic one, and the first to emerge in decades since Indira Gandhi in the 1970s.

Of course, Narendra Modi is neither Lee Kuan Yew nor Hitler. He is what he is, a new kind of hybrid politician—part CEO with incredible management abilities, part rabble-rouser with a fierce ideological following—who is both impressive and disturbing in his own right. Developments in mass communications have led to an evolution in leadership styles, and just as Barack Obama gives hope to millions in the new century, a leader like Modi demonstrates how the century can also go wrong: with unbreachable psychological divisions between religious groups masked by a veneer of cold bureaucratic efficiency. And that is why he is so important. Representing a spirit very different from that of Gandhi, he is very much part of the Indian Ocean story.

Leaders often sum up the geographical, political, and social landscapes out of which they specifically arise, so before I delve further into the character of Narendra Modi and describe my long conversation with him, let me provide a picture of Gujarat, a microcosm in more intense form of twenty-first-century India and the Indian Ocean world itself.

Gujarat has "tremendous locational advantage," explains historian Dwijendra Tripathi. It is near the Indian Ocean's midpoint, yet still close enough to Iran and the Arabian Peninsula to refine oil from there, and re-export it. With two great gulfs—those of Kutch and Cambay—Gujarat has the longest coastline and best natural harbors in India. This immense seaboard fronts westward toward the Middle East and Africa, so throughout history Gujarat has been a land of trade and the broad-based movement of peoples.[3] Camões writes in *The Lusíads:*

> See the most fertile land of Sind
> And the deep-seated Gulf of Kutch
> Where the flood tide is like a torrent
> And the ebb retreats as impetuously;
> See the treasure-laden land of Cambay
> Where the sea bites deeply into the coast;
> I pass by a thousand other cities
> Awaiting you with their amenities[4]

Indeed, Gujaratis, who were excellent sailors, made the Gulf of Cambay the easternmost point for trade in the western Indian Ocean and the westernmost point for trade with the East Indies.[5] Both Levantine rigs and Chinese junks could be found here and along the coast of western India.[6] Thus, Gujarat was at the confluence of several trading systems.[7] Moreover, Gujarat's prodigious textile production has given it a market from the Arabian Peninsula to the Southeast Asian archipelago, making its ports since the medieval centuries international trading hubs. During the age of British imperialism, Gujarati businessmen sold cloth to Yemen and were paid in silver, which they then lent to English merchants to buy Yemeni coffee, so merchants here made a double profit after they were repaid.[8] This business acumen and penchant for innovation were supplanted by a spirit of adventure and risk taking. In the early nineteenth century large Gujarati communities, made up to a large extent of Shiite Ismailis, sprang up in Muscat, Aden, East Africa, and Java, with a heavy concentration especially on Malacca and Zanzibar.[9] The fact that Gandhi began his career as a lawyer and political activist in South Africa rather than in India itself was very much part of this Gujarati tradition of planting roots throughout the Indian Ocean. Later, when the United States beckoned on the horizon and visa restrictions were loosened, Gujaratis flooded to its shores, becoming, among other things, motel proprietors and Silicon Valley software tycoons. It is estimated that 40 percent of the Indian immigrants in New York City are Gujaratis. In particular there are the Patels, village officials who in the nineteenth century amassed property and became landed gentry, and following that traveled to Africa and later the United States in search of commercial opportunities.

Faith—both Hindu and Muslim—became a tool of this business networking, providing a social and cultural framework for advantageous interactions. Thus, in Gujarat, devout, highly distinct ethnic and religious communities have been operating easily within a cosmopolitan framework. Even as the state leads India in the use of computer governance and indexes of economic freedom, it also has the strictest dietary restrictions, with alcohol publicly prohibited in this land of Gandhi, and vegetarianism (partly the result of the religious influence of the Jains) more widespread here than elsewhere in India. Hindus in Gujarat negatively associate meat eating with the tradition of the late-medieval Mughals, Muslim conquerors from Central Asia.

The Gujarati historical experience has been shaped not only by the Arabian Sea and the wider Indian Ocean, but also by Gujarat's situation on a frontier zone of the Subcontinent. Thus it has sustained repeated Muslim invasions from the north and northwest, which have been documented here more excruciatingly than in other Indian states. The worst of the depredations came at the hands of the Turko-Persian ruler Mahmud of Ghazna, who swept down into Gujarat from eastern Afghanistan, and in 1026 utterly destroyed the seaside Hindu temple of Somnath. Whenever I mentioned the events of 2002 to Hindu nationalists, I was lectured about the crimes of Mahmud of Ghazna and those of the Mughals. For these Hindus this is living history, as if it happened yesterday. Indeed, the Islamic architectural genius that created the Taj Mahal and brought a luxurious civilization, blending the material cultures of Persia and Central Asia with that of northern India, is considered a regrettable historical episode in the minds of Hindu nationalists, one of whom, Vijay Chauthaiwale, a molecular biologist, told me, "Muslims in India must de-link themselves from the memory of [Mughal kings] Babur and Akbar, and from terrorism, and should become purely of India."

Purely of India. This is a significant statement, which telegraphs a deliberate revision of history that the Indian media and school textbooks are partly responsible for propagating. The very Islamic migrations that make for today's dazzlingly multicultural India, with many Arabic and Persian loanwords embedded in Hindi and Gujarati, are wholly repudiated because of the undeniably awful sufferings and plunder of cities and religious sites that they brought upon Hindus (although armed conflicts between Muslim rulers probably outnumbered those fought between Muslims and Hindus in Indian history).[10] Even the Mughal emperor Akbar the Great, so named because of the religious pluralism he practiced (though a Muslim, he was accepting of Hinduism and spent his later life in search of a cosmic deity that spanned religious divides), is considered by Hindu nationalists just another Muslim subjugator.

Gone in significant measure in this worldview is the all-inclusive secular Indian version of history, originally subscribed to by the Congress Party during the Nehruvian era of the 1950s and 1960s, which emanated ultimately from Mahatma Gandhi's gentle humanistic vision of excluding no one from the national project, and which sought to bridge the historical differences between religious groups. The aura of legitimacy and romance that invested the Congress Party—the party of independence, after all—was shattered during the dictatorial emergency decrees enacted by Indira Gandhi in the mid-1970s. Following that, a new logic was required to mobilize the Indian masses and particularly the emerging middle class, a segment of the population that arose in Gujarat sooner than in many other Indian states, supported by its history of successful trading.

This logic was provided perversely by information technology and higher education. Information technology has allowed for standardized and ideologized versions of Hinduism and Islam to emerge from the multiplicity of local variants: Just as Shiites became united across the Middle East, Hindus became united across India, and the same for Sunni Muslims here. But it was particularly so with the Hindus, for whom before the age of mass communications their religion existed more as a series of local cults, making a united Hinduism as such an expression rather than an actual fact.[11] Meanwhile, education has made people aware of their own histories for the first time, and thus supplied them with historical grievances that they never previously had. "The Hindu poor are blissfully ignorant of Mahmud of Ghazna. It is the middle class that now knows this history," explained one local human rights worker. That is why Hindu nationalism is strongest not among the poor and uneducated, but among the professional classes: scientists, software engineers, lawyers, and so on. The same phenomenon can be observed among Islamic extremists, from al-Qaeda to the Muslim Brotherhood. In the eyes of this new right-wing middle and upper-middle class, India was a civilization before it was a state, and while the state has had to compromise with minorities, the civilization originally was unpolluted, Hindu that is, even if the truth is more complex.

This search for a reinvented national greatness among middle-class Hindus of India also applies to the new Muslim middle classes of Pakistan and Iran, which is why all three are intoxicated about the idea of nuclear weapons. Whether it is the Mauryan Empire in India, or the Achaemenid Empire in Persia, for millions lifted out of poverty and recently educated, the *bomb* now summons forth these great kingdoms of antiquity.

In India such yearning was further ignited by the economic reforms of the 1990s, which brought India truly into the vanguard of globalization. Because the socialistic nation-state of Hindus and Muslims is increasingly a thing of the past, both groups need a strengthened communal identity to anchor them inside an insipid world civilization. Their newly acquired prosperity has made many Hindus suddenly nervous of their situation, and thus susceptible to an exclusivist ideology. This has been especially apparent among overseas Gujaratis, who while becoming successful immigrants in the West, have engaged in a search for roots that they have transferred back to relatives in the homeland. Again, it is the very encounter with the wider world that has caused a certain narrowing of horizons. Out of this crucible *Hindutva* (Hindu-ness) mightily arose, with Islamic extremism a reaction.

The word *Hindutva* first appeared in a 1923 pamphlet, "Who Is a Hindu?," written by independence activist Vinayak Damodar Savarkar.

But it has really achieved prominence in the last decade with the opening up of the Indian economy, whose social effects have allowed the so-called *Sangh* (family of Hindu organizations) to flourish. They include the RSS, the BJP (Bharatiya Janata Party), and the VHP (Vishwa Hindu Parishad, or World Hindu Council). But the RSS, founded in 1925, is the mother organization, a vast and, in some sense, informal, volunteer-driven self-help corps. Chauthaiwale, the molecular biologist, explained that the RSS provided a "true Hindu voice lost by the pro-Muslim tilt of the Congress Party. Muslims invaded in earlier centuries. They conquered," he said. "We lost. The British conquered. We lost. We were a defeated society. We needed to come together as Hindus."

In the minds of its followers the RSS performed the heroic task of saving many Hindus in Pakistan during the partition in 1947. It was banned after Gandhi was assassinated the next year by a Hindu nationalist, Nathuram Godse, who was linked to the RSS. But in the 1960s, the RSS began to stage a resurgence, entering student movements and, in particular, getting involved in social betterment programs, much like the Muslim Brotherhood in the Middle East. It initiated humanitarian projects in the Hindu tribal areas, and sought to eliminate untouchability, so as to make Hindus more equal among themselves. As the prestige of the Congress Party waned in the 1970s, that of the RSS grew. The BJP was formed to promote RSS ideals at the national political level. All the human rights groups with which I visited in Gujarat, both Hindu and Muslim, called the RSS a fascist organization, which, behind its veneer of humanitarian assistance to fellow Hindus, has a "cultural nationalist" agenda. After the 2001 earthquake here, the RSS reportedly provided relief to Hindu families only.

The throbbing heart of the RSS is the *pracharaks* (propagators, or propagandists). They spread the word of the RSS. They are usually unmarried, and give up their lives to the organization, living sparely, inspiring hundreds of workers while trying to remain faceless themselves, in a deliberate attempt to eliminate their own egos. They are like a priesthood, except that the average *pracharak* serves only two or three years before marrying and resuming a normal life. Narendra Modi is unusual. Born in Gujarat in 1950 into a middle-level caste, he was a *pracharak* for almost a decade before becoming chief minister in late 2001. Modi is unmarried and lives alone. His has been a life devoted to the RSS.

Modi, the Hindu ideologue and the innovative CEO of Company Gujarat, is the culmination of local history and geography at this juncture in time, testimony to Gujarat's hard-edged communal identifications and its innovative business spirit that is right up to cosmopolitan Western standards. He is so honest that gifts for him are regularly deposited in the state treasury—a far cry from the corruption and nepotism that is so much a part of Indian politics. On visits to villages pregnant women regularly touch his feet so that their newborn will be like him.

Modi's office is located on an upper floor of a massive ministry building, made of cheap stone forty years ago and with a scabby facade. It is surrounded by other equally massive and ugly ministry buildings in Gandhinagar, the planned city of government workers north of Ahmedabad that is a monument to some of the flawed architectural schemes of formerly socialist India. Gujarat constitutes only 5 percent of the Indian population, but that is still fifty million people, more than the population of South Korea, so it requires a sizable government bureaucracy.

There was considerable hubbub outside his office, as Western businessmen and investors in expensive suits clustered together after meetings with the chief minister. At 5 p.m. sharp, I was ushered into Modi's office. He sat behind a desk that looked over a long committee table with the chairs empty. He wore traditional pajama pants and a long, elegant brown *korta,* with pens stuck in the pocket, the traditional dress of India that the Muslim Mughals had brought here. Wire-rimmed glasses rested on his face. He had a clipped and distinguished salt-and-pepper beard, and a handsome, welcoming visage. In front of him lay a small stack of documents, which he thrust at me before I even asked my first question. He clearly had little time for small talk. "I heard you were interested in development here, so here are your answers." What he gave me was not the usual promotional brochures, but long lists of sourced statistics put together by an aide. Gujarat had had 10.2 percent annual GDP growth since 2002. It had eight new universities. More than half the new jobs created in India were in Gujarat. It ranked first in poverty alleviation, first in electrical generation. As I had experienced, Gujarat was a far cry from neighboring Sindh in Pakistan where there were only a few hours of power every day. Then there were the new dam projects and microirrigation systems—again, a far cry from Sindh, with its acute shortages of water and dams not improved upon since the era of the British.

Chile and China flashed through my mind. Augusto Pinochet tortured and murdered a few thousand people in his first months as leader in 1973 and 1974, and then went on to create an economic dynamo that benefited the whole country. Deng Xiaoping massacred many hundreds of students at Tiananmen Square in 1989, and then went on to improve the quality of life of more people in a shorter time than perhaps ever before in recorded economic history. In both cases, deliberately planned atrocities had created an atmosphere of shock and fear, which the leader manipulated in order to push through a host of reforms without opposition. It worked, even as it was repugnant. It was a fact almost difficult to admit, that since 2002 there had not been a single act of inter-communal violence in Gujarat.

Was Modi trying to create another Singapore or Dubai in Gujarat, a place that would be, in a positive sense, distinctive from the mother brand of India? I asked him.

"No," came the reply. "Singapore and Dubai are city-states. There can be many Singapores and Dubais here. We will have a Singapore in Kutch," he said, waving his arm dismissively, "and GIFT [the Gujarat International Finance Tec-City, a new high-tech city planned nearby] can be like Dubai. Gujarat as a whole will be like South Korea. Global commerce is in our blood," he went on, lifting his eyebrows for emphasis. There was a practiced theatricality about the way he talked. You could see how he could move a crowd or take over a boardroom. Whenever he opened his mouth he suddenly had real, mesmerizing presence.

His ambition was staggering, whatever his roots as a faceless *pracharak*. South Korea was the world's thirteenth largest economy. Yet I could understanding the comparison: South Korea is a vast peninsula open to major sea-lanes like Gujarat. It had congealed as an industrialized, middle-class dynamo not under democratic rule, but under the benign authoritarianism of Park Chung-hee in the 1960s and 1970s. I mentioned this to Modi. He said he wasn't interested in talking about politics, only about development. Of course, politics constitutes freedom, and his momentary disinterest in politics was not accidental. Modi's entire governing style was anti-democratic, albeit quite effective: emphasizing reliance on a lean, stripped-down bureaucracy over which he had taken complete personal control, even as he had pushed his own political party to the sidelines, almost showing contempt for it.

It was also revealing that he had referred to GIFT as but a detail in his larger game plan. GIFT was the *pièce de résistance* in the effort to make

Gujarat an Indian Ocean economic nerve center. Modi had laid the foundation for this financial services hub in June 2007. The high-tech city would be five hundred acres, twice as large as Dockyards in London, 25 percent larger than La Défense in Paris, and larger even than the vast financial centers of Shanghai and Tokyo. GIFT would feature eleven modernistic skyscrapers, landscaped green zones, the latest in public transportation, waste management up to Western environmental standards, "intelligent buildings" with cutting-edge bandwidth connectivity and data integration, internal roads with storm weather drainage for monsoons, and a walk-to-work concept for its 50,000 residents and daily working population of 400,000. GIFT was to be a city of the future to compete with any in the world. And yet he now referred to it as merely a Dubai inside his larger, South Korean whole.

Modi spoke to me in to-the-point phrases with a didactic tone about the cosmopolitan trading history of Gujarat going back five thousand years, and how Parsees and others had come to its shores and been assimilated into the Hindu culture. I asked him about the contribution of the Muslims, who are 11 percent of the state's population. "We are a spiritual, God-fearing people," he answered. "We are by and large vegetarians. Jainism and Buddhism impacted us positively. We want to create a Buddhist temple here to honor Buddha's remains." He then prompted me for my next question. He had nothing further to say. Of course, Muslims are meat eaters.

I asked if he had any regrets about anything he did or failed to do since becoming chief minister seven years earlier. My question was clearly designed to give him an opening to show remorse, however oblique, about the events of 2002. Again, he had nothing to say. I then asked specifically if he regretted 2002. His answer: "There are so many views about that. Who am I to judge?" He said that a commission would decide about his role in the riots. In fact, a commission from his own state bureaucracy had already absolved him of any wrongdoing.

"There was no Kalinga effect on Modi," Hanif Lakdawala, a Muslim who runs a human rights NGO, told me. Lakdawala was referring to a war fought in the third century B.C. by the Mauryan Empire under King Ashoka against the state of Kalinga on the eastern coast of India. Ashoka's forces slew 100,000 civilians. The slaughter left Ashoka with so much guilt that he forswore further military expansion, and dedicated his life thereafter to nonviolence and the peaceful development of his empire.

Yet to give Modi the benefit of the doubt, I wondered if he wasn't, at least partly, privately remorseful. To admit guilt would be to undermine his position in the Hindu nationalist movement. In any case, in the Indian political context, few admit mistakes. But by all accounts, after the riots, he shut himself up and manically dedicated himself to development, sleeping less than four hours every night, as he told me, up at 5 a.m., checking his email and reading the local papers. Eventually he visited about three thousand of seven thousand villages in the state, developing his own grassroots networks to check on how the state bureaucracy was functioning at the local level, and empowering the lowest reaches of that bureaucracy—those functionaries in most contact with the citizenry— through his slogan, "less government, more governance." As Atul Tandan, director of the Mudra Institute of Communications in Ahmedabad, told me, "You have to separate Modi's political ideology from his management ability. Because there is not a hint of corruption about him, Modi is effective because people believe his decisions are only results-oriented." Indeed, even many Muslims have come to respect Modi for his accomplishments, such as cracking down on gambling and criminal rackets that have infested some of their own communities.

Nevertheless, I was still stuck with the notion that there were so many ingenious ways, direct and indirect, for him to show remorse for the crimes of 2002 without directly admitting guilt, and Modi had shown no interest in doing so at many an opportunity. Or was this Machiavellian? First, do little to stop RSS forces in what many neutral observers said was a methodical killing spree in 2002, and then turn toward development after violence has been used to consolidate power and concentrate the minds of your enemies. But Machiavelli, whose writings are either not carefully read or misunderstood, would not have approved. Machiavelli believed in using only the minimum amount of cruelty to attain a positive collective result, and thus any more cruelty than was absolutely necessary did not, as he put it, qualify as virtue.

"I am from a poor family," Modi told me. "If I had become a teacher it would have made my family happy. But I got involved in a national patriotic movement, the RSS, where one must sacrifice. As a *pracharak,* I was like a Hindu monk in a white dress. My Hindu philosophy: terrorism is the enemy of humanism." I assumed he meant Islamic terrorism, which accounts for most large-scale violent attacks in India. He compared himself to Gandhi: "When the British ruled, so many fought for independence and Gandhi turned this into a mass movement. I have converted economic development into a mass movement psychology." His words echoed throughout the empty room. "I have a toll-free number where callers hear my recorded voice and can make complaints against the government, and the relevant department must respond within a week."

He rolled off his accomplishments: modern roads, private railroads with double-decker containers, 31,000 miles of fiber optical networks, 1367 miles of gas pipelines, 870 miles of drinking water pipelines to 7000 villages, twenty-four-hour uninterrupted power in rural areas, the first Indian state with private ports, a totally integrated coastal development plan, two liquefied natural gas terminals and two new ones coming online. Statistics and lists had a rhythmic, spellbinding effect on him. He quantified everything.

He mentioned, too, the plant to be built in Gujarat by Tata Motors, employing several thousand workers, that will produce the Nano, the world's cheapest car priced at $2500. Luring Tata, perhaps India's most prestigious company, to Gujarat had been a coup for Modi, and billboards around Ahmedabad proclaimed his accomplishment, attesting to the cult of personality forming around him. "For so long the whole coastal area had been subjugated to Mumbai," he said. "But now the richness is coming back home to Gujarat. Gujarat will be the center point for East-West connectivity from Africa to Indonesia."

He was a very driven man, with no personal life from everything that I could gather. He exuded power and control. How could he not have been implicated in the 2002 pogrom? I asked myself.

A number of Hindus, all of them of the enlightened, global cosmopolitan class, as well as Muslims and several foreign writers, told me that there was an element of fascism in Modi's personality. Sophia Khan, the human rights worker, put it bluntly: "He's a fascist man. We Muslims don't exist for him. Our neighborhoods are called mini-Pakistans, while the Hindus live where the malls and multiplexes are."

Is Modi a fascist? The answer I think is ultimately no. Here is where we are too much influenced by leadership models that are rooted in earlier historical periods. But posing the question serves to further illuminate the danger that Modi might represent. Fascism, the scholar Walter Laqueur tells us, comes in many different stripes, though classic fascism of the kind that emerged in Europe in the first half of the twentieth century stems from defeat in war, or at least a very unsatisfactory victory.[12] Fascism is an "anti-movement, it defines itself by the things against which it stands," and in its hatred of the elite and cosmopolitans it is hyper-nationalistic, writes Juan J. Linz, an emeritus professor of political science at Yale. Modi exhibits little hatred of the elite, and his governing message of developing an infrastructure in order to lure business is positive in outlook. There is, too, fascism's distinctive style, with its "chants, ceremonies, and shirts" which had attracted so many young people between the two world wars. There is a romantic appeal to fascism that cannot be understood merely by reference to its ideology. Its cultic obsession with brutality and virility, combined with its glorification of military virtues, stresses action rather than reason. The point is to *act,* and damn the consequences. Between the wars, the uniforms, marches, rallies, and songs all spoke of an almost orgiastic love of the collective—of the group—and consequent hatred of the individual.[13] Because democracy protects the rights of the individual, fascism must be anti-democratic. Indeed, fascism usually comes armed with an authoritarian leader who is both ruthless and charismatic. The results can be truly terrifying. The Romanian Iron Guard, the Hungarian Arrow Cross, and the Croatian Ustashi all featured a deeply reactionary Orthodox Christianity and Catholicism that resulted in the most blood-curdling and theatrical of atrocities against Jews and Serbs. Despite the defeat of the Axis powers, because of the way technology promises social control the will to fascism has not gone away.[14] The phenomenon of Modi is an indication that, despite the claim in Francis Fukuyama's brilliant article of 1989, "The End of History," the battle of ideas continues, even as geography effects how it is played out.

It would appear, therefore, that Modi in February 2002 might have momentarily been a full-fledged fascist, and then quickly declined to being a low-calorie one. "What makes Modi different from Hitler," Prasad Chacko explained, "is that while Hitler thought fascism the end result of political evolution, Modi knows that *Hindutva* is only a phase that cannot last, so now he focuses on development, not communal divides." In fact, Modi has recently gone after the very Hindu nationalists who put him in power, arresting members of the VHP. Because he cannot or will not apologize for 2002, showing that he is less extremist than other Hindu firsters has become his method for becoming acceptable on the national stage, in advance, perhaps, of one day running for prime minister, explained Achyut Yagnik, a journalist and historian.[15]

Modi was helped in his ambition in the first years of the new century by the general atmosphere of civilizational tension around the world and the region. Whether it was the wars in Iraq and Afghanistan, the threat posed by Iran, possible chaos in Pakistan, or Islamic terrorism in Kashmir and India itself, Modi and those like him benefited momentarily from all of this. The global situation reminded Hindus—the overwhelming majority of Indian voters—how much they had to fear from Muslim radicalism, and how much Modi signified a strong bulwark against it, not through any specific act, but by the whole aura of his no-nonsense rule. The central question regarding India in the years ahead is whether an era of worldwide Muslim terrorism will lead more of its majority Hindus to despair and hatred. Based on the results of the 2009 national elections, the answer seems now to be no.

Yet in the immediate aftermath of 2002, Modi did not have to do anything anymore. He had made his point. As much as India fears Pakistan, it fears its collapse even more. The threat of Islamic anarchy in the region helps the cause of Hindu nationalism, even as inter-communal tension represents, arguably, a profounder threat to the country than even the increasingly drastic shortage of water. It is not so much radicalization that I encountered in interviews with Muslim victims of the 2002 violence, but a feeling of no longer being part of India. They have withdrawn into their own communities, afraid to venture among Hindus.

The contrary Hindu fear of Islam runs parallel with a more understated but palpable yearning for order. India's very rise as an economic and naval power has invited comparisons with China, and that, in turn, has led to frustration, particularly among the elites. Whereas the authoritarian government in China can make things happen, development in India occurs only in spite of the government, rarely because of it. The human rights official Hanif Lakdawala told me that, especially because of the nightmarish chaos of Indian cities, "there are at least a few in this country ready to accept a dictator, or at least a very strong leader."

Modi's record since 2002 has been far from perfect. Precisely because of 2002, he has been denied a visa to the United States, and this stigma has had an effect on foreign investment, in which Gujarat ranks third in India, even though it is the prime destination for domestic deal-making. Despite the infrastructure projects, Gujarat still ranks low on scales of human development in India: malnutrition afflicts almost half the population of children under five, anemia afflicts three quarters of the women here, and literacy is only 67 percent—no higher than the average for the country as a whole. There are rumors that GIFT is not being implemented properly, and that the foreign investment required for its takeoff will not be forthcoming in the wake of the global financial downturn.

In fact, what is truly preventing Modi from taking the grand leap of his imagination—that is, from remaking Gujarat into the kind of antiseptic global entrepôt, where, as in Singapore and Dubai, and in many parts of South Korea, you feel you could be literally anywhere—is the ball-and-chain reality of the Indian landscape itself. Take Gandhinagar, Gujarat's political capital, designed to be a highly regulated model city, liberated from the local milieu. Yet the greenery is overgrown and impossible to manage, cows and water buffaloes wander about, and shanties have sprung up along the main roads. Only in one small section of Gandhinagar made up of information technology companies did I feel as if I might have left India, or at least gone to an office park in Bangalore.

Then there is Ahmedabad, encased in tear-inducing smog, jammed with wailing motorbikes and auto rickshaws, treacherous with its broken sidewalks, and punctuated with stray cows and beggars, even as it constitutes a less jarring experience than the epic congestion of a Mumbai or Kolkata. Ahmedabad, founded in 1411 by Ahmed Shah of the Gujarat Sultanate, was something of a playground for internationally renowned architects in the 1950s, when the Western elite placed newly independent India on a pedestal as the hope of humanity. Le Corbusier designed the Textile Mills Association building, Louis Kahn the Indian Institute of Management, and Buckminster Fuller a geodesic dome. But with the exception of a few gems, Ahmedabad, with a population of 4.5 million, remains weighed down by the same affliction that ails other Indian cities: little of architectural note or beauty between a handful of truly magnificent medieval Muslim monuments and the mishmash of steel-and-glass Dubai-style dwellings of the new-rich which are a product of 1990s economic liberalization. Because Ahmedabad was not a political center for the British, there is no colonial architecture here to lighten the burden of the cheap, drab Soviet-style modernism, further defaced by the jumble of rusty signage, which is the visual legacy of Prime Minister Jawaharlal Nehru's long, post-independence rule (even though he was such an inspiring leader in other respects). Of course, Gandhinagar represents this dreary, crumbling modernism at its worst.

India is 37 percent urban. Within the next two decades it will be 50 percent so. Bimal Patel, a local architect, explained that the real governing challenge of India's leaders will be to make cities like Ahmedabad more aesthetically appealing and habitable. Here is where Modi, as dynamic as he has been, has yet to succeed or try hard enough. GIFT is, to some degree, an escape from what needs to be done, though an understandable escape, given that throughout the world old downtowns are degenerating as new suburbs sprout.

Under Modi, a new six-mile-long park and waterfront project, designed by Patel, is being constructed along the Sabarmati River that runs through Ahmedabad. But, for the most part, the chief minister has avoided the local politics of Ahmedabad and other Gujarati cities rather than grapple with them to effect change. Urban politicians in India are generally incorrigible on one hand, and weak on the other, as most of the power is held at the state level, so very little happens in the cities. Neither Modi nor very many other state leaders have truly engaged in consensus building at the municipal level to clean up the urban mess, though, at some point, India's new urban elite may demand that real local politics, however messy and unsatisfactory, be engaged in—the true mark of freedom.

This is to say nothing of the informal communal cantons that have either sprung up or been strengthened under Modi's rule, with the old walled city of Ahmedabad among the only areas where Hindus and Muslims, who compose 9 percent of the city's population, can really mix. Otherwise, the most poignant scene I came across in more than two weeks of wandering around Ahmedabad was at the Sarkhej Roza, the fifteenth-century mosque and tomb complex dedicated to Sheikh Ahmed Khattu, the spiritual advisor to Ahmed Shah. Amidst the medieval domes and balconies overlooking a water tank, families picnicked, young couples whispered, children played ball, and prayer meetings were held. The architecture, with its elegant stucco and grillwork, blended Islamic and Hindu styles, a composite known as Indo-Saracenic. But at least until the park and waterfront project are completed, there is no such mixing of cultures in Ahmedabad today, for the crowd at the Sarkhej Roza was, obviously, exclusively Muslim.

To see more of Gujarat, for ten hours I traveled by bus and car from Ahmedabad south to the coast at Diu, at the southernmost point of Gujarat's Kathiawar Peninsula, the site of Portuguese monuments that have particular relevance to the larger Indian story I wish to relate.

I passed through a never-ending series of hovels along broken roads, past creaking and dusty carts, shanties, and lean-tos made of burlap and rusted corrugated iron that define rural India. Though the Indian landscape, especially as seen in the pages of coffee table books, offers a richness of primary colors, the reality is often a dreary tableau of grays and browns. In many places, though, I found that the roads were paved, and running water and electricity were everywhere. As primitive as the scenes looked, I knew from journeys in poorer Indian states like Bihar and West Bengal that much progress had been made. Still, South Korea? No, not for a few decades at a very minimum. India could be a great regional power and pivot state, but it was not likely to reach the level of development of the East Asian tiger economies. "Modi's very good at hype," one journalist told me, "but he can't completely deliver."

Diu had been a key strategic base for Portugal's Indian Ocean empire, captured from the Ottoman Turks in a decisive sea battle in 1509 by Francisco de Almeida, who had convinced the local Muslim governor to change sides and thus not come to the aid of his religious compatriots. It was this victory that further cemented Portugal's claim to control navigation in these waters. The poet Camões celebrates such conquest and treachery in *The Lusíads:*

> That Portuguese, they prophesy,
> Raiding along the Cambay coast, will
> Be to the Gujaratis such a specter
> As haunted the Greeks in mighty Hector. . . .
> The King of Cambay, for all his pride,
> Will surrender rich Diu's citadel,
> In return for protecting his kingdom
> From the all-conquering Mughal . . .[16]

The sea gently knocked at the ramparts of the Portuguese citadel, the colors of mustard and lead from centuries of wear. The citadel is a triumph of fortress architecture—with a long landing pier, double gateway, rock-cut moat, and double line of seven bastions, each named after a Christian saint. Weeds crept through the stone, wild pigs wandered about, and packs of young male Indians, impervious to the historical explanations in Hindi and Gujarati, loudly ambled along the stone works, seemingly unknowing of the significance of this immense curiosity, topped at its highest point by a lonely white cross. No guidebooks in any language were on sale, nor was there any entry fee or even a gatekeeper. The massive Portuguese churches here, with their colossal white Gothic facades, stood equally forlorn, their walls faded and leprous. You could actually see and hear the plaster falling at the close wing beats of pigeons. Inside these churches, after you had made your way past the tangle of garbage and overgrown white roses and oleanders, were cool, dark aromatic interiors conducive to prayer for the delivery of loved ones from the ravages of the sea. A few hundred years old, these dilapidated monuments are more like relics from antiquity, so divorced do they seem from the local environment.

Empires arise and fall. Only their ideas can remain, adapted to the needs of the people they once ruled. The Portuguese brought few ideas save for their Catholic religion, which sank little root among Hindus and Muslims, so these ruins are merely sad, and, after a manner, beautiful. By contrast, the British brought tangible development, ports and railways, that created the basis for a modern state. More importantly, they brought the framework for parliamentary democracy that Indians, who already possessed indigenous traditions of heterodoxy and pluralism, were able to fit successfully to their own needs.[17] Indeed, the very Hindu pantheon, with its many gods rather than one, works toward the realization of competing truths that enable freedom. Thus, the British, their flaws notwithstanding, advanced an ideal of Indian greatness. And that greatness, as enlightened Indians will tell you, is impossible to complete without a moral component.

As the influence of an economically burgeoning India now seeps both westward and eastward, it can do so only as a force of communal coexistence made possible by being, as the cliché goes, the world's largest democracy. In other words, India, despite its flashy economic growth, is nothing but another gravely troubled developing nation without a minimum of domestic harmony. Mercifully, the forces of Indian democracy have already survived more than sixty years of turmoil, attested to by the stability of coalition governments following the era of Congress Party rule. These forces appear sufficiently grounded to either reject a Modi at the national level or to neuter his worst impulses as he moves at some point from Gandhinagar to New Delhi. After all, the churches and bastions in Diu are ruins not because they represent an idea that failed, but because they represent no idea at all; whereas India has been an idea since Gandhi's Salt March in 1930. Modi's managerial genius will either be fitted to the service of that idea or he will stay where he is. Hindus elsewhere in India are less communal-minded than those in Gujarat, and that will be his dilemma. The coming together of Hindus and Muslims following the seaborne terrorist attack on a hotel and other sites in Mumbai in November 2008, originating from Pakistan, should have been a warning to him.

And if he did not get the message then, he certainly got it in May 2009 when Indian national elections gave the Congress-led coalition a decisive victory over Modi's BJP. Indeed, the decline of Modi, which those elections might suggest, is as sure a sign as any of India's triumphal entry into the twenty-first century. At the end of the day, despite all of the trends I have noted, I believe that enough Hindus will not ultimately give in to hate, regardless of the Muslim threat. We can thank India's democratic spirit for that, a spirit that is truly breathtaking in terms of what it can overcome. That is India's ultimate strength.

But in Gujarat, at least, peace will not come easily. From Diu I hired a car and drove two hours westward along the coast to Somnath, site of the Hindu temple destroyed by Mahmud of Ghazna, as well as by other invaders, and rebuilt for the seventh time starting in 1947.

Adorned with a massive pale ocher *shikhara* (tower) and assemblage of domes, this temple is located at the edge of a vast seascape glazed over with heat. Its coiled and writhing cosmic scenes on the facade are so complex they create the sculptural equivalent of infinity. Prayer blasted from loudspeakers. It was a madhouse on account of the full moon. Hundreds of worshippers checked their bags at a ratty cloak stand and left their shoes in scattered piles. Beggars attached themselves to me; hawkers were everywhere, as at many pilgrimage sites. Signs proclaimed that no mobile phones or other electronic devices would be permitted inside. I knew better, I told myself. I put my BlackBerry in my cargo pocket, not trusting it to the mild chaos of the cloak stand, and expecting the usual, lackadaisical third world frisk. I then joined the long, single file line to enter the temple. At the entrance, I was savagely searched and my Black-Berry discovered. I was rightly yelled at, and beckoned back to the cloak stand. "Muslim terrorism," one worshipper alerted me. From the cloak-room I got back in line and entered the temple.

Semi-darkness enveloped me as worshippers kissed the flower-bedecked idol of a cow. The air was suffocating with packed-together bodies approaching the womb-chamber. I felt as if I were trespassing on a mystery. Though nonbelievers were officially welcomed, I knew that I was outside the boundaries of the single organism of the crowd—philosopher Elias Canetti's word for a large group of people who abandoned their individuality in favor of an intoxicating collective symbol.[18] This sanctum was a pulsating vortex of faith. Some dropped to their hands and knees, and prayed on the stone floor. There was no seduction of outsiders as at the Vatican, a place diluted by global tourism; nor was this the Kali temple in Kolkata, where foreigners are regularly welcomed and accosted by "guides" demanding their money. The universalism of the kind I had experienced at the Sultan Qabus Grand Mosque in Oman, which celebrated material civilization throughout the Indian Ocean, was not missing here, it was simply irrelevant. I had had the same extreme and cloistered sensation inside the shrine of the Black Madonna at Częstochowa in Poland, and in the Imam Ali Mosque in Najaf in Iraq, two of the holiest sites of Catholicism and Shiism, respectively; at the latter unbelievers are expressly forbidden and I had to sneak in with a busload of visiting Turkish businessmen.

Being here you could not help understanding Hindu feelings about Muslim depredations of this temple, one of India's twelve Jyotirlingas (places with signs of light that symbolize the God Shiva). Emotions crackled like electricity, yet I thought of what human rights official Hanif Lakdawala had asked me in a pleading tone: "What can we poor Muslims of today do about Mahmud of Ghazna?"

CHAPTER SEVEN

THE VIEW FROM DELHI

O f all the periods of Indian Ocean history with which Gujarat is associated, and which are pertinent to our larger strategic discussion, among the most important is that of the Mughal Empire. Mughal emperor Akbar the Great marched into Ahmedabad in 1572 and completed the conquest of the province two years later. For the first time, the Mughals were rulers of a full-fledged coastal state with a substantial foothold on the Arabian Sea. Gujarat offered the Mughals not only possession of the busiest seaports of the Subcontinent at the time, but also a maritime kingdom that included vast and rich agricultural lands, and was in addition a powerhouse of textile production. By linking Gujarat with the Indo-Gangetic plain, and with soon-to-be-conquered Bengal, Akbar secured a subcontinental empire that spanned the two great bays of the Indian Ocean: the Arabian Sea and the Bay of Bengal. It was by conquering Gujarat that Akbar saved India from disintegration, and from falling further into the hands of the Portuguese, whose hold on Goa threatened the other Arabian Sea ports.

Few empires have boasted the artistic, religious, and cultural eclecticism of the Mughals. They ruled India and parts of Central Asia from the early 1500s to 1720 (after which the empire declined rapidly). Like the Indian Ocean world of which it was a part, the Mughal Empire was a stunning case in point of early globalization. Take the Taj Mahal, the white marble mausoleum built on the bank of the Yamuna River in Agra by the Mughal emperor Shah Jahan to honor his wife Mumtaz Mahal, who died in childbirth (her fourteenth) on June 17, 1631. The tomb fuses

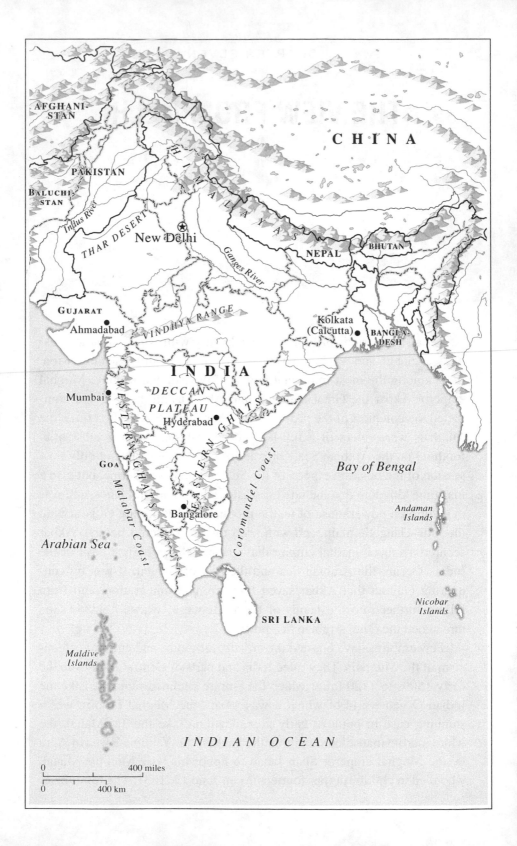

all the liberating grace and symmetry of the best of Persian and Turkic-Mongol architecture, with an added Indian lightness and flair. It is as though, with its globular dome and four slender minarets, it is able to defy gravity and float off the ground itself. There is a romance to the tomb and the story surrounding it that makes one forget that Shah Jahan was an extremely orthodox Muslim whose rule, according to Duke University history professor John F. Richards, represented a "hardening" of relations between the dominant Muslims and those of other faiths in the Subcontinent.[1]

Mughal is the Arabic and Persian form of Mongol, which was applied to all foreign Muslims from the north and northwest of India. The Mughal Empire was founded by Zahir-ud-din-Muhammad Babur, a Chaghatai Turk born in 1483 in the Fergana valley in today's Uzbekistan, who spent his early adulthood trying to capture Tamerlane's (Timur's) old capital of Samarkand. After being defeated decisively by Muhammad Shaybani Khan, a descendant of Genghis Khan, Babur and his followers headed south and captured Kabul. From there Babur swept down with his army from the high plateau of Afghanistan into the Punjab. Thus, he was able to begin his conquest of the Indian Subcontinent. The Mughal, or Timurid, Empire that took form under Akbar the Great, Babur's grandson, had a nobility composed of Rajputs, Afghans, Arabs, Persians, Uzbeks, and Chaghatai Turks, as well as of Indian Sunnis, Shias, and Hindus, not to mention other groups. In religion, too, Akbar's reign of forty-nine years (1556–1605) demonstrated a similar universalism. Akbar, who was illiterate, possibly the result of dyslexia, spent his adult life in the study of comparative religious thought. And as his respect grew for Hinduism and Christianity, he became less enamored with his own, orthodox Sunni Islam. In his later years, writes Richards in his rich yet economical history of the Mughal Empire, Akbar gravitated toward a "self-conceived eclectic form of worship focused on light and the sun."[2] Moreover, he championed an "extraordinarily accommodative, even syncretic style of politics," even as he governed in the courtly style of a traditional Indian maharaja, as demonstrated in the miniature paintings.[3]

All that changed under his successors Jehangir, Shah Jahan, and especially Aurangzeb, who returned the empire to a fierce Sunni theocracy that, nevertheless, tolerated other sects and religions. This very religious dynamic was a factor in the tense relations between Mughal India and Safavid Persia. Although Persian administrators were among the largest ethnic groups in the Mughal nobility, the Safavi Persians, who were fervent Shias, showed contempt for the Sunni Timurids governing India. This extreme dislike was intensified by the uncomfortable cultural similarity between the two empires that shared a common frontier through what is today western Afghanistan, for the Mughal imperium truly conjoined India and the Near East.

This is what makes the Mughal Empire so crucially relevant to an understanding of the destinies of India, Pakistan, and Afghanistan in the twenty-first century. The very term "Indian Subcontinent" instills in us the geographical logic and inevitability of the Indian state as a separate, inviolate unit framed by nature itself, hemmed in as it is by the Indian Ocean on three sides and by the Himalayas in the north. Meanwhile, we also tend to think of Pakistan and Afghanistan as more or less separate units, with their own historical and natural legitimacy, if less so than India. But the Mughals governed what is today Pakistan and much of Afghanistan from their northern Indian heartland, even as they had trouble subduing the Maratha tribes of the Deccan plateau in India's own south.

The Mughals were everywhere, it seems. They fought the Uzbeks in the extreme north of Afghanistan. They had strong bases in Baluchistan, Sindh, and Gujarat on the Arabian Sea, in the two eastern Indian provinces of Orissa and Bengal, and in a sliver of Arakan in western Burma.* In other words, the Mughals united Central Asia with the Indian Ocean, in both the Arabian Sea and the Bay of Bengal, reaching all the way to Southeast Asia. Islam was the adhesive that held this sprawling state together.

Kabul and Kandahar were a natural extension of this venerable Delhi-based dynasty, yet the strongly Hindu area in southern India around present-day Bangalore—India's high-technology capital—was much less so. Aurangzeb, the "world-seizer," under whose rule in the late seventeenth century the Mughal Empire reached the zenith of its expansion, was an old man in his eighties still fighting Maratha insurgents in India's south. He died in 1707 in his camp in the Deccan plateau, unable to subdue them. In fact, it was this long-running and intractable insurgency in southern India that sapped the cohesion and morale of the Mughal elite. Aurangzeb's preoccupation with the Maratha warriors—to the exclusion

---

* Until the Mughals' invasion, Bengal itself had been under the less organized Delhi Sultanate from the end of the twelfth century.

of imperial problems elsewhere—made it easier for the Dutch, French, and British East India companies to gain footholds on the coast, which led eventually to British rule in India.[4]

The British would unite the Subcontinent through a railway system and other tools of modernity, making a stable and united India appear inevitable, even if, for a host of historical and cultural reasons—as Aurangzeb's experience showed—it was not necessarily. Neither, for that matter, is it inevitable that the borders between Afghanistan and Pakistan, and between Pakistan and India, will continue to have the same meaning they have today. Harvard historian Sugata Bose notes that what both the British and ourselves have referred to as the North-West Frontier Province of Pakistan—the current haven of al-Qaeda and the Taliban—is "no frontier at all," but the "heart" of an Indo-Persian and Indo-Islamic continuum that straddled the high plateau of Central Asia and the steamy lowlands of the Subcontinent for millennia.[5] Thus, our struggle to separate Afghanistan from Pakistan may be in vain if geography, history, and culture are any guide. To succeed in Afghanistan means stabilizing both countries, not one. In fact, for negative reasons like cross-border terrorist attacks or for positive ones like the construction of roads and pipelines, this vast region of the Mughal Empire may achieve a new kind of unity, ultimately bringing Sindh and Gujarat, as well as Central Asia and the Subcontinent, together once again, anchoring, that is, South Asia to a Greater Middle East.

The memory of the Mughal Empire suggests a new and borderless world in the process of emergence, in which the old divisions of Cold War area studies are dissolving across Asia. Nowhere in India did I feel the tensions of what this implied as in the capital of New Delhi. Under the Mughal emperors Shah Jahan and his son Aurangzeb, Delhi was the richest and most populous city between Istanbul and Tokyo, and its existing British-built structures re-create that dominating mood. Walking can be difficult in the administrative heart of New Delhi, parts of which are built on too grand a scale, with much open space and often not enough shade, despite the abundance of trees. Erected in the 1920s, after the capital had been moved from Calcutta, the visual effect of its core government buildings, so graceful and yet so overwhelming, is reminiscent of the fortress architecture of the Mughal Empire itself. Each structure demonstrates the same monumental calm and sweeping proportions of Shah Jahan's one-

and-a-half-mile-long Red Fort, constructed in the mid-seventeenth century in the old part of the city. New Delhi's sandstone government edifices, with their various earthen shades of red and ocher, their long walls, lonely pigeon-inhabited porticoes, and distant oriental domes of varying widths and depths—like planets arrayed in the heavens—convey a political power so certain and self-confident that it rises above mere ambition.

The scholar and India expert William Dalrymple sees in New Delhi's architectural panorama vague evocations of Nazi Germany and fascist Italy, both of which were contemporaneous with Britain's own brand of authoritarianism in India, and both of which shared with the British Empire the illusion of permanence.[6] It is said that British architect Sir Edwin Lutyens had bells carved into the columns of the Viceregal Lodge, now the official residence of the President of India, because as they would be silent, British rule would never come to an end. Indeed, some years earlier, Lord Curzon had proclaimed: "The Empire calls, as loudly as it ever did. . . . The Frontiers of Empire continue to beckon."[7] Yet a mere two decades after this building spree the British deserted India, and these gargantuan structures—and all the power and presumption they express— are now the offices of the Indian armed services and government ministries.

The lesson of the fragility of central authority appears to have been internalized by the current occupants. In several days of meetings with top Indian military and civilian officials in New Delhi on separate visits, it became clear to me that although they have plans for India's projection of power throughout the Indian Ocean world, they are also deeply worried about the feebleness of India's own borders, to say nothing of India's internal strife. The voices I heard mixed a determined ambition with a prudent sense of tragedy. Whereas the British had assumed a lot, the current occupants assume less.

It is important to situate these buildings geographically. In terms of architecture, culture, and history, Delhi is where Turko-Persian Central Asia meets the Hindu Gangetic plain, where inner Asia meets the periphery of the Indian Ocean world. As such, it has been the seat of great Asian power since the Middle Ages. In the twenty-first century, according to the U.S. Central Intelligence Agency, India will emerge as the key "swing" state in international politics. As Lord Curzon wrote a century ago:

The central position of India, its magnificent resources, its teeming multitude of men, its great trading harbours, its reserve of military strength . . . all these are assets of precious value. On the West, India must exercise a predominant influence over the destinies of Persia and Afghanistan; on the north, it can veto any rival in Tibet; on the north-east . . . it can exert great pressure upon China, and it is one of the guardians of the autonomous existence of Siam [Thailand].[8]

The British and the Mughal emperors who followed Babur might have been there no longer, but India's current rulers occupied the same geographical position as they did, and in our conversations, therefore, I noted that they looked out at the world similarly.

The Mughals were a land-based empire of Central Asian origin, and the British a sea-based empire. For the moment, India was rising more in the way of the British. Just as the British Royal Navy ruled the seas, allowing for the protection of its crown colonies, notably India, the story of a rising India is, at least in military terms, the story of its navy. Hemmed in on land by a combination of the Himalayan Mountains and failing states from Pakistan and Nepal to Bangladesh and Burma, India can best project power at sea. India stands sentinel astride the major sea-lanes from the Strait of Hormuz to the Strait of Malacca, where the threat of naval or containerized terrorism is very real. And although countries such as Malaysia and China "have reservations about the U.S. pushing its geostrategic objectives in the name of maritime security," in effect, without ever declaring it, India can play the role of the chief balancer vis-à-vis China.[9] The renowned policy analyst of India Stephen P. Cohen argues that New Delhi officials since the time of the Cold War have inculcated the precepts of George Washington's Farewell Address of 1796: that India, like the United States, inhabits its own geographical sphere, in India's case between the Himalayas and the wide Indian Ocean, and thus is in a position of both dominance and detachment.[10] During the Cold War this meant nonengagement; now it means that Indians see themselves with their own separate status as a rising power.

Chinese policy intellectuals are becoming deeply concerned with the emergence of a capable Indian navy.[11] One Chinese analyst even worries that the 244 islands that constitute India's Andaman-Nicobar archipelago can be used as a "metal chain" to lock shut the western entrance of the

Strait of Malacca on which China so desperately depends for its oil deliveries. This analyst, Zhang Ming, reasons further that "once India commands the Indian Ocean, it will not be satisfied with its position and will
continuously seek to extend its influence, and its eastward strategy will
have a particular impact on China." Ming sums up by saying that "India
is perhaps China's most realistic strategic adversary."[12] Of course, this
may bear the sound of a professional worrier from the Chinese equivalent
of Washington's own theory class. But policy elites worry to a serious
purpose, and even if Ming is somewhat exaggerating the extent of the Indian menace, his concerns demonstrate just how seriously Beijing takes
New Delhi as a major sea power in its own right.

One cannot caution enough how subtly this game will have to be
played, for India will never officially join the United States in any anti-
Chinese alliance the way Japan joined the United States in an anti-Soviet
one during the Cold War. Japan was a defeated nation after World War II,
in close proximity to Soviet ports; whereas India is a strong nation with
an independent streak "codified in its policy of non-alignment," far from
the Chinese navy's main ports.[13] Not just the architecture but also New
Delhi's very geopolitical situation make one doubly cognizant of India's
potential as a post-Mughal, post-British power in its own right.

Although his manner was quiet and dull, Admiral Sureesh Mehta, chief
of the Indian naval staff at the time of my visit, was the most sanguine of
the officials I met, liberated as he was from the troublesome land borders
of partition with which India, and particularly its army, was stuck. The
future of the Indian navy could not have looked brighter, for it was slated
in the near future to possibly become the world's third or fourth largest.[14]

India's economy, Admiral Mehta and others said, had been growing
at 9 percent annually, with a 10 percent growth in its industrial output.
Its middle class would grow from 200 million to perhaps 500 million by
2020, and the global economic crisis would slow down but not halt this
trend.* By 2050, India would have the world's third largest economy
after the United States and China. That allowed India's defense budget
to increase by 10 percent, even as it fell in relative terms to under 2 percent of the gross domestic product. Twenty percent of the defense
budget was for the navy, and half of that went into capitalization for new

* India was expected to surpass China around 2032 as the world's most populous country.

ships.* Naval officials said India planned to have two aircraft carrier strike groups by 2015, three by 2022, and was building or acquiring six new submarines and thirty-one new surface warships. It was in discussion to equip seven of its frigates with the Aegis integrated combat system used by the American, Australian, Japanese, South Korean, and a few European navies. All of this activity would result in several brand-new shipyards. There was a new naval training academy on the Malabar coast north of Cochin. In sort of a coming-out party for its growing naval power, in 2008 India hosted an Indian Ocean naval symposium in New Delhi for twenty-seven littoral countries modeled on U.S.-led naval coalitions. It was part of a larger story, in which India would spend as much as $40 billion on weapons procurement, making it one of the largest military markets in the world.[15] Maybe the Chinese had a right to worry seriously after all.

A million ships pass through the various Indian Ocean straits each year. The future was all about the security of energy supplies. Meanwhile, China's so-called string-of-pearls naval strategy was part of an ongoing historical development in which the Chinese, from the strategic perspective of India, had been trying to box India into its subregion. China's 1950 invasion of Tibet, traditionally the buffer between India and China, had established this tendency. There was, too, a 2500-mile-long border dispute arising out of the 1962 Sino-Indian war in which China's victory—the Humiliation in Indian eyes—remains engraved in the local psyche. China still occupied the Aksai Chin region of the western Himalayas and claimed the Indian state of Arunachal Pradesh, which Beijing referred to as lower Tibet. On land India faced an encirclement strategy: top beneficiaries of Chinese arms exports were Pakistan, Bangladesh, and Burma.[16] Moreover, when Nepal's King Gyanendra briefly became a dictator in 2005, suspending political parties and the constitution, Western nations including the United States cut or downgraded military links, even as Beijing dramatically enhanced them, for no other purpose, it seemed, than to balance against India.[17]

The Chinese had a port and road system in Burma. They were building bunkering facilities in Sri Lanka. They had footholds in the Seychelles and Madagascar where they were spending increased amounts on

---

* The navy's share of the Indian defense budget had doubled from the early 1990s. Walter C. Ladwig III, "Delhi's Pacific Ambition: Naval Power, 'Look East,' and India's Emerging Influence in the Asia-Pacific." *Asia Security,* vol. 5, no. 2 (May 2009).

aid. They hoped Gwadar in Pakistan would be a friendly harbor. The Indians were not waiting to see if Gwadar succeeded. Occupying a peninsula connected to the mainland by an isthmus, Gwadar was at present hard for the Chinese to defend.[18] Nevertheless, the Indians' answer to Sino-Pakistani cooperation at Gwadar was a giant new $8 billion naval base at Karwar, south of Goa on India's Arabian Sea coast, the first phase of which opened in 2005. Named INS (Indian Naval Ship) *Kadamba,* it would be India's third operational naval base, after Mumbai farther north and Visakhapatnam on the Bay of Bengal. Karwar had been designed to ultimately berth a whopping forty-two ships, including submarines. The effect would be to decongest Mumbai and maneuver India's fleet fast enough without being hemmed in by merchant vessels.[19] India was not about to let China and Pakistan guard, or indeed block, its entrance to the Gulf of Oman from Gwadar, for this would create for India a "Hormuz dilemma," the equivalent to China's "Malacca dilemma."[20] Beyond American hegemony, the China-Pakistan-India triangle was emerging as the Arabian Sea's decisive geostrategic issue.[21]

To the Arabian Sea's south, in the western Indian Ocean close to Africa, India was establishing naval staging posts, listening stations, and arms relationships in and with the island nations of Madagascar, Mauritius, and the Seychelles. China was countering with its own active military cooperation with these states.

Just as Chinese warships operated in the western Indian Ocean, Indian warships were now in the South China Sea. India was increasing naval cooperation with Indonesia and Vietnam to hedge against the Chinese at the eastern crossroads of the Indian Ocean, and countering in the southwest through its de facto control of Mauritius. Indian naval officers were essentially running the coast guards of both Mauritius and the Seychelles.

Indian officials denied that a naval exercise in late 2007 of five democratic nations—India, the United States, Japan, Australia, and Singapore—off the Malabar coast was an attempt to snub China. Nevertheless, while that exercise witnessed five Western navies—a "concert of democracies," as one Indian official called it—with twenty thousand officers and sailors cooperating at a complex level of operations, India and China were engaged in only the most basic of military exercises—land-based search-and-rescue maneuvers—in which both sides were intent on hiding their advanced systems.

"India has never waited for American permission to balance [against] China," said Indian strategist C. Raja Mohan, confirming the Chinese analyst's fears, adding that India has been balancing against China since the day the Chinese invaded Tibet.*

Concerns about China were born of success. China was the elephant in the room that drove India and the United States closer together.† Nevertheless, "No country has watched China's utterly spectacular rise as closely and jealously as India," write the analysts Mohan and Parag Khanna.[22] India, writes the British journalist Edward Luce, "wants to remain equidistant from both China and the United States. . . . In practice, this would still suit Washington's purposes," for merely by growing economically and becoming more "assertive in its dealings with the world," India would "naturally act as a counterbalance to China."[23] As I have said, India will remain nonaligned, but whereas during the Cold War it tilted toward the Soviet Union, now it will tilt toward the United States.

Yet China was still a problem for India's strategists only—much less so for its security services, or for anyone else in India. Explosions in India were not the work of China-based terrorist outfits, but of Pakistan-based ones. After the United States, China was India's biggest trading partner, for the Indian and Chinese economies were highly complementary. Because of demography, one day China and India would constitute the world's largest trading relationship.[24] It seemed that the two Asian demographic behemoths were bound to cooperate at some basic and crucial level, adding complexity to their relationship, and thus making it unclear whether or not China would ever be so provocative as to establish overt naval bases in the Indian Ocean.

China notwithstanding, from a naval standpoint, India was already a major regional power, with the possibility later in the century of being a great power. Most of India's problems were on land, not at sea. General Deepak Kapoor, chief of the Indian army general staff at the time of my visit, said that "even though we can't deny China's capability, China is our neighbor and we have to get along." Nevertheless, the Indian army

---

* Daniel Twining, "The New Great Game," *Weekly Standard,* Dec. 25, 2006. Only in 2005 did India recognize Chinese sovereignty over Tibet; in return, China recognized Indian sovereignty over the Himalayan state of Sikkim.

† Some Indians liked to point out that China opposed the selling of uranium to India by Australia, for use in India's nuclear program, which suggested to them that China opposed the very emergence of Indian power.

had taken note of three airfields built in Tibet whose arc of operations included India, and of roads and high-altitude rail lines flowing into the Tibetan plateau that abuts the Indian Subcontinent from the Chinese heartland. Then there were the newly constructed thirty-nine transport routes from interior China to its contested border with India.[25]

But as I said, China was an over-the-horizon threat; in the general's eyes, it was meager compared to the real threat represented by Pakistan's Directorate for Inter-Services Intelligence (ISI). In New Delhi, discussions about China still belonged to the more abstract realm of grand strategy, whereas those about Pakistan were up close and personal. People in New Delhi desperately wanted to compare themselves with China, even as the category of worries that kept them up at night was all about Pakistan. Pakistan's Inter-Services Intelligence was "a law unto itself," another Indian army officer had told me. ISI was seen in New Delhi as a state organization that was almost a terrorist outfit, and thus an entity with few equivalents in the world, outside the Lebanese Shiite Hezbollah. ISI was the key supporter of the Taliban and al-Qaeda insurgencies in Afghanistan, and was helping terrorists in Indian-controlled Kashmir. Above all, ISI was operationalizing the infiltration of jihadis into India. "Radical forces are moving east of the Indus, and things will get worse," an Indian intelligence officer told me. He said this before the spectacular 2008 terrorist attack on Mumbai. Indeed, that attack featured a seaborne infiltration, meaning that the maritime borders of the state were also insecure, and thus the Indian navy still had more to do at home in addition to worrying about China.

This was all occurring even as the Pakistan army was redeploying away from the Indian border to Baluchistan and the North-West Frontier Province next door to Afghanistan, in order to deal with insurgents and terrorists inside its own borders. A trend was apparent: the threat to India from Pakistan was less the conventional one of the Pakistani army, as in years and decades past, and more unconventional in the form of infiltrating Muslim terrorists. Still, the Indians spoke about the Pakistani army, which it had defeated in war, with utter derision. The Pakistani army, as one highly placed Indian official put it, "was not a professional army because it has been involved in politics for too long." Moreover, he went on, the political structure in Pakistan could not "deal with or handle its own terrorist elements," so a situation had arisen in which jihadis mixed seamlessly with the bureaucracy itself there. Again, the Mumbai attack would crystallize all of this. The fact that Indian voters, despite this grave threat, had rejected Modi and the other Hindu nationalists in the 2009 election was a further indication of India's rise in stature. The election results heralded a nation that was confident enough not to give in to extremism.

Because of the need for a rear base against Pakistan, the Indian army saw a pro-Western, Taliban-free Afghanistan as a necessity. From India's viewpoint, said General Kapoor, it was more important that the United States maintain a long-term commitment in Afghanistan than in Iraq. "India has a critical interest in the survival of the [Hamid] Karzai regime," said the Indian national security advisor M. K. Narayanan in another meeting. The Afghan war was India's as much as America's. To be sure, Afghanistan has been a prize that Pakistan and India have fought over indirectly for decades. To Pakistan, Afghanistan represented vital strategic real estate that, along with the Islamic nations of former Soviet Central Asia, would offer a united religious front against Hindu-dominated India, and block its rival's access to energy-rich regions. Conversely, for India, a friendly Afghanistan would pressure Pakistan on its western border—just as India itself pressures Pakistan on its eastern border—thus dealing Pakistan a strategic defeat of sorts.

In the 1980s, India backed the secular pro-Soviet regime of Mohammad Najibullah in Kabul, and Pakistan backed Islamic insurgents trying to topple him. Because America's interests at the time were aligned with Pakistan's, the United States encouraged Pakistan's ISI to support the insurgents, many of whom later became allies of the Taliban and al-Qaeda. But in 1991 came the breakup of the Soviet Union, and a decade later 9/11. Although the world changed for America, the importance of Afghanistan to India and Pakistan remained the same. India still needed to back a relatively secular regime in Kabul, just as Pakistan still thought it needed to support Islamic insurgents who wanted to topple it.* Thus, America's interests were now more or less aligned with those of the Soviets of a generation ago.

Besides Pakistan, General Kapoor was also concerned about the tinderbox of Jammu and Kashmir, India's only Muslim-majority state, whose loss or further explosion could ignite "a chain reaction of separatism" across India's kaleidoscopic regions, with their myriad of races,

---

* Pakistan regularly accuses India of using its newly opened consulates in Afghanistan to support the Baluch separatist movement.

languages, and religions.[26] There was, too, Maoist-inspired instability in Nepal, where half the population lived close to the Indian border, and which was in the eyes of Indian security officials under the increasing influence of both ISI and China. Even if this was exaggerated, their insistence of it reflected their own and their country's insecurity on this particular front, especially as the strengthened Maoist position in Nepal might have encouraged terrorist attacks in central and eastern India by Maoist Naxalites.

Rightly obsessed with India's land borders, Indian army officers were worried about a lot of things. They spoke of rising Sunni Islamic fundamentalism in the Maldive Islands to India's southwest; of anti-Indian ethnic insurgent groups in the extreme northeast of the country operating from inside Burma, where China was heavily involved; of illegal immigration in the neighborhood of ten to fifteen million people from Bangladesh; and of the war in Sri Lanka off India's southeast coast, which ended only in 2009. Said one army officer: "We don't have the luxury to go full bore into American-style rapid reaction forces, because we have unsettled borders, and therefore we need boots on the ground in significant numbers."

Then the tone of the discussions lightened, and officials spoke of future energy pipelines connecting India with Turkmenistan and other countries in Central Asia, a region that India—fearing encirclement—is not ready to concede to China and Pakistan. This was witnessed by its recent establishment of a military base in Tajikistan. We spoke of the importance of the Gulf and Southeast Asia for Indian security.

In other words, to sum up this and other briefings, India was weak close by, even as it flexed its muscles farther away. "Pakistan, Afghanistan, Burma, Sri Lanka," said an Indian official, "turmoil, turmoil, turmoil. . . . Everyone expects India to have a tough policy toward Burma and toward Tibet because we are a democracy, but we have land borders with these places, and we can't tolerate a vacuum." It was not for India to stand on ceremony and make black-and-white moral pronouncements in the manner of the United States, which was protected by two oceans, said Shivshankar Menon, India's foreign secretary at the time. "The last thing we want is all eighteen insurgencies up and running in Burma again," said another official. India was strongest in its southern peninsular region by the sea, and most fragile in the north, east, and west.

"We have 155 million Muslims in India. Our concern really is fundamentalism. How do we ensure that things don't get out of control?" said yet another official to me. "Al-Qaeda as a mindset is more dangerous than al-Qaeda as an organization." There was a real fear that instability in the neighborhood would become the norm. "Our calmness and peace are at risk." Indeed, after Iraq, India suffered from the greatest number of terrorist incidents per annum, according to the U.S. State Department.[27] Narayanan mentioned the July 2006 train attacks in Mumbai, consisting of seven bomb blasts, that killed more than two hundred people and injured some seven hundred, which he said "were planned across several countries." Yet, as he went on, "There was no adequate sharing of intelligence" in the region. Vulnerable to terrorism like few other states in the world, India was a natural ally of the United States in the fight against Islamic extremism, whose hub was the Afghanistan-Pakistan frontier in India's own backyard.*

Amid the arcaded porticoes and Mughal miniatures of the Foreign Ministry guesthouse, Menon, the foreign secretary, using the phrase of the scholar Sunil Khilnani, called India a "bridging power"—that is, something between America and China, between a global power and a regional power, between hard power and soft power, between the emerging power of its economy and navy and the poverty of many of its people and its weak borders.[28] Indian cultural influence has always been more widespread and profound than conventional calculations of power would suggest.

It was a nice concept, but how did it help in decision-making? In an even less benign security environment, India might be forced to make choices that would put it firmly in one category or another. Moreover, the nation had often shown a certain ambivalence in asserting its power. Incorporating a much stronger navy and air force into its foreign policy calculations was something that India was still mastering.[29]

India was the ultimate paradox. It dominated the Subcontinent much as the British had, yet unlike the viceroys it was bedeviled by land borders in which the only state within the Subcontinent that was not dysfunctional was India itself. All the others—Pakistan, Nepal, Sri Lanka, Bangladesh, and Burma—were supreme messes of countries. Pakistan and Bangladesh made no geographical sense. They were artificial constructs in places where the political map had changed dramatically over

---

* Facing, in its own view, a missile threat from China and Pakistan, India was also an ally of the United States on the issue of missile defense.

the decades and centuries. Nepal and its dozen ethnic groups had been held together by a Hindu monarchy torn asunder by gruesome murders, and finally replaced by a fragile new democracy. Sri Lanka's rival ethnic groups had been engaged in a generation-long war whose embers were still hot. And Burma's very sprawling and rugged topography made it home to several ethnic insurgencies that had provided the raison d'être for military misrule. Only India, despite its languages, religions, and ethnicities, dominated the Subcontinent from the Himalayas to the Indian Ocean, providing it with geographical logic. Democracy helped immeasurably by giving all these groups a stake in the system. The Naxalite terrorists notwithstanding, India was inherently stable—in other words, it could not fall apart even if it wanted to.

Yet dealing with all of its problems on a daily basis, even as its naval chief contemplated sea power as far away as Mozambique and Indonesia, provided the inhabitants of these awesome government buildings with a sense of modesty that the British, with all of their realpolitik, lacked. Thus, the Indians might occupy this magnificent perch at the confluence of Central Asia and the Hindu plain longer and ultimately more fruitfully than did their predecessors. The real art of statesmanship was to think tragically in order to avoid tragedy.

India stands dramatically at the commanding center of the Indian Ocean, near to where the United States and China are headed for a tryst with destiny. Just as America is evolving into a new kind of two-ocean navy—the Pacific and the Indian oceans, rather than the Pacific and the Atlantic—China, as we shall see in a later chapter, may also be evolving into a two-ocean navy—the Pacific and the Indian ocean, too. The Indian Ocean joined to the western Pacific would truly be at the strategic heart of the world. But before we complete this picture, it is necessary to take a close look at other countries along the Indian Ocean's littoral, particularly those on the Bay of Bengal. Let's start with India's neighbor Bangladesh, which was also part of the Mughal Empire.

CHAPTER EIGHT

BANGLADESH

THE EXISTENTIAL CHALLENGE

The Indian Ocean alone among the world's great bodies of water is, in the words of Alan Villiers, an "embayed" ocean. While the other oceans sweep from north to south, from Arctic to Antarctic ice, the Indian is blocked by the landmass of Asia, with the inverted triangle of peninsular India forming two great bays, the Arabian Sea and the Bay of Bengal.[1] The Arabian Sea is oriented toward the Middle East; the Bay of Bengal toward Southeast Asia, with the Mughals having a perch on both. But it is the monsoon that truly unites them. It ignores national borders with its vast geographical breadth. Pakistanis in Karachi watch closely the progress of the boisterous southwest monsoon northward along India's Malabar coast in the Arabian Sea; Bangladeshis do likewise as this monsoon churns its way up through the Andaman Sea off Burma, culminating at the top of the Bay of Bengal. My visits to the Bay of Bengal were almost always during the spring and summer monsoon rains, so these shores have retained a darker, though not unpleasant cast in my mind compared to the other seaboard farther west, that of the Arabian Sea.

The southwest monsoon that arrives in the Bay of Bengal in early summer provides a new dimension to rain. This is the time of tropical cyclones, and it is as though the ocean was continually emptying itself upon you. For days at a time, the sky is a low, claustrophobic vault of angry clouds. Absent sunlight, the landscape—however intrinsically rich in color, with mountains of hibiscus and bright orange mangoes, and the flowing saris of women—becomes scrubbed over in a grainy mist. Mud

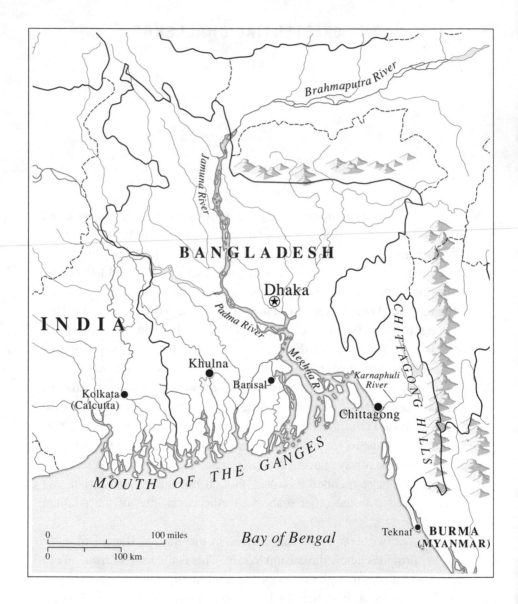

Brahmaputra River

Jamuna River

BANGLADESH

Dhaka

INDIA

Padma River

Meghna R.

Karnaphuli
River

CHITTAGONG HILLS

Khulna

Barisal

Kolkata
(Calcutta)

Chittagong

MOUTH OF THE GANGES

0   100 miles
0   100 km

Bay of Bengal

Teknaf   BURMA
(MYANMAR)

is the primary color, but it is not depressing. It is the coolness that you notice first, not the leaden darkness. You are filled with energy. No longer are your clothes dissolving in sweat or your knees hollow from the heat. No longer is the air something thick and oppressive that your body needs to push against.

The monsoon—from the Arabic *mausim,* meaning "season"—is one of the earth's "greatest weather systems," generated by the planet's very rotation, and also by climate. As the landmass on the Indian Ocean's northern shores near the Tropic of Cancer heats up in the summer, producing spectacularly high temperatures, a low-pressure zone forms near the surface, equalized by cooler air starting to flow in from the sea. When this cool, moist sea air meets the hot dry air of the Asian mainland, the cool moist air rises in upward currents, producing clouds and rain.* There is something truly mathematical about it, as the monsoon's two branches reach Cape Comorin and Bangladesh around June 1, Goa and Kolkata five days after that, then Mumbai and Bihar five days after that, Delhi in mid-June, and Karachi around July 1. It is the monsoon's dependability that inspires such awe, and on which agricultures and local economies consequently depend. A good monsoon means prosperity, so a shift in weather patterns due to possible climate change could spell disaster for the littoral countries. There is already statistical evidence that global warming has caused a more erratic monsoon pattern.[2]

The southwest monsoon in Bangladesh arrived while I was in a shallow draft boat traveling over a village that was now underwater. In its place was a mile-wide channel, created by erosion over the years, which separated the mainland from a *char*—a temporary delta island formed by silt, that would someday just as easily dissolve. As ink-dark, vertical cloud formations slid in from the Bay of Bengal, the small boat made of rotting wood began slapping hard against the waves. Following days of dense soupy heat, rain fell like nails upon us. The boatman, my translator, and I made it to the *char* before the channel water that was splashing into the

---

* Because water is returned to the sky by transpiration through leaves, forests are crucial to the process. As man-made development eats up the forest canopy, it threatens to weaken the monsoon on which agriculture exists. This is a less-discussed form of climate change. Alexander Frater, *Chasing the Monsoon* (New York: Holt, 1990), pp. 31–32, 65, 70, 159; Michael Pearson, *The Indian Ocean* (New York: Routledge, 2003), pp. 19–20.

hull, heavy with silt, threatened the boat's buoyancy. We started bailing. It was a lot of work just to see something that was not there anymore.

Some days later, in order to see a series of dam collapses that had been progressing inland, and which had led to the evacuation of more than a dozen villages, I rode on the back of a motorcycle along an interminable maze of embankments that framed a checkerwork of paddy fields glinting mirror-like in the steamy rain. Once again, the sight at the end of my journey—a few crumbled earth dams—was not dramatic, unless you had a "before" picture with which to compare it.

Climate change and attendant sea-level rises provide few straightforward visuals. Pictures of Arctic ice melt are dramatic only because the Arctic is itself dramatic. As sudden as the changes may be in geological time, to us they still occur in slow motion. Rivers will shift course overnight, and dams will collapse instantly, following a slight but pivotal rise in hydraulic pressure. But in such cases you have to be there when it happens.

Yet, from one end of Bangladesh to the other, in the early weeks of the monsoon, I saw plenty of drama, registered in this singular fact: remoteness and fragility of terrain never once corresponded with a paucity of humanity. Even on the *chars,* I could not get away from people cultivating every inch of alluvial soil. Human beings were everywhere on this dirty wet sponge of a landscape traversed by narrow, potholed roads and grimy, overcrowded ferries, where the beggars and peddlers appeared to sleepwalk between the cars in the pouring rain.

I went through towns that had a formal reality as names on a map, but were little more than rashes of rusted, corrugated iron and bamboo stalls under canopies of jackfruit, mango, and lychee trees. These towns teemed with men wearing traditional skirtlike *longyis* and baseball hats, and women who over the years were increasingly garbed in Muslim burkas that concealed all but their eyes and noses. Between the towns were long lines of water-filled pits, topped with a green scum of algae and hyacinths, where the soil had been removed in order to raise the road a few feet above the unrelenting, sea-level flatness.

Soil is so precious in Bangladesh that riverbeds are dredged in the dry season to find more of it. It is a commodity that is always on the move. When houses are dismantled, the ground on which they stand is transported through wet "slurry pipes" to the new location. "This is a very transient landscape, what's water one year can be land the next, and vice versa," explained an official of the U.S. Agency for International Development in Dhaka, the capital. "A man can dig a pit, sell the soil, then raise fish in the new pond."

In every respect, people were squeezing the last bit of use out of the earth. One day I saw a man carried on a stretcher moments after he had been mauled in the face and ear by a royal Bengal tiger. It is not an uncommon occurrence, as fishing communities crowd in ever closer on to the tigers' last refuge in the mangrove swamps of the Bangladeshi-Indian border area, even as salinity from rising sea levels has led to a sharp reduction in the deer population on which the tigers feed. Neither man nor tiger has anywhere else to go.

The earth has always been unstable. Throughout geological history flooding and erosion, cyclones and tsunamis have been the norm rather than the exception. But never before have the planet's most environmentally frail areas been so crowded. Although the rate at which world population grows continues to drop, the already large base of population guarantees that absolute rises in the number of human beings have never been greater in countries that are most at risk. This means that over the coming decades more people than ever before, in any comparable space of time save for a few periods like the fourteenth century during the Black Death, are likely to be killed or made homeless by Mother Nature. The Indian Ocean tsunami of December 2004 was a curtain raiser for disasters ahead.

People joke sometimes about how thousands of people displaced by floods in Bangladesh equals, in news terms, a handful of people killed or displaced closer to home. But that comparison, in addition to its cruelty, is blind to where natural events may be headed. The U.S. Navy may be destined for a grand power balancing game with China in the Indian and Pacific oceans, but it is more likely to be deployed on account of an environmental emergency, which is what makes Bangladesh and its problems so urgent.

With 150 million people living packed together at sea level, the lives of many millions in Bangladesh are affected by the slightest climatic variation, let alone by the dramatic threat of global warming. The possibility of an eight-inch rise in sea level in the Bay of Bengal by 2030 would devastate more than ten million people, notes Atiq Rahman, executive director of the Bangladesh Centre for Advanced Studies. The partial melting of Greenland ice alone over the course of the twenty-first century could inundate more than half of Bangladesh in salt water. Although such statistics and scenarios are hotly debated by scholars, one thing is certain: Bangladesh is the most likely spot on the planet for the greatest humanitarian catastrophe in history. And as I saw, it would affect almost exclusively the poorest of the poor.

Yet as the case of Bangladesh shows, the future is not strictly about rising sea levels. It is about the interrelationship between them and political phenomena such as religious extremism and the deficiencies of democracy.

Atop the Bay of Bengal, the numberless braids of the Ganges, Brahmaputra, and Meghna rivers have formed the world's largest, youngest, and most dynamic estuarial delta. Squeezed into a territory the size of Iowa— 20 to 60 percent of which floods every year—lives a population half that of the United States and larger than the population of Russia. Bangladesh's Muslim population alone (83 percent of the total) is nearly twice that of Egypt's or Iran's. Bangladesh is considered small only because it is surrounded on three sides by India. Actually, it is vast: a veritable aquatic culture where getting around by boat and vehicle, as I learned, can take many days.

First come the spring floods from the north, originating with the snowmelt in the Himalayas, swelling the three great rivers. Then in June, and lasting for three months, comes the monsoon from the south, up from the Bay of Bengal. Calamity threatens when the amount of water arriving by river, sea, or sky is tampered with, whether by God or by man. Nepal, India, and China are all ravished by man-made deforestation. The result is silt, or loose soil, that traps water in place: hence waterlogging, which prevents water from flowing onward into the great rivers. Moreover, India and China, are appropriating Ganges and Brahmaputra water for irrigation schemes, thus further limiting freshwater flows into Bangladesh from the north, causing drought. Meanwhile, to the south, in the Bay of Bengal, global warming appears to be causing a sea-level rise. This brings salt water and sea-based cyclones deeper inland. Salinity—the face of global warming in Bangladesh—kills trees and crops, and contaminates wells. And with insufficient fresh river water coming down from India and China, this hydrological vacuum is only quickening the ingress of salt water northward into the countryside.

But Bangladesh is less interesting as a basket case than as a model of how humankind copes with an extreme natural environment, for weather and geography have historically worked to cut one village off from another here. Credible central government arrived only with the Mughals from Central Asia in the sixteenth century. But neither they nor their British successors were truly able to penetrate the countryside. The major roads were all built after independence. Hence, this is a society that never waited for a higher authority to provide it with anything. The very isolation effected by floodwaters and monsoon rains has encouraged institutional development at the lowest level. The political culture in rural Bangladesh is more communal than hierarchical, in which women especially play a significant role.

A four-hour drive northwest of Dhaka, I found a village in a mixed Muslim-Hindu area where the women had organized themselves into separate committees to produce baskets and textiles, and invest the profits in new wells and latrines. They showed me a cardboard map they had made of where they would install them. They received help from a local nongovernmental organization that, in turn, had a relationship with CARE. The initial seed money came from outside, but the organizational heft was homegrown.

In a tiger-infested mangrove swamp in the southwest, I found a fishing village where people lived in bamboo-thatched huts along a river. Here I watched a play performed by a local NGO, which taught about climate change, the need to conserve rainwater through catchments, and the importance of planting trees to prevent erosion. Hundreds of villagers were present; I was the only foreigner. Afterwards, they showed me the catchments that they had built to direct rainwater into the wells.

Through similar bottom-up, purely voluntary means, the population growth rate in Bangladesh has been cut from 7 percent per year after independence to 1.5 percent now—an unprecedented achievement, given the value placed on children as laborers in a traditional agricultural society. Polio has been nearly eradicated several times, failing only because of perennial reinfection from India. Despite all of its predicaments, Bangladesh has risen from a state of famine in the mid-1970s to a nation that now feeds itself.

The credit for coping so well under the circumstances rests ultimately with NGOs. NGOs have become a familiar acronym because of the work of relief charities like Save the Children, Doctors Without Borders, and so on. But in Bangladesh the word connotes a new organizational life-form, in which thousands of local NGOs help fill the void between a remote, badly functioning central government and village committees.

Because they are nonprofit enterprises with for-profit elements, some ethical questions have been raised about Bangladeshi NGOs. Take Muhammad Yunus, who, along with his Grameen Bank, won the 2006 Nobel Peace Prize for pioneering micro-credit schemes for poor women; he also operates a cellphone and Internet service. Then there is the Bangladesh Rural Advancement Committee (BRAC), which besides its bounteous relief work, operates dairy, poultry, and clothing businesses. Its head offices, like those of Grameen, occupy a skyscraper that constitutes some of Dhaka's most expensive real estate. Yet to concentrate on the impurities of these NGOs is to ignore their transformative function.

"One thing led to another," explained Mushtaque Chowdhury, BRAC's deputy executive director. "In order not to be dependent on Western charities, we set up our own for-profit printing press in the 1970s. Then we built a plant to pasteurize milk from the cattle bought by poor women with the loans we had provided them. Now we've become a kind of parallel government, with a presence in sixty thousand villages."

Just as cellphones have allowed third world countries to make an end run around the need for a hard-wired communications infrastructure, Bangladesh shows how NGOs can make an end run around too often dysfunctional third world governments. Because local NGOs are supported by international donors, they have been indoctrinated with international norms to an extent that not even the private sector in Bangladesh has been.

The linkage between a global community on the one hand and a village one on the other has made Bangladeshi NGOs intensely aware of the worldwide significance of their country's environmental plight. "Come, come, I will show you the climate change," said Mohan Mondal, a local NGO worker in the southwest, referring to a bridge that had partially collapsed because of rising seawater. To some degree, this is a racket in which every eroded embankment becomes part of an indictment against the United States for abrogating the Kyoto accords. But in almost every other way Muslim Bangladeshis are pro-American—the upshot of historical dislike of former colonial Britain, frequent intimidation by nearby India and China, and lingering hostility toward Pakistan stemming from the 1971 liberation war.

Nevertheless, for the United States to strictly argue the merits of its case is not good enough here. Because it is the world's greatest power, the United States must be seen to take the lead in the struggle against global warming or suffer the fate of being blamed for it. Bangladesh demonstrates how third world misery has acquired—in the form of "climate change"—a powerful new political dimension, tied to the more basic demands for justice and dignity. The future of American power is related directly to how it communicates its concern about issues like climate change to Bangladeshis and others. This matters just as much as the number of warships it has; maybe more so.

NGOs would not have the influence that they do in Bangladeshi villages without a moderate, syncretic form of Islam. Islam arrived in Bengal late, at the beginning of the thirteenth century, with Delhi-based Turkish invaders. It is but one element of a rich, heavily Hinduized cultural stew. In Muslim Bengali villages, *matbors* (village headmen) do not carry the same authority as sheikhs in Arab villages. And below these figureheads, the other layers of social organization can be dominated by women whose committee mentality has been both receptive to, and empowered by, westernized relief workers.

But this mild version of Islam is now giving way to a starker and more assertive Wahabist strain. A poor country that can't say no to money, with an unregulated, shattered coast of islands and inlets, Bangladesh has become a perfect place for al-Qaeda affiliates, which, like westernized NGOs, are another sub-state phenomenon filling the vacuum created by weak central government. Islamic orphanages, madrassas, and cyclone shelters, which operate much like CARE or Save the Children, are mushrooming throughout the country, thanks largely to donations from Saudi Arabia, as well as from Bangladeshi workers returning home from the oil-rich Arabian Peninsula.

But rather than representing something unique in Bengali history, the radicalization of Islam shows how Bengal is part of a heavily Islamized Indian Ocean cultural system. Just as the great Moroccan traveler Ibn Battuta journeyed from Arabia to Bengal in the fourteenth century to gain the spiritual blessing of a renowned holy man, Shah Jalal, Saudi ideas and texts now infiltrate Bengal in the twenty-first century, and Bangladeshi workers, linked by air and sea to the Arabian Peninsula, return to their homeland with new ideas.[3]

From jeans and T-shirts a decade ago, women in the capital of Dhaka, in the port city of Chittagong, and throughout the countryside are increasingly covered in burkas and *shalwar kameezes*. Madrassas now outnumber secondary schools, according to Anupam Sen, the vice chancellor of a private university in Chittagong, who told me that a new class of society is emerging here that is "globally Islamic" rather than "specifically Bengali." Islam is especially acquiring an ideological edge in urban areas, where rural migration is 3 to 4 percent annually, as people flee an increasingly desperate countryside, ravaged by salinity in the south and drought in the northwest. In the process, they lose their tribal and extended family links as they are swept up into the vast anonymity of sprawling slum encampments. Here is where global warming and manmade climate change indirectly feed Islamic extremism.

"We will not have anarchy at the village level, where society is healthy. But we can have it in the ever-enlarging urban areas," warned Atiq Rahman. Such is the abject failure of central authority in Bangladesh after fifteen years of elected governments.

Nearing the second decade of the twenty-first century, Bangladesh is a perfect microcosm of the perils of democracy in the developing world because it is not a spectacular failure like post-invasion Iraq, but one typical of many other places. As in many a third world country that officially subscribes to democracy, civil society intellectuals play almost no role in the political process, the army is trusted more than any of the political parties, and although many champion historic liberalism, everybody I met also dreaded elections, which they feared would lead to gang violence. "We have the best constitution, the best laws, but no one obeys them," lamented one businessman. "The best form of government for a country like ours," he went on, "is a military regime in its first year of power. After that, the military fails, too."

The military was the power behind a caretaker civilian government in the fall of 2006, when the political system appeared on the brink of chaos, with strikes, demonstrations, a spate of killings, and an economy going nowhere. The ruling party was in the process of fixing the upcoming election, even as the opposition was planning a series of attacks by armed gangs in return. Up to that point, democracy had served up two feudal, dynastic parties: the Awami League, headed by Sheikh Hasina Wajid, a daughter of Sheikh Mujibur Rahman, Bangladesh's founding father who was assassinated in a military coup in 1975; and the Bangladesh Nationalist Party (BNP), headed by Khaleda Zia, the widow of another of the country's founders, General Ziaur Rahman, who was assassinated in another coup in 1981. The personal animosity between the two women harks back to the pardon given the killers of Begum Hasina's father by Begum Zia's late husband. This was darkly Shakespearean politics driven by personal vendetta, and as such, very reminiscent of Pakistan.

Because both parties are weak, both require alliances with various Islamic groups, and consequently turn a blind eye to al-Qaeda affiliates such as Jemaah Islamiyah that use Bangladesh as a transit point and training base. When in early 2007 the military-backed caretaker government hanged six militants from the Jama'atul Mujahideen—a local Islamic group responsible for literally thousands of terrorist attacks up through 2005—the conventional wisdom had it that neither political party could have carried out the sentence, compromised as they were by their Islamic coalition partners. In the eerie calm that characterized the time of my visit, with the country more orderly than it had been in years—with no terrorist attacks, with the ports operating without strikes, with army checkpoints everywhere, with hundred of arrests of politicians on charges of corruption, and with technocrats getting promoted over party hacks—nobody I met was enthusiastic about a return to the old two-party system, even as no one wanted the military to continue to play such an overt role in the nation's affairs. The military eventually withdrew from power and Sheikh Hasina was elected prime minister, though soon after her election, she had to deal with a violent mutiny by paramilitary border guards.

Bangladesh illustrates how the kind of government a state has is less important than the degree to which that state is governed—that is, a democracy that cannot control its own population may be worse for human rights than a dictatorship that can. Again, one does not need the extreme example of Iraq to prove this point; the less extreme example of Bangladesh will do. Functioning institutions—rather than mere elections—are critical, particularly in complex societies, for the faster a society progresses, the more and different institutions it will require.[4] Military intervention in Bangladesh is, ultimately, a response to the lack of capable institutions.

Furthermore, while democracy may provide the only cure for radical Islam over the long term, in the short term in Bangladesh, it was the very fear of radical Islam taking advantage of a political void that kept the military from initially returning to the barracks. This is a country where 80 percent of the population subsists on less than $2 per day, even as Jama'atul Mujahideen budgets $1250 per member per month. In addition to the financial incentive of becoming a militant, Bangladesh has porous borders with a barely governable part of India, where more than a dozen regional insurgencies are in progress. Rather than be eliminated in the military crackdown, it was thought that Jama'atul Mujahideen mutated temporarily into smaller groups operating in the frontier zones.

Bangladesh may be destined to be run by an old-fashioned Turkish-style national security regime composed of both civilians and military officers, in which the civilians dominate in public and the military draws red lines behind closed doors. "In the long run, we are hostages to democracy," Mahmudul Islam Chowdhury, a former mayor of Chittagong, told me. "Your Westminster–Capitol Hill system won't work here. But we're poor and need aid and so are required to hold elections." He explained that democracy in India works because there are so many states where different political parties dominate, so state and municipal governments thrive alongside the federal one in a multi-tiered system. But in Bangladesh the central government cannot risk an opposition party gaining control of any of the few big cities; thus all power is hoarded in Dhaka. The result is a vacuum that village committees have filled at the bottom level of government, and NGOs and Islamists struggle to fill in the vast and crucial middle ground.

Barisal, a major river port in southern Bangladesh, is a poster child for that vacuum: a middle-sized city that reeks of garbage and untreated sewage because of the absence of any viable treatment plants and the drying up of canals. This, in turn, is related to the unauthorized building of high-rises that brings ever more people into the urban core. Ahmed Kaisea, the district environmental director, was another official who told me that "the laws are just fine, there is just no enforcement." I had walked in on him without an appointment. He did not seem busy. His phone never rang, and there was no evidence of a computer. With electricity cuts throughout the day, use of the Internet is severely limited here. He was like many a bureaucrat I encountered, with an office but little effective control.

Because cities require more infrastructure than do villages (sewage, street lighting, traffic signals, and so on), the uncontrolled growth of cities like Barisal—because in part of the environmental ravishment of the countryside—makes it increasingly harder for government institutions, such as they exist, to cope.

Whereas Bangladeshi villages are defined by the struggle to find dry soil, cities are defined by the rickshaw economy. There are several hundred thousand bicycle rickshaws in Dhaka alone, a city of more than ten million people. Many of the drivers are migrants from the flood-prone countryside who pay the rickshaw *mustans* (mafia-style bosses, often associated with the political parties) the equivalent of $1.35 per day to rent the rickshaw. From an average passenger a driver collects 30 cents, and ends up making around a dollar a day in profit. His wife will often earn a similar amount breaking bricks into road aggregate, while their children sift through garbage. Such is a typical Bangladeshi family. This is an economic environment perfectly suited for the growth of radical Islam, which offers both answers and spiritual rewards for suffering that a mere conviction in voting periodically cannot. The miracle is not how radical Bangladesh and much of the third world is, but how moderate they remain.

The social cohesion that does exist on the national level is the result not of democracy but of linguistic nationalism. This is an ethnically homogeneous country where—unlike in Pakistan or Iraq—Islam is not required as a glue to hold together disparate ethnic or sectarian groups. What is more, national identity is built on violent struggle. In 1947, Muslim Bengalis rose up against the British and against India to form East Pakistan. Next came the 1971 liberation war against Muslim West Pakistan, which saw widespread rape and executions in Dhaka by a West Pakistani military hell-bent on imposing its Urdu language on the Bengalis. From East *Pakistan* (the "Land of the [Muslim] Pure") *Bangladesh* (the "Land of the Bengali") was created. Thus language replaced religion as the organizing principle of a society.

But that organizing principle is not inviolate. Because it occupies most of the landmass of the Asian Subcontinent, India enjoys a demonstrable geographic logic; not so Bangladesh. As small as Bangladesh is, again, it is vast in its own right. "Whoever comes to power in Dhaka—democratic or military—neglects us here in Chittagong," Emdadul Islam, a local lawyer, complained to me, voicing a sentiment common in the southeastern port city. "We have our own Chittagongian dialect, a mixture of Portuguese, Arabic, Arakanese, Burmese, Bengali, and so on. Historically," he went on, "we are as linked to parts of Burma and India as we are to the rest of Bangladesh. Who knows what will happen when Burma one day opens up and we have new road and rail links with India and southwestern China. Give me my fundamental rights and dignity, and I'll love this soil. If not, I don't know."

He was not calling for secession, but he was indicating how this artificial blotch of territory on the Indian Subcontinent—in succession Bengal, East Bengal, East Pakistan, and Bangladesh—could metamorphose yet again, amid the gale forces of regional politics, religious extremism, and nature itself. After all, look at all the kingdoms that Chittagong had once belonged to: Samatata, Harikela, Tripura, Arakan, and so forth. Chittagong and southeastern Bangladesh were as organically connected with the story of Burma through the ages as with that of India.

He spoke of a new mini-state composed of Chittagong and the Hill Tracts, lying between Burma and a Greater India; with the Barisal and Khulna regions of southwestern Bangladesh merging with Kolkata in India. He mentioned the thousands of Chittagongians who work in nearby states as part of a rich mini-diaspora. He was not a firebrand, just a man thinking out loud late at night, as the rain pounded in a nearby alley, about things that the very chronic instability of this country made it natural to think about.

I was regaled with a history as voluminous as the file folders tipping up toward the ceiling in the lawyer's office. Chittagong's identity, it turns out, is defined by the Bay of Bengal and by the larger Indian Ocean world much more than by Bangladesh. Though briefly part of the independent Muslim sultanate of Bengal in the early fifteenth century (and sporadically in the sixteenth), for most of the fifteenth through seventeenth century "the city and its hinterland were dominated by the kings of Arakan," a predominantly Buddhist kingdom more closely aligned with Burma than with Bengal. Chittagong was a principal South and Southeast Asian port for Muslim pilgrims traveling to and from Mecca, as well as a base for Portuguese renegades operating their own commercial and military enterprises beyond the reach of the Portuguese authorities in Goa on India's Malabar coast.[5] "Behold Chittagong," Camões writes, "the finest city of Bengal."[6]

Sometime in the Middle Ages, from across the Indian Ocean, came twelve Sufi saints, *auliyas* (protectors), who preached Islam and helped establish the city. Foremost among them was Pir Badr Shah, who, according to legend, floated from Arabia on a slab of rock to rid the city of evil spirits. A symbol of the wave upon wave of Arab traders who plied the Indian Ocean between Arabia and Southeast Asia, bearing spices, cotton fabrics, precious stones, and minerals, Badr Shah carried with him an earthen lamp that spread light "on all sides far and near," to ward off the darkness of evil and to help sailors.[7] This lamp may have been confused with a beacon fire atop a nearby hillside that he lit to guide his fellow sailors into the harbor. In any case, he is worshipped by seamen along the eastern shore of the Bay of Bengal as far south as Malaysia.

The earthen lamp and the slab of stone now lie in a rusted glass case under fluorescent lighting, next to the saint's draped sarcophagus, inside a brass cage under a moldy domed roof in the old fort area of Chittagong. Around it are machine-made carpets, simple mats, and green tiles of the kind common to many a kitchen or bathroom. In other words, there is nothing particularly aesthetic about this tomb, yet at sunset it is packed with worshippers. Men naked to the waist in soiled *longyis,* bathed in sweat and rainwater, danced around it. Sari-clad ladies lay on the stone floor, quietly insisting to the saint. Everywhere I saw candles and flowers. It was as though I were inside a Hindu temple. Pir Badr Shah is holy to Hindus as well as Muslims. His very person may be confused with that of Hindu deities. Buddhists and Chinese revere him as an inferior god. The same delicious confusion of worship holds for the tombs of the other Sufi saints in the city. Chittagong is a window to a world much larger and more cosmopolitan than Bangladesh.

Yet there is little architectural sign of it. Dank and mildewed, Chittagong constitutes miles upon miles of low-end signage eaten away by rust. There is no structure other than a handful of mosques that you could identify with any particular historical style. Rather than architecture, I saw only a makeshift assemblage of necessaries—the minimal construction required to meet the needs of the moment. The people who built such structures obviously lacked the luxury to be able to leave a permanent legacy, let alone something beautiful. For them, this slapdash construction represented a step up from the village from which they had migrated. Like the tomb of Badr Shah, Chittagong was ugly but also dynamic. Its history and folklore embraced a vast terrain, yet in other ways it was so void of tradition that little could be taken for granted here.

From a rooftop, Chittagong looked as if it had been dabbed in tar and charcoal dust, as the monsoon mist blocked out the views of the nearby picturesque Hill Tracts: "the mountains that seem to touch the sky," in the words of a seventeenth-century Portuguese traveler. With me was Tanbir ul Islam Siddiqui, the founder of an NGO called Change Makers. Change Makers had one overriding goal: to make Bangladeshis aware of their own constitution. Bangladesh has a perfectly fine constitution, but because it had been violated so many times over the years by both military and civilian rulers, its very existence was an embarrassment to those in control; thus they treated it almost like a state secret. It was hard for ordinary people to obtain a copy. And so Change Makers was dedicated to distributing their own constitution to Bangladeshis. Tanbir had no illusions about what he was up against.

Looking out at the grainy tableau of Chittagong, he told me: "Debates about democracy, military rule are for us. For the elite. All most people down there care about is their daily rice, while they take refuge in their saints. If the military keeps the port running, keeps the buses and factories running, they are content. The real struggle is not who rules, but to make people care about who rules."

Whereas Chittagong sits on the Bay of Bengal, the port itself, from which the city has grown, lies nine miles up the Karnaphuli River. Because of irrigation schemes and waterlogging upriver, there was not enough water flowing downstream to dilute the salt ingressing from the bay on account of rising sea levels. It was the same story as in other parts of the Bangladeshi coastline. The result was a buildup of sediments that made the river too shallow for an increasing number of ships. What's more, the port was in desperate need of a new road network for trucks to meet the ships at dockside. Thus, despite its perfect location—a midpoint between the Middle East and the Far East, what had made Chittagong such an attractive entrepôt for centuries—the port has an uncertain future.

With China building deepwater facilities in next-door Burma, the decades to come could see this part of Bangladesh serviced by truck traffic from Burma. Fifteen years of elected government in Dhaka had little to show for itself in Chittagong. Without major dredging of the river and a new road system, history could move southeast to Burma. Dhaka was only the latest place from where rule over this city emanated, and it had failed Chittagong.

The port could also be dredged and upgraded by private companies. In particular, the Chinese had their eye on Chittagong, helping in the construction of a container port. One morning I watched as local workers streamed into the premises of a South Korean firm that had virtual sovereignty over a large tract of land by the harbor, inside which South Korean standards of efficiency, precision construction, and so forth were maintained. From here jute, textiles, leather, tea, and frozen fish were exported to South Korea, while Bangladeshi laborers, working for low wages compared to those in South Korea, assembled sportswear for export around the world. The failure of government need not lead to even a virtual change of the borders, but to a ceding of responsibility to the private sector.

India and China were nervously watching the destiny of Bangladesh, for Bangladesh holds the key to the reestablishment of a long-dormant historical trade route between the two rising giants of the twenty-first century. As the Chittagong lawyer indicated, this route would pass through Burma and eastern India before needing to traverse Bangladesh on the way to Kolkata, thus giving China's landlocked southwest its long-sought-after access to the Bay of Bengal and the larger Indian Ocean.

But whether this happens may hinge on the interrelationship between the environment and politics in Dhaka. A stable Bangladesh is necessary for this trade route, even as the trade route may lead in the course of time to a weakening of national identity. It is the very melding of languages and cultures—forces of global unity which disregard borders—that makes many lines on the map ultimately temporary.

Indeed, as I headed south from Chittagong along a narrow slice of Bangladeshi territory between the Bay of Bengal and the Indian and Burmese borders, all I kept hearing about were Burmese refugees and the trouble they were causing. The southeasternmost part of Bangladesh was knee-deep in the awful reality of Burma, whose day of reckoning as an oppressive military state, beset with ethnic problems, seemed not far off. This remote part of Bangladesh marked nearly the end of Indo-European civilization, the easternmost bastion of Asia where Persian loanwords were still integrated into the language. Here, rather than a basket case, Bangladesh was a refuge from much worse turmoil next door.

The landscape, half drowned in water, looked more like Southeast

Asia than the Indian Subcontinent, with a right-angled intricacy of paddy embankments, spiky tangles of greenery, and rigid banana leaves stabbing the cloud-curtained sky. Balloon-like jackfruit hung obscenely from trees. There was a sooty, vaporous quality to everything, sifted as it was through water and mud. Many of the paddy fields were empty, the victims of salinity.

Rivers, sea, and forests converged at the border town of Teknaf. In grimy rooms lit by fluorescent lights, a police chief and an intelligence officer complained to me about "criminals and stateless people all from Burma who were raping, looting, begging." Local Bangladeshis were unemployed because the ethnic Rohingyas—Muslim refugees from the western Burmese state of Arakan—were willing to do the same jobs for less money. Muslim solidarity here was wearing thin. One local politician told me, "The Rohingyas deal in arms, drugs, any sort of crime. If you catch three criminals, there will be at least one Rohingya among them."

There were a quarter million Rohingyas in southeastern Bangladesh, with thousands in refugee camps. There were rumors of Saudi NGOs recruiting Rohingyas for terrorist projects. "You can hire a Rohingya to kill anyone you want for a very small price," one local claimed. What these stories really told me was not that the refugees were criminals; only that they were hated.

The Rohingyas were part of a beautiful hybrid Buddhist-Hindu-Muslim civilization in Arakan where the influences of Persia and India crosshatched with those of Siam and the rest of Southeast Asia. Arakan's current isolation and lost Indian Ocean cosmopolitanism, which flourished owing to old trade routes, "is part of Burma's present-day poverty," writes the Burmese intellectual and U.N. official Thant Myint-U.[8] The Arakanese once held Chittagong to the northwest and Pegu to the southeast, even as they were at other times oppressed and brutally vanquished by the Bengal sultanate and the Mandalay-based Burmese kings. It was a rich history, with a culture replete in Sanskrit and Islamic learning.

The Rohingya village I visited near Teknaf was one of the worst refugee camps I have seen anywhere in the world, and I have seen many in some of the most destitute parts of Africa. It housed about ten thousand people, and was literally crawling with small children. The makeshift houses of bamboo and plastic wrap were each built against the other. A recent tropical storm had stripped away 10 percent of the roofs.

Diarrhea, skin diseases, and respiratory infections predominated among the illnesses, a charity worker from Doctors Without Borders–Holland told me. I was surrounded by refugees, and plied with stories about rape and forced labor in Burma, as if this were the late eighteenth century and the Court of Ava (near Mandalay) were rounding up thousands of Arakanese for building and irrigation projects.[9] The Rohingyas have vaguely Asian features, even as their complexions resemble those of Bangladeshis. They embody the racial and cultural linkage between the Indian Subcontinent and Southeast Asia, and as a result are despised both here and in Burma. Only a world of more flexible borders will free them.

Traveling north back to Chittagong, my bus plowed through one newly formed swamp after another. It was only a week into the monsoon: no cyclone, no tropical storm, just normally heavy rains and mudslides that had killed more than 120 people in forty-eight hours nearby. Off to the sides of the raised road on which the bus traveled, the dark brown water reached up to the bottom of the corrugated iron rooftops. In other places, men gripped their skirtlike *longyis* in waist-deep water. Whole tree trunks were being swept downstream as rivers flowed only a foot or two under bridges. On these bridges, hordes of young men had gathered with ropes, fishing for free firewood as it passed beneath. Soon, high mounds of wood were piled up, later to dry. As I said, this was the beginning of the monsoon, with heavier rains expected in July and August.

Society coped as well as it could, often ingeniously. A cascading series of text messages on cellphones warned of danger ahead. Signal flags were set up on beaches to forewarn of incoming water. Disaster supplies had been pre-positioned in some places as part of an increasingly sophisticated early-warning system. The Bangladeshi army and navy were available in case of major catastrophe. Otherwise, in many ways it was up to the villages and the NGOs to deal with the natural world.

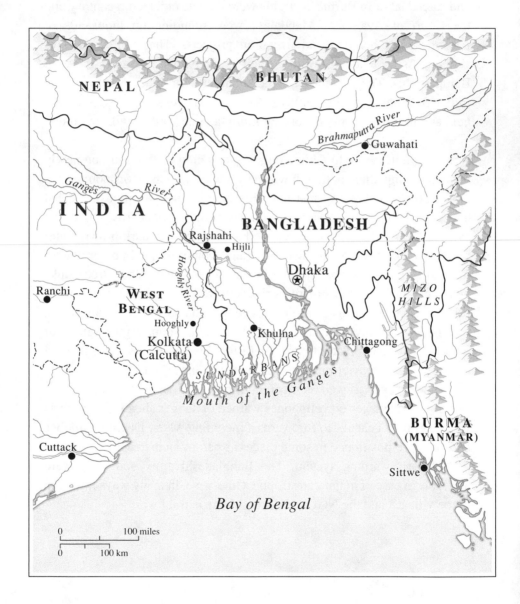

NEPAL

BHUTAN

Brahmaputra River

● Guwahati

Ganges   River

INDIA

BANGLADESH

Rajshahi ●   ● Hijli

Dhaka ☆

Hooghly River

WEST
BENGAL

Ranchi ●

Hooghly ●

Kolkata
(Calcutta) ●

Khulna ●

● Chittagong

*MIZO
HILLS*

S U N D A R B A N S

Mouth of the Ganges

Cuttack ●

BURMA
(MYANMAR)

Sittwe ●

Bay of Bengal

0   100 miles

0   100 km

CHAPTER NINE

KOLKATA

THE NEXT GLOBAL CITY

The low-hanging monsoon clouds shut in the sky like a late afternoon in November. Again I was on a raised road lined with dank, frothy green water pits. Everywhere across the sea-level-flat landscape were bicycle rickshaws, paddy fields, and mountains of logs, bamboo, and jackfruit. The repetition told a story: an economy of subsistence agriculture, where the majority of people lived in bamboo shacks, and where the land was being deforested. Yet it was this landscape, one had to remind oneself, which, along with that of China's, was the basis of capital for the British East India Company, the successor to Portuguese and Dutch power in the Indian Ocean. The wealth of Bengal—its large, dense, hard-working population and vast stores and production of basic commodities like rice, sugar, spices, and vegetable oil—accounted for 50 percent of the company's total trade.[1] Also because of its textiles, Bengal was a trove of riches for earlier empires as well. Bengal, "a land so fertile it transcends them all," writes Camões in *The Lusíads*.[2] Here was where the Arabian Sea and Bay of Bengal trading networks overlapped. Islam spread here in the Middle Ages with the original clearing of the forest and the agrarian expansion that followed, just as in the present-day deforestation and the spread of poor-quality urbanization is leading to an ideological intensification of religiosity. Brick mosques were common: square, with single domes, and occasional terra-cotta ornamentation, inspired, the scholar Richard M. Eaton tells us, by the shape of curved, thatched bamboo huts and pre-Islamic Buddhist temples. Even amidst the most beautiful of these mosques, there was a scraggly wildness to

East Bengal, something that has historically to do with the greater sever-
ity of the monsoon here because of the proximity of the Ganges delta.[3]

After seven hours of driving southwestward from Dhaka, the bus
reached the Bangladeshi-Indian border town of Benapole. A swarm of
beggars, porters, and rickshaw drivers awaited the passengers. Bargaining
commenced. I settled on a bicycle rickshaw that took me the half-mile distance to the actual border for the equivalent of fifty cents. A second man
transported my luggage on a creaky wooden oxcart. A third took my passport. The point was to employ as many people as possible. I tipped half a
dozen people, some of whom handed me—sold me, rather—forms to fill
out. Through the opaque confusion there was a system, though. My passport reappeared later in a filthy shack after it had been stamped. A succession of officials looked warily through my passport and luggage. It
seemed that there just had to be something suspicious about a foreigner
who traveled by bus to Kolkata (formerly Calcutta) rather than fly.

An hour later I walked through a clanging, rusted iron gate into India,
where the same garbage-strewn station awaited me, with makeshift hut-
ments and scrawny dogs, tormented by flies, which I was careful not to
step on. I filled out entry forms in an alley, crouching on the ground next
to the young man who had handed them out, and who also changed my
money. Nowhere on either side of the border did I see a woman.

Land borders expose the naked truth about a country. Crossing once
from Mexico to the United States, in the space of a few feet I journeyed
from a world of beggars, crumbling sidewalks, and rusted signage to an
alienating, protective bubble of precision building standards—that is,
from a third world society to a nervous first world one. What this land
border showed me about Bangladesh was not surprising—a poverty-
wracked country of weak institutions; what it showed about India was
how far it still had to go to be a real global power. It was the very same-
ness of both sides of the border that was shocking, given all the upbeat
media reports about the Indian economy.

Yet, as soon as I reboarded the bus and started out toward Kolkata
there was a dramatic change in the countryside. The strangled-in-
greenery landscape of Bengal continued as before, with the same piles of
logs everywhere. But rather than corrugated iron, I saw clay tiles on the
roofs. There were clotheslines, potted flowers, an elegant if mildewed
balcony here and there, some gabled windows, and actual tea shops:
signs of domesticity that made the ratty sprawl of Bangladeshi towns ap-

pear untamed by comparison. I noticed women in jeans and tight tank tops—yes, I was no longer in a predominantly Muslim country. There were cash machines and many signs in English. In Bangladesh everyone spoke Bengali, so there was no need of English as a lingua franca as in India, with its various languages and dialects.

After three hours the bus reached the outskirts of Kolkata.

"There is beggary all over India, but nowhere is there beggary on the scale of Calcutta's," observes the British travel writer Geoffrey Moorhouse, in the course of describing often-limbless, Brueghelesque figures who invoke one's charity everywhere in this city of more than 14 million, a city whose very name evokes despair.[4] The word "Calcutta" is taken from Kali (Kalikata), the Hindu goddess of disease, death, and destruction. Robert Clive, who consolidated British rule over Bengal in the mid-eighteenth century, labeled it "the most wicked place in the Universe."[5] Rudyard Kipling called it "the city of dreadful night." Lord Curzon, the viceroy of India a hundred years ago, said its "huge and palpitating slums" were a disgrace to British rule.[6] Kolkata's poverty in our own age is famously documented by Dominique Lapierre in *The City of Joy*.[7] It was in Kolkata where Mother Teresa spent a lifetime ministering to the poor, confirming the city's hellhole status.

But when judging a place, it all depends on from where the traveler has arrived. To arrive in Kolkata by bus from Dhaka, the capital of next-door Bangladesh, is like arriving in West Berlin from East Berlin during the Cold War—a trip I made several times. The grayness is gone. Instead of the rusted signage of Dhaka, there is a profusion of giant swanky billboards advertising global products, glowing in the night like backlit computer screens. In Dhaka, traffic is dominated by creaky old bicycle rickshaws; in Kolkata, by late-model cars. There are, too, the sturdy yellow Ambassador taxis, the zippy little Indian-produced Maruti family cars with catalytic converters, and the many luxury vehicles.

Yet the rickshaws that you see in Kolkata provide a signature image of exploitation worse than anything you will see in Dhaka: one human being is not merely being transported by another, who is furiously peddling uphill, but by one who is actually running uphill, pulling the rickshaw like an animal on his bare feet.

Kolkata can be obscene. One day I walked out of a tony espresso bar—its windows cluttered with credit card stickers—that offered an eclectic Indian-cum-globalized cuisine of extravagant mocha cocktails and *paneer tikka* sandwiches. As I left the air-conditioning for the broiling street, I was careful not to step over the whole families sleeping on cardboard along a sidewalk where men and women urinated. A young man began to follow me. After several blocks I still could not shake him. He put his résumé as a documentary film producer in my face, and desperately pleaded with me to hire him. "I realize I am invading your privacy, sir," he said, "but what am I to do? Perhaps you are angry with me. I will stop bothering you, but only if you give me a job." He was neatly if poorly dressed, out to make an impression. In the United States we have the luxury of junk mail offers and telemarketing calls, allowing you to tear up the piece of paper or hang up the phone. In Kolkata, such unwanted entreaties take a very personal form. Street solicitations here are a form of cold calling. Escape is impossible.

Kolkata demonstrates that poverty is neither exotic nor fascinating. It can be dull, numb, devoid of meaning, and monotonous. The poor, like the dead, are invisible except when they confront us with their "loathsomeness," then they are like an "open grave," writes William T. Vollmann in *Poor People,* a book that, by its very calculated repetition, shows just how wretchedly uninteresting poverty is. Poverty is not exotic, it has no saving graces, it is just awful.[8]

In its own perverted way, the caste system grants an individual some rights, and thus alleviates a bit the disgrace of poverty. "The Indian individual has no existence other than within and through his caste; outside it he is lost, no longer a man but a social outcast, a nonentity," writes Madeleine Biardeau, a mid-twentieth-century French Indologist. In traditional India, she explains, "man means nothing in himself." Even among those with large houses, families tend to cluster in the same room, while the others stand empty. "Fear plays a large part in this clinging together . . . an undefined, nameless fear; the fear, quite simply, of being alone."

Though Biardeau wrote those words almost fifty years ago, she foresaw how, because the caste system is bound up in the village, it ultimately would not survive the migration to urban areas, where, because of lack of living space, the patriarchal family would be "thinned out."[9] As the caste system is diluted, even as the achievement of full-fledged individual identity is not complete, there are decades of tumult, as new and more radical forms of group identity help fill the gap—for example, Hindu nationalism and radical Islam.

Kolkata's invasive poverty stopped hippies in their tracks. The hippie trail across Asia in the 1960s and 1970s followed the Ganges east to the holy Hindu city of Varanasi, then veered north to Kathmandu, Nepal, rather than continuing on to Kolkata. "On first acquaintance," Moorhouse writes in *Calcutta: The City Revealed,* the city "is enough to destroy any romantic illusions about gentleness and brotherly love."[10]

The slums may actually be worse in Mumbai (more than four times as many people live in them), but Mumbai slums are a bit more segregated from the wealthier areas; whereas in Kolkata it is much harder, on account of the urban geography—with beggars and street people spread evenly throughout the city—to escape from the poor.

The first days of the monsoon in June—smothering heat followed by pounding rain—are the optimum time to experience Kolkata's two separate and unequal universes: the world with air-conditioning, and the one without. The world with air-conditioning is that of an upwardly mobile, international civilization, whereas the one without constitutes the miserable reality of the street, where 1.5 million Kolkatans live within a few feet of air-conditioning, which they will never experience in their lives. The door to this espresso bar or to that charming bookshop with those Penguin paperbacks constitutes a border as hard to cross as any drawn on a map.

In north Kolkata the pavements are occupied by miles of tarpaulin and burlap lean-tos, inside which whole families live, with older siblings watching younger ones while the mothers work as maids and the fathers as construction workers. But as wrenching as the scene appears, if you wade through the street people, past this partially opened door, or under that chain, you will find another Kolkata: a maze of beautiful and derelict eighteenth- and nineteenth-century mansions built by former rajahs and merchants, with blackened weather-stained walls, intricate brickwork in Muslim, Hindu, and neoclassical styles, and colonnaded courtyards choked in vines and other greenery. The largest of these is the Marble Palace, in whose lightless rooms, which feel like a succession of grimy steam baths during the monsoon, are packed dusty Belgian mirrors, classical statuary, Chinese vases, crystal glass chandeliers, four paintings by Rubens, hookahs, and lithographs. Like this rambling palace in which everything seems to sweat, Kolkata is a rotting, eccentric jumble, of which the poverty is but the outer layer.

Despite the distracting horror of pavement life, the real story of Kolkata is its transformation into a global city, with expatriates coming back from abroad, investing in malls and restaurants, and in the process enforcing standards of service that they learned in the West. In early 2008, a 900,000-square-foot mall, among the largest in India, was opened in the southern part of Kolkata, one of forty new large and small retail centers set to open in Greater Kolkata by 2011. This is in addition to twenty new multiplex cinemas as the city expands to the east. Then there are the luxury condominiums with names like Highland Park and Silver Spring going up closer to downtown. "If you think of the British Empire as the first go at globalization," explained Santosh Ghosh, an urban planner, "then Kolkata, as the capital of British India, with its museums and botanical gardens, was a global city when Singapore and Kuala Lumpur were still villages. Now Kolkata is finally catching up again."

On a return visit in the winter, I saw the spirit of globalization captured by the gusto with which Christmas—another legacy of the British—is celebrated in this Hindu-Muslim city: with streets strung with colored lights, decorations on sale everywhere, and life-sized Santa Clauses made of mud and straw sculpted in the same workshops that produce the myriad Hindu gods. On Christmas Eve, thousands of Kolkatans of different religions converge on Saint Paul's, the nineteenth-century Gothic cathedral built by the British, whose innumerable wall plaques commemorate the various campaigns and skirmishes waged in the course of several hundred years of imperial rule in the Indian Subcontinent. The secularization of Christmas, combined with a vague nostalgia for things British, has invested the holiday here with a cosmopolitan ambience.

The pace of change in Kolkata still is not on the scale of China, but the city is headed in the same direction. There was always a middle class here, in addition to the ubiquitous poor. But the middle class is now more visually apparent because of its consumerist buying sprees. According to a recent study by McKinsey & Company, discretionary spending by Indian consumers accounted for 52 percent of average household consumption in 2005 (up from 39 percent in 1995); by 2025, it may rise to 70 percent. Shikha Mukerjee, who directs a nongovernment organization and has lived her whole life in Kolkata, noted that the world of the leisurely wealthy with their live-in servants is gone, as the upper classes live a less secure, more frantic existence. Concomitantly, there is also a rise in family cars, leading to the most persistent traffic jams I have experienced anywhere in the developing world, as bad as Jakarta, and worse than Teheran, Bangkok, or Cairo.

"It's not the fancy malls, but the low-end centers that are the heart of the change," Mukerjee went on, "the people who have created jobs for themselves by altering clothes, fixing appliances, and so on. I have a tailor who travels from an outlying slum area each day to occupy a particular place on the sidewalk with his sewing machine, where his clients come to him. He's saving money, he told me. That's what Kolkata is really about these days." Indeed, there are the soup kitchens selling noodles and curry dishes on the pavements. Their very expansion in recent years signifies the rise of a lower middle class, up from abject poverty, that requires cheap meals during the workday.

"Sealdah was my own private, childhood nightmare," Professor Sukanta Chaudhuri told me, referring to the railway station that in the late 1940s, after the partition of India, housed thousands of Hindu refugees from Muslim East Bengal who had arrived in Kolkata destitute, with nowhere to go. Even today, Sealdah is unnerving: the terminus for all trains arriving from India's underdeveloped northeast, with its armies of people disgorged onto the platforms, separating out amidst other armies squatting on the station floor with their suitcases.

"But you know what?" the gray-haired English professor said. "Most of those people, with no help from the government, got settled somewhere. They didn't just die or go begging. And the process continues today." The Kolkata street, Professor Chaudhuri and others explained, is less a dead end than a way station to the working classes, the same way that shantytowns are in a country like Turkey. But since India is so much poorer than Turkey, the way station is that much harsher. "If you come back each decade," noted Chaudhuri, "the poverty looks the same, so you think nothing has changed. But the individuals on the street are different. They come from Uttar Pradesh, Bihar, Orissa, and Bangladesh, with no place to live, because on the streets you can earn something, save something, and move on." Opportunity, as much as poverty, creates slums. Indeed, if there is a trend in Kolkata's slums, it is the fitful transition—gentrification in its own way—from *kutcha* (mud) and *jhupri* (burlap and cardboard) temporary housing to the more permanent *pucca* (cement and corrugated iron) housing. Whole areas are changing their appearance, as Kolkata begins to look less like some subcontinental Dickensian nightmare and more like just another dynamic city with great disparities of wealth.

Yet I was still unsure and uncomfortable. It seemed to me too neat and easy to just dismiss the Kolkata street as a beneficial way station to the higher classes. I'm sure that in many cases it was so, but also in too many cases it was not. The street emblemized how India, while emerging as a great power or at least a regional power in its own right, was also a very troubled nation harboring stores of misery.

To a degree Kolkata has always been like this: a place of harsh, unsentimental social interaction that my understandable Western fixation with the brutal visual effects of its poverty obscures. In *Those Days,* a detailed Proustian study of nineteenth-century Calcutta, Sunil Gangopadhyay writes:

> Houses, big, small and medium had mushroomed everywhere to accommodate the new generation of working *babus,* freshly migrated from villages. Weavers, barbers, washermen and oil crushers followed in their wake to minister to their needs. The Permanent Settlement had robbed many poor peasants of their land, not only in Bengal but in Orissa, Bihar and even distant Uttar Pradesh. These landless labourers flocked to the city's environs in thousands, ready to pick up any kind of menial work. . . .[11]

In a city where it has been impossible to avoid the poorest of the poor, urban balkanization—the stratification of the economic classes with the emergence of satellite towns and gated communities—finally makes it possible to do so. It is not so much the crime that these new, upwardly mobile classes wish to avoid, since Kolkata, despite its poverty, is a fairly safe city; it is something deeper. Whereas wealth used to be a secret here, the newly rich now want to flaunt it; and that, in turn, creates a security problem where one did not used to exist. Thus, the well-off need to escape into protected neighborhoods where they can exhibit their fortunes. Along with the birth of gated communities has come an explosion in the number of private security guards, who themselves bestow a sign of status for the new rich.

There is, too, another motivation for these planned communities. As Professor Chaudhuri told me, "The new upper classes are afraid of seeing ugliness." They want to "sanitize themselves" from the exhibition on the streets. They want to see only other well-off people. Wealthy Indians have always acted as if the poor were invisible, but now they have found a means to render them literally so.

The Kolkata street that these new rich want to escape from seeing is a rendering of rural life in the midst of the metropolis. The women line up at the pavement pumps the way they do at the village well. In the village, domestic life is lived out of doors, without a notion of privacy, without bathrooms, so everything is done in public. And because of the heat much of the year, people who live on the street are often in a state of semi-nakedness, grooming themselves with no sense of embarrassment.

In sum, as the new rich in Kolkata become diluted of their distinct Indianness, they have less and less toleration of Indian village life as it is displayed in the city streets. Yet as long as those forced to live on the street have the possibility of upward mobility, they will continue to stream in from the nearby poverty-wracked provinces of Bihar and Orissa, especially as the new construction here attracts cheap labor.

However, by continuing to live on the street and in *bustees* (slums), the poor are getting in the way of government plans for new satellite towns, gated communities, and special economic zones intended to attract foreign investment from Southeast Asian countries like Indonesia and Singapore. In power for three decades, the West Bengal administration constitutes the longest-serving democratically elected communist government in the world. Yet, in order to win over voters unhappy with its statist policies, the Bengali communists have been forced to follow the Chinese path of privatization with a vengeance. The expropriation of land for development projects elsewhere in West Bengal has led to violent protests in Kolkata. In one incident, in which vehicles were burned, windshields smashed, and stones hurled, the army was called out to patrol the streets—one of the rare times in years that the military has been needed to bring peace to a major Indian city.

Of course, in China the land would have been more easily expropriated. In China, a communist regime can act in a rampantly capitalist manner and it is accepted as a matter of course; but not in democratic India, particularly not in Kolkata. Whereas Delhi had a long and grand history under the Mughal emperors, Calcutta was founded only in the late seventeenth century by the British in a tropical swamp as a trading outpost, and has been a place of social conflict ever since: a tendency exacerbated by the Industrial Revolution, which began with a profusion of jute and textile factories and eventually led to West Bengal becoming the Ruhr of India, with most of the country's iron and steel industry. Thus, in recent decades, Kolkata has been at the heart of Indian trade unionism and communism. "Continued exclusion of the poor in Kolkata will only result in outbreaks of riots and destructive violence," V. Ramaswamy, a Kolkata-based business executive and grassroots organizer, told me. For all of Kolkata's aspirations to become a global city, its history suggests that the transition will not be altogether peaceful. When West Bengal's government tried to outlaw rickshaws in December 2006 as a "disgraceful practice," for instance, the city's eighteen thousand rickshaw pullers launched vigorous protests. Kolkata will likely remain a place of strife.

In 2001, Calcutta's name was officially changed to Kolkata, reflecting the native Bengali pronunciation. For generations reared on "Calcutta," the new name is awkward. It carries no evocative association with either British rule or with the city's infamous poverty. That might be for the better. Given that globalization has ironically led to invigorated localisms, "Kolkata" may yet catch on as a new global and Bengali entrepôt for eastern India, Bangladesh, Burma, and southwestern China. Ancient and medieval trade routes are reaffirming themselves and Kolkata is slowly regaining the hinterland it lost after the 1947 partition of the Indian subcontinent that created East Pakistan (later Bangladesh). In particular, as noted, southwestern China has no access to the Pacific Ocean. Its closest outlet is the Bay of Bengal. Whereas in the Middle Ages, tea, horses, and porcelain were traded along this ganglia of silk road offshoots, now Bangladesh and Burma have natural gas to export to China and India. India has iron ore to export to China. China has all kinds of manufactured goods to export to India. Despite the rising naval tensions between the two countries, on another level a natural gas alliance might arise to include India, China, Bangladesh, and Burma.

"Kolkata could once again become the Indian gateway to Southeast Asia, and particularly to China," Monideep Chattopadhyay, another urban planner, told me. It is the only city in India with a real Chinatown. In 2007 a Chinese consulate opened in the city. A new airport will allow Chinese Buddhist pilgrims to transit Kolkata en route to the holy site of Bodh Gaya in Bihar Province, where the Buddha attained enlightenment. These renewed links, particularly the land links, could finally open up insurgency-wracked northeastern India, whose violence and underdevel-

opment have played a significant role in Kolkata's own poverty by rob-
bing the city of a prosperous backcountry that retains its own inhabitants,
rather than forcing many of them to migrate penniless to the nearest big
city.

"Kolkata could also be the Harvard of India," said Kingshuk Chatterjee, a research fellow at the Maulana Abul Kalam Azad Institute of Asian
Studies, explaining that primary and secondary education in Kolkata is
the finest in the country, and Bengalis fill many places at the best universities in Mumbai and Delhi. All that is needed, he said, is for the
communist-left alliance that governs West Bengal to stop making ap-
pointments at local universities based on its own politics. The high level
of education also makes it likely that Kolkata will evolve into another Indian hub for information technology. "Forget Mother Teresa, think IT
and young people with disposable income," one local journalist ex-
claimed about the city.

The most extravagant visions are possible for Kolkata because, for the
time being, the city has one thing that other Indian cities—and many in
the developing world—dangerously lack: sufficient stores of fresh water.
Like Dhaka, Kolkata lies astride the vast estuarial delta of Bengal. To
know this abstractly is different from palpably experiencing it. Just as I
once arrived in Kolkata by bus from Bangladesh, another time I left and
returned to the city by boat on the Hooghly River, a principal tributary of
the Ganges. Arriving anywhere by boat gives one a unique perspective
about a place. This is particularly true in the case of Kolkata, whose very
existence is supported by a river to which it turns its back. The ghats
notwithstanding, there are no waterfront promenades here as in other
river cities; no captivating and embracing smell of warm seas as there is
in Mumbai, fronting the Arabian Sea. Yet without the Hooghly there
would have been no Kolkata.

For the equivalent of $340, with the help of Gautam Chakraborti, an
expert on the river, I chartered a forty-seven-foot wooden boat with a
small crew at the Outram docks near downtown. It was a trip back in
time. Because Kolkata is 60 miles up a narrowing river from the Bay of
Bengal, as the city grew and the Industrial Revolution took hold, the port
had to move by stages closer to the sea, in search of deeper drafts to accommodate bigger and bigger cargoes. Thus, an aura of desertion now
characterizes the city's riverfront, whereas in previous epochs it used to

bustle. The continuous tangled curtain of palms and banyan trees stands in sharp focus on both banks, obscuring the more distant and shadowy city skyline. Here at water level one can imagine the original trading post that Kolkata once was, when Bengal was the world's greatest silk-producing area, ahead of Persia and China. Hundreds of masted ships, including schooners from America and other boats from as far away as China used to ply the Hooghly at this spot. Here on this riverfront a great number of tall-masted, long-sparred opium clippers were built in the eighteenth and nineteenth centuries to transport opium brought from Patna and Benares up the Ganges, to the Canton River and Hong Kong via Singapore.[12]

The first Portuguese vessels sailed up the Hooghly in 1530, doing business in cotton and cloth. Eventually there was a line of Portuguese settlements along the river, principally at the ports of Hooghly and Hijli. By 1628, as many as a hundred Portuguese ships sailed from these ports, carrying rice, butter, oil, and wax. The Portuguese enjoyed a tenuous hold over maritime Bengal, with an agency at the port of Chittagong on the eastern side of the province. Soon, to counter the Portuguese, the Dutch, Danes, Flemish, and French were receiving permission from the Mughal emperors in Delhi to trade along the Hooghly. Here the English enter the story, particularly in the person of Job Charnock, the senior agent of the British East India Company in the region, an old hand who had gone partially native, adopting Indian culture and marrying an Indian widow whom he had rescued from her husband's funeral pyre moments before she was immolated in the traditional practice of *sati*.[13] After a string of failures and frustrations up and down the river, in an attempt to establish a base for the company in Bengal that might one day be an equivalent of Madras or Bombay, in 1690 Charnock finally established a small trading post at a bend in the Hooghly where Kolkata now stands; on the eastern bank, on ground high enough to avoid flooding.

Indeed, Kolkata remains a young start-up city: younger than the founding of European North America at Quebec, Jamestown, and Santa Fe. It is a commercial venture, pure and simple. It lacks those fortifying medieval centuries, whose very accumulation of architecture and other material culture gives not only cities in Europe, but also those in Asia and the Subcontinent a substantial, graceful demeanor. The very distortions of poverty and wealth in Kolkata have a raw, New World edge about them that one does not quite find in other large and older Indian cities.

The history of Kolkata is written along the Hooghly shores: on one side Kolkata, on the other the industrial suburb of Howrah. Peeping out of the bush on both banks are the old deserted garden houses of the British. Here and there is a pastoral scene of people bathing and doing the wash on the steps of the ghats. Surinam Dock, a vacant space on the Kolkata side, stands as a haunting reminder of servitude. It was from here that indentured laborers—slaves, for all intents and purposes—were shipped to the Guianas on the northern shore of South America in the nineteenth century, creating an Indian diaspora in the Caribbean basin. Moorings, the shape of turbans, bob and tilt in the water: gigantic, rusted, and no longer in use. There is the darkened, collapsed, and empty hulk of Garden Reach jetty, one of several such battered ruins of the former downtown port complex. Where jute mills used to be the forest now encroaches, the jute industry having moved to Bangladesh. The river seemed so calm, a smoky still life, though it is anything but. Most of the distance to the Bay of Bengal requires a pilot. Seven-foot tides coming up from the bay and hidden sandbars make it treacherous. Though the Hooghly is three quarters of a mile wide during part of its stretch through Kolkata, the navigable part is much narrower, made worse by hidden shipwrecks.

We passed cargo boats laden with logs from Burma and Malaysia, then a feeder vessel with conventional hydraulic cranes hugging the Howrah side of the river, where its hull would not run aground on a sandbar. The larger cargo ships with gantry cranes cannot come this far upriver because of the shallow draft, so they transfer their containers to feeder vessels a few miles south of here. Though the downtown port still exists, it is greatly diminished because of new harbors closer to the Bay of Bengal. Because of these other harbors spaced miles apart from one another, Kolkata is considered a multi-draft port. The largest and deepest of these is at Haldia near the Bay of Bengal. But as the metropolis ever expands, there is word of developing Diamond Harbor into an even bigger shipping complex.

Just a few miles downriver of the city, the Hooghly opens out to become a vast inland sea of seemingly Amazonian dimensions. Here, amid the "nauseous verdure," in the words of British historian John Keay, civilization is reduced to a bare minimum: nothing but fishing villages with small wooden boats stranded on the beaches against palm jungles.[14] The only sign of a higher civilization is the procession of towering kilns for brick-making that extends on both shorelines almost the entire distance to the Bay of Bengal, for such is the appetite for building materials as Kolkata expands by the day. Availability of water feeds its expansion, even as rising sea levels from global warming threaten the mega-city's survival. The Bali climate conference of 2007 listed Kolkata as among the top ten cities most threatened by coastal flooding and by storm surges caused by rising sea levels that accompany global warming. And by late in the twenty-first century, because of its soaring population, Kolkata is slated to top the list.

Until the expansion of the British railway system in India in the second half of the nineteenth century, you would likely have arrived in Kolkata by boat, up the Hooghly from the Bay of Bengal. Except for the kilns, the scenery—water and junglescape—would have been similar to now. Thus, as my boat continued south along the ever-widening river, turning around close to Diamond Harbor and continuing back north to Kolkata, I could not help thinking about the career of the most pivotal and perhaps colorful character in Kolkata's history, one who traveled up this same river the first time he arrived in the city: Robert Clive.

It was not only that he knew this same river that now made me think of Clive, it was also that he was a perfect counterpoint to the direction of my thinking. The boat journey was a vivid lesson in just how much geography matters. Indeed, the centrality of the Indian Ocean in the twenty-first century is a lesson in geographic and demographic determinism. But on the other hand, one needs to ask: is history only the result of *vast impersonal* forces—geographical, cultural, economic, and technological—about which we can do little? Or is history also the record of ordinary and extraordinary individuals who, in many cases, against great odds, succeed at overcoming these very forces? Is history also an account of sheer luck and misfortune? As Machiavelli indicated, he could only counsel his "prince" in the ways of *virtù,* not in the ways of *fortuna,* which was just as important. The career of Lord Robert Clive provides a dramatic illustration of the individual man theory, with all of the good luck and bad luck and moral choice that goes with it, and thus a refutation of the belief that vast impersonal forces *determine* the future.[15]

In hindsight, Great Britain's domination of India appears inevitable, given the rise of British sea power throughout the Indian Ocean in the eighteenth and nineteenth centuries. Yet without Lord Clive, it is to be sure arguable whether Britain would have gained control of India in the way that it did and to the extent that it did. One might even argue that without Clive's magnetic personality, Britain would not have gotten control of India at all. Clive, in and of his own extraordinary self, constitutes an argument that nothing should be given up to fate; that nothing is inevitable.

The sacred text of Clive's career is the long essay written about him by the English historian and India hand Thomas Babington Macaulay in 1840, nearly a century after the young Clive had captured Calcutta.* Macaulay's essay races along, as though a cover story in a contemporary magazine. It does not seem old at all, not just in its subject matter, but in its poised, cocksure rhythm.

As Macaulay informs us, when Clive set sail for India in 1743 at the age of eighteen, in the service of the British East India Company, India was in a state of political confusion. In a sprawling Subcontinent that stretches two thousand miles from north to south (a greater distance than from Hudson Bay to the Gulf of Mexico), and more than fifteen hundred miles from west to east (nearly the distance from New York City to Denver), the Moghul dynasty was in utter disarray: on its way to becoming an assemblage of independent hereditary princedoms, many of which were besieged by the Marathas, a warrior caste that occupied the mountains east of Bombay, and ravaged the entire Deccan plateau, and—with its own piratical navy—India's western coast. This chaotic landmass, writes Macaulay, was inhabited by a population ten times as numerous as the Aztecs and Incas, whom the Spanish had vanquished, even as the population was as highly civilized as the Spanish themselves.[16] Therefore, the idea that a single foreign power from half a world away would one day hold decisive bureaucratic sway over all these sophisticated people was simply unimaginable.† Yet that is what the charismatic, dynamic, moody, suicidal, corrupt, and fearless Clive was able to set in motion.

---

* Macaulay's *Essay on Lord Clive,* edited with notes and an introduction by Preston C. Farrar (1840; reprint, New York: Longmans, Green, 1910). In many ways Macaulay held a condescending view of India. See Salman Rushdie's summary of Macaulay's attitudes in *The Moor's Last Sigh* (New York: Pantheon, 1995), p. 376. For a fuller biography of Clive, see Robert Harvey, *Clive: The Life and Death of a British Emperor* (New York: St. Martin's, 1998).

† It was a gradual process, however. Following Clive's subjugation of Bengal, the British hold on the Subcontinent was mainly limited to northern India, Bombay, and the Carnatic coastal plain. For a time the rest of the south would be divided among feudals and the Maratha confederacy.

Clive's triumph in Calcutta is a story that starts in Madras, where he began at the age of twenty-one as a "writer," the lowliest category of East India Company bureaucrat. He was drawn into military service owing to the outbreak of hostilities between the British and French East India companies and their rival indigenous princes in southeastern India, an area known as the Carnatic.* It was these Carnatic wars that elevated the European trading companies to territorial powers in their own right. Until this point, the only man with the vision of a European empire built on the ruins of the Mughal dynasty was not a Briton but a Frenchman, Joseph-François Dupleix, who had managed through military maneuver and political manipulation to make himself and his native surrogates masters of southern India. In a few years, Dupleix had gone from appeasing the local native powers to usurping them.[17] In particular, this was a period when the superiority of European arms over indigenous populations became manifest, for in Europe war had already become a science, whereas in places like India it was still sport.[18]

The lone obstacle to French domination was the fortress of Trichinopoly, seventy miles inland from the Bay of Bengal, held by the British surrogate, Mohammed Ali. In the summer of 1751, a Dupleix ally, Chunda Sahib, helped by French auxiliaries, laid siege to it. The situation was dire. As Macaulay writes, "At this moment, the valor and genius of an obscure English youth [Clive] suddenly turned the tide of fortune."[19]

Clive took command of two hundred British soldiers and three hundred Indian sepoys (native soldiers in British service), but did not head to Trichinopoly. Instead, in the midst of a thunderstorm he overwhelmed the provincial capital of Arcot, forcing Chunda Sahib to send reinforcements there from Trichinopoly, thus saving British forces. But the French immediately laid siege to Arcot, where Clive and his followers had holed up in the fort. Their defenses were meager. As Macaulay recounts, the walls were "ruinous," the ditches "dry," and the ramparts too "narrow" to admit their guns. As death and hunger set in, "the devotion of the little band to its chief [Clive] surpassed any thing that is related of the Tenth Legion of Caesar, or of the Old Guard of Napoleon."[20]

Although he had scant training, Clive turned out to be a military natural, given that the essence of soldiering is leadership or "undaunted res-

---

* According to one explanation, the word may come from the local Dravidian terms *kar* (black) and *nadu* (country), a reference to the black soil of the region.

olution"—that is, the ability to rally men to your side, especially in adversity. Indeed, in such fluid little wars and engagements, tipping the balance owed much to improvisation and plain luck.[21] Having successfully withstood a fifty-three-day siege at Arcot through ingenuity, sheer endurance, and seeming ubiquitousness during the fighting, the twenty-six-year-old Clive single-handedly turned the tide against the French. Madras and its interior hinterland were about to be secured for Great Britain.

In 1753, Clive returned to England triumphant, whereas the equally brilliant and psychologically complex Dupleix—more than twice Clive's age—returned to France the following year in disgrace and, stripped of his considerable fortune, died in obscurity.

In 1755, Clive set sail once more for Madras. Arriving there the next year to take command of Fort St. David, where his mission was to complete the expulsion of the French, he nevertheless became embroiled in the affairs of Bengal far to the north, the richest part of India, which had been a main revenue source for the Mughals to fund their Deccan wars. As Macaulay puts it in his matchless prose:

> Of the provinces which had been subject to the House of Tamerlane, the wealthiest was Bengal. . . . The Ganges, rushing through a hundred channels to the sea, has formed a vast plain of rich mould which, even under the tropical sky, rivals the verdure of an English April. The rice fields yield an increase such as is elsewhere unknown. Spices, sugar, vegetable oils, are produced with marvellous exuberance. The rivers afford an inexhaustible supply of fish. . . . The great stream which fertilizes the soil is, at the same time, the chief highway of Eastern commerce. On its banks, and on those of its tributary waters, are the wealthiest marts, the most splendid capitals, and the most sacred shrines of India. The tyranny of man had for ages struggled in vain against the overflowing bounty of nature. In spite of the Mussulman [Muslim] despot, and of the Mahratta freebooter, Bengal was known through the East as the Garden of Eden. . . .[22]

It was also a filthy and sodden fen astride the Tropic of Cancer, consisting of "new mud, old mud, and marsh," in the words of a geographer quoted by the British travel writer Geoffrey Moorhouse.[23] The commercial heart of this fecund and rotting vastness was Calcutta, a port on the Hooghly River that, in turn, emptied into the Bay of Bengal. Here the British East India Company operated under the protection of a nawab (viceroy) who ruled the territories of Bengal, Orissa, and Bihar in the name of a Mughal figurehead. In 1756, the nawab, Aliverdy Khan, died and was succeeded by his grandson, a youth of less than twenty, Surajah Dowlah. Macaulay describes him as cruel, selfish, drunken, debauched, and full of hatred of the English. Furthermore, he surrounded himself with "dregs . . . recommended by nothing but buffoonery and servility."[24]

And so it was that the nawab, after finding some pretext, marched with his army upon Fort William, the English stronghold in Calcutta. Whereas the specter of Dupleix and his army had forced the British in Madras to be not only traders but soldiers and statesmen besides, in Calcutta the English seemed to have only the first quality, and were consequently terrified. Fort William fell without much of a fight. Then what Macaulay calls "that great crime" occurred, to be immortalized in British lore, with its likely exaggerations.[25]

In 1756 the monsoon rains did not arrive until June 21, meaning that the night of June 20 was the most horrid, sultry night of the year, with flesh-disintegrating humidity. On this night the nawab's guards threw dozens of English men and women into the "Black Hole of Calcutta," an eighteen-foot airless cube, where most perished before the guards opened the doors the next morning—after the nawab had "slept off his debauch," in Macaulay's recounting, and "permitted the door to be opened."[26] Though it was claimed that 146 people were thrown into the hole, the actual number was more likely sixty-four, of whom twenty-one survived.*

When news of the events in Calcutta reached Madras that August the cry for vengeance was universal. Clive was put at the head of nine hundred British infantry and fifteen hundred native sepoys to punish a nawab who, as Macaulay points out, "had more subjects than Louis the Fifteenth or the Empress Maria Theresa."[27] They set sail north along the Bay of Bengal in October. However, owing to adverse winds that meant detours to the coasts of Ceylon and Burma, they did not reach Bengal until De-

---

* Geoffrey Moorhouse, *Calcutta: The City Revealed* (London: Weidenfeld and Nicolson, 1971), pp. 44–45. One of the survivors was John Zephaniah Holwell, a brilliant publicist, whose retelling of the incident helped spread the word of the horror. See Keay, *Honourable Company,* p. 304.

cember. Clive was all business, quickly routing the native garrison at Fort William and reconquering Calcutta. The nawab sued for peace, but Clive was against dealing peaceably with him, given the nawab's character and previous actions. But the East India Company in Calcutta was eager to resume business, and in Madras it was anxious for the return of its army and weapons. Thus, Clive consented to negotiate. Macaulay explains:

> With this negotiation commences a new chapter in the life of Clive. Hitherto he had been merely a soldier, carrying into effect, with eminent ability and valour, the plans of others. Henceforth he is to be chiefly regarded as a statesman. . . . That in his new capacity he displayed great ability, and obtained great success, is unquestionable. But it is also unquestionable, that the transactions in which he now began to take a part have left a stain on his moral character.[28]

In fact, Clive lacked slyness and cunning. According to Macaulay, he was "constitutionally the very opposite of a knave." Clive's dynamism— the ability to get things done on and off the battlefield—had arisen not from sleaziness, but simply from a larger-than-life energy and enthusiasm, especially when it came to taking risks. In fact, there is little evidence that he ever acted improperly with a fellow Englishman. As it turned out, this "stain on his moral character" was confined to dealings with Indians: "he considered Oriental politics as a game in which nothing was unfair."[29] In other words, his immorality did not flow naturally from his personality, but rather represented a calculated—we could even say, strategic—decision.

> He seems to have imagined, most erroneously in our opinion, that he could effect nothing against such [Indian] adversaries, if he was content to be bound by ties from which they were free, if he went on telling truth, and hearing none, if he fulfilled, to his own hurt, all his engagements with confederates who never kept an engagement that was not to their advantage. Accordingly this man, in the other parts of his life an honorable English gentleman and a soldier, was no sooner matched against an Indian intriguer, than he became himself an Indian intriguer. . . .[30]

Meanwhile, the nawab, Surajah Dowlah, was nothing if not calculating. He concluded a treaty with Clive, even as he conspired quietly with the French at nearby Chandernagore to drive out Clive's forces from Calcutta. The British, who got wind of the nawab's designs, successfully attacked Chandernagore before the French could send reinforcements from their bases in the Carnatic in southeastern India. "By depriving the French of their most profitable operation," writes Keay, "and of the base from which both Pondicherry [in the Carnatic] and their Mauritius establishment were provisioned, it undermined" France's whole position in the Indian Ocean.[31]

Clive decided next—against the advice of some of his fellow Britons—to support a coup against Surajah Dowlah, to be led by Meer Jaffier, the principal commander of the nawab's troops. When one of the Bengalis involved in planning the coup threatened to reveal it if he was not guaranteed a sum of money, Clive drew up two treaties: a real one with no mention of a reward for this fellow, and a fake contract that did. When a fellow British officer refused, out of conscience, to sign the counterfeit treaty, Clive simply forged the man's signature. His scruples were limited to contacts with his own race, making him in the final analysis, claim his severest critics, reprehensible.*

Though moody and suicidal after the fact, Clive was not given to worry or reflection in the midst of an operation. His bravado was on full display before the battle that—perhaps more than any other individual event—would determine the fate of the Indian Subcontinent. The armies of Surajah Dowlah and Clive had gathered a few miles from each other, when it was agreed that once hostilities commenced Meer Jaffier would desert with his forces to the side of the British. But Meer Jaffier's fears overcame his ambition; he dithered with cold feet.

For Clive at this moment, it was no easy decision to cross a river and engage an army twenty times the size of one's own, so he called a war council. The majority of his fellow officers advised against giving battle, and Clive concurred momentarily. "Long afterwards," Macaulay writes, Clive said "that he had never called but one council of war, and . . . if he

---

* See, in particular, Nick Robins's *The Corporation That Changed the World: How the East India Company Shaped the Modern Multinational* (Hyderabad, India: Orient Longman, 2006). John Keay disagrees, however, noting, "In the context of a revolution, and compared to some of the intrigues conducted by others (British as well as Indian), this little piece of duplicity would scarcely rate a mention." Harvey agrees. Keay, *The Honourable Company: A History of the English East India Company* (London: HarperCollins, 1991), p. 317; Robert Harvey, *Clive: The Life and Death of a British Emperor* (New York: St. Martin's, 1998).

had taken the advice of that council, the British would never have been masters of Bengal," and ultimately of India. According to Macaulay's account, Clive retired under the shade of some trees and passed an hour in thought. "He came back determined to put every thing to the hazard, and gave orders that all should be in readiness for passing the river on the morrow."[32] He decided henceforth to take the responsibility for whatever happened completely on himself.

The next day, upon fording the river, Clive's army set up camp after sunset in a mango grove near Plassey, north of Calcutta, within a mile of the enemy. Clive spent the night lying awake, listening to the drums and cymbals of the enemy camp. It is hard to imagine a person subject to more pressure and consequent anxiety.

The next morning, June 23, 1757, the two armies met at Plassey. The nawab's cavalry alone numbered fifteen thousand. Then there were the forty thousand infantrymen armed with pikes and swords, bows and arrows. But only twelve thousand troops would take part in the battle. The British-led forces numbered a mere three thousand of which a thousand were English. Both sides unleashed their cannons. Whereas Surajah Dowlah's field pieces failed to fire properly, those of the British "produced great effect," killing some of the most distinguished officers in the nawab's ranks. The nawab's forces began to retreat, and one of Clive's officers, seizing the initiative, ordered a full-scale advance. The battle lasted barely an hour. As Macaulay writes, "With the loss of twenty-two soldiers killed and fifty wounded, Clive had scattered an army of nearly sixty thousand men, and subdued an empire larger and more populous than Great Britain."*

With the British victory, Meer Jaffier replaced Surajah Dowlah on the throne. Dowlah was murdered for his crimes, a grisly act, however deserving the victim might have been. While the British played no direct part in it, the murder was one to which they had set the political context.

---

* John Keay, *The Honourable Company: A History of the English East India Company* (London: HarperCollins, 1991), pp. 52–53. Putting words in Clive's mouth, Mark Twain added: "With three thousand I whipped sixty thousand and founded the Empire." Mark Twain, *Following the Equator* (New York: Oxford University Press, 1966), ch. 54. Some writers claim that Plassey was less a battle than a "transaction," by which the nawab's internal enemies negotiated with the East India Company to arrange his defeat. K. M. Panikkar, *Asia and Western Dominance* (London: Allen & Unwin, 1959), pp. 78–79. But Robert Harvey pours scorn on this notion; *Clive: The Life and Death of a British Emperor* (New York: St. Martin's, 1998), p. 221.

More troubling to British sensibilities was the amount of money that changed hands. Meer Jaffier sent 800,000 pounds sterling in silver downriver to Calcutta, of which Clive helped himself to between 200,000 and 300,000. Clive literally "walked between heaps of gold and silver, crowned with rubies and diamonds." There was nothing strictly illegal in this. Clive was a general not of the crown, but of the company, and the company had indicated that its agents could enrich themselves by means of the generosity of the native princes. Macaulay even suggests that it was a wonder that Clive did not take more, but adds:

> we cannot acquit of having done what, if it not in itself was evil, was yet of evil example. . . . It follows that whatever rewards he receives for his services ought to be given either by his own government, or with the full knowledge and approbation of his own government.[33]

The problem with Clive is that being a larger-than-life risk taker, who operated in a savage, frontier environment in which he made up his own rules accordingly, the very traits that allowed him to form the foundations for a British empire in India, were also the ones that make us uneasy. But there was certainly, as Macaulay indicates, an element of hypocrisy in the opprobrium that greeted him back in England. "It was a very easy exercise of virtue to declaim in England against Clive's rapacity; but not one in a hundred of his accusers would have shown so much self-command in the treasury of Moorshedabad."[34]

And not one in a hundred would have shown so much audacity, repeatedly willing to risk an entire reputation on yet another throw of the dice. When in 1759 seven Dutch ships arrived in the Hooghly from Java, Clive would have been within his rights to accept their presence. Meer Jaffier favored the Dutch as a balancer against the British, and Clive was loath to upset his relationship with his own chosen nawab. Moreover, London was already engaged in a war with the French and could least afford another enemy. Yet knowing how the Dutch presence would threaten Britain's emerging hold on India, Clive ordered an attack completely on his own, and the Dutch were subsequently routed.

Indeed, it was Clive whom the British authorities sent back to India in 1765 to clean up the corruption and disorganization in the government of Bengal that had ensued in his absence, and was the result of a system that he was partly responsible for erecting. Though he remained in India only eighteen months, in that time he accomplished a comprehensive reform of the British East India Company, including the way it dealt with the indigenous population. The root of Clive's reforms was his understanding that to give men power, and at the same time to keep them poor, was an invitation to rampant corruption. Thus, a centerpiece of his reform was to raise the salaries of company employees. He accomplished this by giving employees a share of the revenue of the salt trade according to their rank, an act that caused greater damage in some quarters to Clive's reputation than much else that he did. Clive's ultimate tragedy was that he often knew what had to be done, and did not shy away from doing it, even as what had to be done was never for the pure at heart. Of course, this holds true for many men, but it is particularly so with Clive, whose choices and temptations—and their consequences—were of a momentous scope. Here, again, is Macaulay:

> If a man has sold beer on Sunday morning, it is no defence that he has saved the life of a fellow-creature at the risk of his own. . . . But it is not in this way that we ought to deal with men who, raised far above ordinary restraints, and tried by far more than ordinary temptations, are entitled to a more than ordinary measure of indulgence.[35]

In a manner of speaking, Clive gave Britain India, and Britain was not altogether grateful because of the way in which he did it. Thus, he was to be hounded in middle age by critics, to the point where his manic-depressive nature finally caught up with him. He took up the opium habit, and at the age of forty-nine committed suicide (though some belief holds that he might have been murdered).[36]

When he died in 1774, Clive was the greatest English general since James Wolfe died at the victorious Battle of Quebec fifteen years earlier (even as "his corruption would be equally denounced as somehow un-British").[37] Almost alone among Western military leaders, Clive had no experienced generals around him on whose advice he could fall back. He was a military autodidact who, unlike other agents of the British East India Company, saw beyond commercial goals to political and geographical supremacy. Macaulay writes: "The only man, as far as we recollect, who at an equally early age ever gave equal proof of talents of war, was Napoleon Bonaparte."[38]

Macaulay suggests even that had Clive not fallen into illness and depression and taken up opium while still in middle age—had Clive still been what he was when he defeated the Dutch near Calcutta—he might have commanded British forces in North America and the history of the American Revolution might have been different, with independence deferred for some years. Indeed, it is impossible to know for sure what would have happened had George Washington been forced to face Robert Clive in battle.* For history is about more than just geography and other impersonal forces.

Sailing back upriver in the evening and reentering Kolkata, my boat passed under the cantilever Howrah Bridge, the city's urban icon. The bridge was constructed during World War II to provide British divisions access to the Burmese front. From any direction, it appears like a gargantuan Erector set, taking up half the sky, its draperies of steel dwarfing everything around it. Both human and vehicular traffic are bumper-to-bumper, toe-to-heel on its span, as masses of people cross the Hooghly, the color of faded cardboard from the silt that it carries downstream. Even from the water down below, the noise of the crowd and of the cars is like the din of a locomotive perpetually passing. Fancy new motorcycles idle next to hand-pulled rickshaws. People carry everything from briefcases to birdcages; crates and baskets rest on their heads. Just below the entrance to the bridge on the Kolkata side is a bustling flower market with mountains of marigolds and rose petals. Hawkers sell everything from razor blades to textiles. The pleas of beggars and the in-your-face solicitations are unceasing. Nobody gives up here.

---

* But Clive favored a liberal, less confrontational approach to the American colonists. Harvey, *Clive,* p. 349.

CHAPTER TEN

OF STRATEGY AND BEAUTY

wo prominent landmarks, not far from each other in Kolkata, are each associated with a great figure from the city's past, a figure central to the ideas and ideals that will drive politics and culture in the twenty-first century throughout the Indian Ocean and the larger world. One is an imperial statesman; the other a man of arts and letters. The one was a practitioner of realpolitik, concerned with maneuvering amid different political-military forces and other naked geopolitical interests; the other a man concerned with aesthetics, who understood that the ultimate end of consciousness is the appreciation of beauty. The one embodies the British legacy in Greater India; the other that part of the Indian legacy which represents the dreams of many beyond India's frontiers. The one leads us to a discussion of India's foreign policy; the other to a discussion on the search for justice and dignity that the United States needs to better understand. Each man is totemic of Kolkata: Calcutta the imperial capital of British India, and Kolkata the home of millions who seek to be heard.

The first landmark is Government House (the Raj Bhavan in Hindi), the home a little more than a hundred years ago to Lord George Nathaniel Curzon.

Until the early twentieth century, when India's capital was moved to Delhi, Calcutta constituted the throbbing heart of British imperialism in Eurasia. And that India-centric imperialism is associated with no man so much as Lord George Curzon, the viceroy of India from 1899 to 1905. To

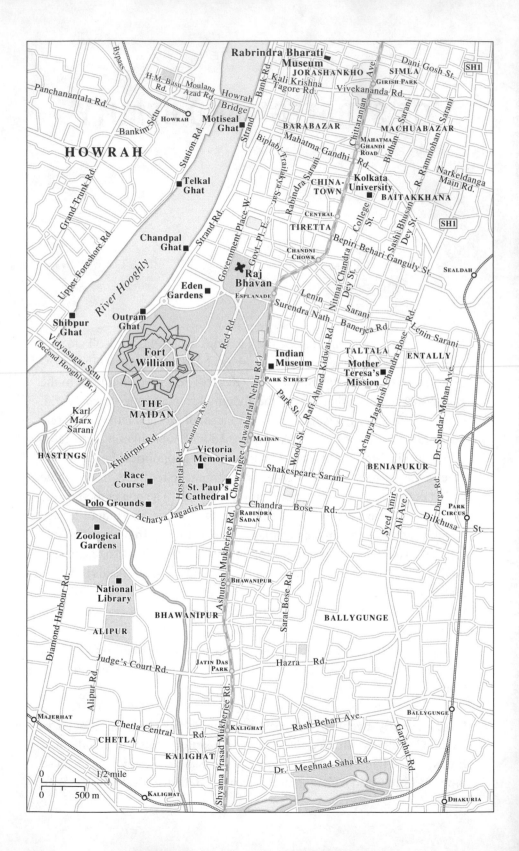

say that Curzon felt at home in India and in Calcutta is quite literally true. In a case of supreme symbolic coincidence, the gorgeous brick Government House—the viceroy's headquarters, completed in Georgian style in 1803—was based on the plan of Kedleston Hall, Curzon's twelfth-century ancestral home in Derbyshire.

Despite their aversion to British rule, Indians have retained a special place in their hearts for Curzon, who did much to rescue the country's architecture and antiquities from ruin. "After every other viceroy has been forgotten," India's first prime minister, Jawaharlal Nehru, once remarked, "Curzon will be remembered because he restored all that was beautiful in India."[1]

Particularly since the end of the Cold War, regard for Curzon has grown in some circles here despite the fact that as viceroy he partitioned Bengal into eastern and western halves: a divide-and-rule tactic that robbed Calcutta of a lucrative, predominantly Muslim hinterland, and established a precedent for the secession of East Pakistan from India and later the emergence of Bangladesh. Indeed, J. N. Dixit, India's foreign secretary in the early 1990s, called Curzon "among the greatest of the Indian nationalists." C. Raja Mohan, a professor at New Delhi's Nehru University, explains that all of his countrymen who now dream of a Greater India—a zone of quiet and informal influence reaching across much of southern Asia and the Indian Ocean—find Curzon "a source of strategic inspiration."[2]

In 1909, Curzon writes:

> the master of India, must, under modern conditions, be the greatest power in the Asiatic Continent, and, therefore, it may be added, in the world.[3]

The India to which Curzon refers (and over which he ruled) now covers four states: India, Pakistan, Bangladesh, and Burma—that is, all the mainland territory from the Iranian border to the Gulf of Thailand. This Greater India naturally required, in Curzon's view, buffer states to the west and north to protect it against Russia and China. Thus, in 1901, under Curzon's direction, the ethnic-Pushtun North-West Frontier Province came into being as a means for British India to apply pressure on Afghanistan by controlling the tribal areas abutting it. Today, the North-West Frontier Province survives in name and fact as a means for Pakistan to do exactly the same.

But it was not only a compliant Central Asia that Curzon sought, but a compliant Persia, too, notes David Gilmour in his comprehensive biography *Curzon: Imperial Statesman.* During Curzon's viceroyalty, British India was the principal power in the Arabian Gulf, with exceptionally strong trading links to Persia, Mesopotamia, and the Gulf sheikhdoms, which, in turn, facilitated India's economic reach farther afield in East Africa. For example, the United Arab Emirates (Dubai, Abu Dhabi, and Sharjah) constitute the former Trucial States, so called because they signed a "truce" with the British to contain piracy in the Gulf, and thus secure the trade route from Europe to India via the Middle East. Meanwhile, on British India's eastern frontier, in Burma, a class of Indian traders and moneymen provided credit and other services to Burmese peasants, thus helping to fortify the viceroy's imperial reach. Whereas Persia and Afghanistan were British buffer states against Russia in the west and northwest, the Shan States of Burma were buffers against France and its empire in Southeast Asia to the east.

The viceroy in Calcutta did not merely take orders from Whitehall, for the "architecture" of the British Empire was built around India.[4] The viceroy was a power in his own right, influencing affairs from Aden to Malacca—the entire span of the Indian Ocean. That power derived ultimately from India's own size and wealth, leveraged by its link to London. Nowadays, if you replace London with Washington—or, perhaps, replace it with a triangular relationship with both Washington *and* Beijing—you have, as some Indians define it, a "neo-Curzonian" situation.

Neo-Curzonism is a tendency among those Indian strategic thinkers who anticipate continued economic growth in their country, and a foreign policy that should follow from it. It might be tempting to compare it to American neoconservatism. After all, it is an imperial-like vision that desires national greatness based on big ideas. But whereas neoconservatives seek to impose America's ideals and system of governance abroad, neo-Curzonians are content with alliances with nondemocratic systems different from India's own. Neo-Curzonians understand limits. They seek a return to Indian preeminence mainly within India's geographical sphere of influence.

This is a vision less crude in spirit than the Greater India (Akhand Bharat) wished for by Hindu nationalists, and should not be confused with it. Whereas neo-Curzonians are more oriented to the Subcontinent's western frontier, seeking to expand India's influence in the Middle East, Hindu nationalists are oriented toward the east—to Southeast Asia and Indonesia—which have been heavily influenced by India's Sanskrit culture. Still, Curzon enjoyed especial prestige during the Hindu nationalist government of the Bharatiya Janata Party in the 1990s, when he was quoted frequently.

Quoting him served as a rebuke to India's foreign policy during the Cold War, a time when (according to Jaswant Singh, the foreign minister from 1998 to 2002) India had lost much of its influence over the shadow zones of the Subcontinent because of Nehru's preoccupation with non-alignment and third world liberation. The upshot was that nations such as Oman to the west and Malaysia to the east no longer took India seriously as a source of security. But with the end of the Cold War, and the unleashing of Indian capitalism in a globalized framework, neo-Curzonians have sought to define a new "forward" strategy for India that concentrates more specifically on Asia and the Indian Ocean, rather than on the world per se.

To be fair to Nehru, his foreign policy could emanate only from India's domestic condition, which in the 1950s and 1960s was one of recent freedom from the British, with the wounds of imperialism still fresh. The result, explains Shashi Tharoor, a biographer of Nehru, was a foreign policy perhaps less appropriate for a state than for a liberation movement.[5] But as the memory of British rule recedes, its more positive attributes can be appreciated. Hence a neo-Curzonian viewpoint represents much less an Indian variant of American neoconservatism than a return to the realpolitik of the viceroys who, while British, still operated from the same position on the map as India's current rulers. Jayanta K. Ray of the Maulana Abul Kalam Azad Institute of Asian Studies in Kolkata told me that the viceroys "simply had great geopolitical sense in terms of projecting soft power throughout Asia, occasionally better sense than our own governments since 1947."

A neo-Curzonian policy would seek to diminish the national borders of Pakistan, Bangladesh, and Burma not through conquest, but through the revival of commercial cooperation with these countries, abetted by the development of roads and regional energy pipelines. Burma, especially, will likely be a zone of contention between India and China. China's deepening transport and commercial links with Burma have compelled democratic India, starting in the late 1990s, to bid for development projects there, train Burmese troops, and do less complaining about the plight of Burmese dissidents, despite the odious nature of the military regime there. If Burma were ever to liberalize and truly open its borders, geography and historical ties might favor India over China (notwithstanding local hostility toward the Indian merchant community early in the twentieth century).

"Greater connectivity" with India's neighbors, declared Indian prime minister Manmohan Singh, can transform "each sub-region of the Sub-continent" into a web of "mutual dependencies for mutual benefit." Translation: India's economy is so much larger than any nearby state that a soft hegemony would be the natural consequence of greater economic cooperation. Asserting political primacy would not only be unnecessary, it would be counterproductive as well.

The difficulty with this vision is that it requires a society secure enough in its own domestic situation so it can dynamically focus outward. But that only partially describes India. While the American media have focused on the country's high-tech "Bangalore" phenomenon, the more immediate reality is of a tumultuous third world society where a third of the population live on a dollar a day. As noted in Chapter Seven, India is beset with political violence between the government and various disaffected groups and castes, as well as by periodic eruptions of Islamic terrorism. Its eight northeastern states are home to no fewer than fifteen insurgencies manned by local tribes seeking self-rule. The country simply lacks the internal stability to open its borders to its neighbors in return for greater influence in its near abroad.

Take relations with Muslim Bangladesh, surrounded on three sides by India. People and goods could get from one part of India to the other most easily by passing through Bangladesh. This would aid economic development in India's unstable northeast, as well as earn Bangladesh significant transit fees. In fact, a natural gas pipeline will be built bringing gas from Burma across Bangladesh to India. Because Bangladesh's political system is in ruins, its only hope is through greater economic involvement with India. But that is precisely what people in Kolkata fear. Whereas an older generation that includes refugees from the 1947 partition harbors nostalgia for a lost hinterland, many others—especially the younger generation—see Bangladesh the way many Americans see Mexico: as a place you should literally erect a wall around. "Keep all those radical mullahs locked up on the other side of the border," one prominent

Kolkata journalist told me. With more than ten million Bangladeshis living in India as economic refugees, Indians do not want more. There is also a certain historical comfort with the current border near Kolkata; as for many decades stretching deep into the nineteenth century, the Hindu elite in Calcutta and West Bengal looked down on the Muslim peasantry in East Bengal. By contrast, in the Punjab, there is an ecumenicalism of sorts toward fellow Punjabis living over India's western border in Pakistan. In general, though, India is still struggling with the borders of partition.

A Greater India that projects its economic dynamism eastward into Southeast Asia, northward into China, and westward into the Middle East must do so first in its own subcontinental backyard. And that will take stores of courage and broad-mindedness that India presently lacks.

But beyond Greater India as a land power, there is the larger Indian Ocean littoral to consider. Curzon was focused on land power because in his day British control of the seas was taken for granted. But India, as we have seen, must now consider its role on the seas and the lands on the other side of them. India, writes Raja Mohan, is discarding the sentimentalism and third worldism with which it once considered eastern and southern Africa. Now it views Africa in terms of strategy and raw materials. The Indian navy currently patrols southern Africa's Mozambique Channel, from where coal is transported to India's increasingly energy-hungry, billion-plus population. When one considers that the Indian navy has occasionally escorted U.S. warships through the Malacca Strait, the picture is completed of a rising power, ever present from one end of the world's third largest ocean to the other.

Of course, it is still the U.S. Navy that dominates the Indian Ocean. But because India's navy is a significant presence in the region, yet obviously no match for America's, neo-Curzonians require a de facto military alliance with the U.S. The word "de facto" is crucial. As I heard again and again in Kolkata, and in New Delhi, just as India was nonaligned during the Cold War, it must remain so in the future. Although it needs to tilt toward the United States to project its own power, it cannot afford to transparently alienate China, with which it will both compete for influence and do abundant trade.

Ultimately, more than any particular strategic vision, it may be the very fact of India's mass democracy that will align it with the United States as well as gradually draw surrounding nations into its orbit, as these nations struggle to replicate India's own noncoercive, yet modestly effective governing authority. And that is something that the paternalistic Lord Curzon, who never thought in terms of Indian self-government, could not have imagined.

Yet, to be sure, Curzon will be a guiding spirit behind India's foreign policy in the Indian Ocean and beyond. The strategic requirements of imperialism in his day are those of Indian nationalism in ours.

"Nationalism is a false god. It is unaesthetic," said the Bengali poet, short story writer, novelist, and artist Rabindranath Tagore, who in 1913 was awarded the Nobel Prize in Literature.* The statement is highlighted among the exhibits at the poet's rambling family home in north Kolkata. With its connecting courtyards softened by ranks of potted plants, and with the walls echoing the haunting sound of his poems put to music and adorned with iconic, modernistic paintings, the Tagore mansion has a small-scale, almost magical human quality to it that stands in opposition to the towering cold dimensions of Government House where Curzon worked.

Certainly there is a mystical quality to the long and white-bearded Tagore, yet to define him as a mystic—the messiah from the East, according to some—is to diminish him, by hinting that there is something windy and undisciplined about his work.[6] The Harvard scholar Amartya Sen notes that to see Tagore, as many in the West have, as some sort of "sermonizing spiritual guru" is to take an astonishingly narrow view of him.[7] In fact, what may give Tagore's art a mystical quality is its studied yet natural universalism, anchored in a specific Indian and Bengali soil. Just as Curzon is the ultimate pragmatist for an age of Asia-centric, multi-polar balance-of-power politics, Tagore's lifelong quest to get beyond nationalism establishes him as among the most relevant writers for an age of globalization even though he has been dead for almost seven decades.

Indeed, to express a deep regard for the work of Tagore is akin to expressing a deep regard for the work of the late Oxford philosopher Isaiah Berlin: it is a way of declaring the free and sanctified individual as the sovereign force in history. Tagore's poems, more than ninety short sto-

---

* Tagore is an anglicized form of *Thakur,* an honorific meaning "Lord," used to address an Indian Brahmin or male deity.

ries, and novels are the artistic equivalent of Berlin's humanistic philosophy. Tagore's output was that of a colossus. Human tears flow throughout his hypnotic stories like the monsoon rains. Like Berlin, he is never preachy; there is "no theory or philosophy" herein.[8] His writings over the course of a lifetime are dominated by poignant tales of individual longing, often in an idyllic rural setting, that leave the heart uneasy: the young man who did not fulfill his ambition and yearns for the love of a woman he once could have had; the skeleton in a medical school that once belonged to a beautiful woman with hopes and dreams all her own; the poor clerk who spends the evenings in Sealdah station to save the cost of light; the ungainly teenage boy in Calcutta who gets critically ill and misses his mother in the countryside; the peddler who befriends a little girl because she reminds him of his own daughter back in Afghanistan; the nine-year-old child bride who takes refuge from her loneliness by writing in an exercise book; the woman who falls in love with a vagrant boy who shows up at her doorstep; a coughing naked boy in the cold who is slapped hard by his mother and thus, in Tagore's vision, bears all the pain in the universe.

The stories go on, each one replete with compassion. Tagore's humanism shines through by the totality of his concentration on small, seemingly insignificant individuals, whose hopes and dreams and fears fill an entire world. There is nothing grandiose about his work; rather, it is always defined by intimacy. A Bengali writer to the core, Tagore writes often of monsoons ("The Padma began to swallow up gardens, villages and fields in great hungry gulps") and of ghats, the steps leading down to a river where people bathe, wash, and gossip, which also, in ways both concrete and symbolic in his literature, are places of arrivals and departures.[9]

Besides a comparison to Berlin, Tagore bears comparison to Leo Tolstoy for his mystical aspect and interest in education in a rural setting. Like Tagore, Tolstoy was the son of a landed noble family and, dissatisfied with formal education, established a school at Yasnaya Polyana just as Tagore did at Santiniketan in West Bengal, north of Calcutta. Both men were members of the gentry who glorified peasants while being somewhat less sympathetic to the rising middle class in the cities.

Above all, Tagore, as Amartya Sen suggests, because of the manner in which he harmonizes Hindu, Islamic, Persian, and British (that is, Western) culture, stands as a counterpoint to those who see the contem-

porary world as a "clash of civilizations."[10] In a poem in his collection
Gitanjali ("Song Offerings"), Tagore declares that he seeks a world

> Where knowledge is free;
> Where the world has not been broken up into fragments by narrow
> Domestic walls . . .[11]

Tagore's "narrow domestic walls" stand for a close-minded nationalism. Though he was a lover of Japanese culture, his words about Japan
are inscribed on the wall of his Calcutta home:

> Japan had vanquished China in naval battle, but it should have real-
> ized it was barbaric and unaesthetic to display the relics of that vic-
> tory all over the country like harsh thorns. Man is often compelled
> by circumstances to undertake cruel deeds but true humanity is to
> forget them. What remains eternal with man for which he builds
> temples and monasteries it is surely not violence.

Herein is the essential Tagore. War may be necessary but it is so piti-
ful that no monuments should be built to it. War, military glory, and the
like are worse than wrong; they are, like nationalism, "unaesthetic."
Beauty, that is to say, is moral and universal. And anything that is not
moral and universal cannot be beautiful.

Tagore was truly a visionary in the sense that his lifetime (1861–1941)
corresponded with the age of nationalism, even as he went beyond it and
saw a larger solidarity group above the state, that of humanity. He was not
opposed to nationalism or patriotism, only to nationalism or patriotism as
the highest good. He understood the yearning that led to patriotism, just as
Saint Augustine understood the yearning that led to tribalism, which in the
late classical age served to unite large groups of people peacefully. But
both men knew these longings as stepping-stones to larger unions.

Tagore was the ultimate syncretist, a constant blender of cultures and
peoples in his work and thoughts. There is no beautiful Bengali landscape in his view, only the glorious "Earth."[12] As such, he was an invet-
erate traveler and pilgrim, writes the Harvard scholar Sugata Bose: to
Iran, Iraq, Southeast Asia, Japan, and so on. Like Curzon, Tagore thought
of a greater India. But whereas Curzon and latter-day Indian nationalists
have had a monolithic political and strategic vision, Tagore had an inter-

woven cultural one, seeing, for example, the "lineaments of a universal brotherhood of Sufi poets bridging the Arabian Sea."[13] Tagore's mental map of Asia was a seamless tapestry of overlapping nationalities and cultures in which, for instance, a greater India dissolved into a greater Persia and into greater Malay and Balinese cultures, in the same way that Hinduism and Islam dissolved into each other in the rural eastern Bengal that he knew so well. There were no borders in Tagore's worldview, only transition zones. He would smile knowingly at discussions about a future Kurdistan, Sunnistan, Pashtunistan, Greater Azerbaijan, and other variations to the current cartography of the Near East, for Tagore thought of the world in terms of a holistic, multidimensional map. For him, a place like Kurdistan has always existed, layered atop Turkey, Iraq, and Iran rather than in contradiction to those states. This is why Tagore could talk about having a "blood relationship" as an Indo-Aryan with the Iranians, without coming across as racist or ethnocentric.[14] Blood relationships are easily acknowledged if one's worldview celebrates all blood relationships, as well as cultural and spiritual ones, as he did.

Nevertheless, Tagore was not a globalist, if that means giving up one's national or ethnic identity. He grasped intuitively that to appreciate other cultures one had to be strongly rooted in one's own. He understood that the "universal" could be implanted only in many rich and vibrant localisms. He was, in other words, a perfectly enlightened man for the early twenty-first century who, as Sugata Bose suggests, encapsulated the spirit of the Indian Ocean world.

In a "poem-painting" signed "Baghdad May 24, 1932," during a trip to Iraq, Tagore writes:

> The night has ended.
> Put out the light of the lamp
> Of thine own narrow corner
> smudged with smoke.
> The great morning which is for all
> appears in the East.
> Let its light reveal us
> to each other
> who walk on
> the same
> path of pilgrimage.[15]

The irony is that for the neo-Curzonian vision to succeed, Tagore's must also, for it is only by getting beyond the narrowing perspective of nationhood that India can gain the trust of its neighbors, in order to organically expand its own sphere of influence. Politics must follow geography and culture in this regard. As Raja Mohan put it to me in conversation, "Kolkata will always be Lhasa's closest outlet to the sea. The goal, then, is make that geographical fact linking Tibet and India a reality, through thinking big enough to overcome borders." Realpolitik with a conscience is what India, and the West, too, require, for in the broader competition with China, the power with the most benign and cosmopolitan vision will ultimately have the upper hand.

CHAPTER ELEVEN

SRI LANKA

THE NEW GEOPOLITICS

stood in a vast wasteland of upturned soil stretching miles to the horizon, as long convoys of trucks moved earth uphill on switchback trails from one part of the construction site to another, with Chinese foremen in hard hats directing the operation in the terrific heat and dust. A deep, man-made canyon with a flat and yawning valley floor was emerging; as well as two jetties, one of which was ten football fields in length. This massive dredging project—literally the creation of a new coastline farther inland—would soon be the inner harbor of the Hambantota seaport, near Sri Lanka's southern extremity, a point close to the world's main shipping lanes where more than thirty thousand vessels per year transport fuel and raw materials from the Middle East to East Asia.

By 2023, Hambantota is projected to have a liquefied natural gas refinery, aviation fuel storage facilities, and three separate docks giving the seaport a transshipment capacity, as well as dry docks for ship repair and construction, not to mention bunkering and refueling facilities.[1]

It was a fifteen-year construction project about which the Sri Lankans were both proud and sensitive: proud that their country could eventually move beyond being a byword for ethnic conflict to emerge as a strategic node of global maritime commerce; sensitive because it was not they, but the Chinese, who were both building and financing the seaport. Thus, access to the site was strictly regulated. To see the enormity of the project I had to trespass into a secure area and ended up under arrest. I was de-

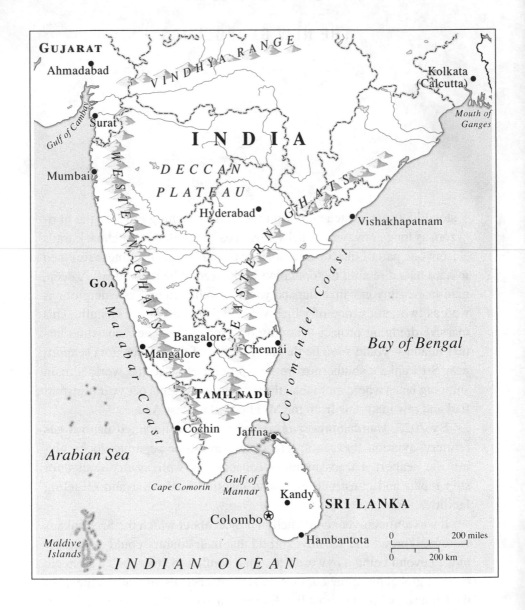

tained in the Hambantota police station for seven hours until charges were dropped.*

Like Gwadar in Pakistan, the Hambantota region constitutes a stunning seascape of thundering surf, poised to be a twenty-first-century place-name. This would be in keeping with the town's situation in antiquity, when as part of the Kingdom of Ruhuna it formed a branch of the maritime silk route. The present-day town of twenty thousand constitutes only a few streets of bustling storefronts, with wooden fishing boats stacked four abreast at the little harbor, as well as jammed onto the beach in low tide. (In many cases, the boats are owned by Muslims of Malay origin).†

The beachfront hotel where I stayed had a truly deserted, edge-of-the-earth feel with only two other guests. It had been reconstructed on the ruins of the hotel destroyed during the 2004 Indian Ocean tsunami, which had also destroyed all the boats on the beach before new ones were built with aid from the international community. The tsunami killed 35,000 people in Sri Lanka and made 400,000 homeless. Indeed, Hambantota constitutes a visual shorthand for the Indian Ocean during the current phase of history, a victim of the tsunami and a beneficiary of China's rise as a great power.

Before the start of the seaport project, Hambantota had been a backwater of Sri Lanka, known only for the time at the beginning of the twentieth century when the great English man of letters Leonard Woolf had been an assistant government agent here. Woolf, later the husband of Virginia Woolf and the director of the famous Hogarth Press, used his time in Hambantota to gather material for a brilliant novel about the cruelties of rural life in this corner of Ceylon, *The Village in the Jungle,* published in 1913. In fact, just behind the town there still lurks the dry-zone, scraggily palm forest with its putty red soil reminiscent of the book.

Azmi Thassim, head of the local chamber of commerce, who proudly told me the story of Leonard Woolf in Hambantota, insisted that the seaport project was a Sri Lankan and not a Chinese one. He noted that Ham-

---

* During the entire period I was detained I was well treated, a testament to the professionalism of the local police, at least in my case, and the intercession of the United States Embassy in Colombo.

† Hambantota means "sampan-harbor," a reference to the flat wooden boats used here in ancient times, and still used in Malaysia, Indonesia, and Vietnam; *Hamban* being a corruption of *sampan*. Ramya Chamalie Jirasinghe, *Rhythm of the Sea* (Hambantota, Sri Lanka: Hambantota District Chamber of Commerce, 2007), p. 23.

bantota's strategic maritime position and deep depths close to shore had made it an ideal place for a new port for decades; in fact, the Canadians had been involved for a time in the drawing-board phase before the Chinese and Sri Lankans initialed their far-reaching deal in 2007. "We lack the funds and expertise, and, therefore, looked for foreign support." Hambantota, he said, also had plans for a conference center and a new airport in which the Chinese likely would not be involved, just as once the seaport was completed, the Chinese probably would not be the ones operating it.

The chamber leader is right in an important sense. China's move into the Indian Ocean constitutes less an aggressive example of empire building than a subtle grand strategy to take advantage of legitimate commercial opportunities wherever they might arise in places that matter to its military and economic interests. China is adroitly riding a wave of economic history rather than plotting it out in the first place. As in Gwadar, where the Port of Singapore Authority will be managing a Chinese-built port, China will have at least one layer of separation between its goals and ground-level reality. China does not need to run any harbor. It requires only state-of-the-art port and bunkering facilities for its merchant fleet and possibly its warships in places where Beijing works hard to maintain excellent diplomatic and military relations. Hambantota and other such ports will constitute flow-through centers where vast quantities of Chinese manufactured goods destined for Middle East, South Asian, and Southeast Asian markets can be temporarily stored. Thus, Hambantota is emblematic of China's budding yet exquisitely elusive empire, built on soft power.[2]

In the world of late antiquity, Ceylon—strategically located at the hinge between the Bay of Bengal and the Arabian Sea—was the entrepôt between China and the Middle East. As George Hourani writes, Chinese ships used to sail as far west as Ceylon, and from Ceylon westward trade was in the hands of the Persians and Axumites (from present-day Ethiopia).[3] Chinese admiral Zheng He broke that pattern by using Ceylon as a base for sailing as far west as the Horn of Africa, making two trips to the island. He erected a trilingual tablet here in 1410 that was unearthed exactly five hundred years later near Galle, close to the southernmost point of Sri Lanka and the Indian Subcontinent. The message inscribed in Chinese, Persian, and Tamil invoked the blessings of the Hindu deities for a peaceful world built on trade. The year before, the Chinese had invaded Ceylon and made their way as far as the Buddhist hill capital of Kandy, where they captured the Sinhalese king and queen and members of the court as retribution for not handing over a sacred relic—a tooth of the Buddha—some years earlier.[4]

The Chinese occupied Ceylon for thirty years in the fifteenth century. This was before the European assault that would include occupations by the Portuguese, Dutch, and British, a historical epoch that ended only in the mid-twentieth century. The fact that the Chinese got here before the island fell under western tutelage makes China's current policy in Sri Lanka and the Indian Ocean compatible with local history, and the expensive commemoration in Beijing of Zheng He's voyages demonstrates that is how the Chinese themselves view it.

China's activities in Sri Lanka reveal that China, in the words of one Indian naval officer, is ready to "drop anchor at India's southern doorstep." China is involved in building a billion-dollar development zone in Hambantota that features the deepwater harbor that I saw being constructed, in addition to a fuel-bunkering facility, oil refinery, and other infrastructure that the chamber leader did not mention.[5] The complex may one day be used as a refueling and docking station for China's navy as it patrols the Indian Ocean and protects Chinese supplies of Saudi Arabian oil. Amid the Indian Ocean's key sea lines of communication, Hambantota is in the same part of the island near where Zheng He's fleet landed six hundred years earlier. With India constrained in providing military assistance to the Buddhist Sinhalese government in the capital of Colombo because of the political sensitivities of its own Hindu Tamil population, China, along with Pakistan, has been filling the gap. China has supplied Sri Lanka with fighter aircraft, armored personnel carriers, anti-aircraft guns, air surveillance radar, missiles, and rocket-propelled grenades. China's aid to Sri Lanka jumped from a few million dollars in 2005 to $1 billion in 2008; by comparison, the United States gave only $7.4 million. The U.S. suspended military aid in 2007 over the human rights abuses of the Sinhalese government in its civil war against ethnic Tamils; China, which is also involved in gas exploration here, as well as the building of a coal power plant at a cost of $455 million, has had no such moral qualms.[6]

Whereas European colonialism ended just over sixty years ago, and while the U.S. is distracted elsewhere, China has now returned to this island at the core of Indian Ocean trade routes. Its military assistance, including six F-7 fighter jets free of charge, was crucial in ending the military stalemate with the Tamil rebels in favor of the Sri Lankan government.[7] Though the U.S. has relatively ignored Sri Lanka as an island in India's geographical orbit that is far from the Middle East, the Chinese correctly see it as key to twenty-first-century sea lines of communication around the Asian rimland. So as the Americans labor in Afghanistan, the Chinese are quietly constructing ports along the Indian Ocean littoral. And even if the American labor succeeds, that will only mean a Central Asia connected by pipelines to the Indian Ocean, creating an economically pulsing new world order that China will be poised to take further advantage of.

And yet China's challenge will ultimately be the same as America's, for as much as China has helped Sri Lanka (and Pakistan, too, for that matter), there is no guarantee that China will have ready access to the very port facilities it is building. It will all depend on the political circumstances between China and the host country at the desired moment. China might eventually find itself in the same frustrating position as the United States, with ports and bases it cannot use in time of need because of unforeseen political tensions. This, again, is the real lesson of the Indian Ocean world: nuanced relationships rather than overt alliances and basing arrangements. I note China's deep involvement in Sri Lanka because that is what I see happening on the ground, but there is little reason for the West to be paranoid about it.

Throughout the twenty-six-year-long civil war here Western strategists had found themselves in a deep moral quandary regarding Sri Lanka, a place that for a generation constituted a human rights catastrophe even as it figures prominently in new geopolitical calculations. Therefore, as Sri Lanka grows in importance in this Indian Ocean–centric world, it is time now to rescue the island from the relative obscurity it has suffered at the hands of the American media.[8]

The very word "Ceylon," so formal and elegant, though a mispronunciation of a Portuguese name, conjures up the most rarefied of paradises. And the landscape, with its sprawling seaboard, pristine forests, and glistening tea plantations, as well as the soaring-to-heaven whiteness of its Buddhist stupas surely does not disappoint. Medieval Arab seafarers called this island that hangs like a pear-shaped teardrop off the southeastern extremity of India "Serendip," or "island of jewels," which allowed an eighteenth-century English writer to coin the word "serendipity." Sri Lanka, the Sinhala name by which the island has been known since 1972, means "resplendent land."

But Sri Lanka is one of those benighted places—one thinks of Cyprus, Kosovo, Nagorno Karabakh—not altogether uncommon to the developing world, whereby the earth is magnificent even as the actions of its human inhabitants have too often been small-minded and ugly. And in each of these places, wholly fresh historical complexities riddle the political landscape, making the possibility of engineering a solution as difficult as finding one's way out of a maze. There is a perversity about the local history of recent decades that suggests it is the very isolation imposed by an island geography, as well as the sectioning of the landscape by hills and mountains—the very features that make Sri Lanka so beautiful—that contribute to the paranoia and narrow-mindedness which has been the hallmark of politics here.

The majority Buddhist Sinhalese, who constitute more than three quarters of Sri Lanka's population of twenty million, have lived in fear of being overwhelmed by the Hindu Tamils, who, though composing only 18 percent of the population, can theoretically call upon their sixty million ethnic and religious compatriots living just across the Palk Strait in southeastern India. The history of Tamil invasions against the only homeland that the Sinhalese possess is not just the stuff of ancient history, but a living reality reinforced by the Tamil terrorism of the present era. Writes the Sri Lankan scholar K. M. de Silva:

> Sri Lanka's location off the coast of South India, and specifically its close proximity to [the Indian state of] Tamilnadu, separated by a shallow and narrow stretch of sea serves to accentuate this sense of a minority status among the Sinhalese. Their own sense of ethnic distinctiveness is identified through religion—Theravada Buddhism— and language—Sinhala. They take pride in the fact that Buddhism thrives in Sri Lanka while it has practically disappeared in its original home, India. Their language, Sinhala, has its roots in classical Indian languages, but it is now a distinctly Sri Lankan language, and one that is not spoken anywhere else.[9]

Indeed, there is a sense of historical destiny among Sinhalese, de Silva writes: of preserving Theravada Buddhism under a Hindu revivalist assault, with southern India the source of scores of these invasions. It is as if the Buddhist Sinhalese were a lonely people, with few ethnic compatriots anywhere, who had been pushed to their last bastion, the southern two thirds of Sri Lanka, by the demographic immensity of largely Hindu India. Therefore, the Sinhalese must fight for every mile of their ethnic homeland, Bradman Weerakoon, an advisor to former Sri Lankan presidents and prime ministers, told me. Adding to the feeling that the majority Buddhist Sinhalese have of being perennially under siege by the more entrepreneurial and dynamic minority-Hindu Tamils is the feeling of religious oppression sustained under the rule of the various European colonial powers, beginning with Christian Portugal, and continuing through the mid-twentieth century with the Dutch and British.[10]

As a result, like the Serbs in the former Yugoslavia and the Shiites in Iran, the Sinhalese are a demographic majority with a dangerous minority complex of persecution. If one may generalize, the Buddhist Sinhalese are less austere and contemplative than other Buddhists; they are militant religionists with a blood-and-soil identity. This identity harks back to the breathtaking architectural and sculptural residue of twenty-three hundred years of Buddhist worship, with its brassware, garish costumes, silver and gold objects, and resplendent statues in red and gold; artistic traditions that arrived here from India as part of the missionary activity of the great Mauryan emperor Ashoka in the third century B.C. Buddhism, just like Christianity, Islam, Judaism, and other faiths, Western and Eastern alike, while principally dedicated to a spiritual and thus nonviolent calling, can become an instigator of violence and hatred in specific circumstances, when ethnicity, struggle over territory, and political ideology are put into the mix. (Repeat: this is not an Eastern failing, for Western religions have been just as guilty in the course of history. And remember that while I refer throughout to Buddhist Sinhalese and Hindu Tamils, for they constitute the broad outlines of the war, in fact, much of the violence has been perpetrated by Christians, and specifically Catholics, on both sides. Indeed, Christians have numbered among the key terrorists and suicide bombers.)

For their part, the Hindu Tamils have been labeled a minority with a majority complex, owing to the triumph of Hinduism over Buddhism in southern India in the fifth and sixth centuries A.D. The subsequent invasions from India's south against the rich and thriving Buddhist city-state of Anuradhapura in north-central Sri Lanka resulted in the creation by the thirteenth century of a Tamil kingdom of its own that, in turn, helped lay the groundwork for Tamil majorities in the north and east of the island today.[11]

The post-independence experience of this country, including a quarter century of civil war between Sinhalese and Tamils, has borne out the worst fears of both communities. The Sinhalese have had to deal with a Tamil guerrilla insurgency every bit as vicious and suicidal as the better known ones in Iraq and Afghanistan. For their part, the Tamils have had to deal with coercion, discrimination, and the utter failure of largely Sinhalese government institutions to protect their communal rights. As Weerakoon and others explain, Sri Lanka is an example of how democracy can be used, over the course of decades, for the expression of the rights of an oppressive ethnic majority rather than, as we in the West understand it, for the rights of the individual.

From as early as a few years following independence in 1948, the Sinhalese and Tamils were at each other's throats. In the 1950s the Sinhalese demonstrated against the government's granting of Tamil minority rights, only to have the Tamils demonstrate after the government backed down from that very pledge. Tamil mobs and gangs attacked Sinhalese homes and shops in the north of the country and Sinhalese did the same to Tamil neighborhoods in the southwest. Meanwhile, government security forces became less and less professional, and in the 1960s more Sinhalese-nationalist in outlook. The Sinhalese government made Tamils scapegoats for its own failures, while promoting Sinhala as the sole official language. Preferential treatment in all public spheres was given to the Sinhalese community: Not only the security forces, but the civil service became dominated by the ethnic majority. Electoral districts were drawn to give overbearing influence to rural Sinhalese.[12]

By the mid-1960s, the model of a secular, multi-ethnic state had been discarded in favor of a Sinhalese one, with Buddhism raised to the status of a state religion and the Hindu Tamils largely disenfranchised. Ironically, this occurred with the connivance of a democratic system that never descended into dictatorship. Sinhalese politicians, including Sirimavo Bandaranaike, who in 1960 became the world's first woman prime minister, remained beholden to the mood of the majority, instead of working to rise above it. Supporting this descent into communal intolerance was the greater part of Buddhist monks who, in the manner of a medieval clergy, have enjoyed the uses of political power and look back to a past when they were the rousing nationalist force behind Ceylonese kings.

Nevertheless, poor economic conditions that included rising oil prices left hordes of Sinhalese youth either unemployed or with limited opportunities, and the result was a guerrilla movement that in the late 1960s and 1970s espoused an ideology that combined Buddhist nationalism with Marxism. Strikes and demonstrations gave way to inter-communal killings. A Marxist-nationalist insurrection in 1971 led to fifteen thousand dead, and one in 1989 that could be likened to Peru's Shining Path insurgency carried a death toll of fifty-five thousand. Women, children, and handicapped people numbered heavily among the victims. It was truly unspeakable. The ability of security forces to end it decisively was what ultimately gave the military two decades later the self-confidence it needed to defeat the Tamil insurrectionists.

By the 1970s the security forces had been hardened into a ruthless criminal organization in their own right. The American scholar John Richardson writes in his book about Sri Lanka, *Paradise Poisoned,* of the emblematic case of a young woman, Premawathi Menamperi, in a Sinhalese district in the extreme south of the island in 1970, who had been taken into police custody for alleged ties to a radical Marxist organization. She was stripped, reportedly raped a number of times, then marched naked through the town where she had reigned as a New Year's festival queen, before being shot to death by a policeman's submachine gun. Sri Lanka may have been a democracy, but a mere two decades after achieving statehood it was no longer a civil society.

This was an era when the elected government itself was drifting toward Titoism and other milder variants of Soviet communism. Meanwhile, in 1972, a certain Vellupilai Prabakharan founded the Tamil New Tigers, whose name later became known by journalists around the world as the Liberation Tigers of Tamil Eelam (LTTE): Tamil Tigers for short. Prabakharan, a Christian actually, is another illustration of human agency, of how despite the tragic record of inter-communal conflict between Sinhalese and Tamils, the civil war might not have been ignited in the first place, or at least might have unfolded differently, had one man—Prabakharan—not existed. Prabakharan, who would develop into one of the world's most hunted terrorists, as well as one of its most feared and capable guerrilla leaders, was a product of two overriding factors: the rank discrimination against Tamils and a particularly wayward middle-class youth. His fertile young mind devoured books about Napoleon's campaigns, even as he pored through comic books and listened to political discussions by his father's side about the ill treatment meted out by the Sinhalese government to his fellow Tamils. His heroes were Clint Eastwood, the legendary Tamil warrior Veerapandia Kattabomman, and Subash Chandra Bose, the Bengali Indian nationalist who rejected Gandhi's pacifism and joined forces with the German Nazis and Japanese fascists to fight the British in India.

The young Prabakharan killed animals with a slingshot and air gun, and practiced making homemade bombs. He stuck pins under his nails to increase his stamina for pain, and killed insects with needles to prepare himself to torture the enemy. In the beginning, he led the Tamil Tigers in robberies to raise money for training camps in remote jungle locations, where the screening of candidates was painstaking. "You intellectuals are afraid of blood," he scolded the academic community in Sri Lanka's northern Tamil city of Jaffna. "No struggle will take place without killings." Ironically, the Sinhalese-dominated security services fulfilled his wishes. Small-scale killings carried out by the Tigers resulted in massive police reprisals against Tamil refugees, aided by Sinhalese thugs. By the early 1980s, decades of inter-communal hatred and democratic misrule had brought Sri Lanka to the verge of a cataclysm.[13]

Prabakharan himself, as I have said, was a Christian, as were other key members of the Tamil Tigers. Religion was less of a factor in this tragedy than ethnicity; the Tigers, it should never be forgotten, oppressed as many Hindus as they did Buddhists.

The civil war began in earnest on July 23, 1983, when Prabakharan orchestrated and personally led an attack on a Sri Lankan army patrol near Jaffna University that included a land mine explosion and automatic weapon fire. Thirteen of the fifteen Sinhalese soldiers taking part in the patrol were killed. A week of rioting followed in the capital, Colombo, and other Sinhalese regions, in which ethnic Tamils who had lived amicably with their Sinhalese neighbors for decades saw their homes and businesses burned and suffered beatings, gang rapes, and murder, including being burned alive. As would happen in Gujarat in 2002, official involvement was alleged after voting rolls had been used to target Tamil families.

Indian prime minister Indira Gandhi attempted to play the role of peacemaker, even as the Research and Analysis Wing of the Indian security bureaucracy—the spy service known as RAW—established training camps for militant Tamil youths to fight the Sinhalese. In the late 1980s the Indian military was dispatched to Sri Lanka as peacekeepers but ended up fighting the Tamil Tigers, the very group it originally had helped train. The Indians ultimately withdrew from the island in utter failure. In 1991 a female Tiger suicide bomber assassinated Indira Gandhi's son Indian prime minister Rajiv Gandhi.

For more than a quarter century since 1983, during a civil war that killed more than seventy thousand people, Sri Lanka occupied a pathetic position in the news: an ongoing tragedy of immense humanitarian proportions that, nevertheless, could be forever relegated to the inside pages. In the United States, especially, it seemed that the worse the war got, the less anyone knew about it, or cared even, for at the time few thought about the island as strategic.

Throughout the course of the war Prabakharan turned the Tamil Tigers into a quasi-cult terrorist group in which he was venerated as a demigod. "To comprehend LTTE," writes the late American scholar Michael Radu, "imagine Jim Jones' Temple cult of Guyana in possession of a 'navy' and 'air force,' as well as (at its height) some 20,000 fanatical and armed zombie followers."[14] Indeed, Prabakharan's Tigers comprised the world's first guerrilla insurgency with its own air force (Czech-made Zlin Z 143s) and, more important, its navy (explosive-packed fishing trawlers and a small submarine force). He imposed a blood tax on the population under his control in the north and east, with each family having to provide a son to the Tigers. There was a wing of the organization, the Black Tigers, dedicated to murder and assassinations. Until the early 1990s the Tigers led the world in suicide bombing, a tactic that, to a large extent, they had pioneered. The Tigers used many tens of thousands of civilians as human shields and children as porters on the battlefield.[15] The very history of the Tamil Tigers shows that perverse violence, the embedding of warriors amid large numbers of civilians, and the rampant use of suicide bombing are not crimes specific to Muslims or to the Arab-Persian world.

The Tigers also symbolized another deeply troubling phenomena: the idea of a seemingly permanent insurgency and the consequent power of statelessness. In the early twenty-first century, mass communications and weapons technology have conspired to embolden groups that have no formal representation at the United Nations, few institutions, and, in many cases, little or no secure territory. Precisely because they do not have to govern, these groups are spared the need for compromise and can subsist on moral abstractions and absolutes.[16] The near permanence and lethality of such groups as Hezbollah, al-Qaeda, the Taliban, and the Tamil Tigers have stemmed directly from their lack of official responsibilities of sovereignty. Just as battling al-Qaeda somewhat dehumanized the United States government—to judge from the revelations about torture—battling the Tamil Tigers did worse to the Sri Lankan authorities, whose institutions of democratic governance are far weaker than those of America.

In late 2008 the Sri Lankan army's most professionally trained elements, numbering some 50,000, began a methodical offensive in the north and west of the country, after defections had liberated the east from Tiger control. From an area of seven thousand square miles, the Tiger-held territory fell to some thirty square miles, surrounded on land and sea by the Sri Lankan military. Between the two armies were as many as 200,000 Tamil civilians that, by some accounts, the Tigers were using as human shields. The Tigers thus carried to an exponential extreme the technique of the Taliban, al-Qaeda, and Hamas to hide amid noncombatants. The Sinhalese government forces did not flinch at this moral predicament, however. With mortars and multi-barreled rocket launchers they shelled and then starved civilians even as they mopped up further territory. Of the 70,000 people killed in the war since 1983, 10 percent, mainly civilians, were reportedly killed in the last few months of fighting in 2009.[17] Moreover, the government's gradual victory over the Tamil Tigers, among the post–World War II era's most ruthless and bloodthirsty organizations, while a good in and of itself, would lead only to a more severe coarsening of politics in Colombo. Not only did Tamil civilians (themselves opposed to the Tigers) have their rights violently abused by the government, but even independent-minded Sinhalese, journalists especially, were hunted down and killed as well.

"Murder has become the primary tool whereby the state seeks to control the organs of liberty," wrote journalist Lasantha Wickramatunga in a self-penned obituary that anticipated his own assassination in early 2009.[18] Sources told me that he had been killed by having iron rods with sharp points driven through his skull. "If Lasantha, with all of his connections, could be killed in broad daylight, then they could do this to any-body," one local journalist told me. This journalist had stories about re-porters being beaten black and blue; the atmosphere in Colombo was one of extreme self-censorship—"the worst and most insidious kind." An-other journalist told me: "Lasantha's fate really scarred us. People like me decided it was more important to stay alive than to report the news." Few journalists I met were willing to cross the line and publicly attack the gov-ernment. The Americans had struggled with how to deal with an inde-pendent world media while conducting a counterinsurgency in Iraq. The Sri Lankan government knew no such frustrations in its path to victory.

Sri Lanka, when I visited it toward the start of the southwest monsoon in the spring of 2009, was a place on the brink of a great victory against the semi-conventional elements of the fascist Tamil Tigers who were down to their last square mile or two of territory in the Mullaitivu district of the northeast, with a few tens of thousands of civilians packed inside as hostages. But Sri Lanka was also a place in the grip of fear. The media, usually the watchdogs of free societies, had been psychologically sepa-rated from the public by the government, whose own human rights abuses were now increasingly tolerated by the population as long as vic-tory on the battlefield was imminent. The civilizational divide between Buddhist and Hindu on this island, at the meeting point of the Arabian Sea and Bay of Bengal, had never been sharper, even as it was not origi-nally a religious dispute.

"Since the Rajapaksas assumed power in 2005, abductions and disap-pearances have gone through the roof," a foreign expert told me. He was referring to the three Sinhalese brothers who ruled the country during my 2009 visit: the elected president, Mahinda Rajapaksa; the defense secre-tary, Gotabhaya Rajapaksa; and the president's most trusted advisor, Basil Rajapaksa. Together they marked a decisive break from previous Sri Lankan governments. Whereas the governments of the Senanayake and Bandaranaike family dynasties hailed from the Colombo-centric elite, the Rajapaksas were more representative of the rural, somewhat xenophobic, semi-illiterate, and collectivist part of the Sinhalese Bud-dhist population. There were both rumors and credible reports from for-eign embassies of deep connections to the underworld, and to narcotics and human trafficking. The brothers' consolidation of power represented the democratic equivalent of a colonels' coup.

Whereas in 2003, aside from the war itself, there had been relatively few human rights problems, by 2009 there were roughly a thousand extrajudicial killings and disappearances annually. These murders and abductions, mainly of young Tamils, but also of journalists, lawyers, and other members of the Colombo elite, were being conducted by shadowy underworld groups controlled by military intelligence, which, in turn, reported to the top leaders of government.

Then there were the more celebrated cases such as the sixteen ethnic Tamil and one Muslim aid workers employed by a French nongovernmental organization, who in 2006 were each shot through the back of the head execution style near the port of Trincomalee in the east. And at a plethora of military and police roadblocks throughout downtown Colombo and the country, young Tamils were being abducted and dispatched to overcrowded internment camps. Because of the unsophisticated backgrounds of members of the regime, the amoral aid from China, and the government's illicit activities combined with the very brutality of its military and security operations, diplomats and human rights workers feared that the pressure of the war had, finally, turned it into the same category of regime as those in Burma and Zimbabwe, with disappearances reminiscent of the Argentina of the 1970s and early 1980s, just as the government was about to achieve an epochal victory. The Rajapaksa brothers, with the full backing of the Sinhalese clergy and population, now constituted something out of the Sinhalese past: a royal and ethnically rooted dynasty, superficially like the Buddhist kingdoms of Kandy of old, dedicated to ethno-national survival, unaccountable to the cabinet and parliament. Democracy had yielded up a family business. Colorful banners were everywhere, even as war heroes in the great struggle against the Tamil Tigers were proclaimed and celebrated.

Except that what the Rajapaksas had wrought was a perversion of the old Buddhist Kandyan kingdom, which, rather than purely Buddhist, was really syncretic. Beleaguered by Portuguese, Dutch, and British attempts to conquer it, Kandy, defended by its mountainous forests in the center of the island, held on as independent until 1815, when finally taken by the British. The ruling dynasty, the Nayakkars, were South Indian and Hindu in origin, even as they patronized Theravada Buddhism, while seeking Hindu brides for their Buddhist male heirs. By ending this dynasty and thus breaking the link between Buddhism and Hinduism, the British helped set the stage for the ethnic polarization of politics in the post-colonial era. The truth was that Theravada Buddhism, so concentrated on ethics and the release from worldly existence, was too austere for the Ceylonese peasantry, and thus required the Hindu pantheon to provide it with the necessary color and magic. A few miles from Kandy, deep in the forest amid shimmering fields of tea, I saw statues of the Buddha and of Hindu gods under the same roofs, together in their dusky magnificence: in dark stone vestibules at the medieval temples of Gadaladeniya, Lankatilaka, and Embeka.

At the temple of Embeka, I lifted aside a Hindu tapestry to behold the Buddha, which the tapestry had been guarding. At Lankatilaka, I saw the Buddha surrounded on all four sides by *devales* (prayer complexes) devoted to the deities Upulvan, Saman, Vibhishana, and Skanda—of mixed Hindu, Buddhist, and Persian origin. At the Buddhist shrine of Gadaladeniya, I saw stone carvings based on the style of the Hindu empire of Vijayanagar in Andhra Pradesh in southern India. The torrential rain of the southwest monsoon invigorated the spiritual and artistic pageant, shrieking and clapping against the leaves as sheets of mist moved across the bosky realm. This was the real legacy of Sri Lanka, I thought, to which primarily the Tamil Tigers, and secondarily the Rajapaksas, had done violence.

One diplomat told me that the West should simply ostracize the Rajapaksa regime and not worry about it becoming a linchpin of Chinese great-power strategy. As he saw it, the hundreds of billions of dollars of Chinese money invested in the U.S. economy was more central to American interests than one more Chinese-built port in the Indian Ocean which, in any case, was of greater concern to the Indian and Japanese navies than to America's. Furthermore, Sri Lanka's Burma-trending regime was simply too corrupt and too incompetent in other spheres to last, despite its battlefield successes.

For their part, the Rajapaksas were dismissive toward the West and the United States, and replete with vindicated righteousness. After all, let us consider the following history:

In 2006, at a time when the new Rajapaksa government withdrew from a meaningless ceasefire with the Tamil Tigers (both sides were still shooting at each other), the Tigers controlled one third of Sri Lanka. The United States had been, up until then, increasing its support for the government as part of a post-9/11 strategy whereby the Tamil Tigers were considered a terrorist organization in a similar category as al-Qaeda. But Mahinda Rajapaksa had been elected to finally win the war, and in 2006 he had a stroke of luck: the Tiger-held east of the country folded up because of the defection of a key ally of Prabakharan—Vinayagamoorthy Muralitharan, known by the nom de guerre Colonel Karuna Amman. Now was the time to push for final victory. Yet, finishing the war meant officially breaking the ceasefire, which, together with Colombo's increasing human rights violations under Rajapaksa, ended American military assistance. Thus, there were no more deliveries of spare parts for Sri Lanka's fire-fighting radar, or for its Huey helicopters and C-130s. The Sri Lankan navy had been especially pleased with its maritime domain awareness radar, but the Americans soon dropped all service and parts for it. The navy had relied on its 30mm Bushmaster cannons from the U.S. as a standoff capability against Tiger suicide craft, but the salt water was hard on the equipment and, again, no more parts were forthcoming. The Sri Lankans felt that the Americans were slamming the door in their face just as they were dealing efficiently with a nihilistic insurgency. "Right at their moment of glory they're getting their ankles bit by the 'international community,' " was how one diplomat in Colombo described it.

Meanwhile, sensing an opportunity, China began supplying Sri Lanka with more and more arms and ammunition. Chinese fire-fighting radar was bad compared to that of the U.S., but at least parts were available. Military aid from Beijing was soon top to bottom: the assault rifles in evidence at military roadblocks were Chinese T-56 knockoffs of Russian AK-47s. China also had Sri Lanka's back at the U.N. Security Council whenever the Western powers wanted to condemn it. China was providing slots for Sri Lankan officers at its war and staff colleges. As in Uzbekistan and Nepal, where the curtailment of political freedoms had caused the West to downsize its relationships, the Chinese were seriously upgrading theirs.

Other military and economic aid was coming from Pakistan, Iran, former Soviet states, Libya, and Israel even, which was supplying the Sri Lankan navy with Dvora patrol boats. Buoyed by the non-Western half of the world that was less obsessed with human rights concerns, military progress against the Tamil Tigers accelerated in 2008 as the army stood up new divisions and special operations task forces. Safe in the knowledge of China's firm backing, the Sri Lankan military moved forward methodically and patiently, not driven by any political timetable, devolving power to its officers in the field. Meanwhile, the Sri Lankan navy sank Tamil Tiger mother ships, or floating warehouses, in the Indian Ocean to the southeast. It was an impressive show, except for the utter lack of a hearts-and-minds element toward ethnic Tamils by an army recruited from the poorest inland villages of the Sinhalese heartland. Indeed, there was little thought of building schools or digging water wells for the Tamils. It was total war with civilians caught in the middle as hostages in the tens and hundreds of thousands. Victory and the deaths of more than a thousand Sinhalese troops in the fighting of 2008 and 2009 put the government in no mood to compromise. Defense secretary Gotabhaya Rajapaksa made official visits to China, Russia, and Israel. With a loan from Libya, oil from Iran, and the Chinese building and financing the state-of-the-art seaport at Hambantota, the West simply had less and less leverage.

Partly because of Chinese strategic concerns, Sri Lanka was able to win a war while rejecting the West. And though the defeat of a group like the Tamil Tigers is certainly something to be welcomed, it was achieved in a manner that demonstrates how the rise of China in Asia and Africa carries with it troubling repercussions for the states and regimes affected. The decline of the West in maritime Asia, while a wholly natural and in some sense benign occurrence in the wider span of history—given the trauma caused since da Gama's voyage—will not be altogether beneficial. As we have seen, Chinese military aid does not come with lectures about human rights the way the West's does. China does not interfere in another state's internal politics and does not tolerate interference in its own. Chinese foreign policy, without being in any way extreme or bellicose, nevertheless represents the bleakest form of realism. It indicates a new bipolarity in the world: between those states that employ human rights as part of their policy calculations and those that do not.

Yet, despite being crucial to Sri Lanka's destruction of the Tamil Tigers, China cannot be wholly triumphant here for the simple reason that political geography locates Sri Lanka within the shadow of India. Yes, there was the disastrous 1987 intervention of the Indian military, in which India essentially invaded Sri Lanka in order to defend ethnic Tamils and ended up fighting the Tamil Tigers, who would not tolerate any power other than their own. Nevertheless, today India enjoys better relations with Sri Lanka than it does with other large and immediate neighbors such as Pakistan and Bangladesh.* Owing to a 1998 free trade agreement, Sri Lankan trade with India is substantial: India dominates imports to Sri Lanka and is Sri Lanka's third largest export market.† India's natural sway over Sri Lanka is so explicit that at the time of independence, Sri Lanka signed a defense pact with Great Britain out of fear of an Indian invasion (as would happen in the cases of Hyderabad and Goa on the Indian mainland). As we have seen, India may be bedeviled by semi-failed states on its borders, but at the same time those states, as irascible as they can be, must make their own geopolitical calculations in reference to India. For example, Pakistan's support of Islamic extremism in Afghanistan is fully explained by its desire to erect an Islamistan of sorts deep into Central Asia with which to confront India. Thus, Sri Lanka's new pro-Chinese tilt is, at the end of the day, only relative; for especially as the Indian-Chinese maritime rivalry heats up Sri Lanka will have to maneuver delicately between the two giants in order to achieve a kind of functional nonalignment. Sri Lanka, with its growing and increasingly influential Muslim minority, its political war debt to China, and its proximity to India, is the ultimate register of geopolitical trends in the Indian Ocean region.

Nonetheless, India, pointed out Paikiasothy Saravanamuttu, executive director of the Centre for Policy Alternatives in Colombo, is itself compromised in its relations with Sri Lanka, less because of its failed intervention in 1987 than because of the signal fact of Tamilnadu, the Indian state practically adjoining Sri Lanka, which is the ethnic homeland of Sri Lanka's embattled minority Tamils. Because of political pressure from Tamilnadu exerted on politicians in New Delhi, India must strive to support Sri Lanka's Tamils, even as it competes with China and Pakistan for friendship with Colombo's Sinhalese authorities. But as Saravanamuttu went on to say, India's very tangled and troubled relationship with the island makes a solution to the Sinhalese-Tamil dispute crucial to its interests. True ethnic reconciliation in Sri Lanka is an Indian goal more than a Chinese one.

In the spring of 2009, the methodical government offensive intensified in take-no-prisoners style. The war was declared over on May 18, when

---

* Though India also enjoys close relations with the Maldives and Bhutan, these are microstates in their own category.

† Sri Lanka's largest export market is the United States, to which it supplies finished textiles such as lingerie.

Prabakharan's body was displayed on television, as the last few hundred yards of Tamil Tiger territory were taken. The next morning, safely out of jail from my trespassing scrap, I drove through the southern coastal heartland of the Sinhalese. Everywhere there were parades and flag-bedecked, horn-honking rickshaw convoys, with young men, many of them unemployed, shouting and setting off masses of firecrackers. Posters of President Rajapaksa were everywhere. Villagers lined the roads offering free food served on palm leaves to passersby. Prabakharan's body was dragged and burned in effigy. In the case of the young men, I sensed a scary and wanton boredom in their actions, as if the same crowds, under different circumstances, could be setting fire to Tamil homes, as had happened in earlier decades. It was noteworthy that the closer I got to the ethnically mixed population center of Colombo, the demonstrations were less in evidence.

Yet it truly was an event to celebrate. Prabakharan had been causing death and destruction to a much greater extent and for a much longer period than Osama bin Laden in the case of the United States. This was the kind of clear-cut, demonstrable victory that any American administration could only hope for, even as the methods used by the Sri Lankan government to attain it could—and should—never be replicated by the U.S.

That same morning I stopped in the town of Tangalla to watch Rajapaksa's victory speech to the parliament broadcast on national television. Gathered before a large screen especially arranged for the event were hundreds of people waving the distinctive Sri Lankan flag: a lion against a maroon background symbolizing the Sinhalese, with smaller orange and green stripes for the Tamil and Muslim communities. It seemed at first a brilliant Machiavellian performance: be absolutely ruthless in war and generous in victory. After gutting the rights of ethnic Tamils and of the media for years, Rajapaksa spoke repeatedly of national reconciliation. He began his speech not in Sinhala but in Tamil. He talked of an ethnically united country: "We must all live as one." Moreover, he mentioned development, education, and health care for the Tamil minority. In the past he had spoken thus in international forums, but never so humanely and comprehensively before a domestic audience. Though no specific programs were announced, there seemed more hope than there had been in years that Sri Lanka was on the path to national recovery.

On the other hand, he had no apologies or remorse for the victims of the war. He would promise the Buddhist monks in Kandy several days later that "our motherland will never be divided [again]." Furthermore, he told them that there were only two types of Sri Lankans, those who love the motherland and those who do not. And yet democracy, as imperfect as it is, has a way of working wonders. Months later, in order to win a national election, Rajapaksa had no choice but to court the Tamil minority. And that, in turn, led the Buddhist leader to do such things as offer public prayer at a Hindu temple. The religious divide in Sri Lanka was never as wide as the ethnic one, and the ethnic one could be bridged, it turned out. With the Christian Prabakharan dead, Sri Lanka now looked set to enter a new and productive phase of history. The diplomats and NGO officials I had met during my visit were by and large skeptical about Rajapaksa's ability to reform himself. But one hoped that their pessimism was misplaced. And if it was, we can thank democracy for it.

As we've seen, it was the Chinese who had partly allowed this victory to happen, since for the West, to its credit, not even the most desirable of ends could justify certain means. Yet, as morally uncomfortable as it may be to countenance, the Chinese aid model does have its logic. In his 1968 classic, *Political Order in Changing Societies,* the late Harvard professor Samuel P. Huntington points out what Thomas Hobbes and Walter Lippmann had observed earlier, that authority, even of a brutal kind, is preferable to none at all. *Oh, how we have learned that lesson in Iraq!* While we in the West scan the developing world for moral purity, decrying corruption in backward societies, the Chinese are content with stability, no matter how illegitimately conceived. Our foreign aid emphasis is on democracy, human rights, and civil society; theirs is on massive infrastructure projects and authority, civil or not.

We should keep in mind that our goals have been determined by our own unique historical experience, which, as Huntington notes, has been about limiting the power of authority, since our institutional practices were imported easily from seventeenth-century England, whereas much of the rest of the world has had to build a legitimate authority from scratch.[19] Thus, America's historical experience is not always irrelevant to many of the very countries that will be at center stage in the new century. Weak, unresponsive, or nonexistent government institutions define significant swathes of geography, as we are still living, and will be for some more decades, with the aftermath of the dismantlement of European empires that have exposed regimes in Eurasia and Africa to the rigors of modernity.

The competition between the development models of America and China is, of course, most pronounced in Africa, at the western end of the Indian Ocean, but it is Burma where I next want to turn, a place where not only the United States and China, but India, too, is deeply involved. Burma will be as pivotal to the Bay of Bengal region as Pakistan will be to the Arabian Sea. Whereas Pakistan is akin to the Balkans, with its tendency for dissolution, Burma is like early-twentieth-century Belgium, with its tendency to be overrun by great contiguous powers.[20]

CHAPTER TWELVE

BURMA

WHERE INDIA AND CHINA COLLIDE

Monsoon clouds crushed the dark, seaweed green landscape of eastern Burma. The steep hillsides glistened with teak, coconut palms, black and ocher mud from the heavy rains, and tall, chaotic grasses. When night fell, the loud buzz saw of cicadas and the pestering croaks of geckos competed with the downpour. I stumbled on three bamboo planks over a fast-moving stream into Burma, guided by an ethnic Karen soldier with a torchlight attached by naked copper wires to an ancient six-volt battery slung around his neck. The danger was less Burmese government troops than the Thai military. Because of logging and other commercial interests, the democratically elected government of Thailand at the time was a close friend of the military regime in Burma. The Thai prime minister Samak Sundaravej had said that the ruling Burmese generals are "good Buddhists" who like to meditate, and that Burma is a country that "lives in peace." Thus, the Thai military was on the lookout for Karen soldiers who as a minority hill tribe have been fighting successive Burmese regimes since 1948.

"It ended in Vietnam, in Cambodia. When will it end in Burma?" asked Saw Roe Key, a Karen I met as soon as I had crossed the border, who lost a leg to a toe-popper anti-personnel mine. It was the kind of mine with which the military regime has littered villages throughout the hill tracts of Burma, which cover 40 percent of the country, and where more than a half dozen ethnic groups, including the Karen, have long been in some stage of revolt. Of about two dozen Karens I met at an outpost just inside Burma, four were missing a leg from a mine. They were

otherwise a motley collection. Some wore green camouflage fatigues, and were armed with M-16s and AK-47s; most were in T-shirts and traditional skirts (*longyis*). The outpost was a jumble of wooden plank huts on stilts, roofed with dried teak leaves, and built into a hillside under the forest canopy. It was continually being devoured by beetles, malarial mosquitoes, and other insects, yet was equipped with a solar panel and an ingenious water system. Beyond it beckoned perfectly rugged guerrilla country at a strategic junction of the Indian Ocean world. Here in this jungle was not only where anti-regime ethnic guerrillas and the Burmese government collided, but where an India looking eastward and a China looking southward did, too.

Sawbawh Pah, fifty, a small, stocky man with a tuft of hair on his scalp, ran a clinic for wounded soldiers and people uprooted from their homes, of which there have been 1.5 million in Burma. With three thousand villages razed in Karen State alone, the *Washington Post* calls Burma a "slow-motion Darfur."[1] Pah told me, with a simple, resigned expression, "My father was killed by the SPDC [State Peace and Development Council, the Burmese junta]. My uncle was killed by the SPDC. My cousin was killed by the SPDC. They shot my uncle in the head and cut off his leg while he was looking for food after the village was destroyed." During a meal of fried noodles and eggs, in which a toilet roll substituted for napkins, I was inundated with life stories like Pah's whose power lay in their grueling repetition.

Major Kea Htoo, the commander of the local battalion of Karen guerrillas, had reddened lips and a swollen left cheek from chewing betel nut his whole life. He saw his village burnt, along with his family's "paddy," or rice. "They raped the women, they killed the buffalo." *They* were the SPDC or, if the event occurred before 1997, the SLORC (State Law and Order Restoration Council), the menacing acronym by which the Burmese junta previously was known. He, like the others I met, including the four with missing limbs, all told me that they saw no end to the war. They were not fighting for strictly a better regime in Burma, composed of more enlightened military officers, nor for a democratic government that would likely be led by ethnic Burmans like Aung San Suu Kyi, but for Karen independence. Tu Lu, missing a leg, had been in the Karen army for twenty years. Kyi Aung, the oldest at fifty-five, had been fighting for thirty-four years. These guerrillas were paid no salaries. They received only food and basic medicine. Life for them had been condensed to a seemingly unrealistic goal of independence, mainly because nobody since Burma first fell under military misrule in 1962 had ever offered them anything resembling a compromise.

For the moment, the war in Burma was on an exceedingly low boil, with the military junta trapping the Karens, Shans, and other ethnics into small redoubts of territory near the Thai border. Yet the regime, beset by its own problems—a corrupt and desertion-plagued armed forces— seemingly lacked the strength for the final kill. And the ethnics were tough, with a strong sense of historical identity that had little connection to the Burmese state. So they tried to fight on.

Burma's agony could be reduced to the singular inconsequential fact that because of endless conflict and gross, regime-inflicted underdevelopment, it is still sufficiently primitive to maintain an aura of romance. Thus, it joins Tibet and Darfur in a trio of *causes,* whose moral urgency in each case is buttressed by an aesthetic fascination for its advocates in the post-industrial West. In 1952 the British writer Norman Lewis published a book about his travels throughout Burma, *Golden Earth,* a spare and haunting masterpiece in which the insurrections of the Karen, Shan, and other hill tribes hover in the background, helping to make the author's travels dangerous and, therefore, extremely uncomfortable. Only a small region in the north, inhabited largely by the Kachin, was "completely free of bandits or insurgent armies." He spent a night tormented by rats, cockroaches, and a scorpion, yet woke none the worse in the morning to the "mighty whirring of hornbills flying overhead." Indeed, his bodily sufferings were a small price to pay for the uncanny monochromatic beauty of a country of broken roads and no adequate hotels where "the condition of the soul replaces that of the stock markets as a topic for polite conversation."[2] What is shocking about this more-than-half-century-old book is how contemporary it seems. Think of all the places where because of globalization even a ten-year-old travel book is already out of date.

But Burma is more than a place for which to feel sorry. And its ethnic struggles are of more than obscurantist interest. For one thing, with a third of the country's population composed of ethnic minorities in its friable borderlands—accounting for seven of Burma's fourteen states—the demands of the Karens and other minorities truly will come to the fore once the regime does collapse. Democracy will not solve Burma's dilemma of being a mini-empire of nationalities, even if it does open the door to a compromise. More than that, however, Burma's hill tribes are part of a new and larger canvas of geopolitics. Burma fronts on the Indian Ocean, by way of the Bay of Bengal. It is bordered by India and China, both of which covet Burma's abundant reserves of oil, natural gas, uranium, coal, zinc, copper, precious stones, timber, and hydropower. China, especially, desires Burma as a vassal state for the construction of deep-water ports, highways, and energy pipelines that will provide China's landlocked south and west access to the sea, from where China's ever-burgeoning middle class can receive deliveries of oil from the Persian Gulf. And these routes must pass from the Indian Ocean north through the very territories plagued historically by Burma's ethnic insurrections.

In short, Burma provides a code for understanding the world to come. It is a prize to be fought over, as China and India are not so subtly doing. Recognizing the importance of what Burma and its neighbors represent at a time of new energy pathways, unstable fuel prices, and seaboard natural disasters like Burma's 2008 cyclone and the Indian Ocean tsunami of 2004, the U.S. Navy has suggested that it will no longer be forward-deployed permanently in the Atlantic, but instead will concentrate in the coming years and decades on the Indian Ocean and western Pacific. For the navy and the marine corps, too, Indian Ocean states like Burma are now, or should be, central to their calculations.

Strategic, romantic, and a moral catastrophe, Burma is a place that tends to consume people. And a very interesting group of Americans are consumed by it. In some cases, I cannot identify them by name, because of the tenuousness of their position in neighboring Thailand, which they use as a base (and where I interviewed them); in other cases, because of the sensitivity of what they do and for whom they work. But their story is worthwhile to tell because of the expertise they bring to bear, and what their own goals say about the geopolitical stakes in Burma.

Lately, it has become fashionable to extol the virtues of cultural area expertise given how the lack of it contributed to the mess in Iraq, even as it is forgotten that America's greatest area experts have been Christian missionaries. American history has seen two strains of missionary-area experts, the old Arab hands and the Asia, or China, hands. The Arab hands were Protestant missionaries who traveled to Lebanon in the early nineteenth century and ended up founding what was to become the American University in Beirut. From their lineage descended the State

Department Arabists of the Cold War era. The Asia hands have a similarly distinguished origin, beginning, too, in the nineteenth century and providing the U.S. government with much of its area expertise through the early Cold War, when a number of them were unjustly purged during the McCarthy-era hearings on China. The American who counseled me on Burma was the descendant of several generations of Baptist missionaries from the Midwest who ministered to the Burmese hill tribes beginning in the late nineteenth century, particularly in the Shan States and across the Chinese border in Yunnan. His father was known as the Blue-eyed Shan. Escaping Burma on the heels of the invading Japanese, his father was conscripted into Britain's Indian Army in which he commanded a Shan battalion during World War II. Thus, my acquaintance had grown up in India and postwar Burma. Among his earliest memories was the sight of Punjabi soldiers ordering work gangs of Japanese prisoners of war to pick up rubble in the Burmese capital of Rangoon. With no formal education, he spoke Shan, Burmese, Hindi, Lao, Thai, and the Yunnan and Mandarin dialects of Chinese. He had spent his life studying Burma, though the 1960s saw him elsewhere in Indochina aiding America's effort in Vietnam.

During our first conversation he sat erect and cross-legged on a raised platform, wearing a traditional Burmese *longyi* in his home. He was gray haired, with a sculpted face and an authoritative Fred Thompson voice that gave him a courtly bearing: very much the wise elder statesman tempered by a certain oriental gentleness. Around him were a few books and photos: of butterfly wings, of the king and queen of Thailand, and of himself as a muscular young man with a bandolier and machete in Vietnam.

"Chinese intelligence is beginning to operate with the anti-regime Burmese ethnic hill tribes," he told me. "The Chinese want the dictatorship in Burma to remain, but being pragmatic, they also have alternative plans for the country. The warning that comes from senior Chinese intelligence officers to the Karens, the Shans, and other ethnics is 'to come to us for help—not the Americans—since we are next door and will never leave the area.' "

At the same time, he explained, the Chinese were beginning to reach out to young military officers in Thailand. In recent years, the Thai royal family and the Thai military, particularly the special forces and cavalry, have been sympathetic to the hill tribes fighting the pro-Chinese military junta in Burma; whereas Thailand's civilian politicians, influenced by various lobbies wanting to do business with resource-rich Burma, have been the junta's best allies. In sum, democracy in Thailand has been at times the enemy of democracy in Burma.

But the Chinese, he implied, are still not satisfied: they want *both* Thailand's democrats and military officers on their side, even as they work with *both* Burma's junta and its ethnic opponents. "A new bamboo curtain may be coming down on Southeast Asia," he worried. If such a thing were to happen, it would not be a hard and fast wall like the iron curtain; nor would it be part of some newly imagined Asian domino theory, similar to what was believed in the Vietnam era. Rather, it would be a discreet zone of Chinese political and economic influence fostered by, among other factors, relative American neglect, which was somewhat the case during the administration of George W. Bush. While the Chinese are operating at every level in Burma and Thailand, top Bush administration officials had periodically missed summits of the Association of Southeast Asian Nations (ASEAN). And while China has launched twenty-seven separate ASEAN-China mechanisms in the past decade, the U.S. has launched only seven in thirty years.[3] My friend wanted the U.S. back in the game. And thus far the Obama administration has obliged him.*

"To topple the regime in Burma," he said, "the ethnics need a full-time advisory capability, not in-and-out soldiers of fortune. This would include a coordination center inside Thailand. There needs to be a platform for all the disaffected officers in the Burmese military to defect to." Again, rather than a return to the early Vietnam era, he was talking about a more subtle and clandestine version of the kind of support the U.S. provided the Afghan mujahidin fighting the Soviets from bases inside Pakistan during the 1980s. The pro-Karen Thai military could yet return to power in Bangkok, and even if it did not, if the U.S. signaled its intent to provide serious support to the Burmese hill tribes against a regime hated the world over, the Thai security apparatus would find a way to assist.

"The Shans and the Kachins near the Chinese border," he went on, "have gotten a raw deal from the Burmese junta, but they are also nervous about a dominant China. They feel squeezed. And unity for the hill

---

* By appointing special envoys for Israel-Palestine, Afghanistan-Pakistan, and North Korea, Secretary of State Hillary Clinton has been freed up to concentrate on the Indian Ocean and Asia-Pacific regions. Structurally, the State Department is now better organized than in decades for adjusting to a rising China and India.

tribes of Burma is almost impossible. Somebody from the outside must provide a mechanism upon which they can all depend."

Burma should not be confused with the Balkans, or with Iraq, where ethnic and sectarian differences simmering for decades under a carapace of authoritarianism erupted once central authority dissolved. The hill tribes have been at war with successive Burmese regimes for decades. War fatigue has set in, and the tribes show little propensity to fight one another were the regime to unravel. They are more disunited than they are at odds. Even among themselves, as he told me, the Shan have been historically subdivided into states led by minor kings. Thus, there might be a quiet organizing role for Americans of his ilk.

He mentioned Singapore leader Lee Kuan Yew's warning that the U.S. must stay engaged in the region as a "counterbalance to the Chinese giant"; the U.S. being the only outsider power with the wherewithal to slow down Beijing's advance, even though it has no territorial designs of its own in Asia. Southeast Asian nations in general, and Vietnam in particular, with its own historic fear of China, wanted Washington to counter Beijing in Burma. Thailand, with a monarchical succession ahead of it that could usher in an era of unstable politics, fears falling further under Chinese influence. Not even the Burmese junta, my friend said, wanted to be part of a Greater China. There are memories still of the long, grueling, and bloody Manchu invasion in the eighteenth century. It is just that the Burmese generals have had no choice, if they want to remain in power.

Burma is destined to be an energy conduit for China in any event. But it need not become a de facto province of China, and be eternally governed by one of the world's most brutal regimes: raped of its natural resources as the generals line their pockets, and veritable slave labor builds its pipelines—financed in part by multinationals in an example of the dark, unconscionable side of globalization. Much may still depend on how the U.S. acts. And my elderly acquaintance, who believes in quietly working in the shadows, armed less with guns than with area expertise, needs people to carry on his life's work, and, more specifically, people to whom he can hand over his networks deep inside Burma.

Another American working inside Burma was Tha-U-Wa-A-Pa, "the Father of the White Monkey" in Burmese, a sobriquet that came from the endearing nickname he calls his daughter. He, too, is the son of Christian missionaries in the region, originally from Texas. Except for nine years in the U.S. Army, including time in Special Forces from which he retired as a major, like his parents he had been a missionary in one form or another his whole adult life. He also spoke a number of the local languages. He was much younger than my other acquaintance. And unlike him, he was very animated, with a ropy, muscular bullet-like physique that is in perpetual motion, as if his system is running on too many candy bars. Whereas my other contact had concentrated his life's work on the Shan tribes near the Chinese border, the Father of the White Monkey worked, for the most part, with the Karen and other tribes in eastern Burma abutting Thailand, though the networks he operated have ranged as far as the Indian border on the opposite side of the country.

In 1996 he met the Burmese democracy leader Aung San Suu Kyi in Rangoon, during a brief period when she was not under house arrest. The meeting inspired him to initiate a "day of prayer" for Burma, and to work for ethnic unity within the country. During the 1997 Burmese army offensive that displaced hundreds of thousands of people, he was deep inside Burma, alone, going to the "worst places," from one burned-out village to another, handing out medicine from his backpack. He told me about this and other army offensives that he has witnessed, in which churches were torched, children disemboweled, and whole families killed. "These stories don't make me numb," he said, his eyes popping open wide, his facial muscles stretched in emotion. "Each is like the first one. I pray always that justice will come and be done."

In 1997, after that trip inside Burma, he started the Free Burma Rangers, which has more than three hundred volunteers working in forty-three small medical teams among the Karen, Karenni, Shan, Chin, Kachin, and Arakanese, virtually the whole of highland Burma that embraces on three sides the central Irrawaddy River valley, home to the majority Burmans.* The Free Burma Rangers are a very unique kind of relief group, or nongovernmental organization.

"We stand with the villagers, we're not above them. If they don't run from the government troops, we don't either. We have a medic, a photographer, and a reporter-intel guy in each team that marks the GPS positions of Burmese government troops, maps the camps and takes pictures with

---

* "Burmese" signifies a nationality, "Burman" an ethnicity.

a telephoto lens, all of which we post on our website. We deal with the Pentagon, with human rights groups. . . . There is a higher moral obligation to intervene on the side of good, since silence is a form of consent.

"NGOs," he went on in a racing voice, "like to claim that they are above politics. Not true. The very act of providing aid assists one side or another, however indirectly. NGOs take sides all the time." There was ample proof of this in recent history. In the 1980s, NGOs working among Afghan refugees in Pakistan's North-West Frontier Province essentially helped the Afghan mujahidin in their struggle against the pro-Moscow Afghan government, just as aid workers in Sudan during the same period helped ethnic Eritreans and Tigreans in their military struggle against the Marxist Ethiopian government. And here on the Thai borderland, an underground railway for guns was mixed in with relief supplies.

The Father of the White Monkey had taken this hard truth several steps further. Whereas the Thais host Burmese refugee camps on their side of the border and the ethnic insurgents run camps inside Burma for internally displaced people—even while the Karens and other ethnics have mobile clinics in forward positions near Burmese army concentrations—the backpacking Free Burma Rangers actually operated behind enemy lines. The Father of the White Monkey was, like my other acquaintance, a very evolved form of special operator: the kind that the U.S. security bureaucracy can barely accept, for he was taking sides and going native to a degree. Yet these special operators command the level of expertise that the U.S. desperately needs if it is to have influence without being overbearing in remote parts of the globe. Here is the Father of the White Monkey talking about the Wa, to whom he had been exposed relatively little, compared to his years of living in the jungle with the Karen and other tribes:

"The Wa were the muscle of the Burmese communists. They were armed by the Chinese. In 1989, around the time of the Tiananmen Square uprising, they declared independence and kicked the Chinese out. They were willing to give up their opium production in return for a crop substitution program and arms to fight the Burmese military government with. But they found no takers in the West for their offer. The Free Burma Rangers now have a small-scale medical aid program for the Wa. The Wa are in bed with Than Shwe [the Burmese junta leader] only because they have nowhere else to turn."

One might suspect that the Free Burma Rangers are on some government payroll in Washington. But the truth is more pathetic. "We are funded by church groups around the world. Our yearly budget is $600,000. We were down to $150 at one point, we all prayed and the next day got a grant for $70,000. We work hand to mouth." On some of his missions inside Burma, the Father of the White Monkey took his wife and three small children along. Like my other acquaintance, Burma was not a job for him, it was his life obsession.

"Burma is not Cambodia under the Khmer Rouge," he told me. "It's not genocide. It's not a car wreck. It's a slow, creeping cancer, in which the regime is working to dominate, control, and radically assimilate all the ethnic peoples of the country." I was reminded of what Jack Dunford, executive director of the Thailand Burma Border Consortium, said to me in Bangkok. The Burmese military regime is "relentless like clockwork, building dams, roads, and huge agricultural projects, taking over mines, laying pipelines," sucking in cash from neighboring powers and foreign companies, selling off natural resources at below-market value, all in order to further entrench itself in power. Burma is a land of mass rape, child soldiers, and large-scale narcotics trafficking, with Wa armies mass-producing amphetamines.

Once, not long ago, the Father of the White Monkey was sitting on a hillside at night in Burma, in an exposed location between the Burmese army and a cluster of internal refugees whom the army had made flee their homes. The Karen soldiers he was with had fired rocket-propelled grenades at the Burmese army position, and in response the Burmese soldiers began firing mortar rounds at them. At this point he got a message from a friend at the Pentagon on the communications gear with which he was equipped asking him why the U.S. should be interested in Burma.

He tapped back a slew of reasons that ranged from totalitarianism to the devastation of hardwood forests, to religious persecution of Buddhist monks, to the use of prisoner labor as minesweepers, and much else. But he did not touch much on strategic or regional security issues. As I said, the Father of the White Monkey is very much the missionary. When I asked him his denomination, he responded, "I'm a Christian." As such, he was doing God's work, engaged morally first and foremost, especially among the Karen, among whom number many Christians, converted by people like his parents.

Army Colonel Timothy Heinemann (Ret.) of Laguna Beach, California, did think strategically. He was also a veteran of Special Forces, whom I met in 2002 at the Command and General Staff College at Fort Leavenworth, Kansas, where he was the dean of academics. He now ran an NGO, Worldwide Impact, which helped ethnic groups, primarily Karens; as well as a number of cross-border projects, with a special emphasis on sending media teams into Burma to record the suffering there. Another evolved type of special operator, Heinemann, in his flip-flops and engaging manner, embodied the indirect approach to conflict emphasized in the 2006 "Quadrennial Defense Review," one of the Pentagon's primary planning documents. Heinemann told me that he "privatizes condition setting." He explained: "We are networkers on both sides of the border. We try to find opportunities for NGOs to collaborate better in supporting ethnic group needs. I do my small part to set conditions so that America can protect national, international, and humanitarian interests with real savvy. Our work is well known to various branches of the U.S. government. The opposition to the Burmese military dictatorship has no strategic and operational planning like Hezbollah does. Aung San Suu Kyi is little more than a symbol of the wrong issue—'Democracy first!' Ethnic rights and the balance of ethnic power are preconditions for democracy in Burma. These issues must be faced first, or little has been learned from Afghanistan and Iraq." Heinemann, like the Father of the White Monkey, lives hand to mouth, grabbing grants and donations from wherever he can, and is sometimes reduced to financing trips himself. He found Burma "exotic, intoxicating."

But Burma is also, he went on, a potential North Korea, as well as a perfect psychological operations target for the U.S. military and other agencies. He and others explained that the Russians were helping the Burmese government in the Kachin and Chin regions in the north and west of the country to mine uranium, with the North Koreans waiting in the wings to help them with nuclear technology. The Burmese junta craves some sort of weapons-of-mass-destruction capacity to provide it with international leverage, in order to help perpetuate itself in power. "But the regime is paranoid," Heinemann pointed out. "It's superstitious. They're rolling chicken bones on the ground to see what to do next.

"Burma's got a 400,000-man army [the active-duty U.S. Army is 500,000] that's prone to mutiny," Heinemann continued. "Only the men at the very top are loyal. You could spread rumors, conduct information warfare. It might not take much to unravel it." Indeed, Burmese soldiers reportedly were getting only a portion of their salaries, and their weapons at major bases were locked up at night. On the other hand, the military constituted the country's most secure social-welfare system, complete with hospitals and schools, and that bought a certain amount of loyalty from the troops.[4] Yet, "there is no trust by the higher-ups in the lower ranks," said a Karen resistance source. The junta leader, Than Shwe, a former postal clerk who has never been to the West, was known along with his wife to consult an astrologer. "He governs out of fear, he is not brave," noted Aung Zaw, editor of *The Irrawaddy,* a magazine run by Burmese exiles in the northwestern Thai city of Chiang Mai. "And Than Shwe rarely speaks publicly, he has even less charisma than Ne Win," the dictator from 1962 to 1988.

Heinemann and Aung Zaw each recounted to me how the regime suddenly deserted Rangoon one day in 2005 and moved the capital north to Naypyidaw ("the abode of kings"), halfway between Rangoon and Mandalay, which it built from scratch, with funds from Burma's natural gas revenues. The new capital lies deep in the forest and is marked by underground bunkers against an American invasion, which the regime fears. The date of the move was astrologically timed. Heinemann viewed China, India, and other Asian nations jockeying for position with one of the world's worst, weirdest, wealthiest, and most strategically placed rogue regimes, which all the while is prone to a coup or disintegration even, if only the U.S. adopted the kind of patient, low-key, and inexpensive approach advocated by him and my other two acquaintances.

Heinemann's last job in the military was as a planner for the occupation phase of the Iraq war, and he was eyewitness to the mistakes of a massive military machine disregarding local realities. He saw Burma as the inverse of Iraq, a place where the U.S. could do itself a lot of good, and do much good besides, if it fought smart.

Another American I met who was consumed by Burma saw me in his suite in one of Bangkok's most expensive hotels. A staff sergeant in Special Forces in the 1970s, he was now a resident of Singapore, where he worked in the security business, and preferred to be identified by his Burmese nickname, Ta Doe Tee ("The Bull That Swims"). His expensive black, tailored clothes barely masked an intimidating muscular physique.

He put on reading glasses and opened a shiny black loose-leaf notebook with a map of the Indian Ocean. There was a line drawn on the map that went from Ethiopia and Somalia across the water past India, and then north up the Bay of Bengal, through the heart of Burma, to China's Yunnan Province. "This map is just an example of how CNOOC [the China National Offshore Oil Corporation] sees the world," the Bull explained.

He showed me another map, which zoomed in on Ethiopia and Somalia, with grid marks on the significant reserves of oil and natural gas in the Ogaden basin on the Ethiopian-Somali border. A circle was drawn around Hobyo, a Somali port visited in the early fifteenth century by the Chinese admiral Zheng He, whose treasure fleets plied back and forth across the Indian Ocean along the same sea-lanes as today's energy routes. "In this scenario, the oil and natural gas would be shipped from Hobyo direct to western Burma," the Bull told me, where the Chinese are building a new port at Kyauk Phru, on Ramree Island there, in Arakan State. It is capable of handling the world's largest containerships. According to the Bull, the map showed how easy it will be for the Chinese to operate all over the Indian Ocean, "tapping into Iran and other Persian Gulf energy suppliers." Their biggest problem, though, will be cutting through Burma. "The Chinese need to acquire Burma, and keep it stable," he said.

China's drive southward and India's drive both westward and eastward—to keep it from being strategically encircled by China's navy—means that both powers collide in Burma. As China and India vie for power and influence, Burma has become a quiet, strategic battleground.

Until 2001, India, the world's largest democracy, took the high road on Burma, condemning it for its repression and providing moral support for the cause of opposition leader Aung San Suu Kyi, who had studied in New Delhi. But as senior Indian leaders had told me on a visit to New Delhi, India could not just stand by and watch Chinese influence expand there unabated. Burma's jungles serve as a rear base for insurgents from eastern India's own mélange of warring ethnic groups. Furthermore, as Greg Sheridan, foreign editor of *The Australian,* writes: India has been "aghast" to see such developments as the establishment of Chinese signals intelligence listening stations along Burma's border with India.[5] So in 2001, India decided to engage Burma comprehensively, providing it with military aid and training, including the sale of tanks, helicopters, shoulder-fired surface-to-air missiles, and rocket launchers.

India has also decided to build its own energy pipeline network through Burma. In fact, during the 2007 crackdown of the monks in Burma, India's petroleum minister signed a deal for deepwater exploration. Off the coast of Burma's western Arakan State adjacent to Bangladesh are the Shwe gas fields, among the largest natural reserves in the world, from which two pipeline systems will likely emerge. One will be China's at the nearby port of Kyauk Phru, which in the future may take deliveries of oil and gas from as far away as the Persian Gulf and the Horn of Africa, as well as from Shwe itself. The hope is that not every China-bound tanker will have to travel from the Middle East across the entire Indian Ocean, then through the Strait of Malacca and the Indonesian archipelago to get to China's middle-class population centers, which lie too close for comfort to the Strait of Taiwan and the U.S. Navy. The other pipeline system is India's. India is spending $100 million to develop the Arakanese port of Sittwe as a trade window to open up its own landlocked, insurgency-wracked northeast. This pipeline will go north through Arakan and Chin provinces, and then split into two sections: one transiting Bangladesh to Kolkata, and the other reaching Kolkata by transiting Indian territory all the way around Bangladesh.

There is nothing sinister about any of this; it is all wholly legitimate, and the consequence of the intense need of hundreds of millions of people in India and in China who will be consuming ever more amounts of energy as their lifestyles improve.

But the devil is in the details. The most direct route into the heart of China is through Burma, not through Pakistan or Bangladesh. And China's attitude toward Burma is, as it happens, similar to its attitude toward North Korea. Beijing is both aware and uncomfortable with the demented natures of Than Shwe and Kim Jong Il. It would surely prefer less morally repulsive rulers as allies. But as we have seen in Sri Lanka, China is not like the U.S., whose leaders, both Democrat and Republican, seek the moral improvement of the world as a basis of foreign policy. China is interested in Burma and North Korea for the long term. It may even foresee democracy in those places on some distant morrow. That is why, in Burma's case, the Chinese have initiated contacts with the ethnic hill tribes and with the democratic opposition. Beijing does not want to be caught by surprise again, as it reportedly was during the revolt of the monks in September 2007. Meanwhile, it makes do in the short term by substantially fortifying one of the world's most repressive regimes.

The moral problem goes beyond China or India, however. For example, Chevron and its French partner, Total, are involved in the Yadana pipeline project that brings Burmese natural gas into Thailand. The problem is that the Burmese army, responsible for pipeline security, at least according to some human rights groups, had confiscated the land from villagers along the pipeline route, conscripted them as forced labor in order to grow rice and carry military supplies, and committed rape and torture. As Indian Ocean energy politics gather force in the twenty-first century, the nearly fifty million people of Burma could be the losers in this process: a victim of the evil confluence of totalitarianism, realpolitik, and corporate profits. In eastern Burma, forests are being destroyed, with truck caravans of timber rolling nonstop into China. In western Burma, whole ecosystems and cultural sites will be under attack from the new pipelines, according to Arakanese resistance sources with whom I spoke.

As indicated in Chapter Eight, Arakan has a large Muslim population composed of Rohingyas, more than 200,000 of whom have taken refuge in Bangladesh from massive military repression in Burma. Each of Burma's many indigenous peoples, all with their own history that usually is marked by centuries of independence, have suffered like the Rohingyas in their own way under the junta, and have different demands. Thus, even if the military regime were to fall tomorrow, Burma could be a political mess for years to come.

This brings me back to the Bull That Swims, who thought a lot, as he told me, about Burma beyond the Than Shwe regime. He explained that grand lines on a map and the plans of master strategists over broad regions of the globe are often bedeviled by the minutiae of tribal and ethnic differences in one particular place. Just look at the former Yugoslavia and Iraq. This led him to talk about the struggles of the Karens, Shans, Arakanese, and other minorities, and how they will constitute the "theater of activity" for his lifetime. Burma is where the U.S. has to build a "UW [unconventional war] capability," he said, for China's problems are only just beginning in Burma.

The discussion went along similar lines as those with the other three Americans. The Bull talked about the need to build and manage networks among the ethnic hill tribes, through the construction of schools, clinics, and irrigation systems. Such would be the unofficial side of America's competition with China, which might be compelled over time to accept a democratic and highly federalized Burma, with strong links to the West.

But the problem is that while the former Green Berets and other Asia hands I interviewed saw Burma as central to American strategy, the active duty Special Operations community did not, because it has been under orders to be focused on al-Qaeda. And except for the Muslim Rohingyas, whose terrorist potential still remains theoretical, Burma lacks an Islamic terrorist theme. U.S. Special Operations Command was preoccupied mainly with the Arab-Persian western half of the Indian Ocean and much less so with the eastern half. This, my acquaintances said, was an example of how America's overwhelming obsession with al-Qaeda has warped its larger strategic vision, which should be dominated by the whole Indian Ocean, from Africa to the Pacific.

The Bull next spoke to me about the Shans, the largest of the ethnic hill tribes with 9 percent of Burma's population but about 20 percent of its territory. A close relationship between the U.S. government and the Shans that would feature substantial amounts of cross-border humanitarian aid could be achieved through cooperation with the Thai military and royal family, which would buttress America's aid with investment of their own in northeastern Burma. Allying with the Shans, he said, would give the U.S. a mechanism to curtail the flow of drugs in the area, and to create a balancing force against China right on its own border. In any democratic scenario for Burma, the Shans would control a sizable portion of the seats in parliament. More could be accomplished through nonlethal aid to a specific Burmese hill tribe, the Bull indicated, than many of the larger defense programs on which the U.S. spends money. The same strategy could be applied to the Chins in western Burma, with the help of India. Not just in Iraq, but in Burma, too, in the coming years, it would be about informal relationships with tribes, he emphasized.

The Bull was passionate about Burma and Southeast Asia, and about a role for people like himself there. He was of the Army Special Forces generation that was frustrated about having just missed service in Vietnam, with little to do overseas during the presidency of Jimmy Carter. *Outpost of Freedom,* published in 1965 by Roger Donlon, was the inspirational book of his youth, about Donlon's experiences as the first Medal of Honor winner in Vietnam. Stationed at Fort Devens, Massachusetts, in the mid-1970s, the Bull was mentored, commanded, and led by some of the Son Tay raiders themselves. "Dick Meadows, Greg McGuire, Jack Joplin, Joe Lupyak" are names he recited with reverence: Green Berets who stormed the Son Tay prison camp near Hanoi in 1970 in a failed attempt to rescue American prisoners of war. "Vietnam and Southeast Asia was all they ever talked about," he told me.

But in 1978, Carter's head of the Central Intelligence Agency, Admiral Stansfield Turner, fired or forced into retirement almost two hundred officers running agents stationed abroad, who had been providing human intelligence, and many of them were in Southeast Asia. The CIA's clandestine service was devastated. As the Bull told the story, many of the fired officers would not simply "be turned off," and decided to maintain self-supporting networks, "picking up kids" like himself along the way, just out of Special Forces. They sent him to learn to sail and fly, and he became a certified ship master for cargo vessels and an FAA-certified pilot. In the 1980s he became involved in operations in Southeast Asia, such as bringing equipment to the Khmer Rouge in Cambodia. He blurred the line between such controversial and shadowy government operations and the illegal means sometimes used to sustain them. In 1988, while trying to bring seventy tons of marijuana to the West Coast of the United States with a Southeast Asian crew under his command, he was boarded by the U.S. Coast Guard. He served five years in a U.S. prison and then went back to Southeast Asia, where he has been ever since. He is older now, as he told me, with a lifetime in the region of leveraging indigenous forces. His business card defined him as a "compradore," an all-purpose factotum with a deep cultural footprint in the region—in fact, the kind of enabler who was vital to the running of the British East India Company. He believed that America's future competition with China will be characterized by ambiguity rather than overt hostility. Uniformed forces will be less necessary than men like himself. Whereas the heroes of his youth were focused on Vietnam, he believed that Burma and its tribes can provide the circumstances for the use of his considerable talents, which, in the case of the Shans, will emphasize both discretion and a humanitarian approach.

I was uneasy with him and with parts of his background. As subtle and responsible as his approach might arguably be, one should not easily discount the dangers of what he and these other Americans recommended. The most important relationship in the twenty-first century likely will be the one between the U.S. and China, and care has to be taken not to casually disrupt it. The U.S. saw the costs of speaking loudly and carrying a small stick in the Russian invasion of Georgia in 2008. Thus, if we are to ramp up support of the ethnics in Burma, one cannot emphasize strongly enough that it will have to be done in a way that quietly pressures China toward better behavior in Burma, rather than quietly enrages it. The result should not be some destructive action that America is powerless to deter.

I say this as Burma prepares for national elections, which were announced in January 2010. As I write, it was impossible to know what the outcome of these elections will be and, more important, how they will be conducted and what pent-up political forces they will unleash. But the very holding of them may indicate that constructive engagement between the West and the Burmese regime will achieve more than any American adventurism with the Burmese ethnics. The ethnics are important, no doubt, and they have been relatively ignored in media analyses of Burmese affairs, so that motivates my concentration on them. Still, democracy may be even more crucial. And the decision to hold elections in the first place seemed at least partly to be the fruit of the Obama administration's outreach to the junta.

If America is destined in some way, as these four Americans believe, to become enmeshed in Burmese politics—as it was with Afghan tribes in the 1980s, Yugoslavian ethnic groups in the 1990s, Sunni and Shiite factions in Iraq in this decade, as well as Afghan tribes once again—then some historical background is in order. For "the most striking aspect of the Burma debate today is its . . . singularly ahistorical nature," writes historian Thant Myint-U, who goes on:

> Dictatorship and the prospects for democracy are seen within the prism of the past ten or twenty years, as if three Anglo-Burmese wars, a century of colonial rule, an immensely destructive Japanese invasion and occupation, and five decades of civil war, foreign intervention, and Communist insurgency had never happened.[6]

So consider the following, therefore, as a very short primer for possible headlines to come in future years.

Burmese history was affected by geographical fluidity on the one hand and by religious-cultural isolation on the other. Whereas trade routes brought Burma into contact with both China and the Indian Subcontinent, Burma's Theravada Buddhism isolated it from both Hindu India and Confucian China.[7] The result is a unique history that was, nevertheless, influenced by outsiders.

In the Middle Ages there were three principal kingdoms in the plains and jungles between India and Siam (Thailand): those of Arakan, Mon, and Myanmar, the last being the Burman word for the central Irrawaddy River valley and its environs. Myanmar eventually conquered the other two kingdoms in the late eighteenth century. Henceforth, the Mon capital of Dagon was renamed Yangon, the Burman word for "The End of Strife," corrupted by foreigners into "Rangoon." In addition, there were the hill kingdoms of the Chin, Kachin, Shan, Karen, and Karenni which remained independent, even as they were attacked by marauders from Myanmar. These hill kingdoms were also divided from within: for example, the strife-torn Shan States were also home to hostile Was, Lahus, Paos, Kayans, and other tribal peoples. Larger than England and France combined, this whole, sprawling crazy quilt of vaguely demarcated states was sectioned by a horseshoe of jungly mountain ranges, as well as by the river valleys of the Irrawaddy, Chindwin, Salween, and Mekong. The considerable ethnic diversity is evinced by the fact that Burma's various peoples trace their historic migrations back to Tibet, China, India, Bangladesh, Thailand, and Cambodia, and so, for example, the Chin in western Burma have almost nothing in common with the Karen in eastern Burma.[8] Nor is there any community of language or culture between the Shans and the Burmans save their Buddhist religion. Indeed, the Shans, who have migrated often in their history, have much more in common with the Thais across the border.* As for the Arakanese, heirs to a cosmopolitan seaboard civilization with influences particularly from Hindu Bengal, they have felt themselves so disconnected from the rest of Burma that they compare their plight to disenfranchised nations in the Middle East and Africa.[9] Only the Karen are spread out rather than restricted to a specific ethnic-national territory, with significant concentrations of them in both the eastern hill tracts and in the Irrawaddy delta.

In 1886 the British toppled the Burmese monarchy and annexed this whole area to their Indian empire. Though colonial rule lasted only sixty-two years, as Martin Smith writes in his comprehensive *Burma: Insurgency and the Politics of Ethnicity,* by moving the center of power from the royal courts at Ava and Mandalay in the heart of Burma to Rangoon and the Irrawaddy delta hundreds of miles south on the Bay of Bengal,

---

* For example, the Ahoms, a Shan people, migrated down the Brahmaputra and clashed with the Mughals in the early seventeenth century.

the British robbed the country of whatever geographic logic it had ever possessed. What's more, the British incorporated into their territory "thousands of square miles of rugged hill tracts and loosely independent mini-states" that were home to diverse minorities.[10]

The destruction of the monarchy stripped the country of centuries of tradition that had fortified society in the Irrawaddy valley since before the Middle Ages. "The new Burma, British Burma, would be adrift," writes Thant Myint-U, "suddenly pushed into the modern world without an anchor to the past," prone to bitter nationalism and extremism.[11] It was as if the British in 1886 threw Burma off a cliff from which it is still falling, 124 years later.[12] The British approach was classic divide and rule. They favored the hill tribes with local autonomy, and recruited Karens, Shans, Kachins, and other ethnics into the local army and police, even as they exerted direct and repressive control over the numerically dominant Burmans of the valley.* Had the Tory leader Winston Churchill won the 1945 election in Great Britain, the hill peoples might have become independent principalities of their own, as a reward for defending the British Empire against the Burmans, who, having chafed under British rule, became Japanese sympathizers. But the Labour Party candidate, Clement Attlee, won the election and decided to give all of Burma independence as a single unit, without a clear-cut road map to ethnic reconciliation.

During World War II the Burmese leader General Aung San and thirty comrades had gone to Japan and raised a nationalist army that would welcome the Japanese into Burma. But when Aung San returned to Burma in the midst of the war, he soon realized that the Japanese were even worse occupiers than the British had been and fortuitously switched sides. After the war he entered into negotiations with Attlee, but the ethnics claimed that Aung San, as an ethnic Burman, could not represent them. In their eyes, he could negotiate only on behalf of *Burma proper*—that is, historic Mon, Arakan, and Myanmar—not the Chin, Shan, Karen, and other hill tracts. So Aung San backtracked and, in a very wise and open-minded gesture, agreed to conduct separate negotiations with the

---

* In Brigadier Bernard Fergusson's memoir of World War II in Burma, *The Wild Green Earth* (London: Collins, 1946), he writes (p. 133): "I can do no more than commend that gallant race [of Kachins] to my countrymen, who are mostly unaware of its heroics and unsupported war against the Japs. To carry on their own, independent way of life, they will need our protection . . . like that other splendid race the Karens." This was typical of the favorable British attitude toward the hill tribes.

ethnics. Aung San looked next door at India and would see how inter-communal carnage following independence had led to a million refugees and tens of thousands dead in Bengal and the Punjab. As India moved toward bloody partition, he was determined that Burma avoid India's strife.

The result was an agreement he made in February 1947 in the little Shan town of Panglong with the local *sabwas* (feudal leaders), which helped produce the Union of Burma. It was based on three principles: a state with a decentralized federal structure, recognition of the ethnic chieftaincies in the hills, and their right of secession after a number of years.

But that July, Aung San was assassinated, and attempts at ethnic reconciliation came to a halt just as the British departed in January 1948. A new constitution was promulgated, featuring more central control, and the Karens and others consequently revolted. As the Indian writer Pankaj Mishra explains:

> Imposing a European model of the linguistically and ethnically homogenous nation-state upon such a diverse country as Burma would have been difficult in any circumstances. It was made more arduous by Japan's prolonged occupation and its ferocious battles with the British, which dispersed the authority of the old colonial state, leaving the country awash with political and ethnic groups with postcolonial ambitions—and guns—of their own.[13]

Indeed, Burma's ethnic morass was made worse by having become a maelstrom of jungle warfare between the British and Japanese. Burma was the theater of battle for the famed irregular warfare campaigns of 1943 and 1944 that the British launched from the northeastern Indian border town of Imphal, their rear base. These campaigns featured the legendary unconventional warrior Major General Orde Wingate, the son of Christian missionaries, who led long-range penetration units known as Chindits (an anglicized corruption of a mythical Burmese lion) deep behind Japanese lines in the Burmese jungles, supported by gliders. Before Wingate's daring missions, the Japanese were at the gates of British India, about to invade. Wingate helped turn the tables on them. He operated in the same area that the Chinese would now have to pacify for the sake of their pipelines, were the junta to collapse. (The Father of the White Monkey, a sort of Wingate figure in his own right, had given me a

1946 first edition of the wartime memoirs of one of Wingate's officers in Burma, with an inscription from the prophet Isaiah.)[14]

The Cold War introduced new actors into the Burmese chaos, even as the warmhearted and charismatic civilian prime minister U Nu tried, ultimately in vain, to unite the country in the wake of Aung San's death. In 1950 more than ten thousand retreating troops of Chiang Kai-shek's Chinese Nationalist Army (Kuomintang), run out of China by Mao Zedong's victorious communist soldiers, ensconced themselves in the Shan States. And in the next decade, Mao's China armed a communist guerrilla insurgency against the Burmese government that operated from the hill tracts. In response to these challenges, civilian power in Rangoon floundered as the Burmese military, now dominated by ethnic Burmans (in which minorities could rise only to the rank of major), grew to 100,000. In 1961 this army under General Ne Win managed to expel the Kuomintang out of Burma and into neighboring Laos and Thailand.

The same year in Taungya, the capital of the Shan States, non-Burman ethnic groups came together and demanded that the constitution be amended according to the spirit of the 1947 Panglong Agreement. The issue was debated in parliament and U Nu was sympathetic to the plight of the Shans in particular. Yet the response to this, and to the generally deteriorating security situation in the country, was a military coup that brought General Ne Win to power in 1962. The coup was a mercy killing for a well-meaning though increasingly ineffectual civilian administration, but it ushered in more than four and a half decades of catastrophic rule, with thus far no sign of abatement. The economy was both mismanaged and nationalized, the entire state apparatus both militarized and Burmanized, while ethnic conflict raged.

Civil conflict boiled over in the streets of Rangoon in 1988 just as Ne Win stepped down. Coincidentally, the late general Aung San's daughter, Aung San Suu Kyi, had come from England to Rangoon at this time to care for her ailing mother. Aung San Suu Kyi ended up leading a spontaneous rising of hundreds of thousands of Burmese, mainly ethnic Burman students, in a freedom movement. But a new military junta, the SLORC (State Law and Order Restoration Council), quickly replaced Ne Win and in 1989 renamed the country Myanmar, after the Burman term for the central valley—a name that the ethnic hill tribes, as well as many liberal Burmans, never accepted. When the freedom movement was crushed, many of the Burman students fled to the ethnic areas. Though they had difficulty adapting to the rough physical conditions there, they established a precedent for cooperation between Burmans and the minorities.

In 1990 the military allowed elections that Aung San Suu Kyi's National League for Democracy won in a landslide, even though she was now under house arrest. The military then abrogated the results. Worse, the end of the Cold War brought an end to covert Thai military support for the hill tribes who were fighting the vaguely socialist SLORC. This led to Thai business interests signing deals with the junta for logging and hydropower concessions in the ethnic borderlands. At the same time, China began to funnel billions of dollars of aid to the junta, which was further helped by the opium business in the Golden Triangle. Soon Singapore, Indonesia, and India began to embrace the regime, lured by the country's natural resources. Thus, while military regimes were falling the world over, Burma continued to suffocate under military tyranny. In 1992, Than Shwe, the current dictator, came to power.

Tellingly, the 2007 Saffron Revolution, which saw large demonstrations and consequent brutal repression of thousands of monks in Rangoon, Mandalay, and nearby Pakokku, went unsupported in the hill tracts. Although the uprising caught the West's imagination, Burma's own ethnics remained unmoved. Burma remains not only one of the most tyrannized countries in the world, along with North Korea and Zimbabwe, but also one of the most divided. Everyone substantially involved in the Saffron Revolution is now in prison, exiled, or in hiding.

Burma today is a country where the government spends $1.10 per capita on health care and 40 cents on education, while maintaining one of the largest standing armies in the world. The Burmese army has cut through its own territory like the army of Alexander the Great through the Near East, plundering the populace while making short-lived peace deals with the Wa and splinter factions of the other tribes. Soldiers bayonet peasants' pots in ethnic areas so that they cannot cook and will go hungry.[15] Hundreds of thousands of Burmese troops are sprawled over the hilly borderlands, where thousands of villages have been destroyed and sown over with land mines, even as hundreds of thousands of people are displaced within the country, and more hundreds of thousands sit in refugee camps in Thailand. Risks of infection from HIV, malaria, and tuberculosis "are among the highest in the world."[16] Despite the energy pipeline and hydropower projects, electricity cuts and gasoline shortages plague Burmese cities. Burma may be a more miserable place now than it was during the heaviest fighting of World War II. The regime, while lacking the chilling, bureaucratic evil of Stalin or Saddam Hussein, is, nevertheless, characterized by a benightedness and careless indifference to its people, which it treats as subjects rather than as citizens.[17]

Meanwhile, U.S. policy toward the Burmese regime has remained more or less unchanged over the course of several administrations. Barack Obama, George H.W. Bush, Bill Clinton, and George W. Bush have all embraced the principle of Burmese democracy, even as they have demonstrated little appetite for aggressively supporting the ethnic insurgencies, however covertly. This feeds the argument that American policy toward Burma is more moralistic than moral, and that former president George W. Bush in particular, despite the intense interest in Burma of former first lady Laura Bush, was prone to the same ineffectual preachiness of which former president Jimmy Carter has often been accused on other issues. According to this logic, the U.S. should either open talks with the junta (as Obama's State Department has recently done) rather than risk being ejected from the whole Bay of Bengal region by India and China, and leaving Burma open to mass exploitation, or support the ethnics in the effective but quiet manner that my American acquaintances in the region recommend. "Right now, we get peanuts from the U.S.," Lian Sakhong, general secretary of the Burmese Ethnic Nationalities Council, told me.

American officials responded that there is, indeed, teeth in their pronouncements. There has been a ban on investment in Burma since 1997 (though it is not retroactive, thereby leaving Chevron, which took over its concession from Unocal, free to engage in pipeline construction). New layers of sanctions were added in 2003 and in 2007, and humanitarian aid is provided through certain NGOs operating from Thailand. Moreover, the U.S., from the standpoint of realpolitik, would rather not get too deeply involved in Burma and is, therefore, happy to see its allies India and Singapore indirectly defend its interests against China. As for any form of cross-border operation in support of the Karen and Shan fighters, officials noted that the moment the word of such a policy got out, America's embassy presence in Burma would be gutted.

Nevertheless, according to Jack Dunford of the Thailand Burma Border Consortium, the United States is the only major power that sends the junta a "tough, moral message, which usefully prevents the International

Monetary Fund and World Bank from dealing with Burma," and thus allowing it to build even more dams and infrastructure to further rape the landscape. U.S. policy, Dunford went on, "also rallies Western and international pressure that has led to cracks in the Burmese military." The regime will collapse one day, according to this line of thinking, maybe sooner than later, and that will put America in excellent stead with the Burmese people.

The regime could founder in a variety of ways. Though the specter of another mass uprising excites the Western imagination, perhaps more likely is another military coup, or something more nuanced—a simple change in leadership, with the septuagenarian Than Shwe, in poor health, allowed to step aside. Then, new generals would open up talks with Aung San Suu Kyi, while releasing her from house arrest. Of course, this, by itself, even with elections, would not solve Burma's fundamental problems. Aung San Suu Kyi, as a Nobel Peace laureate and global media star, could provide a moral rallying point that even the hill tribes would accept. But the country would still be left with no infrastructure, no institutions, and a growing but still frail civil society and NGO community, and with various ethnic groups waiting in the wings that fundamentally distrust the dominant Burmans. The National League for Democracy lacks any managerial skills, according to foreign observers, while the ethnic groups are themselves weak and divided. In this regard, Burma bears comparison with Iraq and Romania after their Stalinist regimes collapsed. Iraq fell into chaos for years, whereas Romania experienced only two weeks of chaos because another branch of the Communist Party, more liberal, wrested power from the demonstrators and led the country through a half-decade transition before finally departing. The lesson, as one international negotiator told me, is: "There will be no choice but to keep the military in a leading role for a while, because without the military there is nothing in Burma." In power for so long, however badly it has ruled, the military has made itself indispensable to any solution.

"It's much more complicated than the 'beauty and the beast' scenario put forth by some in the West—Aung San Suu Kyi versus the generals," said Lian Sakhong. "After all, we must end sixty years of civil war."

In sum, Burma must find a way to return to the spirit of the Panglong Agreement of 1947, which provided for a decentralized Union of Burma. Unfortunately, the agreement was never implemented, and thus was the cause of all the problems since.

Even within the central Irrawaddy valley and delta, away from the hill tracts, large Karen and Mon minorities demand equality with the Burmans, promised to them by Aung San before he was assassinated. While the world demanded relief assistance for the delta inhabitants worst affected by Cyclone Nargis in May 2008, the generals, who in any case have little regard for the Karens living there, were more concerned with the preservation of civil order in nearby Rangoon. For the international community the cyclone was a humanitarian crisis, but for the generals it was only a potential security one.

In the jungle capital of Naypyidaw, the junta may represent the last truly centralized regime in Burma's post-colonial history. Whether through a peaceful, well-managed transition or through a tumultuous or even anarchic one, the Karens and Shans in the east and the Chins and Arakanese in the west will likely see their power increased in a post-junta, democratic Burma. That means the various pipeline agreements may have to be negotiated or renegotiated, at least to some degree, with the ethnic peoples living in the territories through which the pipelines would pass. The struggle over the Indian Ocean, or at least the eastern part of it near the top of the Bay of Bengal, may come down to who deals more adroitly with the Burmese hill tribes.

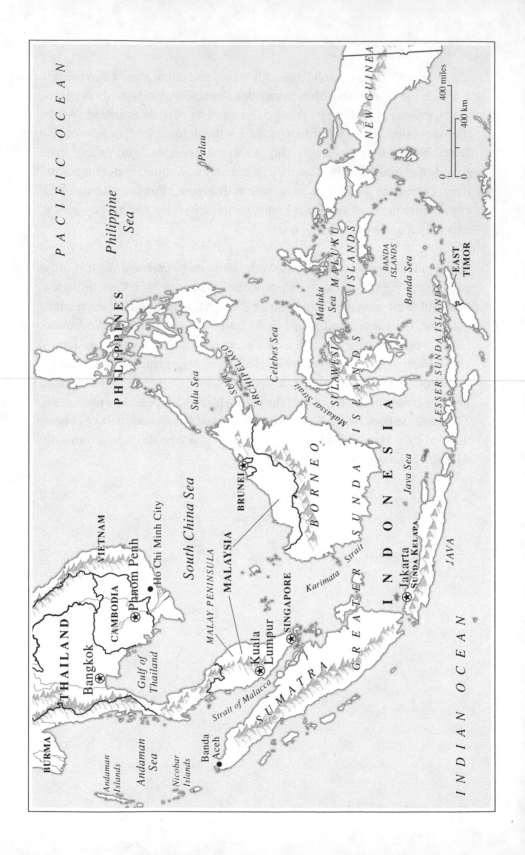

CHAPTER THIRTEEN

INDONESIA'S TROPICAL ISLAM

In early 2005, I was embedded on a United States Navy destroyer conducting relief work in the aftermath of the December 26, 2004, Indian Ocean tsunami, when the waters off Banda Aceh on the northern tip of Sumatra jutting out into the Bay of Bengal were, in one officer's words, like a "floating cemetery." Shoes, clothes, and parts of houses were in the sea; "it was like whole lives were passing by." The tsunami marked the first time that these officers and sailors had seen dead bodies. In the spring of 2003 some of them had fired Tomahawks into Iraq from another destroyer, and then run over to a television to learn from CNN what they had hit. For them Iraq had been an abstraction. But going ashore by helicopter at Banda Aceh they had observed trees, bridges, and houses laid down in an inland direction, as if by high-pressure firehoses. It was a natural disaster, not a war, that had matured these young men and women in uniform.[1]

Whereas the former Special Forces officers I met on the Thai-Burmese border represented the unconventional side of American power projection and relief assistance in the Bay of Bengal, these officers and sailors represented the conventional end of the spectrum. Yet as we shall see, the influence of the United States is limited when set against the vast, deep, and complex array of environmental, religious, and social forces impacting this region.

The earthquake that measured 9.3 on the Richter scale caused a tsunami that traveled at nearly 200 miles per hour at a height of more than 60 feet. It killed close to 250,000 people in Indian Ocean littoral countries: perhaps comparable to the number of people who have died violently in Iraq since the U.S. invasion. The tsunami, which destroyed 126,000 houses in northern Sumatra alone, brought about damage over a radius of thousands of miles in Indonesia, Malaysia, Thailand, Burma, Bangladesh, Sri Lanka, India, the Maldives, the Seychelles, Madagascar, Somalia, Kenya, Tanzania, South Africa, and other nations. Its impact was a demonstration of the fragility of our planet and the natural forces that may be poised to reshape history.

Four years later I returned to the epicenter of this destruction, to an unreal landscape in Banda Aceh of mass graves holding tens of thousands of bodies under mute, empty fields; brand-new mosques, asphalt roads, and little iron-roofed housing communities; and wholly intact ships still stranded far inland where the great wave had deposited them. More than three miles from the beach, in the midst of a field with roosters running through the tall grass, improbably stands the *Ltd. Bapung,* a 2600-ton ship once used for generating 10.5 megawatts of electricity. It is over 200 feet long with a rusted red hull towering 60 feet, atop which is the much taller superstructure and filthy smokestack—like a massive industrial age factory. Close by, almost as an afterthought, is a 70-foot-long fishing boat resting on the roofs of two houses, where it came to settle.

I saw a mosque with buckled pillars—as if a mighty Samson had stood in their midst and pushed them apart—that had somehow survived. Another miracle was the waters that had swept up to the steps of the palatial Grand Mosque itself, only to recede. This is more than local lore. Photos show the truth of these events. The tsunami, like the great natural occurrences of the Bible, has had deep religious—and, therefore, political—significance in the region. The tsunami has clarified northern Sumatra's historically unique and contentious relationship with Indonesia's central government located on the main island of Java, even as it has, more significantly, affected the extraordinarily complex struggle for the soul of Islam itself in Indonesia, the world's most populous Muslim country, and the fourth most populous country in the world.

The future of Islam will be strongly determined by what happens in Indonesia, where Middle Eastern forces from puritanical Saudi Wahabi groups to fashionably global Al Jazeera television compete for people's hearts and minds against local forest deities and the remnants of polytheism. Nothing impacts religions as much as incomprehensible and destructive natural events. Indeed, religion came about as a reaction to the world of nature. All of Indonesia's 240 million people live inside a ring of fire: amid continental fault lines, shifting tectonic plates, massive deforestation, and active volcanoes. Half the people in the world who live within seven miles of an active volcano live in Indonesia. "After the tsunami, Islam here became more self-conscious, more self-aware almost," observed Ria Fitri, a women's activist and law professor.

The tsunami was not the first time in Indonesia's modern history when an environmental event changed the course of religion and politics. As the author Simon Winchester documents, the eruption of Krakatoa in the Sunda Strait between Java and Sumatra in 1883, followed by a tsunami, killed many tens of thousands of people; and in its socially devastating aftermath caused outbreaks of anti-Western Muslim militancy on Java that set a pattern for the century to come.[2] It is not merely fundamentalism per se that is the danger, but as with the case of Bangladesh, the way in which fundamentalism will interact with both the environment and demographic stresses.

During much of its history the region of Aceh in northern Sumatra was an independent sultanate with closer ties to Malaysia and—because of the sure and steady monsoon winds—to the Middle East than to the rest of archipelagic Indonesia. Aceh's many mosques, and its organic relationship—because of the pepper trade and religious pilgrims—to the Arabian Peninsula gave the region the sobriquet "the Verandah of Mecca." Aceh is the only part of Indonesia under Sharia law, yet beer is served in hotels, corporal punishment is limited to soft canings, and there are no forced amputations as in Saudi Arabia. Boys and girls play together in school yards, and women with bewitching smiles wear headscarves (*jilbabs*) but also tight jeans and high heels, and drive motorcycles. Elsewhere in Indonesia it is common to see women, with their hair completely covered, dress in tight blouses and skin-tight hot pants, marked with the latest designer clothes. It is said, though I could not verify it, that there are actually women in Jakarta who wear both *jilbabs* and tank tops with exposed bellies. In Indonesia, modesty stops at the neck.

Yet the helmet-shaped *jilbab* is a mark of modernity, for it indicates that a woman has learned about religion through schooling. Wearing it allows a woman, now armored with symbolic modesty, to enter the professional world of men. "There are few clear-cut lines for women's dress codes, as long as the body is covered. Much is open to personal interpretation," explained Ria Fitri, the women's activist. "The stricter dress codes of some parts of the Middle East and Malaysia are simply not practical here." In a larger sense, women's dress codes in Indonesia are much less a sign of hypocrisy than of wondrous religious diversity, since Islam, even in highly observant Aceh, is enmeshed in a peaceful yet momentous struggle with underlayers of Hinduism and Buddhism that persist to this day.

With well over 200 million of its 240 million inhabitants Muslim, Indonesia represents one of Islam's greatest proselytizing success stories.[3] This is particularly remarkable because Islam came to Indonesia not through military conquest as it did almost everywhere else, from Iberia to the Indian Subcontinent, but, starting in Aceh in the Middle Ages, through seaborne Indian Ocean commerce. In many cases the bearers of Islam were merchants, and thus people with a cosmopolitan outlook who did not seek homogeneity or the destruction of other cultures and religions. The earliest Muslim missionaries in Java are known as the nine saints (Wali Sanga). This myth is similar to that of the twelve Sufi saints (*auliyas*) who brought Islam to Chittagong in Bangladesh. It is quite possible that these saints in the non-Arab eastern reaches of the Indian Ocean were traders.

The places where Islam established early and deep roots were those closest to international trade routes, such as the Malay Peninsula and here on the Sumatran shores of the Strait of Malacca.[4] The farther inland you go, into darkly mauve mountains dripping with greenery, the more idiosyncratic Islam becomes. Rather than being swiftly imposed by imperial armies of the sword, Islam seeped gradually into Indonesia over the course of hundreds of years of business and cultural interchanges, replete with paganistic Sufi influences. Many of the Muslims who came here from the Greater Middle East—Persians, Gujaratis, Hadhramautis—were themselves victims of oppression, and thus open-minded in a doctrinal sense, explained Yusni Saby, the rector of the State Institute of Islamic Studies in Banda Aceh.

"In Indonesia," writes the late and esteemed anthropologist Clifford Geertz, "Islam did not construct a civilization, it appropriated one." That is, Islam became merely the top layer of a richly intricate culture. Whereas Islam, as Geertz explains, when it swept through Arabia and North Africa, moved into "an essentially virgin area, so far as high culture was concerned," in Indonesia, beginning in the thirteenth century, Islam encountered "one of Asia's greatest political, aesthetic, religious, and social creations, the Hindu-Buddhist Javanese state." Even after Islam had spread throughout Indonesia, from the northern tip of Sumatra in Aceh to the easternmost Spice Islands almost three thousand miles away, the Indic tradition, though "stripped . . . of the bulk of its ritual expression," was left intact with its "inward temper." With few exceptions, Geertz goes on, the Indic-Malay "substratum" of "local spirits, domestic rituals, and familiar charms" continued to dominate the lives of the mass of the peasantry. Though Islam as an accepted faith was encountered everywhere in Indonesia by the end of the nineteenth century, as a "body of . . . observed canonical doctrine it was not." Thus, Geertz describes Indonesian Islam as "malleable, tentative, syncretistic, . . . multivoiced," and "Fabian in spirit."[5] Today no more than a third of Muslim Indonesians are orthodox (*santri*); the rest are syncretic (*abangan*).[6] Therefore, Indonesian Islam represents the sum of South and Southeast Asia's nuanced response to Islamic identity, an ideal that has eluded much of the Arab world.*

Indeed, I witnessed throngs of Muslim Indonesian schoolchildren, the girls in *jilbabs,* flocking to Borobudur, a monumental, multi-terraced Buddhist temple complex in central Java built on the scale of Angkor Wat in Cambodia: its 1200-year-old gray stone blocks stained black and ocher with age, its very symmetry deeply mystical. The intricacy of Borobudur's relief work bears testimony to the richness of a culture that long preceded Islam here, and one with which Islam is hard-pressed to compete. I saw the same experience repeated for Muslim Indonesian schoolchildren at the Hindu temples of Prambanan, close to Borobudur. The religious history of imperial Java cannot be defeated, only added to.

Thus, Aceh, although the most Arabian of Indonesian regions, completely lacks the hard atmospheric edge of the Middle East. This is helped by the fact that despite hundreds of years of often tenuous Dutch rule, there is little sense of mass resentment against the West: little sense of having been historically and culturally blighted by foreign intrusion. The age-old hegemony of this island chain was usually more Javanese

---

* Iran, too, has a more nuanced religious identity than is generally assumed. Despite being recruited in recent decades for the purposes of anti-Western ideology, Islam there exists atop an older Persian and Zoroastrian identity.

than European. Javanese imperialism was itself a protective armor against the European variety.

Yet "this could be the beginning of the end of our freedom," worried Aguswandi, an intense and dynamic thirty-one-year-old intellectual and program officer for an Indonesian nongovernmental organization in Banda Aceh, who, like many Indonesians, has only one name. "Sharia law here is intensifying and hijacking post-tsunami Aceh," he told me, explaining, "Why did the tsunami happen? The religious leaders have asked themselves this question. It happened, they have concluded, because the Acehnese were not devout enough. The women were not covered enough, and the foreigners were drinking beer. So the tsunami has had a reactionary effect, even though it brought here the cosmopolitan influences of Western NGOs."

Aguswandi went on: "I first thought that the global influences would win out. After all, Aceh right after the tsunami was the counter-image of Iraq. How can there be a clash of civilizations when you had Jewish money given to Christian charities to build schools in a Muslim town? This is the future, I thought, an Islam with compatibility: a tropical Islam, where it is too hot and humid to be covered."

Continuing in the same vein, Aguswandi told me that helping matters was the very nature of the historical conflict between Aceh and the capital of Jakarta on Java. "There is nothing Islamic about the conflict. It is all about the center versus the periphery in a post-colonial setting, so in and of itself the conflict works against radical Islam." Aceh's geographical situation at the northern tip of the island of Sumatra, jutting out into the Bay of Bengal toward India and Sri Lanka at the entrance to the Strait of Malacca—and crammed between sea and rugged highlands—makes it an easily definable region, distinct from the rest of Indonesia, which contrarily is oriented toward Southeast Asia and the South Seas. For much of its history Aceh was a wealthy sultanate immersed in the Indian Ocean trading system. Its guerrilla struggle against the centralizing hegemony of Javanese Jakarta under both Sukarno and later Suharto was very similar to the struggle it had waged earlier against Dutch Batavia (Jakarta's former name).

But the tsunami brought an abrupt end to this seemingly age-old struggle, and with the newfound security, piracy was reduced dramatically in the Strait of Malacca. The tsunami "killed a lot of the bad guys," one Western observer told me. Or as Yusni Saby explained, with so many people dead and the whole dynamic of Aceh changed by the arrival of international relief organizations, there was, for the time being, nothing left to fight for. It was like the biblical story of the flood with Noah's Ark. It wiped away the previous world.

The Acehnese guerrillas had fought the Jakarta government for nearly three decades, but a peace deal was signed in Helsinki only eight months after the tsunami. Now the former guerrillas, known as the Gerakan Aceh Merdeka (GAM), the Aceh Freedom Movement, have been elected in many Aceh districts through a democratic process operating within Indonesian central authority. This is all the more remarkable given that in 1998 when Suharto was deposed, following the Asian financial crisis of the previous year, many analysts assumed that the Indonesian state would break up with Aceh leading the way. But, improbably, the far-flung archipelago held together and then the tsunami gave centralization a boost by ending the war.

"Indonesia is not an artificial and failed state like Iraq or Pakistan," Aguswandi said; rather, "it is a messy empire" of seventeen thousand islands, in which Islamic parties are incorporated into a weak democratic system, sort of like the way they are in Turkey, even as the system itself tries to grope its way toward an organized decentralization. In this way, regions like Muslim Aceh in the west and Christian and animist Papua thousands of miles away to the east are self-governing within Jakarta's essentially imperial domain. "For centuries it was all about Java, where half of Indonesia's people live," explained Aguswandi, "but now it is all about Aceh, Papua, Kalimantan [Indonesian Borneo]," and so forth.

Whereas Indonesia a decade ago was going in the direction of a failed state, the tsunami was the catalytic event that pushed the Aceh peace agreement across the finish line. Banda Aceh now has little atmosphere of tension. There are no guns in people's houses. But Aguswandi suddenly turned grave and negative as he told me, "The NGO economic bubble here is about to burst and a dangerous vacuum is being created that could be filled by Islamic radicalism and chaos."

In the tsunami's aftermath the United Nations, the World Bank, and the U.S. Agency for International Development poured in, inflating prices, leading to a construction boom in Banda Aceh, a town of close to 300,000 that constitutes a vast sprawl of cruddy houses and storefronts. In 2008 inflation was 42 percent. "The NGOs provided disaster relief and built houses for people," explained Wiratmadinata of the Aceh NGO

Forum, "but not enough was done in the way of infrastructure development. Emergency aid was given, but the building blocks for a local economy are still lacking." Tourism is not the answer because of Sharia law. Meanwhile, the NGOs were dramatically downsizing in 2009 and 2010, and the region—where the majority of people are fishermen or farmers—could be left destitute.

In Pidie, three hours south of Banda Aceh, a region of banana and chili pepper farms in the shadow of volcanoes, I met a former GAM guerrilla, thirty-year-old Suadi Sulaiman, who looked strikingly like Barack Obama. He took me to his humble home behind a storefront and, with no prompting, told me that he was against terrorism and thought that the suicide bombings in Iraq were *haram* (forbidden by Islam). When I asked him why he had left school and joined the GAM in 1999, he spoke to me about the glorious independent Aceh sultanates of yore and the wars against the Portuguese and the Dutch. He went on about the lack of capital despite the presence of oil and mineral deposits, and about the injustice of the Jakarta government. But as I probed further, it turned out that his anger over the lack of freedom and development boiled down to his not finding a job in the crucial period when he enlisted as an Aceh freedom fighter. Now the economy was better and he was running for a seat in the local legislature in the upcoming elections. He supported "self-government, but not independence." He worried that the departure of the NGOs would return the area to the situation it was in when he could not find a job.

As Aguswandi maintained, the initial flowering of cosmopolitanism that came in the immediate aftermath of the tsunami will depart with the NGOs, even as radical Islamists are taking advantage of the political process. This fear was echoed by Fuad Jabali, the deputy director for academic affairs at Jakarta's State Islamic University. "Poverty provides a window for radicalism," Jabali explained, especially in a place like Aceh, which has seen boom-and-bust development. Radicals use democracy but essentially see it as a tool of Western hegemony. "For the radicals, consultation is not for all the people, since you cannot have the corrupt choosing the direction of the state; and because the society is filled with morally corrupt people, in the eyes of the radicals, only the pure should be allowed to choose, or to vote."

But Jabali took care to note that such an exclusivist vision is much more a product of the Middle Eastern experience than of the Southeast Asian one. Again, we are back to the stark difference that the anthropologist Geertz notes: of an Islam that in the brown deserts of the Middle East swallows up a whole culture, and an Islam in a lush, green tropical setting that is layered above and between many centuries of Hindu and Buddhist cultures. While the Middle East enjoys centrality both in the Western news media and in the all-important facts of its being the land of the Prophet and the Arabic language he spoke, nevertheless, in demographic terms, the heart of the religion is in the Indian Subcontinent and particularly archipelagic Southeast Asia. While Western democracy is a very contentious issue in the Middle East, associated as it is with Iraq and the vision of former president George W. Bush, in places like India and Indonesia in South and Southeast Asia, where half a billion Muslims actually live—compared to 300 million in the Arab world—Western democracy is simply beyond reproach. "In Indonesia," said Jabali, a madrassa graduate, "anyone who advocates an Islamic state over democracy will not be supported at the polls. Here maybe five percent of the voters support radical groups like the Majelis Mujahidin Indonesia [Assembly of Holy Warriors] and the Hizbut Tahrir Indonesia [Party of Freedom], which advocate a caliphate, and only ten percent are in favor of dismembering the hands of thieves." The democracy that Bush tried to build violently in Iraq is developing peacefully in Indonesia without his help.

What is so striking about Indonesia, and Aceh in particular, precisely because it is the least syncretic and therefore the most Islamic part of the archipelago, is how, without any prompting, Muslim scholars champion a liberal vision. "We are content here," said Saby. "This is not the Middle East where you fight for the sake of fighting in the name of God. Religion should not focus on enemies. We have good relations with Hindus, Buddhists, Christians, and others. Education and economic empowerment—not ideology—will improve religion." He laments the *pesantren* (madrassas) that focus purely on what separates Muslims from other peoples.* These were the schools that V. S. Naipaul, while traveling through Indonesia more than a generation ago, said did "little more" than teach "the poor to be poor." Writing in 1981, from the standpoint of Indonesia, he observes that Islam

> had the flaw of its origins—the flaw that ran right through Islamic history: to the political issues it raised it offered no political or prac-

* The word *pesantren* comes from *santri* (orthodox).

tical solutions. It offered only the faith. It offered only the Prophet, who would settle everything—but who had ceased to exist. This political Islam was rage, anarchy.[7]

Naipaul's point is certainly relevant to political Islam in parts of the Middle East, but in Indonesia the battle had veered in a different direction since his visit. The *pesantren* he visited do exist, but there are many more throughout the country that teach a broader interpretation of the faith. "Here in Indonesia," Saby told me, "religion is not black or white, but has many grays." Alyasa Abubakar, another Islamic scholar and colleague of Saby at the same institute, informed me that despite the Koran and the Hadith, "geography has given Indonesia a different interpretation of religion. Muslims in the Middle East," he went on, "are obsessed with their glorious past, which means little to us. We are under no such burden." He then ticked off the names of women who were powerful figures in the Aceh sultanate in the seventeenth and eighteenth centuries: "Safiatuddin, Kamalatsyah, Inayatsyah," and so forth.

Then there is former Indonesian president Abdurrahman Wahid, also known as Gus Dur, the grand old man of Islamic pluralism, born in 1940. "Gus" is a Muslim honorific and "Dur" an affectionate shortening of his name. I met him in his Jakarta office, a dark cavernous series of rooms filled with men crouched on chairs smoking. They directed me with their hands toward the inner sanctum. Gus Dur is nearly blind. He sat in the dark, his eyes closed, wearing a traditional batik shirt and tapping on an empty desk hard with his fingers, from side to side. In such gloomy surroundings in the Middle East, filled with chain-smoking males, I had heard many a rant over the years against Israel and the West. But Indonesia is different.

"Radical groups are weak here," Gus Dur told me. "This is the last breath of radicalism before it will be liquidated," he continued, partially lifting his eyelids for emphasis. "Formal Islam is not in demand, unlike in the Middle East. Only in the Middle East has the religion been politicized. With Hamas there is only shouting. The initiatives belong to the Jews, who are working in a systematic way to create a future." He went on: "We are like Turkey, not like the Arabs, or Pakistan. In Pakistan, Islam works against nationalism. Here Islam is a confirmation of [secular] nationalism," that, in turn, encompasses a Buddhist and Hindu past. "There is no longer a threat of disintegration. Though many islands, we are basically one nation. Islam is dynamic in Indonesia." Despite the absoluteness of the Koran, "Islam is not yet finished, it is still in dialogue with itself and with other religions . . ." He continued thus in his peculiar rambling, progressive, preachy, and visionary manner.*

His remarks were not mere platitudes. It was striking how throughout my month-long visit to the country, people kept bringing up spontaneously the necessity of having good relations with Jews and other religious groups. Moreover, Indonesia captured, tried, and executed the terrorists who bombed the discotheque in Bali in 2002, killing more than two hundred people, even as it went on to stabilize its democratic system; nor was there a negative public reaction to the execution of the three terrorists. If the first term of President George W. Bush was about the war on terrorism and the second about spreading freedom and democracy, then Indonesia is the world's best example of what Bush advocated, in the same sequence, although his administration often was too preoccupied to notice.

But the dense story of Indonesian Islam—as complicated as the designs of Javanese batik—does not end with the humanism of Gus Dur. Indeed, the Grand Mosque of Banda Aceh (the Mesjid Raya Baiturrahman) provides a hint of the many contradictions of Islam here. Its striking, six pitch black domes and delightfully ostentatious, sparkling white facade are redolent of both Southeast Asia and the Middle East. It reminded me of the palatial mosques of northern India, full of a happy, floral, and curvaceous blending of different geographical traditions. The severe, fortress-type masculinity of, in particular, mosques in Egypt and North Africa is entirely absent. The prayer hall was full of children playing loudly, mixing with the sounds of tropical birds. Women in *jilbabs* and flowing white *mukennas* were kneeling on the floor in prayer. There were as many women in the mosque as men. It was a real community gathering place. A photograph documented the floating debris that came up to the steps of the mosque following the tsunami. The grounds, complete

---

* Gus Dur died at the end of 2009. He once told former U.S. ambassador to Indonesia Paul Wolfowitz that he had cried while visiting a mosque in Morocco upon seeing an Arabic translation of Aristotle's *Nicomachean Ethics* on display. "If I hadn't read the *Nicomachean Ethics* as a young man, I might have joined the Muslim Brotherhood," Gus Dur said, adding that Aristotle could arrive at deep truths about morality without the aid of religion. Paul Wolfowitz, "Wahid and the Voice of Moderate Islam," *Wall Street Journal,* January 7, 2010.

with a reflecting pool, were rehabilitated with money from Saudi Arabia. The conservative and even radicalizing tendencies of the Middle East are wielding ever greater influence here, even as the peculiar character of the faith in Southeast Asia stubbornly persists.

Besides Saudi money and power, there is the dynamic influence of Middle East–based global television networks such as Al Jazeera, which, while highly professional and entertaining in their own right, bring Indonesians into the mainstream of both Arab and European center-left political thought and sensibilities. Al Jazeera helped crystallize Indonesians' intense and lingering dislike of Bush and, in early 2009, of Israel's air attack on Gaza. "In Indonesia, Israel lost the war of words over Gaza," Aguswandi told me, because of the way it was portrayed on television. This is a new phenomenon, given that Indonesia has never felt itself humiliated by Israel in the way that contiguous countries like Egypt and Syria have.

Compare this with the mass disinterest shown here over the plight of the Muslim Rohingyas, brutally oppressed by the military regime in Burma, with tens of thousands of them living across the border in Bangladesh in some of the world's most squalid refugee camps. In February 2009, when odious elements of the Thai military put boatloads of Rohingyan refugees out to sea with little food or water and Rohingyas came ashore in Aceh, there was little popular outcry here, even though one easily could make the case that the Muslim Rohingyas of Burma's Arakan Province are tyrannized to a greater degree than are the Palestinians. To a significant extent, the contradiction is explained by the effect of Persian Gulf–based global media, which now penetrate the smallest villages; it will only grow in importance, thus helping to close the attitudinal gap with the Middle East.

There is, too, the effect of commercial air travel, which allows 200,000 Indonesians to make the annual haj pilgrimage to Saudi Arabia, the largest contingent of the 1.7 million pilgrims from throughout the Muslim world. Moreover, Yemeni Airways flies to Indonesia four times a week, strengthening the historic Indian Ocean links between the Hadhramaut in Yemen and Java in Indonesia. Previous generations of tradesmen from the Hadhramaut and the Hejaz in Saudi Arabia brought liberal and heterodox Sufi influences to Indonesia. But today, buttressed by Wahabi money that, among other things, translated Hitler's *Mein Kampf* into Indonesia's official national language, Bahasa Indonesia, the influence from the Arabian Peninsula is, to an essential degree, hateful.

This also is globalization, in which various strains of thought are homogenized by mass media, in turn influenced by determined interest groups, into a monochrome, ideological way of thinking.

As is the case with Hindu nationalists in India, those most drawn to radicalism in Indonesia are not the Islamic scholars, whose very knowledge of the religion makes them less susceptible to mass media, but the first generation of professionals, newly liberated from the village, who have wide access to books, news publications, and television, and are still somewhat credulous. In Indonesia, a Muslim radical is much more likely to be a young chemical engineer than an old cleric. An examination of the country's Muslim organizations only adds to the aura of overwhelming complexity that is Indonesian Islam.

Indonesia may be the globe's most populous Muslim society, but it is also home to sizable minorities of Chinese, Christians, and Hindus. Thus, it is functionally a secular state, and this has given rise to Muslim civic organizations that are the largest in the world, because Islamic states like those in the Middle East simply do not require them. "In this way," explained Anies Baswedan, rector of Jakarta's Universitas Paramadina, "the secular state accommodates a vibrant religious life, even as powerful Muslim groups give legitimacy to the secular authorities. Personal piety therefore thrives in a way that it never would in an Islamic state, where religion is by necessity politicized."

The two most prominent organizations are Nahdlatul Ulema (Revivalist Clergy) and Muhammadiyah (Followers of Muhammad). Because of the very size of these groups, with memberships in the millions, their politics are often vague and hard to pin down. Nevertheless, broad themes are discernible.*

Nahdlatul Ulema (NU), of which Gus Dur was a longtime president, was formed in 1926 out of concern for austere and fundamentalist Wahabist influences that began to filter into Indonesia following the establishment of Ibn Saud's kingdom of Saudi Arabia the same year. It is traditional and conservative, loyal to Sufi saints, and, therefore, somewhat counterintuitively, inclusive, syncretist, and supporting of civil society. This is because the deep emphasis on Muslim tradition protects it

---

* The two groups also have geographical bases of support: east Java in the case of Nahdlatul Ulema, and central Java and western Sumatra in the case of Muhammadiyah.

from contemporary Islamic ideology, which seeks to defend Islam from the influences of other religions, such as Hinduism and Buddhism. Because of its anchor in generations of Islamic thought, NU's is a confident belief system that does not feel threatened by other strains of thought and thus does not define itself through enemies. NU is comfortable with the contradictions of the modern world. Thus, it promotes the wearing of the *jilbab* for women, while it also evinces an understanding attitude toward gay rights. Yet NU's record is not entirely clean. For example, NU was caught up in the frenzy of the last years of Sukarno's rule, when, in the fall of 1965, its youth movement went on a killing spree against communists on Java.[8]

Muhammadiyah is the more modern of the two organizations, and therefore, again somewhat counterintuitively, the less open-minded, though it is important not to carry this point very far; this is more of a vague sensibility than a clearly defined policy direction. Muhammadiyah emphasizes literalism, a return to the written words of the Koran and the Hadith that have been corrupted by the pagan and, therefore, reactionary elements of accumulated tradition in this part of the world. Muhammadiyah is conducive to radicalism, even as its very existence and organizational structure keeps many would-be radicals from taking the next step into terrorism.

The popularity of Muhammadiyah among young professionals indicates how the blending of Islam with other cultural and religious traditions here has its limits. For centuries, religious currents direct from the Arab world have continued to influence Indonesian Islam, refusing integration with the local environment. And so the advent of Al Jazeera and commercial airline links are, in the final analysis, an intensification of an old story, rather than the start of something new. To better explain this, a historical and philosophical discursion is in order:

The very encounter with Dutch colonialism only strengthened the Indonesians' sense of Islamic identity, as they became, in Geertz's words, "*oppositional* Muslims."[9] The cry of jihad played a large role in the Acehnese war against the Dutch, who crept up the coast of Sumatra in the 1850s and 1860s before encountering strong guerrilla resistance from the Muslims at Sumatra's northern tip. The war, which began in 1873 and did not end until 1903 with the Sultan of Aceh's surrender, saw not only a full-blown Muslim insurgency against the Dutch, but also the import of pan-Islamic ideas from the Middle East to encourage the mujahidin.

Yet it is also true that this very direct and radicalizing contact with Muslim Middle Eastern lands was encouraged precisely because, as a Dutch colony, Indonesia was denied frequent connections with Muslims of nearby British colonies in South and Southeast Asia, whose inhabitants lived under a rival European power. So it was that Muslims in Indonesia sometimes have been more influenced by the purer ideas of Arabia than from, say, the more syncretic Muslim quarters of India.

To be sure, as the age of steam improved transoceanic communications, waves of immigrants, especially from the Hadhramaut in eastern Yemen, descended upon Aceh and other parts of Indonesia, bringing with them not only Sufistic heterodoxy but also stern and orthodox ideas, forged by their relative proximity to Mecca.[10]

When speaking about the Islamic orthodoxy that began to descend in earnest upon Indonesia in the nineteenth century, we must be careful to say that such a purified Islam, compared, that is, to the Southeast Asian variety, was itself being influenced by new currents of thought within the Middle East. Most significant and exciting in that regard was the modernism of the late-nineteenth-century Egyptian scholar and reformer Muhammad Abduh.

Abduh is crucial to the Indonesian story. The late American Arabist Malcolm H. Kerr explains that Abduh's "historical role was simply to fling open the doors and expose a musty tradition to fresh currents."[11] Abduh deplored the blind acceptance of traditional religious dogma, rife with superstition, that had accumulated over the centuries, and sought answers to Egypt's modern predicament within the pristine faith of the early years of Islam. By giving reasons and explanations to what once was mere simple faith, Abduh did much to bring Islam into the debates of the twentieth century. His was a way of thinking rather than a specific program, said the scholar Yusni Saby. Thus, Abduh unwittingly inspired both secular moderation and fundamentalist radicalism, for both are elements of modernism.[12] In particular, Abduh's efforts to improve religious education, in order to adapt it to contemporary needs, helped to make Middle Eastern Islam a standardized global religion. This gave it the strength to combat the syncretism of Indonesia's Hindu-Buddhist underlayers, as well as its substantial pockets of Christianity, and, just as significantly, its secular nationalism.[13]

Abduh is not only read widely in Indonesia, he constitutes the founding philosophic spirit of Muhammadiyah as well. Organizationally, Indonesia has done more to propagate Abduh's thinking—with its associations to both radicalism and liberalism—than anyplace in the Middle East. Muhammadiyah has helped spawn movements that, like the Ikhwan al-Muslimin (Muslim Brotherhood) in Egypt, are focused on both radicalism and social self-help networks.

So the battle goes on in Indonesia, or rather the process. The latest phase is a fundamentalist attempt to latch on to issues that few people care about and make them into parliamentary controversies, like pornography, suggestive street behavior between young men and women, and who gets to certify *hallal* food (food that conforms to Muslim dietary laws). In this sprawling archipelago, it seems, we are seeing both a so-called clash and a merger of civilizations. Islamic Southeast Asia is welcoming, sensuous, and culturally complex in ways that the desert-baked Middle East is not, even as it features periodic pogroms against ethnic Chinese Christians, and incidents like the 2002 Bali attacks and the bombing of the Marriott Hotel in Jakarta the following year. As these violent acts indicate, there is another enemy besides syncretism that radical Islam faces in Indonesia: westernization itself, the modern world that Indonesia's relative handful of fundamentalists have no choice but to react to. As the Israeli scholar of Indonesian Islam Giora Eliraz puts it: "Radical fundamentalists need worthy adversaries."[14]

According to Geertz, who uses as his examples Indonesia and Morocco—the two geographical end points of the Islamic spectrum—the conversion of religion to radical ideology does not happen because people doubt God, but because they have come to doubt themselves, which, in turn, is something that goes back to their very fear of modernization.[15] It is such doubt and the extreme response it engenders that cannot help influencing Indonesia's fate.

Nevertheless, there are strong grounds for optimism. Although almost 85 percent of the country is Muslim, 85 percent of Indonesians reject the notion that the state should be formally based on Islam, preferring instead the pluralist- and democracy-affirming principles of Pancasila, the moderate nationalist ideology enshrined in the 1945 constitution, with its five principles of belief in God, nationalism, humanism, democracy, and social justice.

Indonesia's very rugged and archipelagic geography, flung out over a seascape as wide as the continental United States—at a place where the Sinic and Indic worlds fuse—has led finally to a democracy that features an increasing dispersal of power following decades of dictatorship under Sukarno and later Suharto.[16] Despite all the pageantry and stagy contrivances of Sukarno's leftist theater state, which developed a useful myth for the new Indonesian nation, and the Dutch- and Japanese-style postcolonialism of Suharto's right-wing military state, which fortified that myth with new institutions, geography has eventually overwhelmed both those attempts at extreme centralization. As it happens, it was reform-minded Islamic groups, with Muhammadiyah in the forefront, loyal to the progressive intentions of Muhammad Abduh, which, more than the secular nationalists, led the pro-democracy struggle against Suharto in the late 1990s. As an Iraqi intellectual once was reported saying, "When I travel to Syria and Iraq I feel that I see Islam's past, but when I travel to Indonesia, I feel that I see its future."[17]

Such religious vibrancy, so intellectually rich that, consequently, it has avoided the ideologizing of faith, could only have occurred within a multi-confessional state that has proved sturdier than many gave it credit for back in the tumultuous days of 1998, after Suharto's downfall. Indonesia now boasts an independent media of eleven national television stations and a press that is the freest in Southeast Asia. Because more people were lifted out of poverty in the 1980s and 1990s here than in any other place in the world save for, perhaps, China, Indonesia is poised to be an economic giant of the twenty-first century. Indonesia is positioned to withstand the rigors of decentralization, and, despite its archipelagic nature, hold together because it is united by a common Malay language: Bahasa Indonesia, which, since it is a traders' tongue not associated with a particular group or island, is embraced enthusiastically by all. And with decentralization comes the potential of applying religious laws differently in each place, according to local traditions, thus further defusing religion itself as a political issue.

Because of the somewhat unexpected success that religious progressives have had against radicals in the democratic environment of the past few years, Indonesian intellectuals are, grudgingly, starting to give Suharto some credit for establishing the basis of a strong modern state, with his promotion of an educated middle class, without which Indonesia could never have held together following his demise. The very students whose demonstrations led immediately to Suharto's exit were the ones who, when they were younger, benefited from the primary and secondary education initiatives he started. I have even heard Suharto compared to Mustafa Kemal Ataturk, the founder of modern Turkey, and to Park Chung-hee, who built the basis of South Korea's industrial might in the 1960s and 1970s. Suharto (and Sukarno, too) helped provide Indonesia with a secular nationalism that has been crucial in the battle against religious extremism. Al-Qaeda-affiliated groups like Jemaah Islamiyah, with their strong Yemeni element, still lurk in the interstices between more moderate Islamic organizations, but they are perceived as weak, and that is partly because Suharto's legacy is not altogether bad.

Whereas Islam arrived on these islands at Aceh, the continuing struggle over the religion's place in modern life in post-Suharto Indonesia will be fought amid the urban slums and skyscrapers of cities like Jakarta. Greater Jakarta has twenty-three million people by some estimates. With skylines in all directions, it exudes the immensity of São Paulo, and in its lazy red-roofed *kampongs* (houses) and grubby storefronts the ratty edginess of Manila. Cars and motorbikes squirm through its streets in traffic jams as bad as Kolkata's and worse than almost everyplace else in Asia. During the rainy season as much as a quarter of the city floods.

Yet, the most interesting places to observe Indonesians are at the spanking new malls, built often with ethnic-Chinese money. While constituting only about 4 percent of Indonesia's population, the Chinese account for well over half of its business dealings. The new malls, packed with Louis Vuitton, Versace, and other designer stores, are the places to observe women in the most fashionable silk *jilbabs* and the most revealing, sophisticated dress. Now that the extremists are at bay, even assuming occasionally spectacular terrorist incidents, the real values' clash here is not between one brand of Islam and another, but the clash between an Islam ostensibly of the Middle East and the rampant materialism of China. The fact that China is nominally still a communist country is, of course, meaningless. China, and the ethnic-Chinese community here, in particular, represent global capitalism, which constitutes the real threat to Indonesian Islam. Nevertheless, these same Islamists wish China well when it clashes with the United States.

The wild card in these tensions is the environment. Remember that Indonesia lies within a ring of seismic fire. Alyasa Abubakar, the Islamic scholar I met in Banda Aceh, told me that because "people accepted the tsunami as the will of God, there was no chaos afterwards. Because of Islam, people didn't become insane with grief despite losing many of their family members. The people here," he went on, "had faith, unlike the people in New Orleans after Katrina. The social reactions to the two catastrophes could not have been more stark."

And so an era of natural disasters will, perforce, strengthen Islam. That will only raise the stakes for the continued evolution of the faith, the debate over which is more pulsating in Indonesia than almost anywhere else, precisely because Indonesia is a non-Arab, virtually secular state. The language of the Prophet is not the spoken language here. The Palestinian-Israeli conflict is geographically distant, despite the widespread presence of Al Jazeera in people's homes and the resultant public relations victory of the Gaza Palestinians. Islamic law is applied sparingly and is not always revered. Most importantly, Indonesia is a democracy where people are unafraid of having their thoughts on religion printed, for fear of retribution from either the government or radical groups. Thus, Indonesia provides the level playing field necessary to establish the true vision and philosophical texture of Islam in the twenty-first century. Along with India, Indonesia is emerging as a vibrant, democratic powerhouse. Monsoon Asia will truly be at the heart of things.

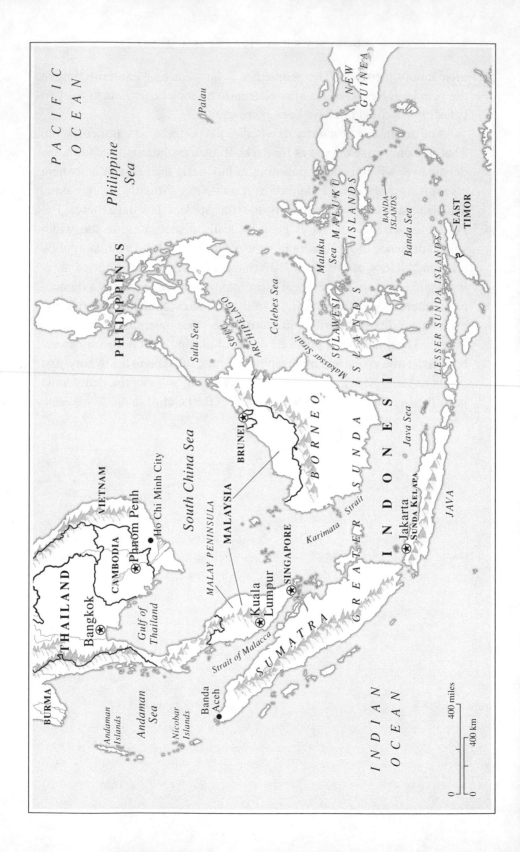

CHAPTER FOURTEEN

THE HEART
OF MARITIME ASIA

ndonesia—in particular, the island of Sumatra—and peninsular Malaysia on the opposite side of the Strait of Malacca form the heart of maritime Asia. The Strait of Malacca is the Fulda Gap of the twenty-first-century multi-polar world, the place where almost all of the shipping lanes between the Red Sea and the Sea of Japan converge at the most vital choke point of world commerce; where the spheres of naval influence of India and China meet; where the Indian Ocean joins the western Pacific. The volume of energy-related tanker traffic will grow in the strait by at least 50 percent by 2020, further increasing its importance.

In and of itself, Indonesia, besides being a major oil producer, will remain East Asia's primary supplier of natural gas for decades. The country's vast archipelagic nature, its energy resources, its ethnic diversity, predominant Muslim religion, institutional weaknesses, and ultra-strategic location will make it a critical hub of world politics.[1] History is instructive: Suharto's consolidation of power in the middle and late 1960s—moving the country in a rightward direction—secured the sea-lanes for the United States, making the war in Vietnam unnecessary, had only we realized it.

I stood again in Banda Aceh, at the entry point of the Strait of Malacca, which is more than five hundred miles in length and two hundred miles wide here at its northern end. But it is only eleven miles across at its heavily congested southern entrance near Singapore, a place made narrower by treacherous shoals and the very volume of ship traffic, from supertankers to small tugs and fishing boats all vying for space.[2] Here geography rules. All the advances in technology since antiquity have thus far done little to reduce commercial dependence on this waterway. Of the fourteen nations constituting East and Southeast Asia, twelve are highly dependent on Middle Eastern oil, which mainly comes through here.[3] The Strait of Malacca drives home the point that whereas the Atlantic and the Pacific are "open oceans," the Indian is "semi-enclosed," which is what makes it so vulnerable and, therefore, for yet one more reason, so important.[4] In fact, in earlier times the very terms "Indian Ocean" and "South China Sea" were not used; rather, in the minds of local merchants, the waters that had to be negotiated constituted a series of separate seas stretching from East Africa all the way to Indonesia's Spice Islands close to New Guinea.[5]

Three quarters of the way down the strait on the Malaysia side, not far from Singapore, is the old emporium of Malacca itself, at the halfway point between the Indian and Chinese trading networks, which were themselves dictated by the reversible monsoonal winds: ships could wait out one monsoon in the town of Malacca and then take advantage of another. In the late Middle Ages, Malacca constituted an Islamic maritime city-state, a thriving Malay market town dependent on Indian Gujarati traders and the protection of the Chinese, with whom it had cemented a relationship following the visit of the eunuch admiral Zheng He. The Portuguese overran Malacca in 1511, and for the next 130 years used it as a headquarters for their monopolistic trading empire. So exorbitant was the Portuguese tax on merchants that many traders simply redirected their ships to other ports, undercutting Portugal's attempts at domination.[6] Forced out of Malacca by a trio of the Portuguese, the Chinese, and Hindu Tamil merchants, the Muslim Gujaratis from India more or less en masse shifted their business across the strait to Aceh, to where they imported Indian cloth in exchange for pepper.

Pepper, the "pungent berry of a tropical vine," which thrives on the wet-and-dry tropical monsoon climate, was the main commercial prize here, just as frankincense was at the other end of the ocean, and just as oil is today. Labor intensive, hard to produce, and craved by all from ancient Rome to China, black pepper (*piper nigrum*—"the true pepper") was known in the way of frankincense for its medicinal properties, as a heart and kidney stimulant. Its importance cannot be overestimated. And northern Sumatra—Aceh—was full of it.[7] In fact, a main reason the Portuguese failed to take over the pepper trade on Sumatra, despite their perch on Malacca, was that the Gujaratis collaborated with their fellow Muslim Acehnese to develop an alternate supply network to the Red Sea via India's Coromandel coast and Iran.[8] While in the late sixteenth century the Portuguese were transporting 1.2 million pounds of pepper annually around the Cape of Good Hope, about four million pounds were being transported via Red Sea. This was when Aceh's maritime kingdom was at its height. Under Sultan Ala-al-din Riayat Shah al-Kahar (1537–71), Aceh was the most powerful kingdom in the Malay world, with international connections as far west as Ottoman Turkey.[9] Under a later sultan, Ala-uddin, the first fleet of the British East India Company sailed into Aceh in 1602.

Roughly in the same period, in the early seventeenth century, the Portuguese were essentially ousted from the East Indies by the Dutch, done in by naval sieges and blockades, and by their own narrow-minded trading practices. The Dutch, greeted first as liberators, went on to develop a trading system just as authoritarian and yet more comprehensive than that of the Portuguese. The Dutch became masters not only of the trade routes, but also of the "commercial agriculture" of much of Indonesia's interior.[10] Given that the Dutch and Portuguese went to war over the Malacca Strait, and that the British in 1786 established a foothold on the small island of Penang on the Malay Peninsula—aided by a trading system far more liberal than that of their European competitors—the strait in the early modern era lay at the heart of great power struggles. Yet the recognition that a violent enmity between Britain and Holland was unsustainable led the two powers into an accommodation in the 1824 Treaty of London, which stipulated that the British would restrict themselves to the Malay Peninsula and the Dutch to the Indonesian archipelago.[11] Thus, the political map of our own era began to take shape.

But let us return to the Dutch, for it was they who created today's Indonesia. Indeed, both Sukarno and Suharto ruled in the baronial and centralizing style of the Dutch, even as they built on and further fortified the messy empire that the Dutch had wrought.

The Dutch were the most utilitarian of imperialists, a character trait that arose out of their own struggle against nature in the Netherlands, where the landscape is a mazework of waters, polders, windmills, and pumping stations. Everywhere "the voice of the waters, telling of endless disaster, was heard and feared." Throughout the Netherlands there was the need for "precise coordination and cooperation—the engineer's mentality," the "drive for order." There developed, too, a corresponding need to be on time, for arriving late was associated with failure and irresponsibility. Discipline was everything. In this culture there was ultimately no room for "Catholic pomp and circumstance" and the "frivolity of Rome." Life was lived according to a strict Calvinistic code.[12]

You could "manage" the water but could not "force" it. Thus, there developed the supreme need for tolerance within their own community, out of which such coordination and cooperation could emerge. It was a culture of "consensus."

But if geography had determined national character, why hadn't such a mechanistic, technological, and cooperative society developed in that other gargantuan estuarial delta: Bengal? In Bengal, as in the Netherlands, watery nature was endlessly on the rampage, and thus it would seem to also require the cooperative hand of man to tame it. But the Bengali character turned out different than that of the Dutch because, again, the choices made by individual men are as important as geography. In Bengal there were "local lords to whom the farmers . . . paid tribute and taxes." If the Ganges changed course and the sea overran the land, the farmers, who did not own the land they tilled, simply moved to the nearest piece of dry land and began tilling again. It was only after the English colonists in Bengal introduced land ownership that the local lords began protecting their new property with dikes and other constructions in order to control the water.[13]

Just as domestic discipline materialized out of the deep insecurity that the encroaching waters imposed on a land of sea-level flatness in northwestern Europe, imperial discipline materialized out of their "tenuous hold" on colonial outposts; indeed, the Dutch "lost their position in Formosa . . . were kicked out of Brazil," and the British threw them out of New York. The whole ocean trade itself "was a gamble."[14] Yet the Dutch empire of the seas grew and prospered, particularly in the Indian Ocean and East Indies. The Dutch writer Geert Mak informs us that at its height in the mid-seventeenth century, the Dutch had more than seven hundred ships at sea, "a fleet larger than the English, Scottish, and French fleets combined."[15] Between 1600 and 1800 a total of 9641 ships sailed from Europe to Asia, nearly half of them Dutch. "By 1648 the Dutch were indisputably the greatest trading nation in the world," writes C. R. Boxer, "with commercial outposts and fortified 'factories' scattered from

Archangel to Recife and from New Amsterdam to Nagasaki," with the Indian Ocean as their centerpiece.[16] Most extraordinary about the dominance of this compact little country was that its ships and outposts were not backed by a strong military.[17] Whereas the Portuguese went to the Indian Ocean as crusaders, the Dutch went as traders first and foremost. Trade was to them a religion.[18] In this way seventeenth-century Holland presages the business and economic empires of major corporations, small and modest-sized Asian states like Singapore and South Korea, and the mega sized European Union in a post-American multi-polar world, in which military might, while certainly a contributing factor to national power, is not necessarily a determining one.

The late British historian J. H. Plumb writes that the faces that stare out of the canvases of Dutch masters such as Rembrandt and Hals are "cautious, prudent, self-satisfied, unostentatious . . . giving little away of their unconscious drives, but speaking eloquently of the sobriety and dedication of their lives."[19] Truly, there is a very modern, in fact, a very corporate steely resolution that these Dutchmen of high empire exhibit. And that is no accident. In addition to having their national character formed by private land ownership and the constant need to prevent coastal flooding, the Dutch, like the British, established an imperialism that was run by a company to a large degree. In 1602 the United Netherlands Chartered East India Company (Vereenigde Oost-Indische Compagnie, or VOC) was allowed a monopoly of trade and navigation east of the Cape of Good Hope across the Indian Ocean and west of the Straits of Magellan across the Pacific.

The company was a state within a state, able to conclude treaties, make alliances, and wage defensive war in the name of the United Provinces, the precursor to the modern Netherlands. The Dutch conquests of the East were not national conquests but those of private merchants, entitled to sell these strongholds to whomever they wished. "In advocating freedom of international trade in general and the freedom of the seas in particular, the merchant-oligarchs of Holland and Zeeland were primarily . . . actuated by self-interest," observes the historian Boxer.[20]

The Dutch empire came into being and expanded its influence in a manner vaguely similar to the present-day European Union. Seven rebellious provinces or states of the north European lowlands, of which Holland was by far the most important, agreed in the 1579 Union of Utrecht to present a common front to the outside world, and consequently put foreign policy in the hands of the States-General at The Hague, a parliament with administrative authority. Gradually, despite their many differences, these seven states cohered around economic and commercial policy, leading to the formation of the East India Company as one of several culminations in this process. It was a progression that made Amsterdam a thriving hub of an international maritime network, which was, in turn, built on the overseas networking zeal of Hollanders, Zeelanders, Flemings, Walloons, and Marranos, whose merchant communities were about to span the globe.

The Indian Ocean presented the Dutch with a natural zone of expansion for their trade in the Mediterranean and the Levant. This tendency was further encouraged by Dutchmen who had sailed with the Portuguese and therefore knew the East Indies well. There was also the lure of the much-sought-after porcelain, tea, and pepper and other spices of the East; not to mention the European desire for Indian textiles, particularly cotton from Gujarat; Persian, Bengali, and Chinese silks; and Javanese coffee and sugar. There was, too, a demand within and from Asia for indigo and saltpeter from India, elephants from Ceylon, and slaves from Arakan and Bali. Thus it was that the early decades of the seventeenth century saw the Dutch compete with, blockade, and over time displace Portuguese settlements in the Moluccas, Malaya, Ceylon, and India, among other places.*

What was the "company" actually like in the Indies? How did the Dutch behave? The answer is: abominably. The historian Holden Furber writes: "In singlemindedness of purpose, in ambition for personal wealth, in callous disregard for human suffering," there was no one worse than the conqueror of the little Javanese port of Jakarta himself, Jan Pieterszoon Coen. Coen was right out of the mold of empire builders in Africa two centuries ahead of his time. He sought to make Jakarta—renamed Batavia by the Dutch—the hub of Asian sea trade between the Persian Gulf and the Sea of Japan. His principles were territorial expansion throughout much of the archipelago, a ruthless monopoly of the

* In fact, the Dutch ascendancy over the Portuguese was relentless. While the English harried them in the Persian Gulf and the Mughals in Bengal, the Portuguese lost the following bases to Holland: the Spice Islands in 1605, Malacca in 1641, Colombo in 1656, the rest of Ceylon in 1658, and Cochin in 1662. A.J.R. Russell-Wood, *The Portuguese Empire, 1415–1808: A World on the Move* (Baltimore: Johns Hopkins University Press, 1992), p. 24.

three main spices—cloves, nutmeg, and mace—and the import of Dutch settlers supported by slave labor.[21] Among Coen's accomplishments was the near-complete extermination of the indigenous population of the Banda Islands in the Moluccas. And Coen was not unique in his ruthlessness. The gulf between the civilized faces drawn by the Dutch masters and the uncivilized criminals who manned Dutch ships was indeed yawning. Although Holland was much further on the path toward modernity than Portugal, it made little difference in terms of its behavior toward the natives of the tropical lands they encountered. The nineteenth-century Islamic scholar Snouck Hurgronje points out:

> The chief actors deserve our admiration for their indomitable energy, but the objective for which they worked, and the means they employed to attain it, were of such a kind that we, even with the full application of the rule that we must judge their deeds and doings by the standard of their times, have difficulty in restraining our aversion.[22]

He goes on to explain that, as it would turn out, the inhabitants of Asia came into contact with the very "dregs of the Dutch nation, who treated them with almost unbearable contempt, and whose task it was to devote all their efforts to the enrichment of a group of shareholders in the Fatherland."[23] The company paid few of its employees a decent wage, forcing them to resort to dishonest means to earn a livelihood. There were, too, the hardships of six to eight months at sea to consider, and the dangers of living in a tropical environment where little was known about disease prevention. Because of the unwillingness of the average Dutchman to sustain such privations, the company's foot soldiers were often the lowest of the low, and the merchants who did choose to go out to the East the most unscrupulous. The crews, which whored, drank, stole, and murdered, had to be ruled with a "rod of iron like untamed beasts."[24] Beatings and lashings were common, and the punishment for homosexuality was throwing the two culprits, bound together, into the sea.

The recruitment of men for the Dutch East India Company, writes the author Geert Mak, was carried out by so-called *zielverkopers* (soul merchants), who plucked homeless men off the streets and gave them food and shelter until making it known to them, "amid much drumming and trumpeting," that it needed hands on deck. The men were then hustled onto the ships, where they died in droves: falling from the masts, swept overboard, murdered by pirates, contracting scurvy, malaria, or dysentery, "or would go down with their ships." One in ten deckhands died on the outbound journey; of 671,000 men who left Amsterdam, 266,000 never returned.[25] Dozens of corpses were thrown overboard every week of delay in the Atlantic doldrums en route to, or returning from, the Cape of Good Hope.[26]

Once east of the cape, many captains, who themselves often enjoyed meat and wine on board, cut down on the crew's rations and pocketed the profit in Batavia. The ships on which they sailed east, called Indiamen, while picturesque on the outside, were dark, cold, dank, and ill ventilated on the inside, with little room to move about, cluttered as the ships were laden with sea chests, buckets of drinking water, and other provisions. Consequently, there was no room either to separate the sick from the healthy. A host of diseases spread fast, particularly as some men did not bother to use the heads and relieved themselves in corners. Dirt and filth abounded. Food was old, full of insects, from the worst cuts of meat. Many became so seasick on the oceanic voyages that they could not even make it to the heads to relieve themselves.

The voyage from Amsterdam southward around the Cape of Good Hope and eastward along the "roaring forties"—36 to 50 degrees south latitude—to Indonesia's Sunda Strait often took seven months. From 1652 when Jan van Riebeeck planted the Dutch flag there until the opening of the Suez Canal more than two centuries later, "the Cape was the half-way house between Europe and Asia," the " 'Tavern of the Indian Ocean,' " where sailors reprovisioned, got drunk, and rested before another long bout of clositered hell on the high seas.[27]

As with the Portuguese, such privations produced cruel men who onshore were inebriated much of the time and mistreated the natives, even as they proclaimed their racial superiority. All cultures contain riffraff, and both the Dutch and the Portuguese sent their worst sorts out to the colonies and outposts. Thus, the natives experienced the bottom social stratum of what these Western nations had to offer.* The strengths and weaknesses of the various imperialisms are determined by who exactly provides the face of it to the indigenous inhabitants. With the British in

* Not all those sent out by Portugal and Holland were Portuguese and Dutch. In the case of the Dutch, German, and Walloon mercenaries numbered among them. But they were also of low social standing.

India, by and large, it was less the worst sorts than simply their mediocrities whom they sent out to the colonies. Because the United States has had no real colonies, but mainly military outposts, it has been highly trained and, in most cases, well-disciplined, working-class troops who have provided the face of great power projection in recent years. (It cannot be denied the invasion of Iraq produced massive cruelties, but these were a result of grand policies emanating from Washington rather than from the behavior of individual troops, exceptions like Abu Ghraib notwithstanding.) As a result, British and American imperialism (such as the latter actually exists) have been generally more benign than the Portuguese and Dutch varieties. Exceptions to this rule include the accommodating behavior with which the Dutch treated the inhabitants of Japan, Formosa, and Persia, whose powerful leaders, whether a shogun or shah, they were bent on cultivating.

Overall, the Dutch left less of a cultural mark on their colonies than the Portuguese did. The Portuguese went native to a degree that the Dutch did not, settling for the rest of their lives in places the Dutch could not wait to leave once their years of service were up. Moreover, the Roman Catholicism of the Portuguese was a gaudy spectacle that transfixed the inhabitants of far-off Indian Ocean lands, and was in some ways quite similar to—with its gorgeous use of rosaries, the cult of saints, and so forth—the religion of the Hindus and, in some cases, Buddhists. Dutch Calvinism, with its cold logic and austere ceremonies, simply could not compete. Furthermore, whereas Portuguese priests were celibates who stayed in one place for many years and consequently developed strong ties with the local community, Dutch ministers were married, had families to care for, and were frequently moved from place to place. The Calvinists also sent out few missionaries compared to the Roman Catholics, preoccupied as they were with religious disputes within Europe. Calvinism simply made little impression on the peoples of the East once the support of the East India Company was dropped. All these factors helped to make Portuguese the lingua franca of coastal Asia for centuries, whereas the only place Dutch, or at least a form of it, took root was in South Africa.

But this was not what ultimately defeated the Dutch empire. As with so many empires, its demise was gradual, and the culprit was imperial overstretch, in the words of the Yale historian Paul Kennedy.[28] It was not per se that the Dutch had too many colonies and outposts in the Indian

Ocean and its tributary waters, as well as in the West Indies. It was that the upkeep of all these places, *combined* with the effort and costs of military adventures in Flanders and the Iberian Peninsula, in which the Dutch were also involved, proved too much. The Dutch navy simply could not keep up with the demand for so much global policing. Of all the United Provinces, only the Amsterdam admiralty found the money to build a sufficient number of warships (thirty-three between 1723 and 1741), compared with seven for Rotterdam, four for Zeeland, one for Friesland, and none for the landlocked provinces.

Here there is a superficial resemblance between American military missions around the world, plus the costs of its heavy land-based involvements in Iraq and Afghanistan, and the decline in shipbuilding for the U.S. Navy, which has seen a reduction of warships from six hundred in the early 1990s to under three hundred near the end of the first decade of the twenty-first century. The United States of the early twenty-first century, like the United Provinces of the eighteenth century, can afford outposts the world over, but not necessarily combined with heavy ground force commitments in a few places.

An awareness of the Dutch empire is the starting point to making sense of Jakarta's urban jumble. The city grows out of the old port, Sunda Kelapa, on the Java Sea. Here are the long, white seventeenth-century spice warehouses of the VOC with their massive teakwood beams and red-tiled roofs blackened with age, and graced with coconut palms lined up alongside them. Nearby are iron-roofed shacks and garbage-strewn canals, which because of the absence of tall buildings in this part of town allow one to conjure up what the Batavia of old was like. Here was where some of Rembrandt's clients made their money. The sea, three and a half centuries ago, was much closer than it is now, because of land reclamation in the interim. Yet, I climbed a tower and beheld ferries and fishing boats in the middle distance, stacked one behind the other near the waterline. From here the city has been spreading south, becoming so big that Jakarta is now less a city than a city-state.

Ever since the Dutch arrived here there has been a large concentration of Chinese. The Chinese did all the middleman trade arising out of the sugar and spice businesses, and to a degree occupied the same position in society as did the Jews in Eastern Europe. As such they were reviled: vital to the economy, while blamed for all the woes. Thousands of Chinese were murdered in riots in 1740, and were henceforth made to live outside the city walls. Anti-Chinese pogroms were a periodic feature of local history as recently as 1998, even as a vibrant Chinatown exists around Sunda Kelapa.

On the next to last day of Chinese New Year, the Year of the Ox, I visited the Chinese temple in old Jakarta, built in 1650. It was a world of red and gold and fire and smoke. Men were burning fake money to symbolically support their ancestors in heaven. There was a forest of massive candles and stone dragons, around which people were holding batches of burning incense sticks toward the sky.

Even today Chinese in Indonesia are effectively barred from the army, judiciary, and other professions, so they dominate the business world. Despite this, and despite the riots, the streets leading to the temple were lined with Indonesians taking part in the New Year's festivities. In fact, the local attitude toward the Chinese is far more nuanced today than a terrible inter-communal history suggests, and it surely helps influence the way in which China itself is perceived.

Since 1998 there has been no anti-Chinese violence and Chinese-language media in Indonesia are flourishing. Neither the Chinese in Jakarta nor in Beijing are becoming Indonesia's enemy. Rather, they signify a growing strategic and economic power that Indonesia must accommodate peacefully, even as Indonesia struggles to find a way to contain it. In 2005, China and Indonesia signed a strategic partnership followed by an agreement in 2007 to collaborate on defense matters. Concomitantly, Indonesia hedges against China by helping to get Australia and New Zealand included in the East Asian summit framework.[29] China is on everyone's mind whenever the discussion turns to the role of the United States and India in Southeast Asia. The more engaged as naval powers Washington and New Delhi become around the Strait of Malacca, the more independent Indonesia remains. Thus, the largest country in the Muslim world secretly welcomes American military might, while at the same time it sees Hindu-dominated India as a fellow, highly nationalistic democracy in the heart of Asia. Top Indonesian officials told me that they hope the U.S. Pacific Command can enmesh China in a Pacific alliance system, thereby effectively neutralizing it.

In fact, resisting China is proving impossible for Indonesia. The China National Offshore Oil Corporation is the largest offshore oil producer in Indonesia, even as China buys rubber and coal from Kalimantan on Borneo. Indonesia is relying on China for the expansion of its electric power grid. There are port visits from Chinese warships.

Precisely because of its progress as a democracy, which has featured a scaled-back internal role for its military, Indonesia is now more vulnerable than ever to Chinese great power intrusion, said Connie Rahakundini Bakrie, executive director of Jakarta's Institute of Defense and Security Studies. As she and others explained it, because of the army's role in propping up Suharto and its sullied human rights record, the army and the military as a whole are somewhat discredited in Indonesia, and as such the victims of low budgets. Indonesia with 240 million people and a geography as vast as America's has a smaller defense budget than the tiny city-state of Singapore, and one the same size as Malaysia's, which has one tenth of Indonesia's population. Singapore has four submarines, Indonesia two that do not work.

Noting that democratization ultimately means decentralization, and with much of the country's coveted natural resources located at its geographic extremes in Aceh and Papua, Rahakundini worries that unless Indonesia can develop some semblance of a world-class, naval-oriented military, "we could be informally broken up, bit by bit, into subtle spheres of outside influence." The irony is that while the Indonesian military has been discredited at home for its inward-focused involvement in domestic politics, that same military is now desperately needed to focus outward toward potential adversaries. As Indonesia, at the confluence of the Indian and Pacific oceans, becomes more and more strategically important, even as it increasingly becomes a democratic and Muslim success story, the rise of regional navies and fishing fleets—China's, India's, Japan's—means it may be about to gradually lose a semblance of its sovereignty.

The strategy of the Indonesian military, Defense Minister Juwono Sudarsono told me, is one of "patience": hold the line while a middle class develops further, providing the tax revenue for a larger military, especially a navy; in the meantime, continue to participate in U.N. peacekeeping operations to raise its international stature, and thus be morally defended by the international community.

Meanwhile, Southeast Asia as a whole, as its various political systems show signs of strain, seems to be falling further under the sway of Chinese mercantile domination. Thailand, once the regional anchor, has an electorate increasingly polarized between an upwardly mobile, rural working class and a Bangkok-based middle class, even as its revered king is aging and his son and heir apparent is very unpopular. As democracy becomes more tumultuous, the Thai state is about to weaken. Meanwhile, both Malaysia and Singapore are heading into challenging democratic transitions of their own, as both of their adept, nation-building strongmen, Mahathir bin Mohammed and Lee Kuan Yew, pass from the scene.[30]

Indeed, Malaysia is the inverse of Indonesia. Whereas around 85 percent of the Indonesian population is Muslim, only 60 percent of Malaysia's is, even as Malaysia is a more overt, hard-edged "Islamic state." Because all ethnic Malays are Muslim, Islam is racialized in Malaysia, and the result is sharp inter-communal divides among the Malay, Chinese, and Indian communities. Creeping Islamization has led to seventy thousand Chinese leaving Malaysia over the past two decades, and those who have remained are sending their children to Chinese-language schools. Political resentments in Malaysia in general are growing as ten thousand Indians rallied in late 2007 against Malay-Islamic political domination. Unsurprisingly, Malaysia, like Indonesia, finds the U.S. naval presence in Southeast Asia a convenient hedge against China, although Kuala Lumpur is courting Beijing with its proposal to build a pipeline across northern Malaysia, which would allow Beijing to be less dependent on the Strait of Malacca for its oil deliveries. In fact, Malaysia is increasingly under the shadow of China, even though its ethnic Malay Muslim rulers are seen by their Chinese subjects as increasingly chauvinist.[31] Translation: the dislike of ethnic Chinese throughout much of Southeast Asia does not necessarily carry over into the foreign policy realm. Beijing is becoming too powerful to be treated with anything but the highest degree of respect. All these countries hope that a continued American naval presence, combined with the rise of the Indian and other navies such as Japan's and South Korea's, will serve to balance against Chinese power.

The quiet fear of China is most clearly revealed by the actions of Singapore, a city-state strategically located near the narrowest point of the Strait of Malacca. In Singapore, the ethnic Chinese dominate the ethnic Malays by a margin of 77 to 14 percent. Nevertheless, Singapore fears becoming a vassal state of China, and consequently has developed a long-standing military training relationship with Taiwan. Minister Mentor Lee Kuan Yew has publicly urged the United States to stay engaged in the region militarily and diplomatically.[32] The degree to which Singapore can maintain its feisty independence will be a gauge of Beijing's regional clout.

This comes at a time when Singapore's mild version of authoritarianism is coming into question. The legitimacy of the ruling People's Action Party has always rested on its economic performance, and as the global downturn affects the region, the party may have no choice but to open up the system.[33] Though democratization benefits both Malaysia and Singapore in the long run, in the short run the rigors of electoral politics will reveal internal weaknesses that could make them more susceptible to Beijing's pressure. Unlike the Dutch and the other Western powers in Southeast Asia, which operated far from their home ports, China is close-by and geographically dominant in the region, giving it the opportunity for a degree of control that will be both more subtle and more comprehensive than anything we have seen in the past.

PART III

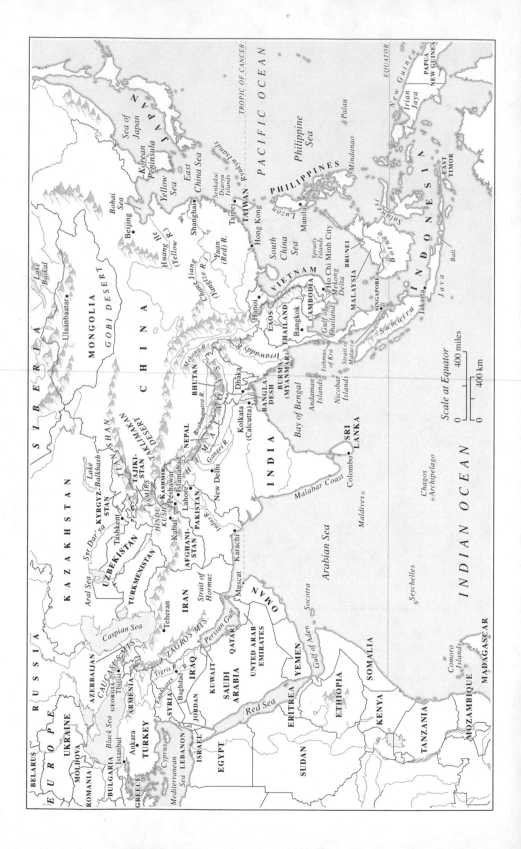

CHAPTER FIFTEEN

CHINA'S TWO-OCEAN STRATEGY?

The Indian Ocean has constituted a stage set for Western conquest going back more than five hundred years. The University of Chicago historian William H. McNeill associates the "advent of the modern era" with the Portuguese command of the African-Eurasian sea-lanes that began with Prince Henry the Navigator and Vasco da Gama.[1] Since the Portuguese we have seen the Spanish, Dutch, French, English, and Americans make their mark in significant tracts of the Indian Ocean and its adjacent seas. These Western conquerors came largely for commercial reasons, with the Americans in particular intent on guarding the sea lines of communication to safely import Middle Eastern oil from the western part of the ocean, even as they have guarded the central part from the coral atoll of Diego Garcia, using the British territory as a base to launch air attacks on Iraq in 1991 and on Afghanistan in 2001.

The Cold War decades saw the United States as the great global maritime power and the Soviet Union as the dominant Eurasian land power. But as the Cold War recedes into the past and China rises economically and politically, taking advantage, in effect, of America's military quagmires in Iraq and Afghanistan, a new and more complex order is gradually emerging in the maritime rimland of Eurasia, which includes not only the Indian Ocean but the western Pacific. What follows is an analysis of a U.S. Navy that has already reached the zenith of its dominance, faced with a rising Chinese maritime presence that, along with the rise of India, could over time herald the end of Western control over these waters.

In retrospect, it might be that we will view the December 2004–January 2005 relief effort mounted by the U.S. military off the coast of Sumatra, on behalf of the victims of the Indian Ocean tsunami, as one of the climaxes of American naval power in Asia. The sight of both carrier and expeditionary strike groups, with their attendant cruisers, destroyers, and frigates—helicopters lifting off decks in ship-to-shore circuits, assisted further by rescue swimmers and medical corpsmen—created a rousing aura of dominance and virtue, two attributes that rarely mix. Although the aim of Operation Unified Assistance was humanitarian, the skills employed—getting a vast array of warships and aircraft across hundreds of miles of ocean at "best speed" on a moment's notice—were those essential to war. The true message of the rescue effort: *Behold the power of the United States Navy!*

Yet the truth that is now hiding in plain sight is the gradual loss of the Indian and western Pacific oceans as veritable American military lakes after more than sixty years of near-total dominion following World War II. A few years down the road, according to the security analysts at the private policy group Strategic Forecasting, Americans will not be the prime deliverers of disaster assistance in South and Southeast Asian seas to the same extent. In the next emergency our ships will share the waters (and the glory) with new "big decks" from Australia, Japan, South Korea, India, and perhaps China. This occurs at the same time that China's production and acquisition of submarines is several times that of America's. Indeed, China is in the midst of a shipbuilding and acquisition craze that will result sometime in the next decade in the People's Liberation Army Navy having more ships than the U.S. Navy. Of course, as we will see, numbers tell only a small part of the story, but they do matter.

Undeniably, over the decades the U.S. Navy has been shrinking. At the end of World War II the United States had 6700 ships. Throughout the Cold War it had around 600 ships. In the 1990s, following the collapse of the Berlin Wall, it had more than 350. Now it is down to fewer than 280. Though the navy has plans to increase that number to more than 310, according to the Congressional Budget Office and the Congressional Research Service, cost overruns of 34 percent, in addition to other factors, mean that such plans may be overly optimistic. Over the next decade and beyond, if the navy continues to build only seven ships per year with a fleet whose life expectancy is thirty years, the total number of its ships could conceivably dwindle to the low two hundreds. Given America's economic recession, the Pentagon's budget will possibly be reduced further, and ship development, which is a very expensive capital item, will pay a price.

This does not mean that the U.S. Navy will cede its preeminent position in the Indian Ocean and western Pacific anytime soon. The figures cited indicate slow-moving trends that are subject to reversal. But it does mean that, closing in on seven decades after World War II, other naval powers all indigenous to the region, as well as non-state actors like pirates, are finally starting to crowd the picture. America's unipolar moment in the world's oceans is starting to fade. And as indicated, this is happening as China—America's most likely peer competitor in the twenty-first century—increasingly translates its economic clout into sea power.

It bears repeating that there is nothing illegitimate about the rise of the Chinese military. China's ascendancy can fairly be compared with that of the United States following its own consolidation of land-based power in the aftermath of the Civil War and the settlement of the American West, which culminated at the turn of the twentieth century with the construction of the Panama Canal. Under the stewardship of some of its most forgettable presidents—Hayes, Garfield, Arthur, Harrison, and so on—the American economy chugged quietly along with high annual growth rates. Consequently, as it traded more with the outside world, it developed for the first time complex economic and strategic interests in far-flung places that led to navy and marine landings in South America and the Pacific, among other military actions. Why should we expect China to follow a radically different path? For China's society is every bit as dynamic now as America's was a century ago.

In 1890 the American military theorist Alfred Thayer Mahan published *The Influence of Sea Power Upon History, 1660–1783,* which argues that a state's power to protect its merchant fleets has been the determining factor in world history. Mahan has always been a favorite of those seeking naval dominance, and both Chinese and Indian strategists read him avidly nowadays. But it is too facile to suggest that China is acquiring naval power strictly as a means to the end of regional or perhaps global hegemony. Empires are often not sought consciously. Rather, as states become stronger, they develop needs and—counterintuitively— a whole new set of insecurities that lead them to expand overseas in an organic fashion.

China is not Iran under President Mahmoud Ahmadinejad. It is not threatening to destroy any country, and it has an intensely developed diplomatic and economic relationship with the United States. The global recession has tied American and Chinese interests even closer together, as the U.S. depends on China for affordable goods and to prop up its currency with trillions of dollars of Chinese deposits, and China depends on the U.S. as its principal consumer market. Strong American-Chinese bilateral relations going forward is not only plausible, but might be the best-case scenario for the global system in the twenty-first century, allowing for true world governance to take shape.

China may not be democratic in a formal sense, but its system admits to intense, vibrant debates over policy and the direction of the society. There is even the possibility that China will face some sort of internal upheaval that will result in splits in the leadership, and delay by years or longer China's march to great power status. Just as Kremlinologists of the 1970s got the Soviet Union wrong in projecting the Cold War lasting several more decades, I among others may be getting China wrong by even assuming in the first place China's continued economic growth. Yet, given current trends, such continued growth must be taken as a serious possibility.

Therefore, the most likely scenario in my mind for relations with China is something quite nuanced: the United States will both compete and cooperate with China. The American-Chinese rivalry of the future could give new meaning to the word "subtlety," especially in its economic and diplomatic arrangements. Yet, if this relationship has its hard edges, I expect one of those will be where the two countries' navies interact: in the Greater Indian Ocean and western Pacific.

While America's ship procurement process has been described as broken, and it struggles to maintain a navy at its current size in the face of reduced GDP growth—amid the worst economic downtown since the Great Depression—China's defense budget has been increasing by double digits for two decades, even as its own economy, despite the deleterious effects of the global crisis, will expand by roughly 8 or 10 percent annually in coming years. China's undersea arsenal includes twelve Kilo-class diesel-electric guided-missile attack submarines, armed with wake-homing torpedoes; thirteen Song-class subs similar to the Kilos; two Shang-class nuclear attack submarines, and one Jin-class nuclear ballistic-missile submarine, with three more on the way.

Obviously, this lineup bears no comparison whatsoever to the U.S. Navy's seventy-four nuclear-powered attack and ballistic-missile submarines now in service. The U.S. boasts twenty-four of the world's thirty-four aircraft carriers, the Chinese have none (but are developing one and maybe two). Such statistics go on. But, to repeat, numbers do not tell the whole story: rather, the story is about underlying trends, asymmetric capabilities, and the creative combination of naval, economic, and territorial power that can create a sphere of influence throughout Asia.

China is catching up slowly, but fast enough to alert Americans that their time of dominance is not forever. Whereas Iraq showed the United States the crude, low-tech end of asymmetry with roadside bombs, the Chinese, with their development of missile and space programs, will show America the subtle, high-tech end of asymmetry through the art of dissuasion and access-denial: making it riskier for the U.S. Navy to move its carrier strike groups close to the Asian mainland in the future, whenever and wherever it likes. Finally, it is China's very geographical centrality to Asia, coupled with its growing navy and burgeoning economic might, that will cause the U.S. to continue to lose influence there.

Therefore, it is crucial to sketch out what may be China's evolving naval strategy in the Indian and Pacific oceans. But before I do that, it is necessary to say more about why China goes to sea in the first place. What exactly are those complex economic and strategic interests it is developing, vaguely comparable to America's own more than a century ago?*

Since antiquity China has been preoccupied with land invasions of one sort or another. The Great Wall of China was begun in the third century B.C. to keep out Turkic invaders; in the mid-twentieth century China was anxious about another invasion from the north, from the Soviet

---

* My thinking about this maritime world depends substantially on a group of scholars at the U.S. Naval War College whose work on China's maritime strategy has been exhaustive, creative, and very moderate in tone. They are Gabriel B. Collins, Andrew S. Erickson, Lyle J. Goldstein, James R. Holmes, William S. Murray, and Toshi Yoshihara. In particular, I am heavily indebted to four publications for statistics and many insights: James R. Holmes and Toshi Yoshihara, *Chinese Naval Strategy in the 21st Century: The Turn to Mahan* (New York: Routledge, 2008); Toshi Yoshihara and James Holmes, "Command of the Sea with Chinese Characteristics," *Orbis*, Fall 2005; Gabriel B. Collins et al., eds., *China's Energy Strategy: The Impact on Beijing's Maritime Policies* (Annapolis, MD: Naval Institute Press, 2008); and Andrew Erickson and Gabe Collins, "Beijing's Energy Security Strategy: The Significance of a Chinese State-Owned Tanker Fleet," *Orbis*, Fall 2007.

Union following the Sino-Soviet split. Thus, under Mao Zedong China concentrated its defense budget on its army and pointedly neglected the seas. But with the collapse of the Soviet Union, such worries dissipated. Moreover, Chinese diplomats, in recent years, have been busy settling remaining border disputes with the Central Asian republics and with its other neighbors. In fact, a reverse invasion is now under way, with Chinese migrants in the slow process of demographically taking over parts of Siberia. So China's pursuit of sea power is, first and foremost, an indication that its land borders are not under threat for the first time in quite a while. Whereas coastal city-states and island nations, big and small, pursue sea power as a matter of course, a continental and historically insular nation like China does so partly as a luxury: the mark of a budding great power. Merely by going to sea in the wide-ranging manner that it has, China demonstrates its dominance on land in the heartland of Asia. To be sure, China is not as secure in its neighborhood as the late-nineteenth-century U.S. was in its own, given America's status as a veritable island nation. Nevertheless, China is right now more secure on land than it has been throughout most of its history.

Another factor pointing China seaward is the dramatic boom in its economy, which has led to an explosion of trade, and thus to the concomitant explosion of commerce along the country's coast. In 2007, Shanghai's ports surpassed Hong Kong as the largest in the world, according to cargo handled. And by 2015, China will become the world's most prolific shipbuilder, overtaking Japan and South Korea. Sea power is partially determined by merchant shipping, and China will lead the world in this area.

Above all, China's demand for energy motivates both its foreign policy and national security policy: the need for an increasing, uninterrupted flow of energy to sustain its dramatic economic growth. Despite its increasing emphasis on coal, biomass, nuclear power, and other alternatives, China requires ever more oil and natural gas, and is the world's second largest consumer of oil after the U.S. Concurrently, Chinese officials see this very need for imported petroleum products as a pressure point that a future adversary might exploit. (The need to diversify its energy sources helps explain why China deals openly with such an odious regime as Sudan's.) China's hydrocarbon use has more than doubled in the past two decades, and will double again in the next decade or two, even as domestic oil production has remained stagnant since 1993, when

China became a net oil importer. That oil and natural gas come overwhelmingly—as much as 85 percent—from the Indian Ocean through the Malacca Strait en route to China's Pacific Ocean ports. Importing oil via pipelines from Central Asia will not be enough; nor will the increased use of domestic coal. In particular, as the years roll on, China may become more dependent on Saudi Arabian oil and Iranian liquefied natural gas. Therefore, vital sea lines of communications (SLOCS) around the southern Eurasian rimland must be protected. Given China's history as a great civilizational power since antiquity, and its relatively recent history as a victim of Western colonialism, why would Chinese leaders want to entrust such a vital defense detail forever to the U.S. Navy, the self-anointed protector of the worldwide maritime commons? If you governed China, with the responsibility of lifting hundreds of millions of Chinese into an energy-ravenous, middle-class lifestyle, you, too, would seek a credible navy in order to protect your merchant fleet across the Indian Ocean and western Pacific.

But the problem is that Chinese leaders are still many years away from having such a navy. Therefore, at the moment, according to the analyst James Mulvenon, they may be content to "free ride" on the "public good" that the U.S. Navy provides.[2] Yet, as the Chinese navy is increasingly able to assume more and more responsibilities, such free ridership will become less necessary and the era of U.S.-China naval competition may begin in earnest, especially if America's own fleet size goes down, bringing the two navies closer together in terms of capabilities.

Keep in mind that increasingly the maritime world from Africa eastward to Indonesia, and then northward to the Korean Peninsula and Japan, will become one sweeping continuum owing to the various canal and land-bridge projects that may provide links in the future between the two oceans, which now are limited to the Malacca, Lombok, and Sunda straits (all in Indonesian waters, the last two being minor passages compared to Malacca). In other words, the geography of maritime Eurasia is destined at some point to become whole and condensed.

One world though it may become, it is still two for the time being, for the Strait of Malacca remains the end of one great oceanic civilization and the beginning of another. And whereas China approaches the Indian Ocean as a landlocked power, seeking port access with littoral countries such as Pakistan, Sri Lanka, Bangladesh, and Burma—thus bringing it into potential conflict with India—China has a long coastline fronting the western Pacific, bringing it into potential conflict with the United States.

So let's turn just beyond the Indian Ocean to the western Pacific. Here the Chinese navy sees little but trouble and frustration in what Chinese strategists call the First Island Chain, which, going from north to south, comprises Japan and the Ryuku Islands, the "half-island" of the Korean Peninsula, Taiwan, the Philippines, Indonesia, and Australia.[3] All of these places save for Australia are potential flashpoints. Scenarios include the collapse of North Korea or an inter-Korean war, a possible struggle with the U.S. over Taiwan, and acts of piracy or terrorism that conceivably impede China's merchant fleet access to the Malacca and other Indonesian straits. There are, too, China's territorial disputes over the likely energy-rich ocean beds in the East and South China seas. In the East China Sea, China and Japan have conflicting claims of sovereignty to the Senkaku/Diaoyu Islands; in the South China Sea, China has conflicting sovereignty claims with the Philippines and Vietnam to some or all of the Spratly Islands. Particularly in the case of the Senkaku/Diaoyu Islands, the dispute does carry the benefit of providing Beijing with a lever to stoke nationalism, whenever it might need to, but otherwise it is a grim seascape for Chinese naval strategists. Looking out from China's Pacific coast on to this First Island Chain, they behold a sort of "Great Wall in reverse," in the words of Naval War College professors James Holmes and Toshi Yoshihara: a well-organized line of American allies, with the equivalent of guard towers on Japan, the Ryukus, South Korea, Taiwan, the Philippines, and Australia, all potentially blocking China's access to the larger ocean. Chinese strategists see this map and bristle at its navy being so boxed in.

Take the two Koreas, the unification of which would be, to say the least, geopolitically inconvenient to China. Jutting out far from the Asian mainland, the Korean Peninsula commands all maritime traffic in northeastern China and, more particularly, traps in its armpit the Bohai Sea, home to China's largest offshore oil reserve. Moreover, a unified Korea would likely be a nationalistic Korea, with distinctly mixed feelings toward its large neighbors, China and Japan, which historically have sought to control and even occupy it. A divided Korea is momentarily useful to China, as North Korea—as many headaches as its hermetic regime gives Beijing—provides a buffer between China and the vibrant and successful democracy that is South Korea.

As for Taiwan, it illustrates something basic in world politics: that moral questions are just, beneath the surface, often questions of power. Taiwan is discussed by all sides purely in moral terms, even as its sovereignty or lack thereof carries pivotal geopolitical consequences. China talks about Taiwan in terms of consolidating the national patrimony, unifying China for the good of all ethnic Chinese. America talks about Taiwan in terms of preserving a model democracy. But Taiwan is something else: in the late army general Douglas MacArthur's words, it is "an unsinkable aircraft carrier" that dominates the center point of China's convex seaboard, from which an outside power like the United States can "radiate" power along China's coastal periphery.[4] As such, nothing irritates Chinese naval planners as much as de facto Taiwanese independence. Of all the guard towers along the reverse maritime Great Wall, Taiwan is, metaphorically, the tallest and most centrally located. With Taiwan returned to the bosom of mainland China, suddenly the Great Wall and the maritime straitjacket it represents would be severed.

China yearns for an authentic blue water, or oceanic, navy, just as the United States once did. To create one, America first had to consolidate the temperate zone of the North American continent through westward expansion and settlement. If China succeeds in, in effect, consolidating Taiwan, not only will its navy suddenly be in an advantageous strategic position vis-à-vis the First Island Chain, but also, just as dramatically, its national energies will be freed up to look outward in terms of power projection, to a degree that has so far been impossible. With Taiwan resolved in China's favor, then, as Holmes and Yoshihara posit, China would be more liberated to pursue a naval grand strategy in both the Indian and Pacific oceans. (And if China could more effectively consolidate ethnic-Han Chinese control over the Muslim Turkic Uighurs in its westernmost province of Xinjiang, that, too, might add an additional spur to its pan-oceanic naval efforts.)

Think of the Chinese resolution of the Taiwan challenge as having a potential impact similar, at least symbolically, to the last major battle of the Indian Wars, the Wounded Knee Massacre of 1890. After that dreadful event the "Wild West" having been consolidated, America's military began in earnest to focus seaward, and a little more than a decade later came the building of the Panama Canal. Though the adjective "multipolar" is thrown around liberally to describe the global situation, it will be the fusing of Taiwan with the mainland that will mark the real emergence of such a multi-polar world.

China is working assiduously in many ways, principally economic, at changing the dynamic of the American-dominated First Island Chain. Countries like the Philippines and Australia will have China as their number-one trading partner. In the case of the Philippines—an American legacy going back more than a hundred years that has included war, occupation, decades-long political interference, and massive economic aid—China has been doing everything it can to boost bilateral ties, even offering the Philippines a defense pact some years back that included an intelligence-sharing agreement. Therefore, one cannot help considering a future with a rearmed Japan, a nationalist Greater Korea, a Taiwan functionally united with the mainland, and a Philippines and Australia that, while nominally pro-American, have been neutralized by trade and other realities related to China's continued economic and military rise. The result would be a far less stable western Pacific in tandem with the diminution of American power, and the breakout of China on all naval fronts.

To the east, in such a scenario, China begins to have designs on what its strategists call the Second Island Chain, dominated by U.S. territories like Guam and the Mariana Islands. Indeed, Oceania in its entirety is a region where China is fast developing interests, even as it broadly strengthens diplomatic and economic ties with many of these small and seemingly obscure island nations.

But it is to the south—where the Indian and Pacific oceans join—in the complex maritime region of the South China and Java seas, dominated by Singapore, peninsular Malaysia, and the many thousands of islands of the southern Philippines and especially of the Indonesia archipelago, where China's naval interests are most pronounced; and where its sea lines of communication to the oil-rich Middle East and Africa are most at risk. Here we have radical Islam, piracy, and the naval rise of India, coupled with the heavily congested geographic bottlenecks of the various Indonesian straits, through which a large proportion of China's oil tankers and merchant fleets must pass. There are also significant deposits of oil that China hopes to exploit, making the South China Sea a "second Persian Gulf" in some estimations.[5] The combination of all these factors, and the opportunities, problems, and nightmares they represent for Chinese planners, make this region at the Indian Ocean's eastern gateway among the most critical seascapes of the coming decades. Just as the U.S. Navy moved a century ago to control the Caribbean basin, so must the Chinese navy move, if not to control, then at least to become as dominant as the Americans in these seas, for the Malacca Strait can be thought of as akin to the Panama Canal, an outlet to the wider world.[6]

The mid-twentieth-century Dutch-American scholar of geopolitics Nicholas J. Spykman notes that throughout history states have engaged in "circumferential and transmarine expansion" to gain control of adjacent seas: Greece sought to control the Aegean, Rome the Mediterranean, the U.S. the Caribbean, and now, according to this logic, China the South China Sea.[7]

Imagine what it must be like for the Chinese to see U.S. Navy carrier and expeditionary strike groups sailing at will throughout their vital backyard. The Indian Ocean tsunami relief effort mounted off Indonesia by the U.S. Navy was for the Chinese a demonstration of their own impotence in their maritime sphere, as they had no aircraft carriers to send to help. The rescue effort further inflamed an ongoing debate in Chinese power circles about whether or not they should acquire a carrier or two of their own, rather than continue concentrating on purely warmaking platforms such as submarines, which have little utility in aid efforts. Future naval dominance of these waters is, in the eyes of the Chinese, a natural right. The tsunami relief effort only intensified their determination in this regard.

When considering maritime Southeast Asia, what immediately impresses one is the danger of radical Islam in the partly ungovernable archipelago of the southern Philippines, Malaysia, and Indonesia. For the Chinese, radical Islam is bad because it brings the U.S. military closer to their shores in the hunt for terrorists. I witnessed this firsthand while covering Operation Enduring Freedom in the Philippines in 2003 and again in 2006. In the hunt for the al-Qaeda–and Jemaah Islamiya–affiliated terrorist group Abu Sayyaf, American Special Operations Forces established a base in Mindanao, to help Filipino soldiers and marines conduct anti-terror operations in the embattled Sulu Archipelago to the south. The effect was to bring the American military back to the Philippines for the first time since the closure of Clark Air Base and Subic Bay Naval Station in 1992, and to deploy American forces south of the main Filipino island of Luzon for the first time since World War II. This was all disheartening news to Chinese strategists. Some Americans I interviewed were very open about the geopolitical implications of their presence, telling me that today the problem was radical Islam, but that such deployments better positioned their military for a future competition with China.

Then there is piracy, which bothers the Chinese for obvious reasons. It potentially threatens China's maritime lifeline to the mainland in these crowded and constricted archipelagic waters. In recent years, cooperation among the navies of Singapore, Malaysia, and Indonesia has reduced piracy greatly, so it is no longer the scourge that it is in the Gulf of Aden, at the opposite end of the Indian Ocean. Nevertheless, given the consequences of a return of piracy to Southeast Asia, where it has been a common feature of sea warfare for many centuries, Chinese admirals cannot afford to be complacent.

As mentioned, there is speculation that in the foreseeable future the Chinese will help finance a canal across the Isthmus of Kra in Thailand that will provide another link between the Indian and Pacific oceans—an engineering project on the scale of the Panama Canal and slated to cost $20 billion. It was across the Kra isthmus that the Chinese portaged goods in antiquity to get to the Indian Ocean side and back.[8] For China, a Kra canal might be as significant as the Grand Canal that in late antiquity connected Hangzhou in central China with Beijing in the north. A Kra canal would offer China new port facilities and oil refineries, warehousing for transshipments, and, in general, a platform from which to expand Beijing's influence in Southeast Asia. Not that far from the Isthmus of Kra is Hainan Island in the South China Sea, where China is increasingly able to project air and sea power from its military base there, which features underground berths for its submarines.[9]

Meanwhile, as you may recall, Dubai Ports World is conducting a feasibility study to construct a nearby land bridge, with ports on either side of the Isthmus of Kra, connected by rails and highways. And the Malaysian government is interested in an east-west pipeline network that will link up ports in the Bay of Bengal and the South China Sea. For some time now the strategic heart of the maritime world has not been the North Atlantic but the western Pacific and Greater Indian Ocean region. Yet that trend may accelerate with the eventual building of at least one or two, if not all three, of these projects, which, in turn, will have an equally dramatic effect on naval deployment patterns. The twin trends of an economically rising Asia and a politically crumbling Middle East will lead to a naval warfare emphasis on the Indian Ocean and surrounding seas, whose choke points are increasingly susceptible to terrorism and piracy.

China will gain immeasurably from all these projects. The potential threats signified by piracy and the rise of the Indian navy dissipate once these Southeast Asian waters become less constricted and less focused on one strait. There is, too, the worry about congestion, pollution, and hazardous cargoes that also will be alleviated. More importantly, the Chinese navy would obviously prefer to be not a one-ocean but a two-ocean power, with multiple access routes between the Indian Ocean and western Pacific to ease the so-called Malacca dilemma. A one-ocean navy in the western Pacific makes China a regional power; a two-ocean navy in both the western Pacific *and* the Indian Ocean makes China a great power, able to project force around the whole navigable Eurasian rimland.

China's Malacca challenge has two long-range solutions. The first is the simple one of providing alternative sea routes from one ocean to the other. The second is to get more of China's energy supplies overland to China from the Middle East and Central Asia, so that less hydrocarbons have to transit from the Indian to Pacific Ocean in the first place. As we have seen, that might include using Indian Ocean ports to eventually transport oil and other energy products via roads and pipelines northward into the heart of China. In fact, it was striking how China leapt at the chance to deploy two destroyers and a supply ship to the Gulf of Aden to protect Chinese vessels against pirates. In addition to getting its sailors hands-on, out-of-area long-voyage experience, it furthered China's claim to the Indian Ocean as a legitimate venue for naval operations.

Here it is worthwhile revisiting the era of great Chinese sea power in the Indian Ocean during the Song and early Ming dynasties, from the late tenth to the early fifteenth century, which culminated in the celebrated voyages of the eunuch admiral Zheng He. These expeditions saw Chinese commercial and political influence extend as far away as East Africa, and featured Chinese landings in such places as Bengal, Ceylon, Hormuz, and Mogadishu. In particular, Zheng He's voyages from 1405 to 1433, which encompassed hundreds of ships and tens of thousands of men, were not merely an extravagant oddity designed to show the Chinese flag in South Asian and Middle Eastern harbors. They were also designed to safeguard the flow of vital goods against pirates, and were in other ways, too, a demonstration of soft, benevolent power. Interestingly, the Chinese navy of the Song and early Ming eras did not seek to establish bases or maintain permanent presences in Indian Ocean ports the way the European powers did later; rather, they sought access through the building of alliances in the form of a tribute system.[10] This more subtle display of power seems to be exactly what the Chinese intend for the future. Take Pakistan as a model: the Chinese have maintained a security and trade relationship with Pakistan, constructing the Karakoram Highway that connects Pakistan with China, as well as a deepwater port at Gwadar on the Arabian Sea. This helps develop the access China desires, even as the Gwadar harbor itself will be run by the Singaporeans. Indeed, full-fledged Chinese naval bases in places like Gwadar and Hambantota would be so provocative to the Indians that it is frankly hard to foresee such an eventuality. "Access" is the key word, not "bases."

The Ming emperors eventually ended their forays into the Indian Ocean, but this happened only after they were pressured by the Mongols on land and thus had to turn their attention to China's northern border. No such difficulties threaten China now. To the contrary, China is making significant progress in stabilizing its land frontiers and has even demographically laid claim to parts of Russian Siberia with Chinese migrants. Thus, the way is clear for China to turn its attention to the sea.

Nevertheless, it is worth keeping in mind that we are talking here of only a likely future. For the present, Chinese officials are focused on Taiwan and the First Island Chain, with the Indian Ocean a comparatively secondary concern. Thus, in the years and decades hence, the Indian Ocean, in addition to everything else, will register the degree to which China becomes a great military power, following in the footsteps of the Portuguese, Dutch, and others. What is China's grand strategy? The Indian Ocean will help show us.

Imagine hence, a Chinese merchant fleet and navy present in some form from the coast of Africa all the way around the two oceans to the Korean Peninsula, covering, in effect, all Asian waters within the temperate and tropical zones, and thus protecting Chinese economic interests and the maritime system within which those interests operate. Imagine, too, India, South Korea, and Japan all adding submarines and other warships to patrol this Afro-Indo-Pacific region. Finally, imagine a United States that is still a hegemon of sorts, still maintaining the world's largest navy and coast guard, but with a smaller difference between it and other world-class navies. That is the world we are likely headed toward.

To be sure, the United States will recover from the greatest crisis in capitalism since the Great Depression, but the gap between it and Asian giants China and India will shrink gradually, and that will affect the size of navies. Of course, American economic and military decline is not a fatalistic *given*. No one can know the future, and decline, as a concept, is overrated. The British Royal Navy began its relative decline in the 1890s, even as Great Britain went on to help save the West in two world wars over the next half century.[11]

Still, a certain pattern has emerged. The United States dominated the world's economy for the Cold War decades. After all, while the other great powers had suffered major infrastructure damage in their homelands in World War II, the U.S. came out of that war unscathed, and thus with a great development advantage. (China, Japan, and Europe were decimated in the 1930s and 1940s, while India was still under colonial rule.) But that world is long gone, the other nations have caught up, and the remaining question is how does the U.S. respond responsibly to a multi-polarity that probably will become more of a feature of the world system in years to come.

Naval power will be as accurate an indicator of an increasingly complex global power arrangement as anything else. Indeed, China's naval rise can present the U.S. with great opportunities. Once more, it is fortunate that the Chinese navy is rising in a legitimate manner, to protect economic and rightful security interests as America's has done, rather than to forge a potentially suicidal insurgency force at sea, as Iran's Islamic Revolutionary Guard Corps Navy appears bent on doing in the Persian Gulf.[12] This provides China and the U.S. with several intersection points of cooperation. Piracy, terrorism, and natural disasters are all problem areas where the two navies can work together, because in these fields China's interests are not dissimilar to America's. Moreover, China may be cagily open to cooperation with the U.S. on the naval aspects of energy issues: jointly patrolling sea lines of communication, that is. Both China and the U.S. will continue to be dependent on hydrocarbons from the Greater Middle East—China especially so in coming years—so the interests of the two nations in this sphere seem to be converging. Therefore, it is not inevitable that two great powers that harbor no territorial disputes, that both require imported energy in large amounts, that inhabit opposite sides of the globe, and whose philosophical systems of governance, while wide apart, are still not as distant as were those between the U.S. and the Soviet Union, will become adversaries.

Thus, leveraging allies like India and Japan against China is responsible in one sense only: it helps provide a mechanism for the U.S. to gradually and elegantly cede great power responsibilities to like-minded others as their own capacities rise, as part of a studied retreat from a unipolar world. But to follow such a strategy in isolation risks unduly and unnecessarily alienating China. Thus, leveraging allies must be part of a wider military strategy that seeks to draw in China as part of an Asia-centric alliance system, in which militaries cooperate on a multitude of issues.

Indeed, "Where the old 'Maritime Strategy' focused on sea control," Admiral Michael Mullen, Chairman of the Joint Chiefs of Staff, said in 2006 (when he was chief of naval operations), "the new one must recognize that the economic tide of all nations rises not when the seas are controlled by one [nation], but rather when they are made safe and free for all."

Admiral Mullen went on: "I'm after that proverbial 1,000-ship Navy—a fleet-in-being, if you will, comprised of all freedom-loving nations, standing watch over the seas, standing watch over each other."

As grandiose and platitudinous as Admiral Mullen's words may sound, it is in fact a realistic response to America's own diminished resources. The U.S. will be less and less able to go it alone and so will rely increasingly on coalitions, for national navies tend to cooperate better than national armies, partly because sailors are united by a kind of fellowship of the sea, born of their shared experience facing violent natural forces. Just as a subtle Cold War of the seas is possible between the American and Chinese navies, conversely, the very tendency of navies to cooperate better than armies may also mean that the two navies can be the leading edge of cooperation between the two powers, working toward the establishment of a stable and prosperous multi-polar system. Given America's civilizational tensions with radical Islam, and its at times quarrelsome relationship with Europe, as well as with a bitter and truculent Russia, the United States must do all that it can to find commonality with China. It cannot take on the whole world by itself.

The United States must eventually see its military not primarily as a land-based meddler, caught up in internal Islamic conflict, but as a naval- and air-centric balancer, lurking close by, ready to intervene in tsunami- and Bangladesh-type humanitarian emergencies, and working in concert with both the Chinese and Indian navies as part of a Eurasian maritime system. This will improve America's image in the former third world. While America must always be ready for war, it must work daily to keep the peace: indispensability, not dominance, should be its goal. Such a strategy will mitigate the possible dangers of China's rise. Even in elegant decline, this is a time of unprecedented opportunity for Washington, which must be seen in Monsoon Asia as the benevolent outside power.

Western penetration of the Indian and western Pacific oceans began bloodily with the Portuguese at the end of the fifteenth century. The supplanting of the Portuguese by the Dutch, and the Dutch by the English, came also with its fair share of blood.* Then there was the supplanting of the English by the Americans in the high seas of Asia, which came via the bloodshed of World War II. Therefore, a peaceful transition away from American unipolarity at sea toward an American-Indian-Chinese condominium of sorts would be the first of its kind. Rather than an abdication of responsibility, such a transition would leave the Greater Indian Ocean in the free and accountable hands of indigenous Asian nations for the first time in five hundred years. The shores of the twenty-first century's most important body of water lack a superpower, and that is, in the final analysis, the central fact of its geography. China's two-ocean strategy, should it ever be realized, will not occur in a vacuum, but will be constrained by the navies of other nations, and that will make all the difference.

---

* One should not forget the French, whose role, particularly in the islands of the southwestern Indian Ocean, is covered expertly by Richard Hall in *Empires of the Monsoon: A History of the Indian Ocean and Its Invaders* (London: HarperCollins, 1996).

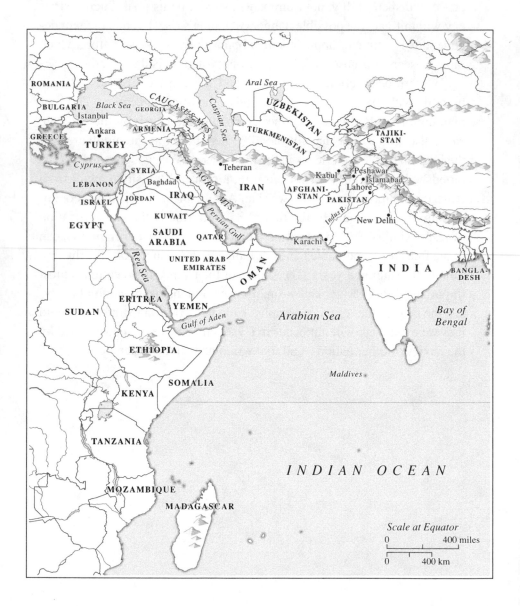

CHAPTER SIXTEEN

UNITY AND ANARCHY

hina is renewing its historical links with Arab and Persian civilizations, and as India never really severed them, the Indian Ocean
world—the universal joint of the Eastern Hemisphere—is hurtling
toward unity. "The rise of China's economy is an accelerant for the Arab
world," writes Ben Simpfendorfer, chief China economist at the Royal
Bank of Scotland. "Its demand for oil has helped fuel the Arab economies.
Its factories churn out consumer goods to fill Dubai's and Riyadh's air-
conditioned malls."[1] For the Arabs, the rise of China offers an alternative
strategic partner to the West. Before the tide turned in the Allies' favor in
World War II, strategists such as Nicholas Spykman concerned themselves with Africa and Eurasia achieving unity through the domination of
fascist powers.[2] That unity may be upon us in coming years and decades,
not through military domination, but through the resurrection of a trading
system, like that established by the medieval Muslims, and perpetuated
by the Portuguese.

And in this increasingly taut web of economic activity, Africa, at the
Indian Ocean's western extremity, is not being left out. Africa's renewal,
however slow and fitful, is being impelled in large measure by investment
from the Middle East and Asia. The third world, as it used to be known,
is disappearing gradually, as the parts of it that have developed are now
concentrating their energies on building up those that have not.

Indeed, globalization is not merely a phenomenon happening between the so-called West and the rest, but between the rest itself. Thus,
Africa is becoming the beneficiary of a resurgent China and also of an

India that is becoming ever more dynamic, as it rises above the confines of Hindu nationalism and Islamic extremism.

China's focus on Africa grows from its ever increasing energy needs. So as not to be too dependent on oil deposits inside the vulnerable Strait of Hormuz, China is hunting Africa for oil. It now gets more than a third of its oil imports from Africa, and President Hu Jintao has made three trips to Africa in three years. In return for equity stakes in African oil fields, China has granted $19 billion in aid and concessionary financing to African governments.[3] China has supplied technical assistance to Africa in the areas of tea planting, soil analysis, irrigation, and rice growing. In return for capitalizing on the natural resources of African nations— Ivorian chocolate, Zambian copper, Zimbabwean iron and steel—China will help modernize African railroads and build highways, power stations, and dams.[4]

Competition with China is pushing India to deepen its engagement with the African continent. India is courting Africa with soft loans, development aid, and political support to win lucrative oil projects. The first India-Africa summit, between India and fourteen African nations, was held in New Delhi in April 2008. India has extended $2 billion worth of credits to African countries. Oil from Nigeria accounts for 10 percent of India's global imports; India now gets a fifth of its energy imports from Africa. Trade between India and Africa has grown from $3.39 billion in 2000 to $30 billion in 2007. In particular, Indian and South African trade has been growing at 30 percent annually. South Africa exports gold, and India polishes South Africa's diamonds. To take another example, India is the single largest offshore investor in Mauritius.[5] Such figures may not be impressive in the larger scheme of things, but they do indicate a trend.

In addition, petrodollars from the Gulf have been flowing into East Africa, from $11 billion in 2000 to more than $50 billion in recent years. Gulf sheikhdoms have been investing in African telecommunications, tourism, mining, real estate, and finance. Half of their developing assistance is targeted for sub-Saharan Africa.

There is little altruistic about what is going on. These Eurasian dynamos are hunting Africa for resources. Their interest in democracy is next to zero, and some of the deals they are making smack more of old-fashioned colonialism than of post–Cold War, Western-style foreign aid. As access to arable land becomes an increasing source of tension in a world where absolute growth in population continues at a significant rate,

Africa, which still awaits a green revolution, looms as the final battle-ground for food resources. In particular, there are arrangements for South Korea to grow grain and palm oil in Madagascar, for Saudi Arabia to grow rice and barley in Ethiopia, for China to grow palm for biofuel in the Congo, and for South Korea, Egypt, and the United Arab Emirates to grow wheat in the Sudan. Unlike traditional agricultural investment schemes, these focus less on cash crops than on staple food items that the country itself may lack, even as the investor countries seek to export the entire production back home.[6] As Africa gets swept into the mainstream of Greater Indian Ocean trade, there will be a fine line between productive investment and exploitation.

All of this Indian Ocean–centric activity occurs within the context of an Africa that has been itself showing steady and impressive economic growth during the first decade of the twenty-first century: 6.5 percent annually since 2003. This is a momentous change from the early 1990s, when economic growth of below one percent meant that sub-Saharan African economies were declining substantially relative to their populations. With these economic advances have come political ones. According to Freedom House, a U.S.-based group, the number of African countries with multi-party governance, civil rights, and a free media has risen to eleven from three in 1977, whereas the number of nations ranked not free at all has fallen from twenty-five to fourteen. Another factor in the opening of these societies has been technology, in which, for example, the development of mobile phone networks has allowed Africa to leapfrog over the lack of hard-wired infrastructure.[7]

Technology, along with monetary inflows from the former third world in the Middle East and Asia, is finally allowing Africa to escape from its geographic isolation, which has always been a principal culprit behind its poverty. Though Africa is the second largest continent, with an area five times that of Europe, its coastline south of the Sahara is little more than a quarter as long. Moreover, this coastline lacks many good natural harbors, with the East African ports that traded vigorously with Arabia and India constituting the exception. Few of tropical Africa's rivers are navigable from the sea, dropping as they do from interior tableland to coastal plains by a series of falls and rapids. The Sahara Desert hindered human contact from the north for too many centuries, so Africa was little exposed to the great Mediterranean civilizations of antiquity and afterwards.[8]

In 1993, when I traveled through West Africa, I saw nothing but trouble ahead, specifically for countries such as Sierra Leone, Liberia, Nigeria, and Côte d'Ivoire.[9] Indeed, in the late 1990s trouble did come to those places in the form of bloody wars and separatist rebellions, even as those years were in development terms a generally bleak decade for the continent. But a new economic and political cycle has been sporadically emerging. The late French anthropologist Germaine Tillion writes "events must run their course before becoming history, so that *all* true history exists only by virtue of its conclusion."[10] After some decades of violence and turmoil, the conclusion of sub-Saharan Africa's postcolonial saga might be integration into a global and specifically Indian Ocean system.

Yet within this overall positive trend there are, and will be, a daunting order of challenges. Just consider: in Kenya, East Africa's wealthiest economy, the average woman has almost five children; in rich countries the average is 1.6 children. In next-door Ethiopia, 70 percent of young adults are jobless.[11] And looming large amid the continent's dilemmas is the failed state of Somalia, bordering both Kenya and Ethiopia at the Horn of Africa, and jutting out into the Indian Ocean with mainland Africa's longest coastline. This vast ungovernable space has allowed for one of the Indian Ocean's principal problems in our era, that of Africa-based piracy.

In the Indian Ocean, writes Alan Villiers, "the profession of piracy is as old as seafaring itself. The first man who ever straddled a drifting log probably knocked the second man from another log. So piracy began. It has been going on ever since." The Malacca Strait and the Gulf of Aden, the Persian Gulf, the Makran coast, the Gulf of Kutch—the whole Arabian Sea in fact—has been crawling with pirates since time immemorial.[12] Ibn Battuta, who was the victim of pirates off the western coast of India, informs us that ships in the Indian Ocean in the fourteenth century traveled in armed convoys as a defense.[13] Ming China's withdrawal from the Indian and Pacific oceans in the second half of the fifteenth century, after the last voyage of Zheng He, led to the seas filling up with many thousands of pirates of various nationalities.[14] In a slightly earlier time frame Marco Polo describes many dozens of pirate vessels off the coast of Gujarat, where the pirates spent the whole summer at sea with their women and children, as they plundered merchant vessels. They formed cordons of twenty or thirty ships at intervals of five or six miles, signaling to one another by fire or smoke. "In the midst of all these troubles," writes the historian George Hourani, "mariner and merchant called readily upon God for help, and the narratives of the sea are full of His name." For as one medieval Arab source lamented, "Man at sea is an insect on a splinter."[15]

Fernand Braudel calls piracy the "secondary form of war" that tends to erupt in the interregnum of conflict between great states. This form of war was "usually instigated by a city acting on its own authority or at any rate only marginally attached to a large state."[16] The scholar Richard J. Norton calls such pirate bases "feral cities": to be sure, the Somalia of our own time.[17]

As can be seen, historically piracy has been endemic to the Indian Ocean, from Aden to Malacca, particularly so after the Western intrusion into these waters beginning with the Portuguese in the early sixteenth century. Pirate groups, sometimes known as sea gypsies, tended to escalate in number and audacity with the burgeoning of trade, so piracy itself has often been a sign of prosperity.[18] "As parasites," pirates "do best when trade is flourishing as then hosts are readily available," writes the Australian scholar Michael Pearson.[19] At the height of Roman commercial expansion, the Emperor Trajan dispatched a retaliatory expedition against pirates that were plaguing the Persian Gulf.[20] In the European view, piracy was central to the eighteenth-century Islamic world of the Sulu sultanate in Southeast Asia, writes Sugata Bose, but from the sultanate's own viewpoint, it was a legitimate response to monopolistic European trading practices. The area around Bahrain and the United Arab Emirates was once so unsafe it was referred to as the Pirate Coast.[21] Until the coming of the British, the coast of East Africa from Somalia south to Mozambique was "pirate country," where Arab dhows came raiding, kidnapping, looting, and taking slaves.[22] Piracy challenged conventional and highly formal notions of sovereignty, proclaimed by the Europeans, that extended to the high seas: one man's pirate was another man's patriot. Not accepting this, the Dutch, English, and French in the days of high empire manned anti-piracy patrols exactly where Somali pirates now threaten shipping.[23] So, the piratical waters of today confirm that the Indian Ocean is reflective of an earlier world, one feature of which was the chaos of petty chieftaincies centered around natural harbors: in places where the state was weak or nonexistent, or subscribed to the notion that ships flying the flags of established nations were fair game.

The British geographer Donald B. Freeman explains that the "spatial concentration of commercial shipping" in the narrow waters of the Strait of Malacca, where Indonesian Sumatra and the Malay Peninsula come together, thus forcing ships laden with rich cargoes to move slowly over treacherous shallows, has made those seas a lair for pirates for many centuries. Malay pirate navies in the early nineteenth century were made up of hundreds of praus, light sailing craft rowed by slaves and manned by pirate warriors in "gaudy armor," armed with spears and krises for close combat. Pirate flotillas from Mindanao and the Sulu Archipelago in the southern Philippines made annual circuits through the Malacca Strait. Opium clippers were a particulary sought-after target.[24] It was a problem that even the British, with their great naval strength, were periodically powerless to deal with, until the advent of steam propulsion in the 1830s gave them and the Dutch an advantage over the pirates of the day.[25]

The resurgence of piracy in our own era speaks volumes about both the robustness of trade and the inability of states to fully protect it. At present, piracy is a large nuisance that has adversely affected trade routes and led to new international coalitions involving both the Indians and the Pakistanis, and the Chinese and the Americans. Thus, piracy in an oblique way, may have a bright side, for it offers up a common enemy—the very symbol of anarchy, in fact—which rival powers can then come into agreement to jointly oppose. In this way, global governance is strengthened, and the balance-of-power system in the Indian Ocean region is helped to become more stable. It was partly to reduce piracy in the Strait of Malacca that the Anglo-Dutch accommodation of 1824 was reached.

As for the romantic image of pirates, it derives mainly from the great age of piracy in the seventeenth-century Caribbean: that of a ship flying the Jolly Roger—the skull and crossbones—and manned by cutthroats with black eye patches and sashes around their heads, who preyed upon Spanish ships and cities. The Indian Ocean pirate of the early twenty-first century is different in some ways but quite similar in others. Only through the distance of time can we find anything charming or romantic about Caribbean pirates, who were murderous thugs just like their modern-day Indian Ocean counterparts. Ask Rory Berke, a U.S. Navy lieutenant commander, who encountered pirates off the Somali coast in January 2006.

Berke was a naval intelligence officer for the USS *Nassau* expeditionary strike group on a six-month Indian Ocean deployment, whose very itinerary constituted a grand lesson in geography. The Tarawa-class amphibious assault ship, its accompanying two destroyers, and other ships left Norfolk, Virginia, in November 2005, with twenty-three hundred marines headed for Iraq. After crossing the Atlantic Ocean and the entire length of the Mediterranean, the strike group sailed through the "ditch"—that is, the Suez Canal. "That's where the excitement starts, when you really know you're on deployment," Lieutenant Commander Berke began. "For weeks you are on the wide open sea in the Atlantic and the Mediterranean, where you are invulnerable. Then suddenly you're among Arabs, with what looks like ten feet of water on each side, and an Egyptian armored personnel convoy following you on land along the canal to prevent attacks on the warships.

"The excitement builds as you sail down the Red Sea, through the Strait of Bab el Mandeb, and along the southern shore of the Arabian Peninsula. Once through the Strait of Hormuz you know you're in the game, with Iran on the starboard side." The *Nassau* strike group sailed up the Persian Gulf to Kuwait, where it deposited the marines. Along the way the Americans passed Iranian corvettes whose sailors gave them friendly waves. The corvettes signified the regular Islamic Republic of Iran Navy, with which the U.S. Navy had had no problems, unlike the case with the Iranian Republican Guard Corps Navy that is ideologically closer to the Teheran regime.

From Kuwait the *Nassau* headed back south, halfway down the Persian Gulf to Bahrain, headquarters of the U.S. Fifth Fleet, where it got orders to join an international naval task force in the northwest Indian Ocean, off the coasts of Arabia and the Horn of Africa. The Americans found themselves patrolling the lawless Somali coast in international waters, from the twelve-mile territorial limit to five hundred miles out. Here pirates preyed on all manner of ships, from small dhows, to cruise liners, to liquefied natural gas carriers. Only a few weeks earlier in the region the cruise ship *Seaburn Spirit* had been attacked unsuccessfully by pirates. Most of the time, though, the victims were Asian fishing boats.

It was no coincidence that Somalia was a failed African state and that these were the most dangerous waters in the world. Piracy constitutes the maritime ripple effect of anarchy on land. The job of the international task force, which at the time included ships from the Netherlands, Great Britain, France, Pakistan, and Australia, as well as from the United States, was simply to "suppress through presence."

On the morning of January 21, 2006, Berke's ship, the USS *Nassau*, 150 miles off the Somali coast, got a distress call from the Bahamian-flagged cargo ship *Delta Ranger*, which had sped up to avoid capture by pirates. The *Delta Ranger* had a twenty-five-foot freeboard, meaning the pirates would have had to climb twenty-five feet to reach the deck of the cargo ship while under fire from the *Delta Ranger*'s crew. The willingness to attack the high freeboard indicated just how brazen and unafraid these Somali pirates were.

The U.S. Navy dispatched a P-3 surveillance plane to the area around the *Delta Ranger* to hunt for the pirates. Soon the P-3 located exactly what it was looking for: several skiffs pulling a dhow fishing boat. The Somali pirate confederations are often broken up into cells of ten men, each cell distributed among three skiffs. The skiffs are old, ratty, roach infested, rarely painted, made of decaying wood or fiberglass, and offer no shade. The pirates navigate by the stars. West is home—Somalia; east is the open ocean. A typical pirate cell goes out into the open ocean for about three weeks at a time. The pirates come equipped with drinking water, gasoline for their single-engine outboards, knives, grappling hooks, short ladders, AK-47 assault rifles, and rocket-propelled grenades. They also bring along millet, narcotic qat to chew, and lines and nets with which to catch fish, which they eat raw. One captured pirate skiff held a hunk of shark meat with teeth marks all over it.

The idea is to take over a larger dhow, usually a fishing ship manned by Indians, Taiwanese, or South Koreans, and then live on it, with the skiffs attached. Once in possession of a dhow, the pirates are then in a position to take and seize an even bigger ship. As they leapfrog to ever bigger ships, they allow the smaller ships that they plundered earlier to go free.

The sea is vast. Only when a large ship issued a distress call did the *Nassau* know where to look for pirates. If all the pirates ever did was hunt small ships, none of the warships in the international coalition, with all of their electronic paraphernalia, would have known of it.

Once the P-3 spotted the dhow and three skiffs, it alerted the warship closest to the area, the destroyer USS *Winston S. Churchill*. The *Churchill* immediately got between the pirates and the twelve-mile limit that marked the entrance into Somali territorial waters. If the pirates made it back to within those twelve miles, they were not legally liable to capture except by the Somali government, which barely exists. Once alongside the pirates, the destroyer fired warning shots from its loud and massively reverberating five-inch gun, in addition to sending helicopters low over the captured dhow and attached skiffs. The ten pirates surrendered, and the sixteen-man Indian crew from the dhow, *Bahkti Sagar,* was rescued fifty-four miles off the Somali coast. All were transferred to the *Nassau,* where Lieutenant Commander Berke debriefed them, with the help of his translators.

The pirates had beaten, bullied, and semi-starved the Indian crew for the previous six days. They had thrown overboard a live monkey that the crew was transporting to Dubai.*

What did the pirates wear? What were they like? I asked Berke.

"Tank tops, light jackets, flip-flops, and 1980s shorts. They were arrogant and petrified at the same time. They assumed that since we had caught them, we would soon kill them, and that we, being Americans, would also eat them." The youngest kept pleading, "Please don't shoot me." They were severely malnourished, dehydrated, and needed dental work, which the U.S. Navy provided to them.

Berke's references to "due process" and "the police" brought blank stares from the pirates. "Their concept of the police was guys in parts of uniforms in Somali towns who robbed you," Berke told me. The pirates looked to be between the ages of fifteen and thirty. Only one of the ten had family members to contact. Two of the ten knew their birth dates. The others knew only that they had been born during "the fighting" and had no family. In Somali culture, they were untouchable, without any clan affiliation. Though the civil war in Somalia began in the 1990s, the country had in effect been broken up since a decade earlier. About half of the pirates had scars from old bullet and knife wounds.

From their own point of view, Berke explained, they had done nothing wrong. "They were guys hanging around the docks who were dispatched by a local warlord to bring back income for him and to defend local waters.

---

* Berke was assisted in his debriefing of both the pirates and their captives by a Somali linguist, provided by a private contractor, that the *Nassau* had brought along on the deployment; and by a Hindi-speaking enlisted American sailor of Indian descent. The crew of the *Bahkti Sagar* were Gujaratis who also spoke Hindi.

They saw themselves as a rudimentary coast guard, trying to make a living, and exacting a form of taxation from foreign ships in their own brutal way."

The strike group's staff judge advocate, Lieutenant Michael Bahar, asked them about the weapons they had. One pirate replied: "I am a Somali. In Somalia, the gun is our government."

Why did they choose to be pirates? Lieutenant Bahar asked them. Their answer: because the chances of getting killed on land in Somalia were even greater, they braved the open ocean. Piracy is organized crime. Like roving gangs, each cell patrols specific parts of the sea. "Forget the Johnny Depp charm," Bahar said. "Theirs was a savage brutality not born of malice or evil, like a lion killing an antelope. There was almost a natural innocence about it."

The Somali piracy crisis merely confirms a critical feature of the post–Cold War era: the rise of sub-state actors. For example, it is the pirate-state of Puntland in northeastern Somalia that, like Hezbollah and al-Qaeda, confounds the international community.

The international community has largely misdiagnosed the issue of Somalia because of insistence on viewing Somalia as one static, albeit failed, state. In fact, Somalia is three separate entities, and thus exhibits different levels of governance: independent Somaliland in the northwest, the autonomous region of Puntland in the northeast, and the chaotic southern area where an extremely weak Somali government continues to combat the rising power of *al-Shabab* (the youth) Islamist extremists. It is largely from Puntland where piracy has originated, and it is largely through Puntland that it can be addressed.

Named after the ancient Land of Punt mentioned in Egyptian hieroglyphics, Puntland declared limited autonomy from the rest of Somalia in 1998, opting against a declaration of full independence because of obligations to fellow members of the Majerteyn clan across the border in the southern Somali city of Kismayo. Throughout Somali history, clans have served as the preeminent form of political, legal, and social representation—a reality reflected in the organization of the Puntland government, which gives significant influence to local elders, and largely relies on clan militias instead of more formal defense forces like those found in neighboring Somaliland. Thus, while not as functional as the government of Somaliland, the Puntland government is still a significantly greater presence than anything found in the south of the country.

Puntland has an organized parliament, and in January 2009 a new president, Abdirahman Mohamed Faroole, was elected. Because it is here where pirates are based, the spoils of piracy are overwhelmingly in evidence, compared to the rest of the country.

For example, in the town of Eyl—widely regarded as the hub of piracy in the Gulf of Aden region—piracy is a veritable industry, with an influx of large amounts of cash from ransoms fueling a surge of growth in the city. Although the nature of clan politics in Puntland makes it almost inconceivable that the government is not in some way involved tacitly, the Puntland government ostensibly has taken a hard line on piracy, claiming that it is simply not powerful enough to curtail piracy and even issuing convictions in some circumstances. Indeed, since the widely publicized April 2009 incident involving the *Maersk Alabama,* a U.S.-flagged ship that was attacked by pirates—who were later killed by U.S. Navy SEALs—the government of Puntland has requested international aid to build an anti-piracy task force.

In Puntland, piracy is popularly seen as both a lucrative and legitimate practice—lucrative in as much as pirate ransoms are comparable in one of the poorest areas on earth to the entire budget of the Puntland government, and legitimate inasmuch as piracy is seen as helping to curtail the rampant illegal fishing and dumping of toxic waste in Somalia's territorial waters. An extremely weak but nonetheless viable sub-state entity thus has produced ripe conditions for a criminal enterprise now threatening to subsume the entire governmental apparatus.

Whereas the emergence of a de facto pirate state is greatly problematic to the international community, the existence of an organized central authority of sorts in the region also creates an opportunity to address the problem at its roots. In other words, the international community will need to offer the carrot of aid and the stick of retaliation on land to concentrate the mind of the clan-based government. After all, Somali piracy cannot be addressed solely as a sea-based issue. And unless the United States is willing to commit significant numbers of troops on the ground to engage in nation building (highly unlikely), it must accept the necessity of working with the government of Puntland to combat piracy in the Gulf of Aden and Indian Ocean, regardless of its lack of international legitimacy. Because the government of Puntland has been in conflict with the *al-Shabab* extremists, bolstering Puntland's institutional capacity could point a way to not only deter piracy, but also to fight radical Islam in the

Horn of Africa. Puntland is important because it shows that so-called anarchy in Somalia and elsewhere is often something else: the slow breakdown of European-drawn states and the restoration of sturdier forms of identity built on clan and tribe and region.

Indeed, as we have seen, from antiquity onward, pirate states like Puntland and pirate confederations have been very much a part of the Indian Ocean reality, and a direct consequence of lucrative trade routes. Though the Cold War, by providing a certain order in the third world, obscured this historical truth, pirates are back because in a sense they never left. The Romans, the Chinese of the Song and Ming dynasties, and the Portuguese, Dutch, French, and English imperialists all confronted pirates in these waters, and now it is the turn of the United States and its allies. Especially as India and China rise, the scourge of piracy will provide opportunities for cooperation among these new powers in the region. But for the time being, American power remains essential. Lieutenant Commander Berke's experience is emblematic in this regard.

CHAPTER SEVENTEEN

ZANZIBAR

THE LAST FRONTIER

From Somalia to South Africa, the western side of the Indian Ocean is bordered by four thousand miles of African coastline, much of it Muslim and Swahili-speaking. If Puntland and its environs concentrate the mind on African chaos, then Zanzibar, farther south, might suggest an equally strong case for African possibilities. For centuries, the island of Zanzibar, "land of the blacks" in Arabic, lying off the Tanzanian seaboard, has been a principal node of Indian Ocean commerce and culture, a melting pot of Islamic and Hindu civilizations. Truly, in the latter Middle Ages, an Islamic scholar from the Hadhramaut in Yemen would have felt just as comfortable in Zanzibar as he would have in Indonesia. In the early nineteenth century hundreds of dhows clogged this port, laden with haj pilgrims, drugs, coffee, fish, ivory, hides, red pepper, ambergris, beeswax, cloves, maize, sorghum, and spices. For the Omani sultans who governed it, Zanzibar was not just an Indian Ocean port, but, in historian Richard Hall's words, "the hub of a vast trading empire with its tentacles deep into Africa," reaching into the Kenyan highlands, the Great Lakes, and the eastern Congo.[1] And this hub continued thus well into the twentieth century. On one March day in 1937, Alan Villiers counted more than fifty dhows at the anchorage, thirty-four of them Arab, and the others from the Comoro Islands, India, and nearby Somalia.[2]

I awoke before dawn my first night on the island to rain crashing on the rusted and rattling corrugated iron roofs of Stone Town, the heart of old Zanzibar. I was renting two rooms from a friend above the cassava souk. From my wooden and cast-iron balcony, with its simple floral designs, I

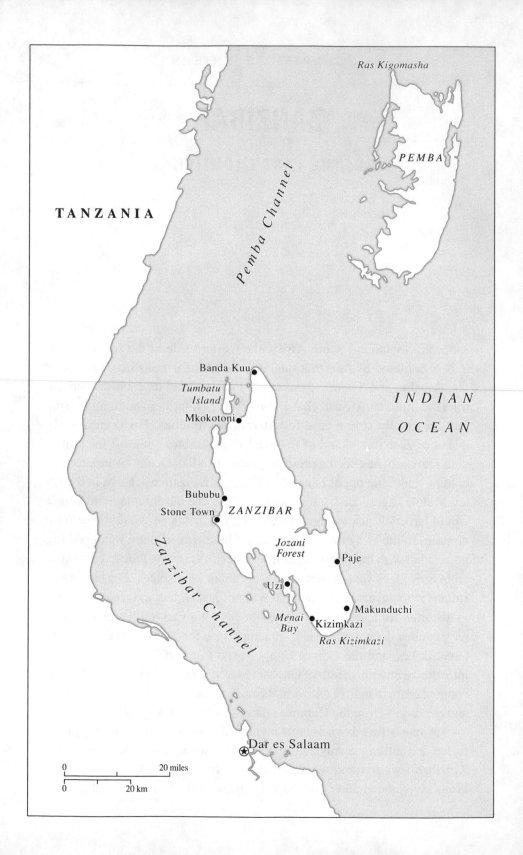

TANZANIA

Pemba Channel

Ras Kigomasha

PEMBA

INDIAN

OCEAN

Banda Kuu

Tumbatu Island

Mkokotoni

Bububu

Stone Town *ZANZIBAR*

Jozani Forest

Paje

Zanzibar Channel

Uzi

Menai Bay Kizimkazi Makunduchi

Ras Kizimkazi

Dar es Salaam

0   20 miles

0   20 km

could almost touch the opposite lime-washed wall of the snaking alley. My rooms featured the usual oriental carpets, a poster bed with mosquito netting, colored-glass windows, and furniture made of wood and brass and copper: an effortless confection of Arab, Persian, Indian, and African aesthetics. In the morning I ascended to the "tea house" on the roof, a raised and open platform embraced by bougainvillea and the boisterous sea winds that granted a prospect of Stone Town's dizzying roofscape. Below the slanting roofs were the building materials that gave this vast maze of an urban quarter its name: stones mixed with mortarized mud and sand, and covered with lime wash. The view was punctuated by Mughal-style minarets with their triple folio arches and the scabby, weather-beaten steeples of a late-nineteenth-century French cathedral. There were, too, the pencil-thin cast-iron pillars of the House of Wonders, a palace built in 1883 for Omani Sultan Barghash bin Said in tropical Victorian industrial style. With iron and rust so ever present, this was a vista that, rather than merely picturesque, seemed bursting with a sturdy spirit. My eyes met the horizon with freighters, outriggers, dugouts, and plank-built dhows all plopped in the milk-turquoise water of the Indian Ocean, so unreal a shade that it conjured up a water color more than it did the sea itself.

Tracing the rooftops with his finger, from one end of the cassava souk to the other, my host, Emerson Skeens, an American who has lived in Stone Town for twenty-two years, registered for me his neighbors: Indian Hindus, Pembans (from the adjacent island), Indian Muslims, Yemenis, Persian Shiites, Ithna'sheris (Twelve Shiites, in this case from Pakistan), Bohras (another branch of Shiites, from Gujarat), Omanis, Goans, more Bohras, Africans, Shirazis, more Africans, and Comorians. "Zanzibar is African, yet different from Africa. It is Arabian and Persian, yet different from Arabia and Persia; and Indian, yet different from India," said Ismail Jussa, a Zanzibari friend from the Gulf of Kutch in Gujarat. From different parts of the ocean they came, united by Islam and eventually, too, by the Swahili language, which, with its Arabic gutturals and loanwords, and its Bantu grammar, functions as pure, heated expression.*

After the indigenous Africans, the Shirazis arrived here with their dhows from the coast of Iran around a thousand years ago, when Zanzibar, primarily owing to the winds of the northeast monsoon, was already

---

* Twenty-five percent of Swahili is composed of Arabic words, with a smattering of Persian (Farsi), Cushite, and Hindustani.

being visited by traders from as far away as China. The Shirazis were not only Persians, but minority Arabs, too, from the city of Shiraz, who might well have been refugees from ethnic oppression. The Portuguese were the first westerners in Zanzibar, plying the East African coast since the time of da Gama at the end of the fifteenth century, and introducing cassava and maize. They built a chapel that the Omanis, who were importing silk from China, destroyed in the early eighteenth century, using the stones to build a fort. The Stone Town that the visitor sees today is mainly an Omani architectural affair, with strong Indian influences.

Yet above all, Zanzibar, and Stone Town in particular, was, well into the nineteenth century, a "sad, dark star, a grim address" of the slave trade, in the words of the late Polish journalist Ryszard Kapuscinski.[3] Hundreds and even thousands of slaves domesticated by years of captivity—men, women, and children—roamed through every street, along with those slaves who had just arrived from the interior, half mad and half dead through maltreatment. It was a scene that was like "looking into another age and another world," somberly writes the journalist and historian Alan Moorehead about mid-nineteenth-century Zanzibar, which was the jumping-off point for Richard Burton and John Hanning Speke's expedition to discover the source of the Nile.[4] So as captivating as Zanzibar was to me, let me say at the outset that this island is not without its ghosts. First and above all there was slavery, the original sin and the lifeblood of the Omani Indian Ocean empire.

In fact, Stone Town, rather than a cute Greek island village of a place, is a battered, roughened, gritty, exhausting, salt-stained monument to the historical process itself, somewhat intimidating and easy to get lost in, especially at night. Wandering around the first morning, when women with rapid broom strokes were spreading away the water from the nighttime rains, I first noticed the doors, more elaborate and replete with stories than the houses themselves. John Baptist Da Silva, an artist and lifelong resident of Stone Town from Portuguese Goa, in western India, read the doors for me as if they were books, with words between the lines. There was the simple, square Omani mango wood door with large cast-iron nails. Along the frames were designs of fish scales indicating fertility, and lotus flowers indicating power and wealth. The geometrical patterns were symbols of mathematics and, hence, of navigation. The rope patterns evinced the dhow trade, so this had been the home of a wealthy Omani merchant trader with many children.

There are the Gujarati doors made of teakwood with massive nails and square patterns below semicircular frames carved with plants and sunflowers, each sect painting its door a different color. Whereas these Indian doors are primarily square and floral, the Arabic doors, made of wood from mahogany, breadfruit, and jackfruit trees, among others, feature Koranic inscriptions. The Persian and Baluch door frames are carved into the shape of pillars, evincing a neoclassical bent. The Swahili doors are shorter than the other ones and painted in garish colors.

The breath of early morning carried with it the scents of sweet basil, lemongrass, and jasmine . . . of cloves, nutmeg, cinnamon, and cardamom. The yams and cassavas laid out on the *barazas* (stone benches) looked like petrified stones. The *barazas* were built primarily for gossiping and socializing, ignited by sips of Omani coffee, and were already getting crowded. Everyone had their favorite *baraza,* which need not be near their home. Men wore knitted caps (*kofias*) and traditional white Omani robes called *kanzus* in Zanzibar. Women wore *khangas* (patterned cotton dresses in African style). There was a pellucid intimacy to the morning here, with everything and every person manifesting an iconic aura that made it memorable.

Here and there palm and tamarind leaves whistled in the wind. I noticed a Jain temple and a Persian bath built on a Roman design, stuck in the midst of fifty-three mosques. A Swahili woman in a loud *khanga* was making an Indian *chapatti* (flatbread) and a Middle Eastern falafel while frying a cassava. Zanzibar is the global village writ small. It makes globalization seem altogether a normal function of human nature, requiring only technology to allow it.

Yet globalization brings its own tensions, bred of the very close quarters with which different cultures and civilizations now find themselves, for all was not well in Zanzibar. The glittering mixture of races and customs that I observed were actually vestiges of what once had been. Indeed, anyone who had known Zanzibar before independence from Great Britain in 1963 would have been saddened by the monochrome dullness of the urban environment. I had been impressed with its vitality only because it was my first visit here.

In the heart of Stone Town, I wandered into an Arab house, renovated in an expensive but somewhat tasteless, mass-produced style, where several men dressed in immaculate *kanzus* and *kofias* were sipping cardamom-scented coffee and munching on dates imported from Oman.

They invited me to join them. The owner of the house was an engaging, welcoming man, rotund, with a perfectly groomed short white beard. He told me that this had been the house of his father and grandfather. A black and white portrait of the latter in turban and beard graced the sitting room, evocative of Omani imperial days. Pointing at the photo, my host said, "And this house had been the house of *his* grandfather." Though he now divided his time between Oman and Zanzibar, he thought of Zanzibar as his true home, even as he considered himself a pure Omani. He had renovated this house, in part, he said, to make a statement. In polished English diction he then explained that what I was seeing here were the mere leftovers of a far more cosmopolitan world: of Omani sultans ruling under British tutelage, before steam travel mitigated the benefit of the monsoon winds, and before the building of the Suez Canal ended the need of Zanzibar as a stopover on the route between Europe and India.

But now there was post-colonial history to consider, he told me: the period since 1963, when Zanzibar was not only troubled, but also experienced some of the worst ravages of violence, and in particular ethnic-racial clashes, that sub-Saharan Africa has had to offer. "The [African] mainland has corrupted this island," my Omani host declared bluntly. "They must apologize for the revolution." From the "revolution" onward, it seemed that, at least in his mind, Zanzibar has been less an illustration of early globalization than of a latter-day clash of civilizations.

On one side of the cultural divide stood the British and their Omani surrogates, who were backed by the local Arab community as well as by the minorities from the Indian Subcontinent. On the other side stood the much poorer, indigenous Africans—embittered in too many cases by the history of slavery, and by the dispossession of their land at the hands of the Omanis. Standing with the Africans were the Shirazis, who, because they had come to Zanzibar in the early medieval centuries, before the other immigrants, and often as refugees, had become almost completely enmeshed through intermarriage with the Africans. Local elections in the period just before the British withdrew resulted in the two sides splitting the vote down the middle. The inconclusive consequences only increased ethnic and racial tensions.

"Race and ethnicity were never issues before the coming of politics," explained Ismail Jussa, the Gujarati who is foreign affairs spokesman for the opposition Civic United Front, mainly composed of ethnic Indians and Arabs. In other words, empires submerge communal politics because power is hoarded under a single absolute sovereignty. But once imperial law collapses, and its divide-and-rule legacy exposed, communal politics consumes everything. It was so in Cyprus, in Palestine, the Indian Subcontinent, and many other places in Afro-Asia, and so it was in Zanzibar. That is the real inheritance of many, if not all, forms of colonialism.

The British left in December 1963, with the Omani sultan literally holding down the fort on his own. It took only a month, until January 1964, for the sultan to be sent packing on his yacht, as an anti-Arab pogrom exploded through the streets of Stone Town: many Africans actually believed that with the British gone, the Omanis would reintroduce slavery or, at a minimum, mete out unfair treatment. "The politics of race espoused by Zanzibar's African nationalists," writes the American academic G. Thomas Burgess, "was based on the premise that cosmopolitanism had not produced wealth and harmony but an exotic, deceptive façade for cultural chauvinism and racial injustice."[5] The result was, according to a Western diplomat and African area expert I met, nothing less than a "mini-Rwanda" that took the lives of men, women, and children in equal proportions, as Afro-Shirazi mobs, speaking the language of revolution and mainland African nationalism and unity, went on a rampage with racial implications. Zanzibari historian Abdul Sheriff, who heads the Zanzibar Indian Ocean Research Institute, describes the violence as "genocidal in proportions."[6] Burgess notes that one third of all Arabs on the island were either killed or forced into immediate exile.

The Zanzibari novelist Abdulrazak Gurnah remembers:

> We like to think of ourselves as a moderate and mild people. Arab African Indian Comorian: we lived alongside each other, quarreled and sometimes intermarried. . . . In reality, we were nowhere near *we,* but us in our separate yards, locked in our historical ghettoes, self-forgiving and seething with intolerances, with racisms, and with resentments.[7]

Anarchy, rather than a new post-revolutionary stability, was the result. The Afro-Shirazis who grabbed power were divided among themselves, with doctrinaire communists pitted against plain mad killers. Julius Nyerere, the leader of mainland Tanganyika, though himself a socialist, was nevertheless afraid that Fidel Castro's Cubans would take advantage of the chaos and set up a puppet state right off his coastline. Ali

Sultan Issa, one of the leading revolutionaries from that period, now an old man afflicted with cancer, openly admitted to me his love of Castro and Che Guevara, both of whom he had met often and whose photos graced his bedroom. And yet, rather than an Afro-Shirazi, Issa was of Yemeni-Omani ancestry, just as other revolutionaries from that period were of Arab and Indian descent, according to the pictures he showed me. Likewise, Issa insisted that the revolution was a class struggle rather than a racial one. "It was a Marxist revolution, and ideology spans the boundaries of skin color," he insisted, a cigarette dripping from his mouth. "For example, Pemban Africans were against the revolution, while some Arabs were for it. No Indians in Pemba were harmed. To define the revolution as racial is to miss the point. Still, a revolution is not a tea party."

No, it certainly was not. In order to prevent another Cuba, as well as to shore up the political chaos, Nyerere negotiated a deal in April 1964 to bring Zanzibar into a union with Tanganyika, creating Tanzania. Nyerere had the new Zanzibari president, Abeid Karume, protected by police and soldiers from the mainland against the more radical members of Karume's own coalition. Still, a hard-line socialist regime emerged that expropriated the property of Omanis and other minorities in Stone Town and resettled Africans here. Because the new inhabitants were poor, they could not afford house repairs, and that set the context for Stone Town's dilapidation. Stone Town today, beyond the rash of trinket and handicraft shops for the tourist, is a hovel of a place when you look at it with careful eyes. Sadly, it is truly representative of Zanzibar as a whole, with an overwhelming African majority and a smattering of Arabs, Indians, and other ethnic groups constituting the inhabitants of the cassava souk, the minorities large in variety but small in absolute numbers (although Stone Town, because of its multicultural demographics compared to the rest of the island, is a stronghold of the political opposition).

The scholar Abdul Sheriff puts the 1964 revolution into perspective. "It was about both class and race," he told me, "but the racial aspect was more visible. True, not all the Omanis were rich and not all the Africans were poor. Yet even the poor Arabs felt comfortable with the sultan's regime, while the many Africans who had never been enslaved nevertheless felt comfortable with the new revolutionary authorities." The nationalizations and other recriminations that followed in the late 1960s sent many Arabs fleeing back to Oman, he added.

In 1972, Karume was assassinated by his own hard-line faction, and Ali Sultan Issa and others, who had been the guiding ideological lights of the revolution, were imprisoned and tortured, as suspicion reigned generally. The revolutionary regime held on, buttressed by the politics of race, as its handling of the economy has generally been a shambles throughout all these recent decades. "We came to power through the machete, we will not give up through the ballot," regime members have been known to declare.

Nassor Mohammed, a lawyer with close ties to the opposition, told me that Zanzibar had more of an authentic multi-party system under the last phase of British and Omani rule than it does now. In 1992 opposition parties were finally established because of pressure from Western donors, in the wake of the democratic revolutions in Eastern Europe. But the "revolutionary government," as it still calls itself, maintains power through intimidation and the doling out of government jobs and subsidies. Elections held every five years have only exacerbated tensions—identified as the political parties still are with racial groups—and have been an occasion for mainland troops to occupy the island temporarily. The investment that there is in Zanzibar tends to dry up before elections and picks up afterwards when everyone exhibits a sigh of relief that, once again, chaos has been averted. In fact, what has kept Zanzibar peaceful, according to Mohammed, is the very cosmopolitanism that struggles to survive despite the dismal post-1964 experience.

"Zanzibar is an embarrassment to the mainland," one foreign diplomat told me. Indeed, as mainland Tanzania and neighboring Mozambique make modest economic and political progress, even as Kenya following its inter-tribal violence is still fragile, and Somalia barely existent, Zanzibar, all its cosmopolitanism notwithstanding, is still stuck in the post-colonial past of the 1960s and 1970s, with essentially one-party rule and a regime that has not done nearly enough to attract the foreign capital necessary to soak up the large pool of unemployed male youth, which is the real key to stability in the developing world, especially Africa. Zanzibar exemplifies why the East African seaboard remains the Indian Ocean's final frontier. And that frontier is not about the holding of elections, but about the building of strong, impersonal institutions that do not discriminate according to race, ethnic group, tribe, or personal connections.

"If we were free of the mainland, we would grow up in a matter of days, and the sons of Zanzibar would return from points all around the Indian Ocean, for our true history is written in the monsoon winds," Sheikh Salah Idriss Mohammed told me. Sheikh Idriss, a historian, maintains his small apartment as a museum, cluttered to the ceilings with photos of former Omani sultans and with diagrams of the lineage of Omani royal families. Everywhere there are books and maps and manuscripts, concerning pre-1964 days, yellowing and rotting. Plying me with coffee scented with cloves and ginger, he lamented, "We have no democracy at all. In America you elected Obama, a black man, that's democracy!"

I tried to be hopeful. Compared to the earlier post-colonial era in the 1960s and 1970s, thoughts of race and revolutionary ideology did appear to be in retreat. The dynamism that existed favored the increasingly vibrant opposition, as well as contacts with the outside world through trade and tourism. I refused to believe that the Gulf states, India, China, and Indonesia could keep mightily developing without East and Southern Africa as a whole being eventually, positively affected. Arabs were trickling back, and a new wave of globalization could yet return to Zanzibar what had been lost, without the oppression that had led to the revolution.

In any event, because East Africa was still a frontier, its situation was critical: for its eventual full-blown incorporation into the Greater Indian Ocean trading system would make that system, which would also have to include East Asia, the true, throbbing heart of the twenty-first-century world. No great power—not even the Chinese—would conquer the maritime rim of the Eastern Hemisphere, but a trading system would. Such a trading system would be a power in its own right, able to compete with the European Union and the United States. And Zanzibar, with its cosmopolitan tradition of old, was as good a place as any to watch for it to happen.

Nothing and no one summed up for me the *idea* of Africa and the Indian Ocean as much as the novels of Abdulrazak Gurnah, born in 1948 in Zanzibar and now teaching literature in England. Gurnah's Zanzibar is a "tumble-down raft floating on the edges of the Indian Ocean," decrepit and unassuming, international yet parochial.[8] It is a place populated by native Africans, Somalis, Omanis, Baluchis, Gujaratis, Arabs, and Persians, all seeing the same streets and shoreline through different personal, family, and collective historical experiences, even as Islam is a commonality, like the air everyone breathes. In one way or another, commerce and the monsoon winds have brought them all to this shore. "This is what we're on this earth to do," declares one of Gurnah's characters. "To trade." To go inland in search of goods to bring back to the coast, to travel to the bleakest deserts or most impenetrable forests, in order to do business with "a king or a savage. . . . It's all the same to us."[9] Trade delivers peace and prosperity. Trade is the great equalizer among people and nations; it does more than perhaps any other activity to prevent war.

Yet in the novelist's elegiac vision Zanzibar's cosmopolitan population has made for a world of separations and abandonment, and the severest personal loss. Trade entails opportunity and movement, and therefore the rending of family ties forever. As one character says, "such pain never ends . . . nothing which means so much is ever over."[10] Another character, a young boy taken away from his parents in order to pay off his father's debt and to find a livelihood with a trader, "wondered" years later "if his parents still thought of him, if they still lived, and he knew that he would rather not find out." At the same time this boy is "numbed by guilt that he had been unable to keep the memory of his parents fresh in his life."[11]

Such deeply felt personal loss is partially appeased by the shock of new landscapes and experiences that the protagonists encounter in their one-way journeys away from loved ones. This sad and beautiful world, of permanent partings and dhow journeys—captured in totally different ways by Camões and Gurnah—is made all the more tragic by the experience of colonialism. A typical Gurnah character is a young East African student sent to study and live a marginal existence in England, who ends up never seeing his family again, and is thus at home nowhere. Referring to the people he meets in England, one such character observes, "How chilling and belittling blue eyes can be."[12] Indeed, even as the imperial power strives to maintain the highest traditions of justice and liberty, the very relationship between the colonizer and its subjects leads to cruel misunderstandings and a feeling of inferiority and servitude on the part of the indigenous inhabitants.

But Gurnah is even more unsparing of his homeland's own postcolonial failure, which only makes the humiliation experienced by his characters that much worse. Barbarism, in the form of the 1964 revolution, quickly follows independence. "There was hardly time to get used to the [new] flag" before "murder, expulsion, detention, rape, you name it." Gangs roamed the street. There is a local dictator for whom "no meanness was too petty," even as he himself was cut down by "mean bastards" with machine guns, a clear reference to Karume.[13] Then there are the petty "deprivations and wretchedness" of self-rule: blocked toilets, running water and electricity only a few hours a day. Historic houses kept up by the English are "turned into hovels." It is a series of uglinesses.

As Gurnah writes: "We don't know how to make anything for ourselves, not anything we use or desire, not even a bar of soap or a packet of razor blades."[14]

Following the British departure, rather than forge a better world, this supposed cosmopolitan and intermarried Indian Ocean civilization of Arabs, Persians, Indians, and Africans comes undone by "seething" intolerances and "racisms," all brought to the surface by post-independence politics. Colonialism, having rent the fabric of traditional island culture, leaves it exposed to every indignity, self-inflicted and otherwise, after independence. It is like a complex organism without any defenses left. Taking a walk, "going nowhere in particular," is, according to the novelist, the "postcolonial condition."[15]

And yet at some point a direction must emerge for the walker, because the post-colonial period itself must pass into a new era; the era, in fact, that I experienced in my travels. Looking at the myriad faces and skin complexions around me, I knew that each had borne a family's separate and unique experience of departures and leave-takings, of struggles and abandonments. And all for what purpose? "To trade."

Gurnah has much to teach. "Imagination is a kind of truth," he writes, for to imagine is to be able to put yourself in another's shoes. And the more you imagine, the more aware you are of how little you know, for "to be too certain of anything is the beginning of bigotry."[16]

From Stone Town I traveled for an hour and a half to the southeastern tip of Zanzibar, to the coastal town of Makunduchi. It was late July, and the Shirazi festival of Mwaka Kogwa was at hand, a celebration of the Zoroastrian new year, long ago absorbed into the culture of the African Swahili inhabitants. Tradition held that through the catharsis of ritual combat the locals would be cleansed of all their grudges and other bad feelings built up between them in the course of the year.

On any open field of red laterite several long lines of fighters jogged in from various directions, loudly chanting fight songs. These Africans were dressed in every outlandish manner of cheap hand-me-down, including fake fur coats, old motorcycle and construction helmets, and torn woollen ski caps. Some of the men were even dressed like women, with small coconuts strapped to their chests to indicate breasts. Each man carried a banana stem to use as a weapon. Small boys tagged behind them. The atmosphere was menacing, as if real violence would occur. Then individual fights broke out. Soon there was a vast melee, with battles raging on every front, and the crowd of onlookers rushing out of the way in this direction and that to avoid being trampled by the fighters. Dust flew. After an exhausting hour of combat, the village women in loud *khangas* marched in from all sides, singing. Soon the fighting died down, a fire was set, and the Persian festival celebrated by Africans was brought to an end.

Later, people gathered at the beach for a picnic. Dhows, like ideograms of the wind itself drawn in rapid ink strokes, went out from the shallows. Small waves broke and it was as if the whole universe reverberated. Beyond a coral reef several miles out lay the entire expanse of the Indian Ocean, stretching all the way to Indonesia. I thought of Oman and India, and the other places in between where I had been. In particular, with the Shirazi festival uppermost in my mind, I thought of an old Persian trader whom I had met many months before in Kolkata.

To his friends his name was Habib Khalili. To Indians in Kolkata, his name was Habib Khalili al-Shirazi — that is, Habib Khalili from Shiraz, in Persia. In Persia his name was Habib Khalili al-Shirazi al-Hindi—that is, Habib Khalili from Shiraz, and more recently of India. Habib Khalili was a tea merchant. He claimed to have forty relatives in Singapore, and more in Malaysia and Abu Dhabi. "My real country is the Indian Ocean," he had told me, his fingers racing through the noisy night air, as though hankering for prayer beads.

We were in the house in Kolkata where he had been born in 1928, full of potted plants, piles of old newspapers, and the moan of traffic through neoclassical columns and the French windows left open for the sake of the monsoon breezes. By the end of our conversation it was dark enough so I could no longer see his face. He had been reduced to a mere excited voice, leaping up and down like his fingers, a vestige in the flesh of the powerful magnetism of Iranian culture and language, whose veins still reach unto Bengal, on the border with Southeast Asia, and southwest unto Sofala in northern Mozambique.

"There are more Persian graves in the Deccan than there are trees," he said, referring to India's southern plateau region. "Fifty percent of Bengali used to be Persian loanwords. With the severing of Muslim East Bengal in 1947, it is now 30 percent. Iran," he went on, "is a country that has never been conquered, and yet has never been free." His conversation was like that, jumping without transitions from one issue to another. I could not hold him still.

I did not bother to check his figures: Persian influence in the Indian Subcontinent has always been substantial. Farsi was the official lingua franca in India until 1835, when English finally replaced it, and until the early modern era it was universally understood in Bengal. Sunil Gangopadhyay's novel about nineteenth-century Calcutta, *Those Days,* intimates how Persian was a second language.[17] In the seventeenth century, many of Dhaka's artists, poets, generals, and administrators were Shias who had migrated from Iran.[18] Mughal rule from the sixteenth through eighteenth century bore a heavy Persian imprint. The Subcontinent, no less than Mesopotamia, illustrated the importance of Iran. And Iran, as the trader intimated, while never colonized, had its affairs constantly interfered with by European powers. Unable to claim formal oppression, Iran developed feelings of oppression that became that much worse.

"My family ultimately traces its roots back to Hebron, in the Holy Land, whose Arabic name is Khalil, 'dear friend of God.' My great-great-grandfather was a merchant in Kashmiri shawls. He trekked three hundred years ago from Kashmir to Shiraz, city of Hafiz, *ahh,*" the trader said, referring to the fourteenth-century poet who was a Sufi mystic— and whose sensuous verses about pagan fire and red wine presaged the chivalric ballads of late medieval Europe. "My great-great-grandfather's wife's family was from Madras. Her brother, who had made a fortune in trade, needed a son-in-law for his daughter. So it was that my great-grandfather trekked from Shiraz to Madras to marry his cousin by marriage. He, too, made a fortune. Persians came to India for the same reason Europeans came to America—for opportunity. A portion of the family eventually went to Calcutta from Madras because of the indigo and opium trade. After opium, we became tea brokers.

"My father was a tea exporter. The tea would be packed in wooden chests that were stitched over with cowhide. The boxes of tea crossed India from Bengal to Rajasthan, then by camel into Baluchistan, and to Zahedan in Iran. Northward to Mashad and Ashgabat [now in Turkmenistan] where we had depots. Ashgabat was lost to Russia by the Qajars. The cowhide shrunk in the dry heat, sealing the boxes tighter. That raised the quality and the price of the tea."

He began talking about the cherry red tea made from Nile water that they drank in Sudan, and about Darjeeling tea that in his mind was of a higher quality than some of the teas in Sri Lanka.

"I would like the whole of the Indian Subcontinent to be reunited. Look at us and Bangladesh: same script, same language, same accent, same food," he asserted, even as he admitted that India itself was not pure. Interrupting himself once again, he spoke about how the *shulwar kameez,* unlike the sari, was not Indian in origin but Persian. "We're all gypsies," he said. "Where are you going to draw the borders?" He was like a man with dementia, whose disconnected thoughts and memories kept whirling around a single theme that he struggled hard to hold on to.

"Have you been to the Omayyad Mosque in Damascus?" he asked.

"Yes," I said.

"Then you know that it is a pagan fire temple, a Hellenistic beauty, a synagogue, a church, and a mosque. To call it one thing separated from any other is to miss the whole point."

This dense, fluid, interconnected world comprising Africa and the southern rimland of Eurasia is, as the Persian trader intimated, hard to disaggregate geographically and culturally, thanks in part to the monsoon winds. Greater Indian Ocean civilization speaks in a plethora of voices, yet it also maintains the element of an integrated whole. The scholar Vali Nasr adds a component to this in his 2009 book, *Forces of Fortune: The Rise of the New Muslim Middle Class and What It Will Mean for Our World.* Nasr's thesis says, in effect, that by concentrating so one-dimensionally on al-Qaeda and radicalism, we have missed the real development of this epoch: the emergence of a bourgeoisie in the Greater Middle East and beyond. This, I may add, is happening alongside the destabilizing effects of extreme poverty, environmental devastation, and unresponsive governments in too many places. Hence, the challenges that most people in the Indian Ocean region face are only indirectly, if at all, related to Islamic terrorism and the military rise of China. Precisely because so many of the challenges—and hopes and dreams—of this new middle class are personal and materialistic, there will be increasing calls for better government and, yes, democracy. Iran's regime will become a thing of the past in this vision, and even in Oman some change will have to come, for its one-man rule, as impressive and relatively liberal as it has been, will not be ultimately sustainable. Indonesia's moderating democracy could become the lodestar of the Muslim world.

There is no more clarifying example of this middle-class phenomenon than the editorial slant of the Qatar-based Arab television channel Al Jazeera, whose English-language version constitutes a feast of vivid, pathbreaking coverage of the travails of the weak and the oppressed throughout the Indian Ocean region and larger former third world. As I watched Al Jazeera many a night throughout my travels, it became the vicarious equivalent of the conversations I was having from Oman to Zanzibar, of which the one with the Persian trader was the most emblematic. The fact that Doha, Qatar's capital, is not the headquarters of a great power—even as it is geographically in the center of the Indian Ocean world—liberates Al Jazeera to focus equally on the four corners of the Earth rather than on just the flash points of any imperial or post-imperial interest. Some in the United States see Al Jazeera as biased, but that only reflects their own biases. Al Jazeera's reporters cry out for *justice,* even as they are honestly representative of an emerging middle-of-the-road, middle-class viewpoint in developing nations. To wit, a new bourgeoisie arises, even as its members are insecure, and see in a new light injustice all around them. The vicissitudes of extremism notwithstanding, a replica of the pre-Portuguese Muslim-Hindu trading cosmopolis is now being rebuilt, buttressed by Chinese investment. In this new Indian Ocean world, it is hoped that Sri Lanka will achieve a new stability, putting its ethnic differences behind it as its government is gradually forced to adjust to the rigors of peace. Meanwhile, new trade routes will open between India, Bangladesh, Burma, and China, with the linkages between great and small powers as dynamic as the tensions.

Indeed, the challenge to America, ultimately, is less the rise of China than communicating at a basic level with this emerging global civilization of Africans and Asians. As for China, I've already indicated that it is rising militarily in a responsible manner. It will have its own problems in expanding its maritime influence into the Indian Ocean. And in any case China is not necessarily America's adversary. But unless America makes its peace with these billions symbolized by the Greater Indian Ocean map, many of whom are Muslim, American power will not be seen as wholly legitimate. And legitimacy, remember, is a primary feature of power in the first place. In an earlier chapter I said that strong American-

Chinese bilateral relations going forward are not only plausible but might be the best-case scenario for the global system in the twenty-first century, allowing for true world governance to take shape. But that is true only so far as the bilateral world of nation-states is concerned. As the former third world forges a new kind of unity, driven by mass media like Al Jazeera that abets an underlying cultural synthesis, the Afro-Asian multitudes will increasingly be in a pivotal position to bestow prestige or condemnation on America, China, and other powerful states, depending upon the merits of each particular crisis. They, in addition to being participants, are the supreme audience for power politics in the twenty-first century.

Great-power politics will go on as they always have, with the American and Chinese navies quietly competing and jockeying for position in the First Island Chain, and India and China competing for sea routes and influence. But these activities will be framed more and more by a global civilization, the product of a new bourgeoisie that in and of itself constitutes a moral force with which to be reckoned.

Hundreds of millions of Muslims and others, quietly elevated into the middle classes, are seeking to live peaceful, productive lives, even as they confer legitimacy on the great power or powers whose actions help them in what my Persian friend and the novelist Abdulrazak Gurnah both say man is ultimately on earth to do—"to trade." Trade is what Zheng He did, and while the Chinese navy celebrates his Indian Ocean exploits, America, too, could learn much from this Ming Dynasty explorer, who saw military activity as an expression not only of hard but of soft power as well: to help protect the global commons and a trading system for the benefit of all. Only by seeking at every opportunity to identify its struggles with those of the larger Indian Ocean world can American power finally be preserved.

ACKNOWLEDGMENTS

Perhaps the most unforeseen pleasure of this project was my introduction to various academic works that constituted an inspiration in the course of my journalistic research. These are books whose standard of excellence and level of detail I cannot hope to attain. Let me name just a few; the rest are in the various footnotes scattered throughout the text: Janet L. Abu-Lughod's *Before European Hegemony: The World System A.D. 1250–1350* (1989), C. R. Boxer's *The Portuguese Seaborne Empire 1415–1825* (1969), Richard M. Eaton's *The Rise of Islam and the Bengal Frontier, 1204–1760* (1993), K. M. Panikkar's *Asia and Western Dominance* (1959), John F. Richards's *The Mughal Empire* (1995), and André Wink's *Al-Hind: The Making of the Indo-Islamic World,* volume 1 (1990).

My assistant, Elizabeth Lockyer, is without peer, and took the lead in arranging the maps for this book. My editors at Random House, Kate Medina and Millicent Bennett, played a crucial role in making this exploration possible and in shaping the manuscript. Thanks, too, to Frankie Jones and Lindsey Schwoeri. *The Atlantic Monthly* published several chapters of this book in abbreviated form, and in this regard I am grateful for the editorial help and fact-checking of James Bennet, Justine Isola, and Scott Stossel, and especially that of James Gibney. I also published an essay on the Indian Ocean in *Foreign Affairs,* and I thank the editors there—James F. Hoge Jr., Gideon Rose, and Stephanie Giry—for their expert help and the prominent placement they awarded the piece.

Once again I thank my agents, Carl D. Brandt and Marianne Merola, for looking after my career and interests the way they have.

The Center for a New American Security (CNAS) in Washington, D.C., provided me with an institutional home while I researched and wrote this book. I cannot thank CNAS enough for all the help and encouragement that came in so many forms. To name a few people there would seem to slight the many others at CNAS who also assisted me. Nevertheless, let me name the former management team of Kurt Campbell, Michèle Flournoy, and James N. Miller Jr., now all members of the Obama administration, and the new team of Nathaniel Fick and John Nagl, as well as the research assistance of Seth Myers. The Smith Richardson Foundation provided me with financial help for this project, and there I thank, in particular, Nadia Schadlow for helping me through the grant process. I am also grateful to the Aspen Strategy Group for allowing me to participate in the U.S.-India Strategic Dialogue.

In Kolkata, Gautam Chakraporti arranged a memorable trip along the Hooghly River for me. In Islamabad and Jakarta, Kathy Gannon and Henk and Emmeline Mulder provided me with the warmth, friendship, and accommodations of their respective lovely homes. In Zanzibar, Emerson Skeens rented me a charming little apartment, and provided much help besides. Lieutenant Colonel Larry Smith literally got me out of jail in Sri Lanka. Brannon Wheeler, my colleague at the U.S. Naval Academy, and Abdulrahman Al-Salimi of the Ministry of Religious Endowments worked together to arrange a series of lectures for me to deliver in Oman, allowing me to visit that country.

Other crucial help came from Jeffrey Anderson, Michael H. Anderson, Robert Arbuckle, Claude Berube, Gary Thomas Burgess, Robin Bush, Jon Cebra, Kingshuk Chatterjee, Eugene Galbraith, Kiki Skagen Harris, Timothy Heinemann, Fauzan Ijazah, Dilshika Jayamaha, Tissa Jayatilaka, Shahzad Shah Jillani, Douglas Kelly, Joanna Lokhande, Edward Luce, Mohan Malik, Harsh Mander, Scott Merrillees, C. Raja Mohan, Kiran Pasricha, Ralph Peters, Indi Samarajiva, Nick Schmidle, Professor Stuart Schwartz, Mubashar Shah, Arun Shourie, SinhaRaja Tammita-Delgoda, Shashi Tharoor, and Paul Wolfowitz.

I once again thank my loving wife of twenty-seven years, Maria Cabral, without whom much of this would have been impossible.

GLOSSARY

abangan: the population of Indonesians who practice a syncretic version of Islam.

Abu Sayyaf: Islamic separatist group based in the southern Philippines.

Akhand Bharat: Greater India (Hindi).

alluvial soil: earth deposited by a river or other running water.

amphora: an ancient vase or jar with handles.

ASEAN: Association of Southeast Asian Nations.

astrolabe: an astronomical instrument used until the seventeenth century to calculate the positions of celestial bodies, survey, triangulate, and determine local time and latitude.

auliya: protector, saint (Arabic).

Awami League: a center-left political party in Bangladesh.

bamboo curtain: euphemism for the boundary separating China and other communist states of East Asia from their noncommunist neighbors.

baraza: stone bench, sitting area, meeting place (Swahili).

bhangra: traditional folk music and dance originating in Punjab.

BJP: Bharatiya Janata Party, a Hindu nationalist party.

BNP: Bangladesh Nationalist Party, a center-right political party.

BRAC: Bangladesh Rural Advancement Committee, a nongovernmental development organization.

bunkering: the refueling of a ship.

burka: a loose, all-enveloping garment with net holes for the eyes worn by some traditional Muslim women in public.

bustee: slum (Hindi).

caliph: successor of Muhammad and spiritual leader of Islam.

canton: a territory or division of a country.

carrack: a Portuguese sailing ship of the fifteenth and sixteenth centuries.

chapatti: an unleavened bread originating in India.

char: a temporary delta island formed by silt.

charpoy: a bed with a frame woven with rope, used primarily in India.

Chindits: a British India military unit serving in India and Burma during World War II. The name is an anglicized corruption of the name of a mythical Burmese lion.

Civic United Front: a liberal political party in Tanzania composed mainly of ethnic Indians and Arabs.

close-hauled: sailing as close to the wind as possible with a tight trim.

C-130: a four-engine U.S. Air Force troop and cargo transport aircraft that can airdrop into a combat zone.

corsair: privateer, pirate.

corvette: a small warship that is easy to maneuver.

dacoit: bandit.

devale: prayer complex, shrine (Sri Lanka).

dhow: a traditional Arab boat with lateen sails.

dishdasha: a long traditional white shirtdress worn by men throughout the Middle East.

doldrums: nautical term for the zone near the equator where the winds are generally calm.

draft: the vertical measurement of the submerged portion of a ship.

entrepôt: trading post.

Ethnic Nationalities Council: coalition of ethnic political organizations in Burma.

faience: earthenware with a tin glaze.

falaj: a system of tunnels, small dams, and storage tanks used to provide reliable irrigation in arid climates.

foist: a small galley ship.

forward base: a base established in a friendly territory to extend command and control of communications, or to provide support for training and tactical operations.

Free Burma Rangers: humanitarian group working in Burma.

galleon: a large, heavy, primarily European sailing ship with multiple decks and armed with cannon.

galley: a ship propelled by oars.

GAM: Gerakan Aceh Merdeka (Aceh Freedom Movement), a separatist group in Indonesia.

gantry crane: cargo hoisted by this type of crane hangs below a trolley that rolls along horizontal tracks attached to a long beam, and in this way is moved between ship and port.

GIFT: Gujarat International Finance Tec-City, a planned high-tech city to be located eight kilometers from Gandhinagar in the Indian state of Gujarat.

Golden Triangle: an area overlapping the countries of Burma, Laos, Thailand, and Vietnam, where opium is produced in large quantities.

Gulf Cooperation Council: a political and economic organization of Arab countries in the Persian Gulf.

haj: the annual pilgrimage to Mecca, Saudi Arabia, considered a religious duty in Islam.

hallal: food that conforms to Muslim dietary laws (Arabic).

halwa: a dense, sweet confection made with flour or nut butters (Arabic).

haram: forbidden by Islam (Arabic).

Hegira: the migration in A.D. 622 of the prophet Muhammad and his followers to Medina.

Hindutva: "Hindu-ness"; also used to describe Hindu nationalist movements.

Hizbut Tahrir Indonesia: Party of Freedom, the Indonesian branch of an international Islamic organization advocating for a caliphate.

Huey: U.S. Army and Marine gunship helicopter.

imam: the leader of a mosque or a Muslim leader claiming descent from Muhammad.

Indiamen: large sailing ships used in the sixteenth through nineteenth century for trade between Europe and the East Indies.

Indo-Saracenic: a style of architecture combining Islamic and Hindu styles.

ISI: [Directorate for] Inter-Services Intelligence, Pakistan's largest intelligence organization.

jahazi: a large dhow used for cargo and passengers (Persian).

Jama'atul Mujahideen: a militant Islamic organization operating in Bangladesh.

Jemaah Islamiyah: a militant Islamic organization dedicated to establishing an Islamic state in Southeast Asia.

jilbab: in Indonesia, a head scarf worn by a Muslim woman (Arabic).

junk: derived from the Southeast Asian term *jong,* a range of advanced Chinese vessels that were developed by the Song dynasty in the tenth century.

Jyotirlinga: a shrine to the Hindu god Shiva.

kampong: in Indonesia, house (Javanese).

kanzu: a white or light colored robe worn by men in East Africa (Swahili).

katchiabaadi: a squatter settlement in Karachi, Pakistan.

khanga: colorful patterned garment worn by women and some men in East Africa (Swahili).

khanjar: a curved dagger traditionally worn by men in Oman (Arabic).

khareef: in Oman and Yemen, the local Arabic term for the southeast monsoon (Arabic).

kofia: a cylindrical, brimless knitted cap worn by men in East Africa (Swahili).

lateen: a triangular sail, running fore to aft, that is extended by a long yard mounted at an angle on a low mast.

load-shedding: the maintenance of a rolling blackout to prevent the complete collapse of a power system.

longyi: traditional skirt worn by men in Burma (Burmese).

LTTE: Liberation Tigers of Tamil Eelam (Tamil Tigers), a separatist organization that sought to establish an independent state in northeastern Sri Lanka.

lubban: frankincense (Arabic).

madrassa: school (Arabic).

Majelis Mujahidin Indonesia: Assembly of Holy Warriors, an Indonesian Islamic group.

masala: a mixture of spices used in South Asian cuisine.

mashua: a small dhow used for fishing (Swahili).

matbor: head or chief of a Muslim Bengali village.

mausim: season (Arabic).

Mercator projection: a map presentation in which longitudes appear as parallel lines and latitudes, also parallel, are spaced more widely farther from the equator, which tends to distort the size and shape of larger objects.

mohajir: immigrant, emigrant (Arabic). In Pakistan, Muslim refugees from post-independence India.

Muhammadiyah: Followers of Muhammad, an Indonesian Muslim civic organization.

mustan: in Bangladesh, a Mafia-style boss.

nawab: viceroy of the Mughal empire.

Naxalites: militant Maoist communist group in India.

NGO: nongovernmental organization.

Nizam: term for the sovereign of the Indian state of Hyderabad from the eighteenth century until Indian independence.

NU: Nahdlatul Ulema (Revivalist Clergy), an Indonesian Muslim civic organization.

oikoumene: an ancient term for (the known part of) the inhabited world (Greek).

Operation Enduring Freedom: U.S. military response, primarily in Afghanistan, to the September 11, 2001, attacks.

Operation Unified Assistance: U.S. military response to the 2004 Indian Ocean earthquake and tsunami.

Pancasila: the pluralist- and democracy-affirming philosophical foundation of the Indonesian constitution, based on belief in God, nationalism, humanism, democracy, and social justice.

pesantren: Indonesian Muslim boarding schools or madrassas; the word derives from *santri,* meaning orthodox (Javanese).

port tack: sailing with the wind coming over the port (left) side of the boat.

pracharak: a full-time activist for the Rashtriya Swayamsevak Sangh (Hindi). See RSS.

prau: a light sailing craft with two hulls used primarily in the Malay Archipelago and the South Pacific.

qasr: fortress (Arabic).

Raj: the period of British rule in India, 1858–1947; also the Mughal Empire, 1526–1857.

RAW: Research and Analysis Wing (of the Indian security bureaucracy).

Rohingya: Muslim from the state of Arakan in southwestern Burma.

RSS: Rashtriya Swayamsevak Sangh (Organization of National Volunteers), the umbrella group of the Hindu nationalist movement.

Saffron Revolution (2007): antigovernment protests in Burma, named for the saffron-colored robes worn by Buddhist monks.

sampan: a Chinese flat-bottomed wooden boat.

Sangh: the family of Hindu organizations.

santri: the population of Indonesians who practice an orthodox version of Islam.

sari: a length of cloth draped over the body in different styles by South Asian women.

sati: Hindu practice in which a widow is immolated on her husband's funeral pyre.

saudade: nostalgia, homesickness (Portuguese).

SEAL: commando team of the U.S. Navy. ("SEAL" is an acronym for "sea, air, land.")

sepoy: a native Indian soldier in British service.

shalwar kameez: pajama-like trousers (*shalwar*) gathered at the waist and ankles, and worn underneath a long loose tunic (*kameez*).

shikhara: in Hindu temple architecture, a tower (Sanskrit).

SLOC: sea lines of communication, the primary routes between ports.

SLORC: State Law and Order Restoration Council, the Burmese military junta from 1988 to 1997.

souk: a market or market stall in North Africa and the Middle East.

SPDC: State Peace and Development Council, the Burmese military junta, which in 1997 replaced the SLORC.

square rigging: the rigging of a sailing ship in which the principal sails are carried on yards, which are fastened perpendicularly to the masts.

string-of-pearls strategy: China's attempts to increase its sea lines of communication across the Indian Ocean by establishing or cultivating posts at, among others, the Pakistani port of Gwadar, the Pakistani port of Pasni, the Sri Lankan port of Hambantota, the Bangladeshi port of Chittagong, commercial and naval bases in Burma, and surveillance facilities on the Coco Islands.

stupa: a dome-shaped Buddhist shrine.

Tamil Tigers: see LTTE.

Thailand Burma Border Consortium: a consortium of twelve nongovernmental organizations providing assistance to refugees from Burma.

Thakur: an Indian honorific meaning "Lord" (Hindi).

toe-popper: a small plastic anti-personnel land mine.

topi: originally from India, a lightweight, insulated, brimmed helmet made of pith or cork, worn as a sun hat.

trades: trade winds, a pattern of surface winds in the tropics blowing primarily from the northeast in the Northern Hemisphere and from the southeast in the Southern Hemisphere.

transship: to change from one ship to another.

VHP: Vishwa Hindu Parishad (World Hindu Council), a Hindu nationalist party.

westerlies: a pattern of surface winds in the middle latitudes blowing primarily from west to east.

NOTES

Preface: The Rimland of Eurasia

1. C. R. Boxer, *The Portuguese Seaborne Empire, 1415–1825* (London: Hutchinson, 1969), p. 65.
2. Luiz Vaz de Camões, *The Lusíads,* transl. Landeg White (1572; reprint, New York: Oxford University Press, 1997), Canto Six: 93.
3. Charles Verlinden, "The Indian Ocean: The Ancient Period and the Middle Ages," in Satish Chandra, *The Indian Ocean: Explorations in History, Commerce and Politics* (New Delhi: Safe, 1987), p. 27.

PART I

Chapter 1: China Expands Vertically, India Horizontally

1. Sugata Bose, *A Hundred Horizons: The Indian Ocean in the Age of Global Empire* (Cambridge, MA: Harvard University Press, 2006), pp. 10, 34.
2. Ibid., pp. 12–13.
3. Michael Pearson, *The Indian Ocean* (New York: Routledge, 2003), p. 12.
4. Fareed Zakaria, *The Post-American World* (New York: Norton, 2008).
5. Felipe Fernández-Armesto, *Pathfinders: A Global History of Exploration* (New York: Norton, 2006), p. 31.
6. Janet L. Abu-Lughod, *Before European Hegemony: The World System A.D. 1250–1350* (New York: Oxford University Press, 1989), p. 291, quoting Tomé Pires.
7. John Keay, *The Honourable Company: A History of the English East India Company* (London: HarperCollins, 1991), p. 104.
8. Heather Timmons and Somini Sengupta, "Building a Modern Arsenal in India," *New York Times,* Aug. 31, 2007. Quote from Sitanshu Kar, Indian defense ministry spokesman.
9. International Energy Agency, "World Energy Outlook 2007," Paris, 2007.
10. Bethany Danyluk, Juli A. MacDonald, and Ryan Tuggle, "Energy Futures in Asia: Perspectives on India's Energy Security Strategy and Policies," Booz Allen Hamilton, 2007.

11. Andrew Erickson and Gabe Collins, "Beijing's Energy Security Strategy: The Significance of a Chinese State-Owned Tanker Fleet," *Orbis,* Fall 2007.
12. Martin Walker, "CHIMEA: The Emerging Hub of the Global Economy," A. T. Kearney report, Washington, D.C., 2008. Ten ships an hour on a 24/7 basis pass through the Malacca Strait.
13. Thomas P.M. Barnett, "India's 12 Steps to a World-Class Navy," *Proceedings,* Annapolis, MD, July 2001.
14. James R. Holmes and Toshi Yoshihara, "China and the United States in the Indian Ocean: An Emerging Strategic Triangle?" *Naval War College Review,* Summer 2008.
15. Juli A. MacDonald, Amy Donahue, and Bethany Danyluk, "Energy Futures in Asia: Final Report," Booz Allen Hamilton, November 2004. The quote was originally reported by the China expert Ross Munro.
16. Holmes and Yoshihara, "China and the United States in the Indian Ocean."
17. China is building similar facilities in Cambodia by the Gulf of Thailand and the South China Sea. MacDonald, Donahue, and Danyluk, "Energy Futures in Asia"; Malik, "Energy Flows and Maritime Rivalries in the Indian Ocean Region."
18. Andrew Erickson and Lyle Goldstein, "Gunboats for China's New 'Grand Canals'?" *Naval War College Review,* Spring 2009.
19. Louise Levathes, *When China Ruled the Seas: The Treasury Fleet of the Dragon Throne* (New York: Oxford University Press, 1994); Thant Myint-U, *The River of Lost Footsteps: A Personal History of Burma* (New York: Farrar, Straus and Giroux, 2006), p. 66; Richard Hall, *Empires of the Monsoon: A History of the Indian Ocean and Its Invaders* (London: HarperCollins, 1996), p. 79.
20. M. Shamsur Rabb Khan, "Time to Revive India-Iran Relations," IndiaPost.com, Jan. 27, 2008.
21. Kemp, "East Moves West."
22. Ramtanu Maitra, "India-US Security: All at Sea in the Indian Ocean," *Asia Times,* Dec. 6, 2007.
23. MacDonald, Donahue, and Danyluk, "Energy Futures in Asia."
24. Greg Sheridan, "East Meets West," *National Interest,* November/December, 2006.
25. Ibid.
26. Walker, "CHIMEA."

PART II

Chapter 2: Oman Is Everywhere

1. Felipe Fernández-Armesto, *Pathfinders: A Global History of Exploration* (New York: Norton, 2006), p. 36.
2. Alan Villiers, *Monsoon Seas: The Story of the Indian Ocean* (New York: McGraw-Hill, 1952), p. 55.
3. Juliet Highet, *Frankincense: Oman's Gift to the World* (New York: Prestel, 2006).
4. Ministry of National Heritage and Culture, *Oman: A Seafaring Nation* (Muscat: Sultanate of Oman, 2005).
5. *The Travels of Marco Polo,* ch. 37.
6. Janet L. Abu-Lughod, *Before European Hegemony: The World System A.D. 1250–1350* (New York: Oxford University Press, 1989), p. 203; Richard Hall, *Empires of the Monsoon: A History of the Indian Ocean and Its Invaders* (London: HarperCollins, 1996), p. 8.

7. Keay, *Honourable Company,* pp. 16–17.
8. André Wink, *Al-Hind: The Making of the Indo-Islamic World,* vol. 1, *Early Medieval India and the Expansion of Islam, 7th–11th Centuries* (Boston and Leiden, the Netherlands: Brill, 1990, 2002), p. 4.
9. Halford Mackinder, "The Geographical Pivot of History," *Geographical Journal,* London, April 1904.
10. Fernández-Armesto, *Pathfinders,* p. 33.
11. Abu-Lughod, *Before European Hegemony,* pp. 198–99. See, too, Hourani, pp. 47, 62; Wink, *Al-Hind,* p. 50.
12. Abu-Lughod, *Before European Hegemony,* pp. 200, 208, 261.
13. Fernández-Armesto, *Pathfinders,* p. 64.
14. Patricia Risso, *Merchants & Faith: Muslim Commerce and Culture in the Indian Ocean* (Boulder, CO: Westview, 1995), p. 46; Philip D. Curtin, *Cross-Cultural Trade in World History* (New York: Cambridge University Press, 1984), p. 121.
15. George F. Hourani, *Arab Seafaring in the Indian Ocean in Ancient and Early Medieval Times* (Princeton, NJ: Princeton University Press, 1951), pp. 4, 23.
16. Abu-Lughod, *Before European Hegemony,* p. 242.
17. Marshall G.S. Hodgson, *The Venture of Islam,* vol. 2, *The Expansion of Islam in the Middle Periods* (Chicago: University of Chicago Press, 1961), pp. 542–43.
18. Risso, *Merchants & Faith,* p. 53.
19. Ibid., pp. 5–6, 54, 71–72.
20. Ibid., pp. 23–24.
21. Peter Boxhall, "Portuguese Seafarers in the Indian Ocean," *Asian Affairs,* vol. 23, no. 3 (1992).
22. Nayan Chandra, "When Asia Was One," *GlobalAsia: A Journal of the East Asia Foundation,* September 2006.
23. Hall, *Empires of the Monsoon,* pp. 24–25, 63.
24. Chanda, "When Asia Was One."
25. Abu-Lughod, *Before European Hegemony,* p. 253.

Chapter 3: Curzon's Frontiers

1. George N. Curzon, *Frontiers: The Romanes Lecture 1907,* (1907; reprint, Boston: Elibron Classics, 2006).
2. Ibid., pp. 13–16.
3. Peter Mansfield, *The Arabs* (Harmondsworth, Eng.: Penguin, 1976), p. 371 of Penguin; Curzon, *Frontiers,* p. 42.
4. Bernard Lewis, *The Middle East: A Brief History of the Last 2000 Years* (New York: Simon & Schuster, 1995), p. 66. See, too, Ayesha Jalal, *Partisans of Allah* (Cambridge, MA: Harvard University Press, 2008).
5. Calvin H. Allen Jr., "Oman: A Separate Place," *Wilson Quarterly,* New Year's 1987.
6. Ibid.
7. Richard Hall, *Empires of the Monsoon: A History of the Indian Ocean and Its Invaders* (London: HarperCollins, 1996), p. 355.
8. Ibid.
9. Samuel P. Huntington, *Political Order in Changing Societies* (New Haven, CT: Yale University Press, 1968), pp. 5–6.
10. Engseng Ho, Harvard University professor of anthropology, presentation for a conference on "Port City States of the Indian Ocean," Harvard University and the Dubai Initiative, Feb. 9–10, 2008.

Chapter 4: "Lands of India"

1. C. R. Boxer, *The Portuguese Seaborne Empire, 1415–1825,* with an introduction by J. H. Plumb (London: Hutchinson, 1969), p. 354.
2. Landeg White, Introduction to Luiz Vaz de Camões, *The Lusíads,* (New York: Oxford University Press, 1997).
3. George F. Hourani, *Arab Seafaring in the Indian Ocean in Ancient and Early Medieval Times* (Princeton, NJ: Princeton University Press, 1951), p. 35.
4. Edward Gibbon, *The Decline and Fall of the Roman Empire* (1776; reprint, New York: Knopf, 1993), ch. 2. See, too, Janet L. Abu-Lughod, *Before European Hegemony: The World System A.D. 1250–1350* (New York: Oxford University Press, 1989), p. 265.
5. Abu-Lughod, *Before European Hegemony,* p. 265.
6. Burton Stein, *A History of India* (Oxford, Eng.: Blackwell, 1998), pp. 100–104, 127–28.
7. Richard Hall, *Empires of the Monsoon: A History of the Indian Ocean and Its Invaders* (London: HarperCollins, 1996), p. 323.
8. For more details, see Fernand Braudel, *The Mediterranean and the Mediterranean World in the Age of Philip II,* vol. 2 (1949; New York: Harper & Row, 1973), pp. 1174–76.
9. A.J.R. Russell-Wood, *The Portuguese Empire, 1415–1808: A World on the Move* (Baltimore: Johns Hopkins University Press, 1992), p. 22.
10. K. M. Pannikar, *Asia and Western Dominance* (London: Allen & Unwin, 1959), p. 17.
11. Ibid., p. 24.
12. Hall, *Empires of the Monsoon,* p. 190.
13. Panikkar, *Asia and Western Dominance,* pp. 17, 24, 313.
14. Ibid., p. 25.
15. Peter Russell, *Prince Henry "the Navigator": A Life* (New Haven, CT: Yale University Press, 2000).
16. *Saudi Aramco World,* June/July 1962.
17. Patricia Risso, *Merchants & Faith: Muslim Commerce and Culture in the Indian Ocean* (Boulder, CO: Westview, 1995), p. 36; Jakub J. Grygiel, *Great Powers and Geopolitical Change* (Baltimore: Johns Hopkins University Press, 2006), pp. 41–42.
18. This section draws broadly from Boxer's *Portuguese Seaborne Empire.*
19. Grygiel, *Great Powers and Geopolitical Change,* p. 43.
20. William Dalrymple, *The Age of Kali: Indian Travels and Encounters* (London: HarperCollins, 1998), p. 238.
21. Alan Villiers, *Monsoon Seas: The Story of the Indian Ocean* (New York: McGraw-Hill, 1952), pp. 161–65.
22. Fernández-Armesto, *Pathfinders,* p. 181.
23. R. B. Sergeant, *The Portuguese Off the South Arabian Coast* (Oxford, Eng.: Clarendon, 1963,) p. 15.
24. Michael Pearson, *The Indian Ocean* (New York: Routledge, 2003), p. 125.
25. Plumb in Boxer, *Portuguese Seaborne Empire,* p. xxiii.
26. Hall, *Empires of the Monsoon,* pp. 172, 198. See, too, Gaspar Correa, *The Three Voyages of Vasco da Gama* (1869; reprint, Ann Arbor, MI: University Microfilms, 1964); and Nick Robins, *The Corporation That Changed the World: How the East India Company Shaped the Modern Multinational* (Hyderabad, India: Orient Longman, 2006), pp. 41–42.

27. T. E. Lawrence, *Seven Pillars of Wisdom: A Triumph* (London: Jonathan Cape, 1926, 1935), ch. 3.
28. Boxer, *Portuguese Seaborne Empire*, pp. 377–78.
29. Ibid., p. 296.
30. Ibid., pp. 39–43.
31. Risso, *Merchants & Faith*, p. 52.
32. Russell-Wood, *Portuguese Empire*, pp. 15, 18–20.
33. Ibid., p. 21.
34. Fernándo Pessoa, *The Book of Disquiet*, trans. Margaret Jull Costa (1982; reprint, New York: Serpent's Tail, 1991), p. 52.
35. Russell-Wood, *The Portuguese Empire*, pp. 23, 198.
36. C. M. Bowra, "Camões and the Epic of Portugal," in his *From Virgil to Milton* (1945; reprint, London: Macmillan, 1967), pp. 99–100; Luiz Vaz de Camões, *The Lusíads*, trans. Landeg White (New York: Oxford University Press, 1997), Canto Five: 81.
37. Camões, *Lusíads*, Canto Eight: 86.
38. Ibid., Canto Four: 87; Six: 80–84.
39. White, Introduction to *The Lusíads*. See, too, Sanjay Subrahmanyam, *The Career and Legend of Vasco da Gama* (New York: Cambridge University Press, 1997), pp. 154–59.
40. Camões, *Lusíads*, Canto Five: 86.
41. Bowra, *From Virgil to Milton*, p. 86.
42. Camões, Canto One: 27.
43. Camões, Canto Five: 16.
44. Bowra, *From Virgil to Milton*, p. 97; Camões, Canto One: 64, and Ten: 102, 122.
45. *Encyclopaedia Britannica*, 11th ed. (New York, 1910).
46. Camões, Canto One: 3.
47. Ibid., Canto One: 99.
48. Ibid., Canto Nine: 1.
49. Bowra, *From Virgil to Milton*, pp. 133, 136.
50. Camoes, Canto Four: 99.

Chapter 5: Baluchistan and Sindh

1. André Wink, *Al-Hind: The Making of the Indo-Islamic World*, vol. 1, *Early Medieval India and the Expansion of Islam, 7th–11th Centuries* (Boston and Leiden, the Netherlands: Brill, 1990, 2002), p. 129.
2. John Keay, *The Honourable Company: A History of the English East India Company* (London: HarperCollins, 1991), p. 103.
3. B. Raman, "Hambantota and Gwadar—an Update," Institute for Topical Studies, Chennai, India, 2009.
4. Robert G. Wirsing, "Baloch Nationalism and the Geopolitics of Energy Resources: The Changing Context of Separatism in Pakistan," Strategic Studies Institute, U.S. Army War College, Carlisle, PA, Apr. 17, 2008.
5. Wilfred Thesiger, *Arabian Sands* (New York: Dutton, 1959), p. 276.
6. "The Great Land Robbery: Gwadar," *The Herald*, Karachi, Pakistan, June 2008.
7. Selig S. Harrison, "Ethnic Tensions and the Future of Pakistan," working paper prepared for the Center for International Policy, 2008.
8. Harrison, "Pakistan's Baluch Insurgency," *Le Monde Diplomatique*, October 2006.

9. International Crisis Group, "Pakistan: The Forgotten Conflict in Balochistan," (Islamabad/Brussels, Oct. 22, 2007).
10. Ibid.
11. Ibid.
12. Ibid.
13. Wirsing, "Baloch Nationalism and the Geopolitics of Energy Resources."
14. Ibid.
15. Wink, *Al-Hind,* pp. 173, 175.
16. Aryn Baker, "Karachi Dreams Big," *Time* (Asia), Feb. 8, 2008.
17. Robert D. Kaplan, *Imperial Grunts: The American Military on the Ground* (New York: Random House, 2005), p. 37.
18. Ibid.
19. Freya Stark, *East Is West* (London: John Murray, 1945), p. 198.
20. John F. Richards, *Mughal Empire* (New York: Cambridge University Press, 1995), p. 51.
21. William Dalrymple, "Pakistan in Peril," *New York Review of Books,* Feb. 12, 2009.
22. Wink, *Al-Hind,* p. 213.
23. Joseph A. Tainter, *The Collapse of Complex Societies* (New York: Cambridge University Press, 1988), p. 6.
24. Burton Stein, *A History of India* (Oxford, Eng.: Blackwell, 1998), p. 22.
25. W. Gordon East, *The Geography Behind History* (New York: Norton, 1965), p. 142.
26. Asif Raza Morio, *Moen Jo Daro, Mysterious City of [the] Indus Valley Civilization* (Larkana, Pakistan: Editions, 2007).
27. Mary Anne Weaver, *Pakistan: In the Shadow of Jihad and Afghanistan* (New York: Farrar, Straus and Giroux, 2002), p. 181.
28. Tainter, *Collapse of Complex Societies,* p. 1.
29. Richard F. Burton, *Sindh: and the Races That Inhabit the Valley of the Indus; with Notices of the Topography and History of the Province* (London: Allen, 1851), pp. 3, 362.

Chapter 6: The Troubled Rise of Gujarat

1. Edward Luce, *In Spite of the Gods: The Strange Rise of Modern India* (New York: Doubleday, 2007), pp. 158–62.
2. Citizens for Justice and Peace, "Summary of the CJP's Activities Between April 2002 and October 2003," Mumbai.
3. André Wink, *Al-Hind: The Making of the Indo-Islamic World,* vol. 2, *The Slave Kings and the Islamic Conquest, 11th–13th Centuries* (New Delhi: Oxford University Press, 1997), p. 269.
4. Luiz Vaz de Camões, *The Lusíads,* trans. Landeg White (1572; reprint, New York: Oxford University Press, 1997), Canto Ten: 106.
5. Marshall G.S. Hodgson, *The Venture of Islam,* vol. 2, *The Expansion of Islam in the Middle Periods* (Chicago: University of Chicago Press, 1961), p. 546; Alan Villiers, *Monsoon Seas: The Story of the Indian Ocean* (New York: McGraw-Hill, 1952), p. 109.
6. R.A.L.H. Gunawardana, "Changing Patterns of Navigation in the Indian Ocean and Their Impact on Pre-Colonial Sri Lanka," in Satish Chandra, *The Indian Ocean: Explorations in History, Commerce and Politics* (New Delhi: Sage, 1987), p. 81.
7. S. Arasaratnam, "India and the Indian Ocean in the Seventeenth Century," in As hin

Das Gupta and M. N. Pearson, eds., *India and the Indian Ocean, 1500–1800* (Kolkata: Oxford University Press, 1987).

8. Engseng Ho, "Port City States of the Indian Ocean," Harvard University and the Dubai Initiative, Feb. 9–10, 2008.

9. Sugata Bose, *A Hundred Horizons: The Indian Ocean in the Age of Global Empire* (Cambridge, MA: Harvard University Press, 2006), p. 75. Charles Verlinden, "The Indian Ocean: The Ancient Period and the Middle Ages," in Chandra, *Indian Ocean*, p. 49.

10. Dwijendra Tripathi, "Crisis of Indian Polity and the Historian," Indian History Congress, Amritsar, 2002.

11. See in this context Susanne Hoeber Rudolph and Lloyd I. Rudolph, "Modern Hate: How Ancient Animosities Get Invented," *New Republic*, Mar. 22, 1993.

12. Walter Laqueur, ed., *Fascism: A Reader's Guide; Analyses, Interpretations, Bibliography* (London: Wildwood, 1976).

13. Juan J. Linz, "Some Notes Toward a Comparative Study of Fascism in Sociological Historical Perspective." See, too, Zeev Sternhell's "Fascist Ideology." Both in Laqueur's *Fascism*.

14. Thomas Pynchon, Foreword to George Orwell, *Nineteen Eighty-Four* (New York: Penguin, 2003).

15. See Achyut Yagnik and Suchitra Sheth, *The Shaping of Modern Gujarat: Plurality, Hindutva and Beyond* (New Delhi: Penguin India, 2005).

16. Camões, *The Lusíads,* Canto Ten: 60, 64.

17. Amartya Sen, "Why Democratization Is Not the Same as Westernization: Democracy and Its Global Roots," *New Republic,* Oct. 6, 2003.

18. Elias Canetti, *Crowds and Power* (New York: Viking, 1960).

Chapter 7: The View from Delhi

1. John F. Richards, *The Mughal Empire* (New York: Cambridge University Press, 1995), p. 122.

2. Ibid., p. 35.

3. Richard M. Eaton, *The Rise of Islam and the Bengal Frontier, 1204–1760* (Berkeley: University of California Press, 1993), pp. 159–60.

4. Richards, *Mughal Empire,* pp. 239, 242.

5. Sugata Bose, *A Hundred Horizons: The Indian Ocean in the Age of Global Empire* (Cambridge, MA: Harvard University Press, 2006), p. 56.

6. William Dalrymple, *City of Djinns: A Year in Delhi* (London: HarperCollins, 1993), pp. 82–83.

7. George N. Curzon, *Frontiers: The Romanes Lecture 1907* (1907; reprint, Boston: Elibron Classics, 2006), pp. 57–58.

8. Lord Curzon of Kedleston, *The Place of India in the Empire* (London: John Murray, 1909), p. 12.

9. Parag Khanna and C. Raja Mohan, "Getting India Right," *Policy Review,* February/March 2006.

10. Stephen P. Cohen, *India: Emerging Power* (Washington, DC: Brookings, 2001), p. 55.

11. James R. Holmes, Andrew C. Winner, and Toshi Yoshihara, *Indian Naval Strategy in the 21st Century* (London: Routledge, 2009), p. 131.

12. Holmes and Yoshihara, "China and the United States in the Indian Ocean: An

Emerging Strategic Triangle?" *Naval War College Review,* Summer 2008. From Ming's articles, "The Indian Navy Energetically Steps Toward the High Seas" and "The Malacca Dilemma and the Chinese Navy's Strategic Choices."

13. Holmes and Yoshihara, "China and the United States in the Indian Ocean."
14. Geoffrey Kemp, "The East Moves West," *National Interest,* Summer 2006.
15. Heather Timmons and Somini Sengupta, "Building a Modern Arsenal in India," *New York Times,* Aug. 31, 2007.
16. Daniel Twining, "The New Great Game," *Weekly Standard,* Dec. 25, 2006.
17. Greg Sheridan, "East Meets West," *National Interest,* November/December, 2006.
18. Holmes, Winner, and Toshihara, *Indian Naval Strategy in the 21st Century,* p. 142.
19. *Defense Industry Daily,* June 6, 2005.
20. Mohan Malik, "Energy Flows and Maritime Rivalries in the Indian Ocean Region" (Honolulu: Asia-Pacific Center for Security Studies, 2008).
21. Adam Wolfe, Yevgeny Bendersky, and Federico Bordonaro, *Power and Interest News Report,* July 20, 2005.
22. Khanna and Mohan, "Getting India Right."
23. Edward Luce, *In Spite of the Gods: The Strange Rise of Modern India* (New York: Doubleday, 2007), p. 287.
24. Ibid., p. 275.
25. Twining, "New Great Game."
26. Stanley Weiss, "India: The Incredible and the Vulnerable," *International Herald Tribune,* Apr. 23, 2008.
27. Khanna and Mohan, "Getting India Right."
28. Sunil Khilnani, "India as a Bridging Power," The Foreign Policy Centre, 2005.
29. Harsh V. Pant, "A Rising India's Search for a Foreign Policy," *Orbis,* Spring 2009.

Chapter 8: Bangladesh: The Existential Challenge

1. Alan Villiers, *Monsoon Seas: The Story of the Indian Ocean* (New York: McGraw-Hill, 1952), p. 5.
2. Interview with Jay Gulledge, senior scientist, Pew Center on Global Climate Change, 2009.
3. Richard M. Eaton, *The Rise of Islam and the Bengal Frontier, 1204–1760* (Berkeley: University of California Press, 1993), p. 306.
4. Samuel P. Huntington, *Political Order in Changing Societies* (New Haven, CT: Yale University Press, 1968), pp. 1, 9, 47.
5. Eaton, *Rise of Islam and the Bengal Frontier,* p. 235.
6. Luiz Vaz de Camões, *The Lusíads,* trans. Landeg White (New York: Oxford University Press, 1997), Canto Ten: 121.
7. Suniti Bhushan Qanungo, *A History of Chittagong* (Chittagong, Bangladesh: Signet, 1988, p. 468. I have relied on this book for much of the historical background material.
8. Thant Myint-U, *The River of Lost Footsteps: A Personal History of Burma* (New York: Farrar, Straus and Giroux, 2006), p. 72.
9. Ibid., p. 110.

Chapter 9: Kolkata: The Next Global City

1. John Keay, *The Honourable Company: A History of the English East India Company* (London: HarperCollins, 1991), pp. 220, 272.

2. Luiz Vaz de Camões, *The Lusíads,* trans. Landeg White (New York: Oxford University Press, 1997), Canto Seven: 20.
3. Richard M. Eaton, *The Rise of Islam and the Bengal Frontier, 1204–1760* (Berkeley: University of California Press, 1993), pp. 12–13, 19–20, 61–62, 313.
4. Geoffrey Moorhouse, *Calcutta: The City Revealed* (London: Weidenfeld and Nicolson, 1971), p. 93.
5. Ibid., p. 18.
6. David Gilmour, *Curzon: Imperial Statesman* (New York: Farrar, Straus and Giroux, 1994), p. 145.
7. Dominique Lapierre, *The City of Joy* (New York: Doubleday, 1985).
8. William T. Vollmann, *Poor People* (New York: Ecco, 2007), pp. xiv, 111, 123–24, 239.
9. Madeleine Biardeau, *India,* transl. F. Carter (London: Vista, 1960), pp. 65, 73.
10. Moorhouse, *Calcutta,* p. 128.
11. Sunil Gangopadhyay, *Those Days,* transl. by Aruna Chakravarti (New York: Penguin, 1981, 1997), p. 581.
12. Basil Lubbock, *The Opium Clippers* (Boston: Lauriat, 1933), pp. 13–14, 16–17, 28. For an example of the profits, opium purchased for 70 rupees in Bengal could be sold for 225 rupees in Batavia in the Dutch East Indies. See C. R. Boxer, *The Dutch Seaborne Empire, 1600–1800* (London: Hutchinson, 1965), p. 228.
13. Simon and Rupert Winchester, *Calcutta* (Oakland, CA: Lonely Planet, 2004). p. 32.
14. Keay, *Honourable Company,* p. 193.
15. The term "vast impersonal forces" was used by T. S. Eliot. See Isaiah Berlin's essay "Historical Inevitability," first delivered as a lecture in 1953 and published in his book *Four Essays on Liberty* (London: Oxford University Press, 1969).
16. Thomas Babington Macaulay, *Essay on Lord Clive,* edited with notes and an introduction by Preston C. Farrar (1840; reprint, New York: Longmans, Green, 1910), pp. xxx, 3, 16–17.
17. Keay, *Honourable Company,* p. 289.
18. Ibid., p. 281.
19. Macaulay, *Essay on Lord Clive,* p. 22.
20. Ibid., pp. 24–25.
21. Keay, *Honourable Company,* p. 290.
22. Ibid., pp. 36–37.
23. Moorhouse, *Calcutta,* pp. 25–26.
24. Macaulay, *Essay on Lord Clive,* p. 39.
25. Ibid., p. 40.
26. Ibid., p. 41.
27. Macaulay, *Essay on Lord Clive,* p. 43.
28. Ibid., p. 44.
29. Ibid., p. 45.
30. Ibid., pp. 45–46.
31. Keay, *Honourable Company,* p. 315.
32. Ibid., p. 51.
33. Macaulay, *Essay on Lord Clive,* pp. 59–60.
34. Ibid., p. 61.
35. Macaulay, *Essay on Lord Clive,* p. 97.
36. Harvey, *Clive,* pp. 375–76.
37. Nick Robins, *The Corporation That Changed the World: How the East India*

Company Shaped the Modern Multinational (Hyderabad, India: Orient Longman, 2006), p. 168.
38. Ibid., p. 103.

Chapter 10: Of Strategy and Beauty

1. David Gilmour, *Curzon: Imperial Statesman* (New York: Farrar, Straus and Giroux, 1994), p. 181.
2. C. Raja Mohan, *Crossing the Rubicon: The Shaping of India's New Foreign Policy* (New York: Penguin, 2003), p. 204.
3. Ibid.
4. George Friedman, "The Geopolitics of India: A Shifting, Self-Contained World," Stratfor, December 2008.
5. Shashi Tharoor, *Nehru: The Invention of India* (New York: Arcade, 2003), p. 185.
6. Simon and Rupert Winchester, *Calcutta* (Oakland, CA: Lonely Planet, 2004), p. 78.
7. Amartya Sen, "Tagore and His India," *New York Review of Books,* June 26, 1997.
8. Rabindranath Tagore, "Passing Time in the Rain," in his *Selected Short Stories,* trans. William Radice (New Delhi: Penguin, 1991), appendix.
9. See the story "Little Master's Return" and the translator's introduction in ibid.
10. Samuel Huntington, "The Clash of Civilizations?," *Foreign Affairs,* Summer 1993.
11. Quoted in Sen, "Tagore and His India."
12. See the letters, Appendix B, in Tagore's *Selected Stories.*
13. Sugata Bose, *A Hundred Horizons: The Indian Ocean in the Age of Global Empire* (Cambridge, MA: Harvard University Press, 2006), p. 235.
14. Ibid., p. 261.
15. Quoted in ibid., pp. 270–71. See, too, Bose's footnote, p. 312, and Chapter Seven, on Tagore, near the end of *A Hundred Horizons.*

Chapter 11: Sri Lanka: The New Geopolitics

1. B. Raman, "Hambantota and Gwadar—an Update," Institute for Topical Studies, Chennai, India, 2009.
2. For a report on China's soft power, see Joshua Kurlantzick's *Charm Offensive: How China's Soft Power Is Transforming the World* (New Haven, CT: Yale University Press, 2007).
3. George F. Hourani, *Arab Seafaring in the Indian Ocean in Ancient and Early Medieval Times* (Princeton, NJ: Princeton University Press, 1951), p. 40.
4. Richard Hall, *Empires of the Monsoon: A History of the Indian Ocean and Its Invaders* (London: HarperCollins, 1996), pp. 80 and 92.
5. Sudha Ramachandran, "China Moves into India's Backyard," *Asia Times,* Mar. 13, 2007; Bethany Danyluk, Juli A. MacDonald, and Ryan Tuggle, "Energy Futures in Asia: Perspectives on India's Energy Security Strategy and Policies," Booz Allen Hamilton, 2007.
6. Harsh V. Pant, "End Game in Sri Lanka," *Jakarta Post,* Feb. 25, 2009.
7. Jeremy Page, "Chinese Billions in Sri Lanka Fund Battle Against Tamil Tigers," *The Times* (London), May 2, 2009.
8. Non-American media outlets such as the BBC and Al Jazeera have covered Sri Lanka in greater depth.

9. K. M. de Silva, *Reaping the Whirlwind: Ethnic Conflict, Ethnic Politics in Sri Lanka* (New Delhi: Penguin, 1998), p. 8.
10. Ibid., pp. 19, 82.
11. John Richardson, *Paradise Poisoned: Learning About Conflict, Terrorism and Development from Sri Lanka's Civil Wars* (Kandy, Sri Lanka: International Centre for Ethnic Studies, 2005), pp. 24–27; Kingsley M. de Silva, *Managing Ethnic Tensions in Multi-Ethnic Societies* (Lanham, MD: University Press of America, 1986), pp. 361–68; Tom Lowenstein, *Treasures of the Buddha: The Glories of Sacred Asia* (London: Duncan Baird, 2006), pp. 62–66.
12. Much of the background on the Sinhalese-Tamil conflict comes from Richardson's neutral and exhaustive book, as well as from de Silva's equally comprehensive *Reaping the Whirlwind.*
13. Narayan Swamy, *Tigers of Lanka: From Boys to Guerrillas* (New Delhi: Konark, 1994), pp. 40–92; Mary Anne Weaver, "The Gods and the Stars," *New Yorker,* Mar. 21, 1988; Richardson, *Paradise Poisoned,* pp. 351–52, 479–80.
14. Michael Radu, "How to Kill Civilians in the Name of 'Human Rights': Lessons from Sri Lanka," E-Note, Forein Policy Research Institute, fpri.org, February 2009.
15. Ibid.
16. Jakub J. Grygiel, "The Power of Statelessness," *Policy Review,* April/May 2009.
17. Al Jazeera, May 20, 2009.
18. Emily Wax, "Editor's Killing Underscores Perils of Reporting in Sri Lanka," *Washington Post,* Jan. 15, 2009.
19. Samuel P. Huntington, *Political Order in Changing Societies* (New Haven, CT: Yale University Press, 1968), p. 7.
20. Interview with Pat Garrett, senior associate, Booz Allen Hamilton.

Chapter 12: Burma: Where India and China Collide

1. *Washington Post,* editorial, Aug. 30, 2007.
2. Norman Lewis, *Golden Earth: Travels in Burma* (1952; reprint, London: Eland, 2003), pp. 137–38, 151, 205.
3. Dana Dillon and John J. Tkacik Jr., "China's Quest for Asia," *Policy Review,* December 2005/January 2006.
4. Joshua Kurlantzik, "The Survivalists: How Burma's Junta Hangs On," *New Republic,* June 11, 2008.
5. Greg Sheridan, "East Meets West," *National Interest,* November/December 2006.
6. Thant Myint-U, *The River of Lost Footsteps: A Personal History of Burma* (New York: Farrar, Straus and Giroux, 2006), p. 41.
7. Ibid., pp. 47, 59.
8. Pankaj Mishra, "The Revolt of the Monks," *New York Review of Books,* Feb. 14, 2008.
9. Martin Smith, *Burma: Insurgency and the Politics of Ethnicity* (London: Zed, 1991), ch. 2.
10. Ibid.
11. Thant Myint-U, *River of Lost Footsteps,* p. 162.
12. In *The Glass Palace* (New York: Random House, 2000), Amitav Ghosh provides a rich, novelistic study of this historical rupture.
13. Mishra, "Revolt of the Monks."

14. Brigadier Bernard Fergusson, *The Wild Green Earth* (London: Collins, 1946).
15. *Washington Post,* Aug. 30, 2007.
16. Mishra, "Revolt of the Monks."
17. James Fallows, "Evil in Burma," TheAtlantic.com, May 11, 2008.

Chapter 13: Indonesia's Tropical Islam

1. Robert D. Kaplan, *Hog Pilots, Blue Water Grunts: The American Military in the Air, at Sea, and on the Ground* (New York: Random House, 2007), ch. 3.
2. Simon Winchester, *Krakatoa: The Day the World Exploded; August 27, 1883* (New York: HarperCollins, 2003), pp. 40–41, 320–21.
3. Ibid., p. 326.
4. M. C. Ricklefs, *A History of Modern Indonesia Since C. 1200* (Stanford, CA: Stanford University Press, 1981), p. 10.
5. Clifford Geertz, *Islam Observed: Religious Development in Morocco and Indonesia* (Chicago: University of Chicago Press, 1968), pp. 11–12, 16, 66. Fabian is a reference to the British movement of a century ago that sought social democracy and liberal reform through a gradual, nonrevolutionary approach.
6. Giora Eliraz, *Islam in Indonesia: Modernism, Radicalism, and the Middle East Dimension* (Brighton, Eng.: Sussex, 2004), p. 74.
7. V. S. Naipaul, *Among the Believers: An Islamic Journey* (New York: Penguin, 1981), pp. 304, 331.
8. John Hughes, *The End of Sukarno: A Coup That Misfired; a Purge That Ran Wild* (Singapore: Archipelago, 1967, 2002), pp. 166–69.
9. Geertz, *Islam Observed,* p. 65.
10. Eliraz, *Islam in Indonesia,* pp. 42–43; Winchester, *Krakatoa,* pp. 333–34.
11. Malcolm H. Kerr, *Islamic Reform: The Political and Legal Theories of Muhammad Abduh and Rashid Rida* (Berkeley: University of California Press, 1966), p. 15.
12. Geertz, *Islam Observed,* p. 17.
13. Eliraz, *Islam in Indonesia,* pp. 6–8, 14, 20.
14. Ibid., p. 31.
15. Geertz, *Islam Observed,* pp. 61–62.
16. Andrew MacIntyre and Douglas E. Ramage, "Seeing Indonesia as a Normal Country," Australian Strategic Policy Institute, Barton, 2008.
17. Told to the scholar Robert W. Hefner, in Eliraz, *Islam in Indonesia,* p. 67.

Chapter 14: The Heart of Maritime Asia

1. Juli A. MacDonald, Amy Donahue, and Bethany Danyluk, "Energy Futures in Asia: Final Report," Booz Allen Hamilton, November 2004.
2. I profiled Singapore in my previous book, *Hog Pilots, Blue Water Grunts: The American Military in the Air, at Sea, and on the Ground* (New York: Random House, 2007), ch. 3.
3. Mohan Malik, "Energy Flows and Maritime Rivalries in the Indian Ocean Region" (Honolulu: Asia-Pacific Center for Security Studies, 2008).
4. Ian W. Porter, "The Indian Ocean Rim," *African Security Review,* vol. 6, no. 6 (1997). Mentioned by Malik.
5. G. B. Souza, "Maritime Trade and Politics in China and the South China Sea,"

included in Ashin Das Gupta and M. N. Pearson, eds., *India and the Indian Ocean, 1500–1800* (Kolkata: Oxford University Press, 1987).

6. Dorothy Van Duyne, "The Straits of Malacca: Strategic Considerations," United States Naval Academy, 2007.

7. Donald B. Freeman, *The Straits of Malacca: Gateway or Gauntlet?* (Montreal: McGill-Queen's University Press, 2003), p. 55.

8. Patricia Risso, *Merchants & Faith: Muslim Commerce and Culture in the Indian Ocean* (Boulder, CO: Westview, 1995), p. 90.

9. Arun Das Gupta, "The Maritime Trade of Indonesia: 1500–1800," in Ashin Das Gupta and Pearson, *India and the Indian Ocean* (New Delhi: Sage, 1987); Satish Chandra, *The Indian Ocean: Explorations in History, Commerce and Politics* (New Delhi: Sage, 1987), pp. 181–82.

10. Michael Leifer, *Malacca, Singapore, and Indonesia* (Alphen aan den Rijn, the Netherlands: Sijthoff & Noordhoff, 1978), p. 9. See, too, Van Duyne, "Straits of Malacca."

11. Van Duyne, "Straits of Malacca."

12. Han van der Horst, *The Low Sky: Understanding the Dutch,* trans. Andy Brown (The Hague: Scriptum, 1996), pp. 29, 85, 127; Geert Mak, *Amsterdam: A Brief Life of the City,* trans. by Philipp Blom (London: Harvill, 1995, 2001), p. 1.

13. Van der Horst, *Low Sky,* pp. 90–91.

14. J. H. Plumb, introduction to C. R. Boxer, *The Dutch Seaborne Empire, 1600–1800* (London: Hutchinson, 1965).

15. Mak, *Amsterdam,* p. 120.

16. Boxer, *Dutch Seaborne Empire,* p. 29. Much of the material in this section on the Dutch empire is based on this classic book.

17. Mak, *Amsterdam,* pp. 120–21.

18. Alan Villers, *Monsoon Seas: The Story of the Indian Ocean* (New York: McGraw-Hill, 1952), pp. 166–67.

19. Plumb, introduction to Boxer, *Dutch Seaborne Empire.*

20. Boxer, *Dutch Seaborne Empire,* pp. 50, 102.

21. Holden Furber, *Rival Empires of Trade in the Orient, 1600–1800* (New Delhi: Oxford University Press, 2004), p. 36.

22. Apud E. du Perron, *De Muze van Jan Compagnie* (Indonesia: Bandung, 1948), p. 13; also see Boxer, *Dutch Seaborne Empire,* p. 56.

23. Ibid.

24. Boxer, *Dutch Seaborne Empire,* p. 78.

25. Mak, *Amsterdam,* pp. 160–61.

26. Villiers, *Monsoon Seas,* p. 177.

27. Boxer, *Dutch Seaborne Empire,* p. 273.

28. Paul Kennedy, *The Rise and Fall of the Great Powers: Economic Change and Military Conflict from 1500 to 2000* (New York: Random House, 1987).

29. Andrew MacIntyre and Douglas E. Ramage, "Seeing Indonesia as a Normal Country," Australian Strategic Policy Institute, Barton, 2008.

30. For a profile of Lee Kuan Yew, see my *Hog Pilots, Blue Water Grunts,* ch. 3.

31. Ioannis Gatsiounis, "Year of the Rat: A Letter from Kuala Lumpur," *American Interest,* May/June 2008.

32. Dana Dillon and John J. Tkacik Jr., "China's Quest for Asia," *Policy Review,* December 2005/January 2006.

33. Hugo Restall, "Pressure Builds on Singapore's System," *Far Eastern Economic Review,* Sept. 5, 2008.

PART III

Chapter 15: China's Two-Ocean Strategy?

1. William H. McNeill, *The Rise of the West: A History of the Human Community* (Chicago: University of Chicago Press, 1963), p. 565.
2. Gabriel B. Collins et al., eds., *China's Energy Strategy: The Impact on Beijing's Maritime Policies* (Annapolis, MD: Naval Institute Press, 2008).
3. Toshi Yoshihara and James Holmes, "Command of the Sea with Chinese Characteristics," *Orbis,* Fall 2005.
4. Ibid.
5. Andrew Erickson and Lyle Goldstein, "Gunboats for China's New 'Grand Canals'?" *Naval War College Review,* Spring 2009.
6. James R. Holmes and Toshi Yoshihara, *Chinese Naval Strategy in the 21st Century: The Turn to Mahan* (New York: Routledge, 2008), pp. 52–53.
7. Nicholas J. Spykman, *America's Strategy in World Politics: The United States and the Balance of Power,* with an introduction by Francis P. Sempa (1942; New Brunswick, NJ: Transaction, 2007), p. xvi. The phrase first appeared in Spykman and Abbie A. Rollins, "Geographic Objectives in Foreign Policy II," *American Political Science Review,* August 1939.
8. Donald B. Freeman, *The Straits of Malacca: Gateway or Gauntlet?* (Montreal: McGill-Queen's University Press, 2003), p. 77.
9. Juli A. MacDonald, Amy Donahue, and Bethany Danyluk, "Energy Futures in Asia: Final Report," Booz Allen Hamilton, 2004.
10. Jakub J. Grygiel, *Great Powers and Geopolitical Change* (Baltimore: Johns Hopkins University Press, 2006), pp. 142–48.
11. Aaron L. Friedberg, *The Weary Titan: Britain and the Experience of Relative Decline, 1895–1905* (Princeton, NJ: Princeton University Press, 1988).
12. Fariborz Haghshenass, "Iran's Asymmetric Naval Warfare," Washington Institute for Near East Policy, September 2008.

Chapter 16: Unity and Anarchy

1. Ben Simpfendorfer, *The New Silk Road: How a Rising Arab World Is Turning Away from the West and Rediscovering China* (London: Palgrave Macmillan, 2009), p. 1.
2. Nicholas J. Spykman, *America's Strategy in World Politics: The United States and the Balance of Power* (1942; reprint, New Brunswick, NJ: Transaction, 2008).
3. Simpfendorfer, *New Silk Road,* p. 40; Ulrich Jacoby, "Getting Together," *Finance and Development,* International Monetary Fund, June 2007.
4. Andrew Droddy, "The Silent Scramble for Africa," United States Naval Academy, 2006.
5. Alex Vines and Elizabeth Sidiropolous, "India and Africa," TheWorldToday.org, 2008; Vibhuti Hate, *South Asia Monitor,* Center for Strategic and International Studies, June 10, 2008.
6. Sharon Burke, "Natural Security," working paper, Center for a New American Security, June 2009.
7. Mohan Malik, "Energy Flows and Maritime Rivalries in the Indian Ocean Region" (Honolulu: Asia-Pacific Center for Security Studies, 2008); "Opportunity Knocks:

Africa's Prospects" and "Everything to Play For: Middle East and Africa," *Economist,* Oct. 9 and Nov. 19, 2008; Sarah Childress, "In Africa, Democracy Gains Amid Turmoil," *Wall Street Journal,* June 18, 2008; Tony Elumelu, "Africa Stands Out," TheWorldToday.org, May 2009.

8. Robert D. Kaplan, *The Ends of the Earth* (New York: Random House, 1996), p. 7; Spykman, *America's Strategy in World Politics,* p. 92.

9. Robert D. Kaplan, "The Coming Anarchy," *Atlantic Monthly,* February 1994.

10. Janet L. Abu-Lughod, *Before European Hegemony: The World System A.D. 1250– 1350* (New York: Oxford University Press, 1989), p. 12.

11. "Opportunity Knocks," *Economist.*

12. Alan Villiers, *Monsoon Seas: The Story of the Indian Ocean* (New York: McGraw-Hill, 1952), pp. 208, 210.

13. Ross E. Dunn, *The Adventures of Ibn Battuta: A Muslim Traveler of the 14th Century* (London; Croom Helm, 1986), p. 219; Simon Digby, "The Maritime Trade of India," in Tapan Ray Chaudhuri and Irfan Habib, eds., *The Cambridge Economic History of India,* vol. I (Cambridge, Eng.: Cambridge University Press, 1982), p. 152. See, too, Patricia Risso, *Merchants & Faith: Muslim Commerce and Culture in the Indian Ocean* (Boulder, CO: Westview, 1995), p. 53.

14. Jakub J. Grygiel, *Great Powers and Geopolitical Change* (Baltimore: Johns Hopkins University Press, 2006), p. 153.

15. George F. Hourani, *Arab Seafaring in the Indian Ocean in Ancient and Early Medieval Times* (Princeton, NJ: Princeton University Press, 1951), pp. 55, 113–14.

16. Fernand Braudel, *The Mediterranean and the Mediterranean World in the Age of Philip II,* vol. 2 (Berkeley: University of California Press, 1996), pp. 865, 869.

17. Richard J. Norton, "Feral Cities," *Naval War College Review,* Fall 2003. See, too, Matthew M. Frick, "Feral Cities, Pirate Havens," *Proceedings,* Annapolis, MD, December 2008.

18. Donald B. Freeman, *The Straits of Malacca: Gateway or Gauntlet?* (Montreal: McGill-Queen's University Press, 2003), p. 175.

19. Michael Pearson, *The Indian Ocean* (New York: Routledge, 2003), p. 127.

20. Freeman, *Straits of Malacca,* p. 175.

21. Sugata Bose, *A Hundred Horizons: The Indian Ocean in the Age of Golden Empire* (Cambridge, MA: Harvard University Press, 2006), pp. 45–47.

22. Abdulrazak Gurnah, *Desertion* (New York: Anchor, 2005), p. 83.

23. John Keay, *The Honourable Company: A History of the English East India Company* (London: HarperCollins, 1991), pp. 255–56.

24. Basil Lubbock, *The Opium Clippers* (Boston: Lauriat, 1933), pp. 8, 181.

25. Freeman, *Straits of Malacca,* pp. 174–79, 181–83.

Chapter 17: Zanzibar: The Last Frontier

1. Richard Hall, *Empires of the Monsoon: A History of the Indian Ocean and Its Invaders* (London: HarperCollins, 1996), pp. 397, 415, 446.

2. Alan Villiers, *Monsoon Seas: The Story of the Indian Ocean* (New York: McGraw-Hill, 1952), p. 87.

3. Ryszard Kapuscinski, *The Shadow of the Sun,* trans. Klara Glowczewska (New York: Vintage, 2001), p. 83.

4. Alan Moorehead, *The White Nile* (London: Hamish Hamilton, 1960), ch. 1.

5. G. Thomas Burgess, "Cosmopolitanism and Its Discontents," in *Race, Revolution, and the Struggle for Human Rights in Zanzibar* (Athens: Ohio University Press, 2009).
6. Abdul Sheriff, "Race and Class in the Politics of Zanzibar," *Afrika Spectrum,* vol. 36, no. 3 (2001).
7. Abdulrazak Gurnah, *Admiring Silence* (New York: The New Press, 1996), pp. 66–67.
8. Ibid., p. 151.
9. Abdulrazak Gurnah, *Paradise* (New York: The New Press, 1994), p. 119.
10. Gurnah, *Admiring Silence,* p. 131.
11. Gurnah, *Paradise,* p. 174.
12. Abdulrazak Gurnah, *Desertion* (New York: Anchor, 2005), p. 212.
13. Gurnah, *Admiring Silence,* pp. 69, 144, 121, 150.
14. Gurnah, *Desertion,* p. 256.
15. Gurnah, *Admiring Silence,* pp. 67, 134.
16. Gurnah, *Desertion,* pp. 110, 225.
17. Sunil Gangopadhyay, *Those Days,* trans. Aruna Chakravarti (New York: Penguin, 1981, 1997), p. 7.
18. Richard M. Eaton, *The Rise of Islam and the Bengal Frontier, 1204–1760* (Berkeley: University of California Press, 1993), pp. 60, 167–68.

INDEX

and, 50, 51–52, 56–57, 60, 65, 116,
265; in Sri Lanka, violence
perpetrated by, 198, 201
Christmas, in Kolkata, 160
Chunda Sahib, 170
Churchill, Winston, 233
CIA (Central Intelligence Agency), 124, 230
clan politics. *See* tribalism and clan politics
climate change, 137, 138, 139–40, 141,
142–43, 168
Clinton, Bill, 237
Clinton, Hillary, 219n
Clive, Lord Robert, 157, 168–78; East
India Company reformed by, 176–77;
as military leader, 170–73, 174–75,
176; riches accumulated by, 176; as
statesman, 173–74
CNOOC (China National Offshore Oil
Corporation), 226, 271
coal, 46, 271; China's energy needs and, 10,
195, 271, 282, 283; India's imports of,
8, 185
Coco Islands, 10
Coen, Jan Pieterszoon, 266–67
Cohen, Stephen P., 125
Cold War, 6, 11, 13, 14–15, 123, 125, 126,
129, 157, 183, 218, 235, 236, 277,
278, 280, 291
colonialism, 268–69, 296, 317; aftermath of
dismantlement of European empires
and, 211–12; ethnic-racial tensions
and, 312–13, 318. *See also specific
colonial powers and former colonies*
communism, 254; in India, 163, 164
Comoro Islands, 307
Congo, 297, 307
Congress Party, 97, 100, 103, 105, 116, 117
Coromandel coast, India, 21n, 30, 49, 263
Côte d'Ivoire, 298
Counter-Reformation, 60
Crusades, 51, 52
Cuba, 313–14
Curzon, Lord George Nathaniel, 33–34,
124–25, 157, 179–86; Greater India
envisioned by, 181–82, 185, 188; neo-
Curzonism and, 182–86, 190
Cyclone Nargis (2008), 217, 239
cyclones, 139

Dalrymple, William, 91, 124
Darius I, 27

Da Silva, John Baptist, 310
Dauletabad natural gas field, Turkmenistan,
14, 70
Deccan plateau, India, 21n, 58, 122, 169,
171, 319–20
deforestation, 140, 155, 228
Delhi, India, 58, 83, 122n, 123–24, 137,
163, 165, 166, 179
Delta Ranger, 302
democracy, 41–42, 296; in Bangladesh, 43,
144–46, 150; Burma and, 43, 216–17,
219, 224, 227, 231, 237, 239, Bush's
advocacy of, 249, 251; fascism vs.,
111; Ibadis and, 37; in India, 88, 97,
98, 116, 117, 132, 146, 163, 185–86,
259, 271; in Indonesia, 247, 249, 251,
256–58, 259, 272, 322; as interpreted
by U.S., 41; in Malaysia, 273, 274;
Omani perspective on, 39, 41–42,
43–44; radical Islamists' views on,
248, 249; in Singapore, 274; in
Southeast Asia vs. Middle East, 249;
in Sri Lanka, 199, 200, 205, 211; in
Taiwan, 285; in Thailand, 273; in
Zanzibar, 315
Deng Xiaoping, 107
Denmark, 166
deserts: as barriers, 33, 34; tribal conflict
in, 34–36, 37–39
Dhaka, Bangladesh, 142, 144, 157, 165,
320; bicycle rickshaws in, 147, 157; as
seat of power, 146, 147–48, 150, 151
Dhofar, Oman, 22–23, 23–24, 27, 30, 39,
45, 46
dhows, 22, 38, 50, 307, 309–10, 319;
building of, 72–73; piracy and, 299,
302–3
Diaoyu/Senkaku Islands, 284
Dias, Bartolomeu, 52–53
Diego Garcia (island), 9
dishdasha (traditional white shirtdress
worn by Middle Eastern men), 40
Diu, India, 47, 114–17
Dixit, J. N., 181
Donlon, Roger, 229
Don Quixote (Cervantes), 64
Dubai, 81, 82, 107, 113; Disney-style
globalization of, 42, 43, 47;
governance of, 74; before
transformation by petrodollars,
71–72; as transshipment hub, 43, 46

ABOUT THE AUTHOR

ROBERT D. KAPLAN is a senior fellow at the Center for a New American Security in Washington and a national correspondent for *The Atlantic*. He was recently the Distinguished Visiting Professor in National Security at the U.S. Naval Academy in Annapolis. His twelve previous books include *Balkan Ghosts, Eastward to Tartary,* and *Warrior Politics*. He is a member of the Pentagon's Defense Policy Board.